WORDGLOSS

For Mary

Shall I compare thee to a summer's day?

WORDGLOSS

A Cultural Lexicon

JIM O'DONNELL

THE LILLIPUT PRESS
DUBLIN

First published 2005 by
THE LILLIPUT PRESS
62–63 Sitric Road, Arbour Hill
Dublin 7, Ireland
www.lilliputpress.ie

ISBN 1 84351 073 1

A CIP record for this title is available
from The British Library.

10 9 8 7 6 5 4 3 2

Set in Dante and GillSans
Printed by MPG Books, Bodmin, Cornwall, England

CONTENTS

FOREWORD

John Banville

'The limits of my language are the limits of my world,' says Wittgenstein. As so often, this great maker of metaphors, which is what he claimed primarily to be, presents us with an ambiguity. Does he mean to say that language is a natural limit to our thoughts and perceptions, or that language being limitless—the combinational power of words is infinite, after all—our world is also without limits?

Wittgenstein's first, great work, the *Tractatus Logico-Philosophicus*, is much concerned with setting the boundaries of what can be said, boundaries beyond which there will be 'simply nonsense'. The book will, he wrote, 'draw a limit to thinking, or rather—not to thinking, but to the expression of thoughts ...' The famous, final proposition of the book has the look of a commandment carved in stone: 'Whereof one cannot speak, thereof one must be silent.' To all this, Wittgenstein's mentor, Bertrand Russell, gave a tartly witty response: 'What causes hesitation is the fact that, after all, Mr Wittgenstein manages to say a good deal about what cannot be said.'

The *Tractatus*, Wittgenstein thought, was literally the last word on philosophy; the book had laid out, so he believed, the essential truths of philosophy, an achievement that he freely acknowledged showed only how little had been achieved. Everything that was important lay *beyond* the limits of language, in that area 'whereof one cannot speak'. Later in his life, however, he had a radical change of mind, and in *Philosophical Investigations* he abandoned the icy heights of his earlier work for homelier lowlands where language may not be able to *say* many things but nevertheless can *show* them, often in moments of luminous epiphany. Rilke had put it well in the *Duino Elegies*:

> Are we, perhaps, here just for saying: House,
> Bridge, Fountain, Gate, Jug, Fruit tree, Window,—
> possibly: Pillar, Tower? ... but for saying, remember,
> oh, for such saying as never the things themselves
> hoped so intensely to be.

There is a case to be argued that language does not limit our world but rather *makes* it: makes our thoughts, makes our perceptions, makes even our selves. Our laws, as Ezra Pound pointed out, are graven in words. To speak is to act, and is to act positively, even when we are saying *No*. And the hoard of words is a treasure trove, is riches beyond compare. 'Words have been my only love,' says one of Beckett's various narrators, those inveterate glossers of the hoard of language.

One of the greatest cultural losses we have experienced in our time is the virtual abandonment of the teaching of the classical languages, Latin and Greek. Dead words in dead worlds, they drift away from us farther and farther every year, yet their essence remains, though increasingly unacknowledged. Every schoolboy watches television, 'an apparatus for receiving sound and pictures broadcast from a distant place,' as Jim

O'Donnell defines it, at his poker-faced best, but how many schoolboys know that the word is an amalgam of Greek and Latin terms?—*tēle*, which is Greek for far, and the Latin verb *videre*, to see. Words are wrapped up in themselves, petal upon petal; our attentiveness unfurls them.

Does it matter, it may be asked, that we no longer have the necessary knowledge to break words up into their derivations? Yes, it matters. *The limits of my language are the limits of my world.*

Jim O'Donnell has set out to recuperate for us something of the range of classical reference that our education no longer gives us. *Wordgloss* is a vast grid of knowledge and information, as dense as chain mail and as intricate as a spiderweb. It is wide-ranging, erudite, accommodating and witty. What it is not is a bluffer's guide to logodaedaly, but a real reference work that will carry the reader far beyond the dictionary. In what the author rightly calls this 'voyage among words' we visit other seas, other realms, and recognize them as our own.

PREFACE & ACKNOWLEDGMENTS

Wordgloss is full of the words and concepts you always meant to look up. It tells you where they came from and how they acquired the meaning or meanings they now have. As a long-time general reader myself, I know how easily the need to know arises and how extensive it can become. It is a beautiful summer's day. You are lying at the end of a boat, a book propped against your knees, the fingers of your left hand are trailing in the slipstream. Suddenly the author hits you with the word mephitic. You do not know what it means. You have forgotten to bring your shorter English dictionary, and the twenty-volume *The Oxford English Dictionary* that everyone swears by is in a trailer in the driveway at home. You resolve to look up mephitic later. You never do. Over the years many other words share the fate of mephitic – eschatology, uxorious, dystopia, oneirocritic, interstice, nemesis, thaumaturge – I could go on. You either let them sink into oblivion (and add to the number of dead notes on your literary keyboard) or rely on encountering them a number of times in different contexts to define them. Since writers do not invariably use words and phrases with exactitude and subtlety that approach is unlikely to reveal the distinctive sharpness with which the words or phrases were freshly minted.

We also encounter words in conversation. If we hear a word we don't know, are we not too embarrassed to say, What does that mean? It may be a phrase – say *éminence grise* – which you know translates into 'grey eminence' but the origins of which completely elude you. Are you prepared to engage a mellow group with the questions: Is that expression applied only to men who are sixty or more years old? Or could you apply it to a thirty-year-old blonde? No. No one wants to be seen as an acolyte of Nicholas the Meticulous.

The problem *Wordgloss* seeks to meet can be examined systemically. The extraordinary expansion of modern knowledge and its fission into micro-specialisms has created a situation in which all of us, even if we are educated in a number of academic areas, encounter what can seem like a niagara of words and concepts flowing from a wide range of disciplines that we have never explored.

The problems created by the knowledge explosion are most keenly felt in third-level education institutions. The faculties do not tackle the general communications problem. Each faculty seeks to develop a verbal universe sufficient for its own students, often by the production of specialized dictionaries. This, by definition, is not serving the verbal universe of third-level institutions as a whole, where the richest markets in cultural exchange are conducted. Conceivably, if one were to master each of the dictionaries in turn, one would emerge as the paragon of general readers. But think of the plodding endeavour! Think of the information overload!

The nature of English and the history of our cultural development allow us to develop a different coping strategy. English can usefully be thought of as having two registers. The lower register contains the Anglo-Saxon words we first grew up with – monosyllabic and concrete in the main, such as rain, dog, tree, grass, water, moon. We use this register to describe the world about us. Poets favour it for its simple, earthy directness. The upper register contains the words derived from Latin and Greek – polysyllabic and abstract in the main, transmitted firstly through Norman French and Church Latin and then during the Renaissance directly from the classical texts themselves. It is favoured for sophisticated discourse because the Greeks and Romans created the classic vocabulary for discussing religion, philosophy, science and the arts – the four different approaches we take to acquire knowledge – and supplied the linguistic elements out of which that vocabulary continues to be developed. The information technology (IT) term 'database' (from the Latin *data* – 'things given' and the Greek *basis* – 'support') provides an apposite contemporary example of the process.

The upper register is of paramount importance to the general reader. In a previous era when Latin and Greek were part of the school curriculum, people had a ready grip on the etymology of the words in this register. They studied them in the classical texts and saw them in their pristine state – as clearly as if they were pebbles in the bed of a stream. Few people now study Latin and Greek. In order to appreciate the loss that has to be made up one has only to reflect on how Greek and Latin suffuse the vocabularies of the traditional core disciplines – philosophy, law, medicine, history, geography, mathematics – and on how the newer disciplines like psychology, sociology, anthropology and linguistics develop their nomenclature from Latin and Greek roots. Moreover, modern democracy requires that every citizen should have a grasp of the words and concepts used in the discussion of public affairs. Great numbers of these are drawn from the classics. The Greeks did not invent politics but they were the first to discuss it in a sophisticated way. The Romans did not invent law but our legal terms and concepts are largely a legacy from them.

The general reader is deprived of the assuredness in the use of the upper register that flows from an understanding of the roots of the words that comprise it and the literary contexts that determine their primary meaning. *Wordgloss* seeks to meet this deficiency. It breaks the words into their components, shows where they came from, and explores the myth or history that clings to them. In effect, it restores the gloss to the set of words and concepts that largely carry the stream of consciousness created by thinkers and writers.

How has this set of words been established? By monitoring over a number of years some well-known interdisciplinary commentaries – *Time* and *Newsweek* magazines, the *Times Literary Supplement*, the *Economist*, the *New York Review of Books*, the *London Review of Books*. There is to be found the wide range of issues that engage the general reader and there too is the set of words and concepts that specialists, who are typically the contributors, feel they can employ to reach their non-specialist readers. As one would expect, the set is largely from the upper register of English. Tranches of experience other than the classical give such expressions as quisling, fifth columnist, Neanderthal, admiral, mesmerize. Other languages give such words as *Götterdämmerung*, *glasnost*, graffito, *roman à clef*, kibbutz.

It is a matter of judgment as to when the set should be regarded as complete.

Reading through *Wordgloss* gives one a general sense of how ample the selection is. A sharper sense can be achieved by using a highlighter to reveal how many words in *Wordgloss* subserve the reader of any single issue of one of the interdisciplinary commentaries. I have done that a number of times myself (who else would?) and the results have been invariably – I blush that the *mot juste* should be one that conveys satisfaction creamed with complacency – gratifying.

A book on words usually presents as a dictionary, a thesaurus or an encyclopaedia. *Wordgloss* is not any of these, although it shares some of the characteristics of all of them. Each of those forms is scientific in structure. That means that each entry in them is freighted with material far more heavily than the general reader needs. A dictionary requires the treatment of all the forms of a word – nounal, adjectival and adverbial – when one form is often sufficient. A thesaurus requires that all the synonyms and all the antonyms of each entry word are listed. But the general reader may require that service in the case of a relatively small number of concepts. An encyclopaedia requires that if one treats a particular subject in a category one must treat all the subjects in that category. *Wordgloss* is not developed in the linear way a scientific text is – and thus avoids the treatment of unnecessary areas. It is developed in an associative way and is characteristically more varied, more unpredictable than a scientific work. The associative style is pedagogically effective. I believe it allows the mind to cluster items and more readily recall them.

Wordgloss uses headline words arranged in alphabetical order to organize its voyage among words. It usually explores many more words than the headline word itself. That is why, if you are wondering whether a particular word is treated in *Wordgloss*, it is advisable to consult the index. The treatment given under headline words varies widely in length, colour, density, diversity and pace. This is so there will be a wide variety of contexts in which to set the words and make them memorable. Thus, by associating 'telluric' with Lorca, and 'chthonian' and 'autochthonous' with Melanchthon, *Wordgloss* casts a net under words that would otherwise free fall into oblivion.

Where a difficult word such as vatic, hegemony or cloaca occurs in the text, *Wordgloss* supplies that glory of the consumer society – instant satisfaction – by explaining it straightaway or providing in the index the page in the text where it is exlained. (Almost every difficult word used in the text is explained in the text.) When explaining a word, *Wordgloss* often uses the opportunity to explain a cluster of words, such as Francophone, monoglot and polyglot along with Anglophone; and natural and supernatural along with praeternatural. The cluster may be based on dissimilarity as well as similarity, such as centripetal and centrifugal; or upon apparent similarity, such as privilege and sacrilege.

In reading, we encounter the work of writers who seek to express themselves with some of man's oldest artefacts – words. Skilled writers know a wide range of words. They know where they came from. They know their meaning and their shades of meaning. They have observed how other writers have used them to striking effect. They have learned those verbal inventions called concepts and use them to give depth to their writing the way artists use perspective to give depth to their painting. They have learned how other writers have combined words or even bits of words to create new words, and so enrich their range, the way artists mix paints on their palettes. It may be too much to claim that *Wordgloss* puts that understanding and skill within the grasp of the general reader. What do you think?

ACKNOWLEDGMENTS

Anyone who writes about words in English is inevitably grateful to the astonishing *Oxford English Dictionary.* Anyone who writes about anything else in English is likely to be grateful to the equally astonishing *Encyclopaedia Britannica. Wordgloss* draws on those sources but also, for instance, on *The Oxford Classical Dictionary* edited by Simon Hornblower and Anthony Spawforth, and *The Greek Myths* by Robert Graves (for the classical world); on *The Penguin Dictionary of Literary Terms and Literary Theory* by J.A. Cuddon (for literature); on *The Fontana Dictionary of Modern Thought* edited by Alan Bullock, Oliver Stallybrass and Stephen Trombley; and *Grand Dictionnaire de Culture Générale* by Bruno Hongre, Philippe Forest and Bernard Baritaud (for general culture); and the *Collins English Dictionary* (for a useful general companion). *Wordgloss* in truth draws on a very wide range of sources, often in small but helpful ways. It all adds up to a need to acknowledge a general indebtedness to a great number of authors. I have managed to mention many of them in the text without weighing it down with academic paraphernalia.

Of its nature *Wordgloss* grew and grew. Many people read parts of the text or even large tracts of it, and gave me useful comments, but no one read it fully. Therefore only such merits as the text has and not any of its shortcomings can be securely associated with them. I wish to thank especially:

Dr Donal de Buitléir, Professor Anthony Clare, Jane Clare, Dr Donal Costigan, Rebecca Daly, Professor Brian Farrell, Seán de Fréine, Jane Gregory, Rev. Terence McCaughey, Dr Edward McParland, Dr Michael Mulreany, Noel Murphy, Professor Séamus Ó Cinnéide, Aiden O'Donnell, E.F. O'Donnell, Dr Don Thornhill and Sarah Woodcock. My old friends Tom Turley and Oliver McQuillan, implicated in the project from an early stage, must come out with their hands up, admitting incitement.

About 30 per cent of the original (1990) text of *Wordgloss* has been carried over into the new text. I would like to acknowledge once more the generous help I got with that text from Fr Fergal O'Connor OP and the late great philhellene Jack Henderson.

Jim O'Donnell
October 2005

USING WORDGLOSS

1. Almost every difficult word used in the text is explained in the text, whether by way of providing its etymology or a fuller note. The explanation often occurs straightaway. If it doesn't, consult the index. To help the reader track down all the words treated in the text, the index is a detailed one.
2. Latin and Greek nouns are normally quoted in their nominative and genitive cases (thus the Latin word for 'judge' *judex, judicis* and the Greek word for 'light' *phōs, phōtos*) because the words derived from them are usually derived from the genitive form (thus 'judicial' and 'photo').
3. Similarly, Latin verbs are quoted in their infinitive and past participle forms because the words derived from them are usually derived from the past participle form – thus the Latin word 'to suffer' *pati, passum* is the source of passion and passionate.
4. The straight dash above a vowel in a Greek word indicates the long form of the vowel. *Wordgloss* conforms to this technicality partly to help restrain the reader from presuming that an s ending indicates a plural (thus *politēs*, the Greek word for 'citizen', would otherwise appear as *polites*).
5. The Greek *k* and *u* transliterate into English as c and y respectively.
6. Where a word is a compound of two words of the same language, the language of the second compound is to be presumed to be the same as that of the first (thus making for a small economy in the use of space).
7. Statements in quotations that illustrate usage were originated for this text, save for the attributed ones, drawn from printed sources. The acronyms *NYRB* and *LRB* stand for *New York Review of Books* and *London Review of Books*.
8. For the sake of directness words are referred to as words rather than nouns, adjectives, verbs, adverbs, etc., except in a small number of cases where distinctions are necessary. For the same reason a certain amount of repetition is allowed in the text.
9. *Wordgloss* uses an alphabetically ordered dictionary style of presentation. The body of the text, however, is frequently associative rather than linear in its development because *Wordgloss* is primarily pedagogic in intent.
10. Marginal glosses are used to supplement the body of the text and are placed as closely as possible to the word glossed.

A

A – ab before a vowel – is the Latin 'from'; *origo, originis* is 'beginning' or 'origin', from which we also derive original and originally. When we wish to indicate something as an ultimate source we may refer to it as the *fons et origo* (*fons* being the Latin 'fountain', *et* being 'and'). *Ab initio* (*initium* is the Latin 'beginning', which also gives us initiate, initiative and initial) and *ab ovo* (*ovum* is the Latin 'egg') mean 'from the beginning'. The aborigines of Latium, the district around Rome, were a tribe called the Latini – hence Latin. The Aborigines of Australia, sometimes offensively referred to as Abos, are the race who occupied that continent before the Europeans discovered it. The peoples popularly known as the American Indians, but now more generally described as Native Americans, are the aborigines of North America. The Caribs (after whom the Caribbean is called) were the aborigines of the West Indies.

The term aborigines tends to be used to suggest a primitive race. When the colonists had respect for the race in possession, they would refer to them as the indigenous people (*indi* is a strengthened form of the Latin *in* meaning 'in' and *gignere,* from which we derive the *gen* particle, is the Latin 'to produce'); or they might refer to them as the natives (from the Latin *nasci, natum* 'to be born'; nascent, meaning starting to grow, as in the nascent revolt, also derives from *nasci*).

Natives who met the colonists with violence were called savages. Savage comes by way of the modern French *sauvage* from the Old French *salvage. Salvage* was derived from the Latin *silva* 'a wood'; woods were uncleared areas and therefore wild.

From the seventeenth century on, the colonizing Europeans encountered primitive peoples in the Americas, in Australasia, and in the South Seas generally, and developed the concept of the noble savage – a condition of human existence that seemed to display excellences of life that civilized man had lost. Throughout history, the notion of an early era when life was lived in perfect harmony with nature has been part of man's thought and mythology. The Greeks and Romans harked back to a golden age – a paradise on earth, with ease, plenty and pleasure. Paradise derives from the Old Persian

aboriginal
pertaining to the earliest known inhabitants

silva
also gives us silvan and sylvan, meaning wooded; *sylvania* is a suffix indicating wooded country, hence Transylvania in Romania and Pennsylvania, one of the original thirteen states in the American union, founded by the Quaker William Penn with Philadelphia (the 'city of brotherly love' – from the Greek *philein* 'to love' and *adelphos* 'brother') as its capital. Sylph, a slender, graceful girl, is also derived from *silva*

civilized
Civilis, from the Latin *civis* 'citizen', means 'pertaining to a citizen', i.e. a city-dweller, in its original sense; civilization is characterized by the peaceful coming together of groups of people to achieve objectives individuals could not achieve alone. Cities with their elaborate economic, social and cultural organization have always been regarded as centres of civilization

pairidaēza 'enclosure, park', which the Greeks borrowed in the form *paradeisos* 'pleasure ground'. Xenophon, writing in his *Anabasis*, tells us of the Persian King Cyrus: '[He] had a palace there and a large pleasure-ground [*paradeisos*] full of wild animals, which he used to hunt on horseback ... Through the middle of the pleasure-ground the river Meander flows.' (The Meander was a proverbially slow, winding river – it gave us the verb to meander.) The Hebrews harked back to the Garden of Eden where in a prelapsarian world pleasure went unchecked by guilt or shame (prelapsarian derives from the Latin *prae* 'before' and *lapsus* 'the Fall'). With the discovery of the noble savage a modern form of primitivism found expression in such literature as Longfellow's *Song of Hiawatha*. The concept of the noble savage is explicitly referred to in *The Conquest of Granada* by John Dryden:

> I am as free as nature first made man,
> Ere the base laws of servitude began,
> When wild in woods the noble savage ran.

It appealed naturally to sentimentalists, but it also appealed to certain political thinkers because it seemed to contradict the biblical doctrine of original sin: they believed that in undermining revealed religion the concept would threaten the political thinking based on it – and encourage the development of new political thinking based on reason rather than tradition.

However, in their discussions about the origins of society (and therefore of the basis of authority in human affairs) modern philosophers viewed the state of nature in either a positive or a negative manner. Jean-Jacques Rousseau, one of the most influential of modern political thinkers, asserted the natural goodness, equality and freedom of men and women – in stark contrast to the conditions of his own time. He traced the corruption of society to the development in men of *amour propre* (French 'self-esteem' or 'vanity') and of the drive to assert their own worth before and against other men.

positive
ive is a Latin suffix indicating 'a tending towards'; *positum* is a formation meaning 'something placed'. Positive in its basic sense means definite; here it means marked by the presence of good qualities. Its opposite is negative (*negare* is the Latin 'to deny')

Agriculture and metallurgy, by leading to the establishment of private property, provided a physical means of asserting one's social position – the more you owned the more you were respected. States, Rousseau believed, were brought into being by the wealthy to provide the means of protecting private property – that is why they were not concerned with liberty and equality. The poor assented to the arrangements for the sake of security.

His remedy was a new social contract under which the general will would be expressed through a vote on all laws by the body of free and equal citizens; it would be the duty of the state executive (in whatever form it took) to apply the laws equally to all.

the executive
is the branch of government that executes, i.e. carries out, laws, plans, agreements, etc. (*ex* is the Latin 'out'; *sequi* is 'to follow')

The English philosopher Thomas Hobbes took a negative view of man in the state of nature – men with their contrary desires were naturally prone to violence and injustice; a sovereign power, in whatever form, is needed to impose order and stability; the State is a creation of man – it may be well or badly built.

A people respected ostensibly because they have been in possession of a particular territory from time immemorial, but in reality because they are powerful, may be described as autochthonous (*autos* is the Greek 'self'; *chthōn* is 'earth' – autochthonous, therefore, means sprung from the earth itself). The Athenians claimed they were autochthonous.

chthon
appears unexpectedly in the name of the brilliant Protestant reformer Philipp Melanchthon who in 1518 Graecized – *Graecia* is the Latin 'Greece' – his surname Schwarzerd (German *Schwartz* 'black' and *Erd* 'earth') using *melas, melanos* 'black' and *chthōn*

academic
as a noun, a professional member of the staff of a university or other institution of higher learning; as an adjective, pertaining to an institution of higher learning, or impractical and theoretical

Outside Athens in ancient times there was a garden that was linked with a legendary hero called Academus. When in 387 BC the philosopher Plato established a school there, it came to be called the Academy. The ten-year course of studies that Plato laid down was aimed not at helping the students earn a living but at making them examine the world and man's place in it. It was said that the Academy was so solemnly dedicated to study that it was forbidden to laugh there.

The Latin poet Horace (Horatian, derived from his name, means relating to, in the manner of, Horace) made a famous reference to Plato's Academy: '*Atque inter silvas Academi quaerere verum*' – 'And seek truth in the groves of Academus'. So did Milton in *Paradise Regained:*

> The groves of Academe,
> Plato's retirement, where the Attic bird
> Trills her thick-warbled notes the summer long.

platonic
as in a platonic relationship, is applied to love free from physical desire. We rely largely on Plato for biographical material on Socrates; platonic love was a synonym for Socratic love – the kind of non-sexual interest in young men that Plato shows Socrates as having

Academe (also sometimes academia, *ia* being a suffix commonly used for places, e.g. Australia, Indonesia, sylvania) is used to refer to a university environment.

People have long observed the *odium academicum* academics are wont to show to one another (*odium* is the Latin 'hatred', from which we derive odious; the Latin lyric poet Catullus famously employs *odere* 'to hate', from which odium derives, to express the frustration of a lover dazzled by a beautiful but heartless woman. He addresses Lesbia, '*Odi et amo*' ('I hate you yet I love you'). Academicism is used by art and literary critics to indicate that an artist or writer follows rigidly the rules and traditions of his or her genre. The word usually has pejorative connotations.

Academy may nowadays be applied to any institution where a skill may be learned, from a dancing academy to a great military training establishment such as West Point.

Plato's Academy continued for nine hundred years and so had a history longer than any university that exists today. It was closed by the Emperor Justinian in 529 AD because it was the last stronghold of ancient pagan learning. How third-level education might have developed had the Academy survived till our own time is, of course, an academic question.

act
a law made by a national parliament (also called a statute) as distinct from a law based on another source such as the judgments of judges or custom

Agere, actum, from which act is derived, is the Latin 'to do' – an act is a thing done, in this instance by the legislature. The word's association with legislation goes back to Roman times when a daily account of the various matters brought before the Senate, the opinions of the chief speakers, and the decisions of the house was published under the title *Acta Senatus* (Acts of the Senate). The word actor usually describes a male member of the cast of a play – originally a doing rather than a mere recitation of an event – but it may also be used simply to describe someone who does something. Sociologists use it in that sense.

ad hoc
for this purpose

Ad is the Latin 'to' or 'for'; *hoc* is 'this thing'. The expression is frequently used about committees. An *ad hoc* committee is a temporary committee set up to do a particular task. It is disbanded when the task is done. Used of arrangements – *ad hoc* arrangements – it connotes improvization.

ad nauseam
literally, to the point of causing sickness

Ad is the Latin 'to' or 'for'; *nauseam* is a form of *nausea* 'seasickness'. A bore often creates his or her effect by going on *ad nauseam* about a topic of exceedingly limited interest to the hearer(s). Nausea is itself derived from the Greek *nausia*, also meaning 'seasickness', which in turn derives from *naus* the Greek 'ship' (*nautikos* 'of a ship' from *naus* gives us nautical). *Navis* is the Latin 'ship' (hence navy, naval, navigator and circumnavigate, *circum* being the Latin 'around').

ad rem
to the point, pertinent

Ad is the Latin 'to' or 'for'; *rem* is a form of *res* 'thing' or 'matter'. A speaker who makes pertinent or relevant points is said to speak *ad rem*.

advocatus diaboli
the devil's advocate

Before a Pope canonizes a saint, a long, thorough examination of the candidate's life is carried out. Before 1983 one official was assigned the task of arguing against the proposal to canonize. He was known as the *advocatus diaboli* (*advocatus* means 'advocate', one who pleads the cause of another, from the Latin *advocare* 'to call in'; *diaboli* is a form of *diabolus* 'devil', from which we derive diabolical). *Advocatus diaboli* may be applied generally to anyone who tests an argument by arguing the opposite case: 'Acting as *advocatus diaboli*, I put it to you that …' Sometimes when the term is applied to someone who takes the unpopular side of an argument, there is a suggestion that he or she is simply being argumentative.

to canonize
is to officially list a dead person among the saints. Canon means the criterion for establishing what books are divinely inspired and by transference the list of such books (*kanōn* is the Greek 'measuring rod'). It is also applied to a Church law and a Church rank. In secular usage the word canon applies to the recognized list of a writer's works – 'the Hemingway canon'

aegis
protection, patronage

Aix, aigos is the Greek 'goat'. The *aegis* was the goatskin covering on the shield of Zeus, the chief of the Greek gods, often transferred to mean the shield itself. To be under the aegis of Zeus was to be protected, and therefore favoured, by Zeus. In Homer's *Iliad*, the epic poem that tells of the Trojan War, the gods and goddesses are depicted as showing great interest in the affairs of mortals, even to the extent of intervening in their battles. Thus Apollo and Pallas Athene borrow the aegis to protect their heroes. Homer describes the shield as follows:

> Athene, daughter of aegis-bearing Zeus … equipped herself for the terrible business of war with the arms of Zeus the Cloud-Gatherer. About her shoulders she threw the dreaded tasselled aegis, all round which the figure of Panic was depicted, while within

> it was Strife and Valour and blood-chilling Rout; within it, too, was the head of the ghastly monster Gorgon, fearful and terrible, the emblem of aegis-bearing Zeus.

Time has long ago leached the divine potency from the word. Nowadays you might find yourself attending a conference held under the aegis of a voluntary organization.

aesthetics
the study of the rules and principles both of art and beauty (whether natural or man-made)

The term aesthetics was introduced by the German philosopher A.G. Baumgarten, who derived it from the Greek *aesthētikos* 'perceptible by the senses'; anaesthetics was later derived from the same source. Immanuel Kant adopted the word and in *The Critique of Judgement* might be said to have laid the basis on which the theory of art and beauty has subsequently been developed. While the ancients did not write about aesthetics *per se* they did concern themselves with aesthetic issues: Plato famously banned flute-playing from his ideal State because it would enervate the youth, Aristotle ruled that a dramatic plot should have 'a beginning, a middle and an end' and Longinus in *On the Sublime* concluded that great writing can only proceed from a great mind.

enervate
(to deprive of strength or vitality) derives from the Latin *enervare* 'to remove the nerves from', *nervus* being the Latin 'nerve' or 'sinew' and e 'from'

Aestheticism was a nineteenth-century movement that placed an exaggerated value on art. It contributed to the modern attitude that the creation and appreciation of beautiful art are self-rewarding activities that do not necessarily proceed from moral, political, social or financial motives.

The principles of aesthetics are often challenged by popular culture. George Bernard Shaw's plays attracted the interest of Hollywood's moguls but Shaw was averse to having his work reshaped by their box-office values. When Sam ('Gentlemen, include me out') Goldwyn visited Shaw in 1920 he assured the distinguished author that he would treat his plays with velvet gloves, that their integrity would be protected, commercial considerations be damned. Later, Shaw told a newspaperman, anxious to know how the meeting between the famous Irishman and the famous Jew had gone, 'There is only one difference between Mr Goldwyn and me: whereas he is after art, I am after money.'

Affidare is a medieval Latin word, literally meaning 'to swear an oath', from which we derive affidavit. By definition an affidavit must be confirmed by oath or affirmation.

affidavit
a written statement that may be produced in evidence in court

A – *ab* before a vowel – is the Latin 'from'; *fortis* is 'strong'; *fortior* is a form of it that means 'stronger'. The expression is used in the context of logical argument. Thus someone might assert: 'If I would not let my best friend drive my car, *a fortiori* I would not let a complete stranger drive it!'

a fortiori
with all the more reason

Agere, actum is the Latin 'to do'. *Agenda* is a form of it that means 'things to be done'. A hidden agenda is the objective or objectives an individual or cabal wishes to achieve through group action without letting the rest of the group know.

In discussion of education the concept of the hidden curriculum occurs. A school curriculum lays down, for everybody to see, the subjects to be pursued by the students – mathematics, English, science, etc. However, in the way in which it teaches the subjects, in the atmosphere it creates, in the extracurricular (*extra* means 'outside' in Latin) activities it arranges, a school may seek to achieve certain hidden objectives such as moral courage, honesty, persistence and conformity. Education(al)ists call the set of such objectives the hidden curriculum.

agenda
things to be done; items of business requiring consideration or decision at a meeting

atmosphere
derives from the Greek *atmos* 'air' or 'vapour' and *sphaira* 'globe' and means in its primary sense the gaseous envelope surrounding the earth or any other celestial body

Agent is a French word derived from the Latin *agere, actum* 'to do'; *provocateur* is a French word meaning 'provoking'. Governments have been known to use *agents provocateurs* to provide them with excuses to move their forces against certain groups.

agent provocateur
someone secretly employed to induce others to engage in disruptive or provocative actions

Ager, agri is the Latin 'field'. From it we also derive agriculture and agribusiness. Its Greek equivalent is *agros*, from which we derive a series of words beginning with *agro*, such as agronomy (the science of the cultivation of land) and agrochemical (a chemical such as a pesticide used for agricultural purposes). Chemical derives from alchemy, the incunabular form of chemistry (*incunabula* is the Latin 'cradle') that sought to transmute base metals into gold; alchemy derives from the Arabic *al* 'the' and *kimiya* 'transmutation'; pesticide

agrarian
relating to land

derives from the Latin *pestis* 'plague' and *cide*, from *caedere* 'to kill'.

alias
an assumed name

context
is the setting in which something occurs (*con* is a Latin particle meaning 'with', *texere, tectum* is 'to weave')

Alias is the Latin 'on other occasions'. It is often used in a legal context and specifically where an accused has used a name other than his or her own to establish a new identity, for instance to facilitate the committing of a crime (thus in court an accused might be identified as 'Tom Brown alias Tom Green').

For various reasons writers may use a name other than their own. This is called a pen-name (in French *nom de plume*), not an alias. One of the greatest novelists in English literature, George Eliot, the author of *Middlemarch*, was a woman, Mary Ann Evans.

If you wish to send a message to someone without revealing your name, you may use a pseudonym (in French a *nom de guerre*, literally a 'war name'), a false name (*pseudos* is the Greek 'false'), or no name at all, and so remain anonymous (*onoma* is the Greek 'name'; *a* – *an* before a vowel – is a prefix that negatives a word).

An acronym is a word formed from the initial letters of other words, for example NATO from North Atlantic Treaty Organization (*acro* is from the Greek *akros* 'topmost', which also gives us acrobat, *bat* being derived from the Greek *bainein* 'to walk', and acropolis, the citadel of an ancient Greek city, *polis* being the Greek 'city').

An antonym is a word opposite in meaning to another (*anti* is the Greek 'against'). Thus black is the antonym of white.

A heteronym is one of two or more words that have the same spelling but a different (*heteros* is the Greek 'other') sound and meaning. Thus two English words are spelled bow but they are pronounced differently and mean different things.

A homonym is a word with the same (*homos* in Greek) sound as another but a different meaning. Air and heir are homonyms.

A metonym is a figure of speech in which a word or phrase indicates a feature of the word for which it is substituted – thus 'wheels' for car and 'a bit of skirt' for a girl (the *met* particle is from the Greek *meta* indicating 'change').

Names are said to be patronymic if they are derived from a father or other ancestor (*patēr* is the Greek 'father') or metronymic (less commonly matronymic) if derived from a mother or other ancestress (*mētēr* is the Greek 'mother'). Patronyms have been employed far more frequently than metronyms in most societies for naming people. In modern times names usually take the form of a forename and surname (the French *sur*, from the Latin *super*, means 'over', 'above' or 'beyond').

A synonym is a word that means the same thing as another word: lift and elevator are synonyms (*sun*, transliterated *syn* in English, is the Greek 'with'). We tend to use the word loosely because to be truly synonymous words must denote the same thing, connote the same things and have the same range, that is be capable of being interchanged in all usages. Our example fails in respect of range: 'I stopped the car to give the woman a lift,' is fine; 'to give her an elevator' raises eyebrows.

transliterate
means to write in letters of another alphabet, from *trans* the Latin 'across' or 'beyond' and *litera* 'letter'. Translate means to remove from one place to another and, in relation to languages, to transfer meaning from one language to another (the *late* formation derives from the irregular Latin verb *ferre* 'to carry')

Nomen, nominis is the Latin 'name', from which we derive nominal, nominee, nominate, denomination and nominalism (the philosophic doctrine associated with Aristotle that general ideas like goodness or beauty are simply names that have no reality apart from the particular people or things from which they are abstracted; the opposite view, called both idealism and realism, was held by Plato's Socrates: general ideas or universals are real things that exist eternally; the things in the world about us share in the reality of universals but only fleetingly).

alibi
the defence that a person was elsewhere at the time of an alleged crime

Alibi is derived from the Latin *alius* 'other' and *ubi* 'where'. It is also used for the evidence given in proof of the defence.

alienation
a feeling of being cut off from others

Alienus is the Latin 'belonging to another' and conveys the sense of estrangement, which is the essence of alienation. (An alien is someone who is not a citizen of the country in which he or she resides but who belongs to another country. It is also used as a synonym for an extraterrestrial.) Alienation, like many other terms, came into vogue with the spread of Marxism. It was borrowed from Hegel.

For Marx, the capitalist system produced a crippling sense of alienation in the industrial worker by such effects as estranging the worker from the product of his labour (it was not his) and from his fellow-workers (because it distinguished between types of labour and created a competitive labour market). The worker, Marx asserted, could achieve his human potential only if he were released from the capitalist system.

Broadly speaking, alienation is used in modern social thinking to describe the sense of isolation the individual feels in modern society (adversely contrasted with the warmth of the extended families and the small communities of earlier times). The word anomie is used in this sense too. Derived from the Greek negative particle *a* and *nomos* 'law', it was used by the French sociologist Émile Durkheim to convey the feeling of hopelessness that follows upon the loss of meaning and purpose in a prevailing culture. (It could be applied, for example, to the inability of French aristocrats to accept the new bourgeois culture after the Revolution.) The Greek historian Thucydides, in his famous account of the plague in Athens, uses this word to describe the behaviour of the Athenians at that time:

> The plague first introduced into the city a greater lawlessness [anomia]. For, where men hitherto practised concealment, they now showed a more careless daring. They saw how sudden was the change of fortune in the case both of those who were prosperous and suddenly died, and of those who before had nothing, but in a moment were in possession of the property of others. And so they resolved to get out of life the pleasures which could be had speedily and would satisfy their lusts, regarding their bodies and their wealth alike as transitory.

transitory
means of short duration, transient, ephemeral, and derives from the Latin *transire, transitum* 'to go across'

inalienable
In is a Latin negative prefix; *alienus* is 'belonging to another' – inalienable, then, means incapable of being transferred to another and therefore incapable of being taken away and is applied to fundamental human rights; imprescriptible, not capable of being limited by law, is also used in relation to rights, from *in – im* before a word beginning with b, m or p – the Latin prefix that negatives a word, and *praescribere*, the Latin 'to lay down as a rule'

The word acedia, derived from the Greek negative particle *a* and *kēdos* 'care', is used to describe the dark night of the soul – the sense of alienation from God that sometimes afflicts contemplatives. More generally it means torpor. Accidie is another form of the word.

In law, alienation means the disposal of property. Property that cannot legally be disposed of, because it would deprive one's heirs, is referred to as inalienable.

alphabet
the letters of a language set forth in a fixed order

Alpha is the first letter of the Greek alphabet and beta is the second. The Greek alphabet is derived from the Phoenician script (the Phoenicians were Semitic traders). Alpha is derived from the Semitic *aleph* meaning 'ox', originally 'ox-head', represented as ᗅ. The Greeks, who did not know the meaning of *aleph,* thought the letter looked better standing up – hence A. Beta is derived from the Semitic *beth*. *Beth* means 'house' (as in Bethlehem – house of bread – so called because it was in a prosperous grain-growing area) and was represented as ⌂ – hence B.

Alphanumeric is used to describe a typewriter, computer or other machine that uses both letters and numbers (*numerus* is the Latin 'number', which also gives us numerate, innumerable, innumerate, numerous, numerology and numeric).

Gamma is the third letter of the Greek alphabet. John Gribbin in his *Almost Everyone's Guide to Science* tells us that the first evidence for energetic processes going on inside atoms had come in 1895 when Wilhelm Röntgen discovered X-rays (given that name because in mathematics X is traditionally the unknown quantity). This discovery stimulated the search for other forms of radiation from atoms. Shortly three such forms were discovered and given the names of the first three letters of the Greek alphabet – alpha, beta and gamma.

Delta is the fourth letter of the Greek alphabet. In Aldous Huxley's dystopian *Brave New World* the deltas are the lowest grade of worker (it was customary for academics to rate their students' work using the first four letters of the Greek alphabet, alpha being the highest grade, delta the lowest). Zoologists use alpha to distinguish the leader in a group of animals from others, for example an alpha male as opposed to a beta male. The capital form of delta is triangular and so aeroplanes with triangular wings are described as delta-winged. An alluvial tract at the mouth of a river is called a delta (because that of the Nile was delta-shaped).

Iota is the Greek letter i, the smallest in the alphabet. It is used as a word meaning something very small: 'The bargaining was very tough but she did not concede one iota.' One of the bitterest schisms in the early Christian Church occurred because of an iota of difference between two sides – that between those who believed the Father and Son were of the same (*homos* in Greek) substance and those who believed they were of like (*homoios* in Greek) substance.

Chi (for ch) is the twenty-second letter of the Greek alphabet and rho (for r) is the seventeenth. Combined, they form the first three letters of Christ's name: so the chi superimposed on the rho was used as a

Α α alpha
Β β beta
Γ γ gamma
Δ δ delta
Ι ι iota
Ρ ρ rho
Σ σ sigma
Υ υ upsilon
Χ κ chi
Ω ω omega
capital and lower-case forms of Greek letters referred to here

schism
is the Anglicization of *schisma*, the Greek 'split', derived from *schizein* 'to split'; from it we also derive schizophrenia, a condition in which the mind – Greek *phrēn* – divides itself between reality and illusion; from *phrēn* we also derive frenetic – frantic – and phrenology, the study of the human brain. Schizophrenia was coined by Jung's teacher Eugen Bleuler

monogram
means a design of one or more letters, especially initials, embroidered on clothing or printed on stationery etc., from the Greek *monos* 'alone' or 'single' and *gramma* 'letter'

monogram for Christ. One of the most famous pages in the Book of Kells – the Chi-Rho page – is lovingly devoted to this monogram.

Sigma is the eighteenth letter of the Greek alphabet. Anything S-shaped, such as the necks of certain birds, may be said to be sigmoid. In mathematics the symbol S indicates the summation of figures or quantities.

Omega is the last letter of the Greek alphabet; when God is called the Alpha and the Omega what is meant is that He is the beginning and the end of all things.

The Russians and the Serbs use the Cyrillic alphabet, which is based on the Greek alphabet. The Russians were converted in the ninth century by St Cyril and other Greek Orthodox Christians who brought writing with them.

Having bequeathed the word alphabet to the world, the Greeks themselves over time proceeded to abandon several of the original sounds. Beta has become vita, a v sound, the g of gamma has become mostly a y sound, delta's d has become a th, and u (upsilon) has become ee. In the process, modern Greek has ended up without a letter for b; improvization has led to the substitution of mp where a b sound is called for, so that *bíra*, the word for 'beer', is spelt *mpura*.

An alphabet is distinguished from a syllabary (*syllaba* is the Latin 'syllable'). An alphabet gives visual representation to what the Greeks saw as the components of syllables, that is vowels and consonants. Syllabaries, such as in Sanskrit and Hebrew, give visual representation to the initials of each syllable. Hebrew newspapers today present only what we regard as the consonants, leaving the reader to construe the vowels from the context. Jehovah, the personal name of God, revealed to Moses, from the Hebrew *YHVH*, is construed by some theologians as Yahweh.

amanuensis
someone employed in taking dictation or keeping notes; a secretary or literary assistant

The Latin *amanuensis* may be divided in two parts: *amanu* derived from the Latin expression *servus a manu* 'a slave at hand', that is for handwriting, and *ensis* a suffix indicating 'a person from' – thus *Cambrensis* means 'a person from *Cambria*' (the Latin 'Wales'; *Cymry* is Welsh for 'the people of Wales'). In *Galileo's Daughter* Dava Sobel writes: 'And having served as Galileo's amanuensis, Viviani later gathered all of his papers to publish, in 1656, the first edition of the collected works of Galileo – without the *Dialogue*, of course.'

Amazonian
relating to the Amazons or to the Amazon river

In Greek myth the Amazons were a race of women-warriors who fought on horseback with bows and arrows, and javelins. They were located north of the Black Sea. Their name is popularly taken to derive from their practice of cutting off the right breast so as not to impede the bowstring (*mazos* is the Greek 'breast' and *a* is a negative particle – *amazos* is 'without a breast'). The battles they engaged in with men were called Amazonomachies (*machē* is 'battle'), and were a favourite subject of artists.

The Amazons once invaded Scythia and began ravaging the countryside. When the Scythians discovered that the invaders were women, they sent out a group of young men to offer the Amazons love rather than battle. The strategem worked and the Amazons settled down to happy, if somewhat asymmetrical, married life.

The Amazon river has no connection with the ancient Amazons. That name is believed to be based on a local native Indian word *amassone*.

ambivalent
having at one and the same time opposing attitudes towards an object

Ambi is a Latin prefix 'on both sides'; *valere* is 'to be strong'. To be ambivalent is to be strong on both sides, to be for and against something at the same time.

Ambiguous, applied to statements, now means capable of more than one meaning although it originally meant capable of two meanings (from *ambi* and *agere* the Latin 'to drive'). Equivocal is a synonym for ambiguous (*aequi* is a Latin prefix meaning 'equal'; *vox, vocis* is 'voice'). People often resort to ambiguity (or equivocation) to avoid giving a lie direct.

They may also prevaricate, that is to say, shift about from side to side to evade the truth (*praevaricari* is the Latin 'to walk crookedly'). A medieval Irish tax-farmer, Shaen, suspected of remitting to the treasury in Dublin far less of the tax he collected than was due, prevaricated. His performance before a tribunal of enquiry was recorded with *Schadenfreude*: 'Many were his windings, shiftings and obscurities.'

Schadenfreude
means delight in another's misfortune (from the German *Schaden* 'hurt' and *Freude* 'joy')

amnesty
a general pardon extended to a large group of people

Amnēstia is the Greek 'forgetfulness' derived from the Greek negative *a* and *mnēstia* 'remembering'. An amnesty is an overlooking of past wrongs. The victor often grants an amnesty to the defeated so as to put behind the rancour of war (indeed the weaker side may make the granting of an amnesty a *sine qua non* of surrender).

tabula rasa
This phrase is often attributed to the English philosopher John Locke but it was used much earlier by Thomas Aquinas to describe the state of a child's mind when it is born

An amnesty provides a society with a *tabula rasa* (a clean slate). *Tabula* is the Latin 'table' or (as here) 'writing-tablet'. For writing exercises Roman schoolchildren often used a wooden tablet over which wax was spread. The letters were cut into the wax. The tablet could be re-used indefinitely by scraping the wax smooth (*radere, rasum* is the Latin 'to scrape', from which we derive razor and eraser).

A pointed instrument called a *stilus* ('stylus') was used for writing. From it the Italians derived the word for a small dagger with a slender tapered blade – a *stiletto*. *Stilus* also gives us style in its various senses. The Greek *stylos* 'column' gives us stylite for a hermit who lived on the top of a pillar, the most notable of whom was the Syrian St Simeon Stylites, and peristyle, the classical architectural form consisting of a range of columns round a building or a square, *peri* being the Greek 'around'.

international
means between nations, from the Latin *inter* 'between' or 'among' and *natio, nationis* 'nation'; *inter alia* means 'among other things', *alia* being 'other things' in Latin; *inter alios* means 'among other persons', *alios* being 'other persons' in Latin

Amnesty International is the name of the independent worldwide movement that works for the release of all prisoners of conscience, fair and prompt trials for political prisoners, and an end to torture and execution.

Amnesia, derived from the same word as amnesty, is the clinical condition of loss of memory (*memoria* is the Latin 'memory'). The amnesiac may present with an inability to register new memories (anterograde amnesia, *anterior* being the Latin 'previous' and *gradi* 'to go') or a loss of access to previously stored memories (retrograde amnesia, *retrogradi* being the Latin 'to go backwards'). Because of the dramatic possibilities, most TV and movie amnesiacs suffer from psychogenic predominantly retrograde amnesia. Research shows that our first memories date from just beyond our third year. Freud held that infantile amnesia was due to repression (Latin *re* 'back' and *primere, pressum* 'to push') – the consignment by people of their earliest sexual experiences to the unconscious.

Mnēmnē is the Greek 'memory' and *mnēmōn* is 'mindful'. A mnemonic is a device to help the memory. For example, to remember a list, a person could associate each item with a house on the street they grew up in. Mnemosyne, the Greek goddess of memory, was the mother of the Muses and Zeus was their father.

analogy
a correspondence in certain respects between things otherwise different

Analogia was a term used by Greek mathematicians to denote equality of ratios (*ana* is the Greek 'up' and *logos* is 'word', 'reason', 'account' or, as here, 'ratio'). The term analogue is still used in scientific fields. In common speech an analogy is often used to convince us that there is a correspondence between a process we know well and one we do not: 'There is an analogy between how a row breaks out between youngsters and how a war breaks out between nations.'

In the theory of language, words are classified as univocal, equivocal, or analogical. A word is univocal if it has the same core meaning in all its uses – thus the word cow means the same when it is used of many different cows (*unus* is the Latin 'one' and *vox, vocis* is 'voice'). A word is equivocal when it can have different meanings in the same usage, thus 'His aunt brought him to see the picture' (painting? film?). *Aequus* is the Latin 'equal'. To equivocate in argument is to draw inferences from different uses of the same word or concept within a discussion without acknowledging the shift of meaning (jokes often hinge on equivocation and therefore are often untranslatable). A word is analogical when it has a core meaning that varies with usage – thus the meaning of good differs when it is applied to a field and a boy. Awareness of the analogical character of words protects us from false inferences (deductions, from *inferre* the Latin 'to bring into').

An allegory is a form of analogy (*allos* is the Greek 'other'; *agoreuein* means 'to speak'). Among the most famous allegories in literature are *Aesop's Fables*. The concept is especially important in biblical studies where it has been argued from an early date that certain texts, for example Song of Songs, should be understood allegorically rather than literally – as, in that case, Christ's love for His Church, rather than the expression of a man's love for a woman.

Simile is probably the most common form of analogy (*similis* is the Latin 'like', from which we also derive similar, assimilate and verisimilitude – semblance of truth – *verus* being 'true'): 'He ran like the hammers of hell.'

Metaphor is a more daring form of analogy than simile (*meta* is here the Greek 'with' and *pherein* is 'to carry'), where we say something is not like, but is, something else: 'She was the apple of his eye.' On occasion

ratio
derives from the Latin *reri* 'to think'; to ratiocinate is to think or argue logically or rationally; reason comes through French from *ratio*. In English ratio is used for a measure of the relative size of two classes expressible as a proportion: 'The ratio of women to men in the dance hall was two to one.'

an author begins with metaphoric speech and then intensifies it with a simile:

> They melted from the field [metaphor], as snow,
> When streams are swollen, and south winds blow,
> Dissolves in silent dew [simile].
>
> –Walter Scott

Analogy allows us to understand one thing in terms of another and thereby makes possible many different sorts of discourse. Thus believers proceed to some understanding of God by using words derived from the created world – they say He is wise or good, but not in the way humans are wise or good. More generally, the analogical character of thought and discourse points to the fact that the human mind attains knowledge and understanding indirectly, that is, it knows of one thing in terms of others. But it is this very feature that allows us to equivocate in our discourse – to intend a meaning other than the apparent one. We must be careful not to draw false inferences from analogies. We cannot infer from the fact that a good typewriter makes little noise that a good rocket launcher makes little noise.

anarchism
a political doctrine that holds that governments should be abolished and in their place a cooperative system established

A – *an* before a vowel – is a Greek prefix that negatives a word; *archein* is 'to rule'. Anarchists prize freedom, not disorder. They feel that humans, being social animals, should be free to combine with their fellows on a voluntary basis (but anarchists have differed in their ideas on how this should be done). Because they see the modern State as forcing people to work together (and as providing an apparatus that some people can use to force others to do what they want), they regard it as intrinsically evil. Since governments seek to impose control from the centre, anarchists lay stress on local control.

century
derives from the Latin *centum* 'hundred'. A centurion was a Roman officer who commanded a hundred men. A centenarian is someone who is a hundred or more years old

In the nineteenth century, some anarchists sought to promote their beliefs through violence, often of a singularly desperate kind such as the assassination of Czar Alexander II of Russia in 1881. Such acts gave anarchists their dominant popular image of swarthy conspirators priming a bomb in a cellar. Other anarchists have sought to promote their beliefs by non-violent means such as civil disobedience, non-cooperation and strikes.

Pierre Joseph Proudhon, a Frenchman, is regarded

as the first modern anarchist: *'la propriété, c'est le vol'* (French, 'property is theft'). He called his form of anarchism mutualism because he envisaged, in place of the bourgeois State, a collection of autonomous communities cooperating with one another for their mutual benefit. His emphasis on the rights of the individual rather than those of the collective brought him into conflict with Marx, who emphasized the need for a strong central authority.

autonomous
means self-governing, from the Greek *autos* 'self' and *nomos* 'law'; the Greeks first applied the word to city-states that made their own laws; while the word is often used as the equivalent of independent there can be degrees of autonomy

Anarchists have never formed a very significant movement. However, they provided Marx with the idea of 'the withering away of the State' as the ultimate condition of communism and, in combination with syndicalists (people who believed trades-union power should be used to destroy the bourgeois State), they were influential in France and Italy before World War I and in Spain before and during the Civil War (1936–9).

Religious principle has also been adduced in support of anarchism. The great Russian novelist Leo Tolstoy was a religious anarchist: he felt the State was inconsistent with love, the quintessential Christian virtue. In modern times one finds religious anarchists of a different kind – people who find the institutional Church unhelpful and seek to practise their religion outside it.

ancestor
one from whom a person is descended, forefather

Ancestor is derived from the Latin *ante* 'before' and *cedere, cessum* 'to go'. The *or* suffix is a Latin form indicating 'masculinity' – thus actor, emperor, mediator and dominator. The *ress* and *rix* suffixes are forms indicating 'femininity' – thus ancestress, actress, empress, mediatrix and dominatrix. (The Latin *meretrix, meretricis* 'prostitute' derives from *merere* 'to earn money'. From it we get meretricious, meaning garishly attractive or insincere.)

Posterity, from the Latin *post* 'after', means future or succeeding generations. Sir Boyle Roche, the classic exponent of the Irish bull – a bull is an expression containing a contradiction unperceived by the speaker – once dismissed the claims of posterity with the remark, 'Damn posterity, sir! What has posterity done for us?' Irish bulls are distinguished from others by their epigrammatic character. John Pentland Mahaffy, Oscar Wilde's professor in Trinity College Dublin, observed, 'Irish bulls are always pregnant.' Boyle Roche once protested, 'I am not a bird – I cannot be in two places at

a papal bull
is a formal document issued by a Pope, which used to be authenticated by a leaden seal (*bulla* in Latin). A bill – a bill of fare, a parliamentary bill – also derives from *bulla*. A bulletin, from a diminutive form of *bulla*, is an official statement on a matter of public interest. Papal, papist, papistry and Pope, referring to the Bishop of Rome as head of the Roman Catholic Church, all derive from the Greek *papas* 'father-in-God', itself derived from the Greek *pappas* 'father'

once!' In a letter to a friend in England he sought to convey the parlous security situation in Ireland: 'I write this with a sword in one hand and a pistol in the other.'

anomaly
irregularity, abnormality

A – *an* before a vowel – is a Greek prefix that negatives a word; *homalos* is 'even'. Bureaucrats and other people who draw up policies must have sufficient imagination to foresee anomalies if they are to do their work effectively. In science the application and development of theories may throw up anomalies. These may be ignored or dealt with incrementally (*incrementum* is the Latin 'growth'), that is by a succession of small *ad hoc* changes in theory. Eventually such anomalies may be fully resolved only by a paradigm shift.

anthology
a printed collection of literary works, especially poems

Anthos is the Greek 'flower' and *legein* is 'to gather'. The Greeks would hail a beautiful short poem, especially an epigram, as a flower of poetry. They sometimes collected a number of such flowers into a book. *Florilegium* is the Latin synonym for anthology (*flos, floris,* from which we derive floral, flora, florid and Florida, is the Latin 'flower' and *legere* is 'to gather').

Analecta (also analects), derived from the Greek *ana* 'up' and *legein*, are selected passages from one or more works, or collections of sayings: 'The only (nearly) direct source of Confucius's thought is *The Analects,* a collection of his *obiter dicta* compiled by disciples after his death.' (*The Economist,* 25 July 1998)

the flora and fauna
means all the plant and animal life of a particular place (Faunus was an Italian deity of the countryside). Wild animals such as wolves and bears are said to be feral (untamed or savage, *fera* being the Latin 'wild beast')

anti-Semitism
hatred of the Jewish race

Shem was one of the three sons of Noah. Abraham, from whom the Jews derive their race (our father Abraham), was one of the many descendants of Shem. The term Semitic, therefore, applies strictly to other races as well as the Jews. *Anti* is the Greek 'against'. Anti-Jewish feeling was common among Christians, who blamed the Jews for the death of Christ. This was a religious rather than a racial prejudice. (However, racism was displayed by the Spanish Inquisition in its especial zeal to test the bona fides of converted Jews.) It was not until 1965 that the Catholic Church formally declared that, while authorities of the Jews and those who followed their lead pressed for the death of Christ, all the Jews then living and their descendants, including the Jews of today, could not be blamed for the death of Christ, that is, were not guilty of deicide.

Hatred of the Jews because of their race rather than their religion, a persistent historical phenomenon, culminated in the Holocaust – the physical destruction of the Jews decided on by the Nazis as the final solution of 'the Jewish problem' at the Wannsee Conference in Berlin in 1942. Many reasons have been advanced for the strange phenomenon of anti-Semitism. In general, the Jews sought, wherever they were, to maintain their religious and cultural identity. This lack of assimilation, sometimes combined with a desire to return to the Holy Land, gave those in whose countries they settled a basis for seeing them as alien.

culminate
is to reach the highest point (*culmen, culminis* is the Latin 'roof' and therefore 'summit'; *apex* is another Latin word for 'top'; *acme* is a Greek word for 'top': 'He reached the acme of his profession.') To fulminate (against) is to denounce violently, from the Latin *fulmen, fulminis* 'lightning' or 'thunderbolt' – the classical expression of divine wrath – itself derived from *fulgere* 'to shine'. Fulgent means shining; refulgent means radiant, the prefix *re* being an intensifier

In Poland and Russia, where there were large numbers of impoverished Jews, the Jews were a convenient minority to blame for political or economic setbacks. In 1905, following the defeat of Russia by the Japanese, the czarist police published a forged document called *The Protocols of the Elders of Zion*. This purported to reveal a Jewish conspiracy to enslave the world. It later fed Hitler's lunatic fantasies about the Jews.

luna
is the Latin 'moon'; in ancient times the influence of the moon was thought to make people mad. *Selēnē* is the Greek 'moon'. Selenology is the study of the moon (*ology* here means 'study of', from the Greek *logos* 'word', 'reason' or 'account')

In Western Europe and America many Jews achieved glittering material success and were conspicuous in art, literature, music, medicine, science and thought: the envy this provoked in some people was visited upon the whole race of Jews. As Barnet Litvinoff in *The Burning Bush: Anti-Semitism and World History* epigrammatically puts it: 'Wealth was not equally shared among the Jews, only the resentment attaching to it.' Most perniciously of all, at the beginning of the twentieth century certain pseudo-scientific theories about race were developed that suggested the Jews were degenerate (*degenerare* is the Latin 'to depart from its kind' or 'to be inclined to become base'). These theories became part of Nazi ideology.

There were few survivors of the final solution. Survivor derives from the French *survivre*, *sur* derives from the Latin *super* 'over' or 'beyond', *vivre* derives from *vivere* 'to live'. Final derives from the Latin *finis* 'end' or 'limit'. Hence define, confine, and infinite – without limit.

apartheid
the unique system of unequal separation of races established by the

Apartheid means 'separateness' in Afrikaans. The word gained universal currency after the election of the National Party of Afrikaners in South Africa in 1948. Legislation was passed to cover nearly every aspect of

white authorities of South Africa solely on the basis of skin colour

life in order to maintain white supremacy and economic privilege through the disenfranchisement and oppression of the majority black population (85 per cent). Following the release from jail in 1990 of Nelson Mandela, the African National Congress (ANC) leader, the whole apartheid system was dismantled and democratic government installed under a new constitution.

aphorism
a pithy saying expressing a general truth

Aphorizein is the Greek 'to define' or 'mark boundaries', from which aphorism and aphoristic derive:

> [Nietzsche's] conviction that art was the highest form of human activity found expression in his own philosophical style, which is poetic and aphoristic rather than argumentative or deductive.
>
> –Anthony Kenny,
> *A Brief History of Western Philosophy*

The following are synonyms of aphorism: apothegm or apophthegm from the Greek *apo*, here 'forth', and *phthengesthai* 'to utter': 'Happiness is no laughing matter' (Archbishop Whately of Dublin, *Apothegms);* gnome and gnomic, from the Greek *gignōskein* 'to know'; proverb, from the Latin *proverbium*; adage, from the Latin *adagium*; maxim, from the Latin *maxima (sententia)* 'the best opinion'; and dictum, from the Latin *dicere, dictum* 'to say'.

apocalyptic
relating to the final destruction of the world

Apo is a Greek prefix, here meaning 'from' or 'un' (like the Latin *a* and *ab*); *calyptein* is 'to cover'. Apocalyptic refers primarily to the last book of the New Testament, the Apocalypse (the Uncovering), or the Book of Revelation as it is called in English, where a graphic account is given of the destruction of the world. The word is frequently used nowadays to describe the conditions that would attend the unleashing of a nuclear war. Armageddon, a mountain district in northern Palestine, is the name of the imaginary battlefield on which the climactic struggle between good and evil is conceived to take place in the Apocalypse. It is often used as a symbol of the destruction of the world.

One of the most famous pieces in European art is Albrecht Dürer's 'The Four Horsemen of the Apocalypse'. Described in the Apocalypse, the horsemen bring war, pestilence, famine and death. The dynamism of the cavalcade was without precedent in European graphic art – and made Dürer famous almost overnight. Cavalcade means a company of riders, and derives from *caballus* the Latin 'horse'. The Greek for 'horse' is *hippos* – a hippopotamus is a river-horse (*potamos* is the Greek 'river'), a hippodrome is a course for horse races (*dromos* is the Greek 'race' or 'course').

apocryphal
fictitious, sham

Apocruptein is the Greek 'to hide away', from which apocryphal is derived. Apart from the four gospels and other works in the list of recognized writings (the canon) of the New Testament, there were writings that purported to tell us more about the life of Christ, especially his youth, which is only summarily treated in the canonical writings. These works were hidden away because they were of dubious (*dubius* is the Latin 'wavering'; dubiety is the state of being doubtful) origin and so were called Apocrypha. The word occurs nowadays often in discussion of the character of public figures: many of the stories told about them are said to be apocryphal.

apologist
one who defends by argument

In everyday speech an apology is an excuse, tendered with an expression of regret, for some action. Its basic sense, however, is a reasoned defence (from the Greek *apo*, here 'off', and *logos*, here 'speaking'). Plato's first philosophical work, the *Apology*, records the speeches Socrates made at his trial. It appears in the form *apologia* in the Latin title Cardinal Newman gave to the book in which he defended his religious convictions – *Apologia Pro Vita Sua*. The second- and third-century writers who wrote in defence of Christianity against the attacks of their pagan contemporaries are known as the Christian apologists. Apologetics describes a process in which written defences are built up for a doctrine or position. We might refer to Marxist apologetics.

apostate
a defector

Apostate and apostasy originally applied to someone who had abandoned his or her religious faith (*apo* is Greek, here 'apart from'; *stasis*, from which the *stasy* formation derives, means 'standing'). They are now applied more generally: 'Unlike other CIA apostates, Snepp revealed no secrets in his book.' (*NYRB*, 23 September 1999)

Stasis may be used literally or figuratively to mean a state of stopped flow – stagnation (from *stagnum*, the

Latin 'pool'). In medicine it indicates a stoppage of any of the bodily fluids. Homeostasis describes the tendency of the body to achieve equilibrium in its physiological processes (*homoios* is the Greek 'like', from which *homeo* is derived). Freud employed the concept to explain a tendency towards constancy of psychic phenomena: just as a high salt intake into the body is followed by increased fluid loss to carry the excess away, so drives that upset the psychic equilibrium tend towards tension-reducing gratification.

Static, which has the same derivation as stasis, means stationary or inactive and is opposed to dynamic.

apotheosis
deification; deified ideal or highest development

Theos is the Greek 'god'; the suffix *osis* denotes process or condition. Among the Romans, apotheosis signified the elevation of a deceased emperor to divine honours, that is, the deification of the emperor (*deus* is the Latin 'god' and the *fication* element derives from *facere* 'to make').

When an emperor died he was given a splendid funeral. In addition, a wax image resembling him in every detail was made and displayed in the imperial palace for seven days. Then, with solemn religious ceremony, the image was borne through Rome to the Campus Martius (the Field of Mars, *campus* being the Latin 'field', now applied to the grounds and buildings of a university or, mainly in the US, to the outside area of a college or university) where it was placed on a great pile of wood, which was set alight. As the flames mounted, an eagle was released from the pile of wood, soaring, so the Romans believed, to carry the emperor's soul from earth to heaven. From that time the emperor was worshipped with Jupiter and the other gods. The practice invited satire. The philosopher Seneca, who was exiled by the Emperor Claudius, wrote a skit on the deification of that emperor called *The Apocolocyntosis* [that is, 'Pumpkinification'] *of Claudius,* which is extant.

We use apotheosis in a figurative sense. Thus, 'In his painting of the coronation of Napoleon – possibly his masterpiece – David apotheosized the French emperor.'

Jupiter was the Roman equivalent of Zeus, the chief of the Greek gods. The eagle – the king of the birds – was associated with Jupiter. The Romans used the eagle as a symbol of their imperial power – a practice in which they were to be imitated (in the first instance by Charlemagne when he was crowned as the first Holy Roman Emperor in 800 AD). The largest planet in the solar system is named felicitously (*felix, felicis* is the Latin 'happy') after Jupiter.

Jove, as in the exclamation 'By Jove!', derives from a form of Jupiter. Jovial is derived from Jove and means good-humoured because astrologers believed those born under the influence of the planet Jupiter were fated to be cheerful like the sportive god. Those born under the influence of the planet Mars, the Roman god of war, were fated to be martial. Those born under the influence of the planet Mercury, the messenger of the gods, represented with winged feet, were fated to be mercurial, that is, active and explosively emotional. Those born under the influence of the planet Saturn were fated to be saturnine, i.e. heavy and gloomy in temperament – Saturn was the old god of agriculture whom the Romans equated with Cronus (the father of Zeus), haunted by the knowledge that one of his children would usurp him. We refer to the satellites of Jupiter as the Jovian moons: satellite derives from the Latin *satelles, satellitis* 'attendant' or 'servant' – hence also the expression a satellite state. We refer to anything related to the planet Mars as Martian, and to the planet Venus as Venusian.

planets
are celestial bodies that revolve around stars and are illuminated by light from them, from the Greek *planētēs* 'wanderer'. The nine planets in our solar system are Mercury, Venus, Earth, Mars, Jupiter, Saturn, Uranus, Neptune and Pluto

a priori
pertaining to reasoning that proceeds from causes to effects. Reasoning that proceeds from effects to causes is called *a posteriori*

A is the Latin 'from'; *priori* is a form of *prior* 'before'. *A priori* literally means 'from something previous'. *Posteriori* is a form of the Latin *posterior* meaning 'later'. *A posteriori* literally means 'from something later'. Something preposterous is literally something before (Latin *pre*) and after (Latin *post*) at the same time.

Logicians use the term *a priori* to describe an argument or process of reasoning that starts from some assumed general abstract definitions or theorems and moves to conclusions that it is hoped will reveal to us some knowledge of the world. This mode of reasoning is also called deductive (*de* is a Latin particle meaning 'from'; *ducere, ductum* is 'to lead'). It is typical of mathematics and science (theorems and laws lead to conclusions) and is an integral part of all theory construction.

Logicians use the term *a posteriori* to describe an argument or process of reasoning that starts from our concrete beliefs about the world and seeks to derive more general and abstract truths from them. This mode

abstract
means literally drawn away (from the Latin *ab* 'away from' and *trahere, tractum* 'to draw'). In this context it means existing only as a mental concept as opposed to something concrete, that is, existing in a form perceptible by the senses like the construction material invented by the Romans from cement, sand, stone and water – concrete, from the Latin *con* 'with' or 'together' and *crescere, cretum* 'to grow'

of reasoning is also called inductive (*in* is a Latin particle meaning 'in' or 'into'). It is typical of philosophic, artistic and moral reasoning and is an intrinsic part of the preparatory work of scientific thinking also. In practice, our thinking is always a combination of both types of reasoning. In the history of thought an almost exclusive resort to the inductive method heralded the beginning of the scientific age. The decisive influence was the English lawyer and philosopher Francis Bacon, who in his book *Novum Organum Scientiarum* explored how the scientific observation of a number of individual instances may be used to discover a general principle.

Philosophers have used the two terms in their efforts to understand the nature of human knowledge. Does our knowledge of the world presuppose some given ideas or beliefs that are innate or at least not dependent on what we call experience (*a priori* knowledge) or is all our knowledge derived from what we call experience (*a posteriori* knowledge)?

Some philosphers have argued that there must be some given principles or categories present in the mind for it to begin to work at all. There are two versions of this theory. The more extreme argues that all knowledge that merits the name is simply a deduction from some innate ideas and beliefs (thus the rationalists). The other version of the theory sees these innate ideas or categories as a precondition for experience – one needs the concepts of space and time, for example, before one can understand the world in such terms. These categories are, as it were, part of the furniture of the mind but their content is filled out by experience. They make experience possible (thus the constructionists).

Other philosophers (the realists) reject the idea of innate knowledge, whether of ideas or categories. For them, all knowledge is derived ultimately from experience (*a posteriori*). The mind constructs its ideas and beliefs in its endeavours to know the world. There is nothing in the mind that has not come to it in its encounter with the world. But the way things are in the mind is different to the way things are in the world. For these philosophers our world is a linguistic world (*lingua* is the Latin 'tongue') and our language is a worldly language. What we know is the real world. Ideas and language are simply the media in and through which we experience the world.

logician
is a master of logic, the science of reasoning (*logos* is the Greek 'word', 'reason' or 'account')

intrinsic
means relating to the essential nature of a thing, inherent, from the Latin *intra* 'within'. Extrinsic means not included or contained within something, extraneous, external, from the Latin *extra* 'outside' or 'beyond'

innate
means inborn or inherent from the Latin *in* 'in' and *natus* 'born'; native (Latin *nativus*) means born in

relativism
is the doctrine that knowledge is relative, i.e. it derives its meaning by reference to something else (*relativus* is the late Latin 'having reference to', which is itself derived from *referre, relatum* 'to carry back'). Absolute is the opposite of relative and means existing without relation to anything else (*absolutus* is the Latin 'loosened from'). Scepticism is the ancient doctrine that real knowledge of things, whether relative or absolute, is impossible and that therefore one can only reflect on things but never draw conclusions about them (*skeptikos* is the Greek 'one who reflects upon')

The idealists, in contrast, believe that we only know our own ideas and that therefore we have no direct knowledge of the world. Among idealists we have three schools – rationalists, empiricists and mixed – the last-mentioned believe that some aspects of knowledge are innate and that others derive from experience.

Behind all *a priori* theories of the origins of knowledge lie the desire for certitude and for foundations to all our thinking. In that way, such theorists seek to ensure against both relativism and scepticism.

Arcadian
of a simple, rustic, fun-loving character

Arcadia (in English Arcady) was a district in Greece whose people lived a simple pastoral life (*pastor* is the Latin 'shepherd'). They were much given to music and dance. Greek poets wrote short poems capturing scenes or episodes from their lives called *idylls* (from the Greek *eidyllion* 'little image'), and so idyllic, meaning gloriously carefree and happy, comes to us from the content rather than the form of these poems.

Pan, the Greek god of woodlands, pastures and flocks, is the exemplary Arcadian (*exemplum* is the Latin 'example'). He was born with horns, a beard, a tail and goat legs. He led an idyllic life in Arcadia, guarding his flocks of sheep, sporting with mountain-nymphs, playing his pipes and resting in the shade. It was his custom to frighten away anyone who disturbed his noonday rest with a sudden shout.

Sudden terror (panic) was attributed to his influence. They say it was a sudden shout let out by Pan that panicked the Titans and led to Zeus's victory over them.

Not every nymph yielded to the fun-loving goat-god. Syrinx escaped him when the other gods took pity on her and turned her into a shudder of reeds along the river Ladon.

Pan cut the reeds and, since they made a gentle singing sound in the breeze, bound them together and invented the pan pipes. (A syringe, used to withdraw or inject fluids, derives from the Greek *syrinx, syringos* 'pipe'; doctors use the term syringomyelia for a spinal-cord disease in which cavities form in the grey matter of the cord, sometimes extending over its whole length, *muelos* being the Greek 'marrow'.)

Of all the gods, Pan was the only one whose death was announced. Plutarch, who wrote at the beginning of the Christian era, tells us that a sailor on a ship

metamorphosis
Syrinx's change into reeds is an example of metamorphosis, the transformation of something into another form of animal, vegetable or mineral, common in myth and folklore (*meta* is a Greek prefix here connoting 'change'; *morphē* is 'shape': modern film technique allows directors to morph characters from one form to another). Ovid's *Metamorphoses* (plural form), one of the most celebrated of Latin texts, is a retelling of those Greek myths that feature such transformations. Metempsychosis also implies change, being used to describe the Hindu and Orphic doctrines of the transmigration of the soul (Greek *psychē*) after death into some other body – reincarnation is its Latin-based synonym. In James Joyce's *Ulysses* the sensual Molly Bloom is puzzled by the word metempsychosis, which she encounters in *Ruby: the Pride of the Ring* by her favourite author, Paul de Kock, and asks her husband Leopold – himself a brilliant representation of *l'homme moyen sensuel* (French, 'your average sensual man') – to explain it: 'It's Greek: from the Greek,' he tells her

bound for Italy heard a voice shout over the waves telling him to proclaim, when he reached port, 'The great god Pan is dead!' When the ship reached shore the sailor did as he was told. And the whole countryside lamented. Pan appears in *The Wind in the Willows* by Kenneth Graham and in *The Crock of Gold* by James Stephens; however, because of Christian antipathy, his features characterize the Devil.

archive
records or the place they are kept in

The word originally applied to public records: *archeion* is the Greek 'public office' (derived from *archein* 'to rule'). For historians as well as lawyers written documents, whether from public or private archives, are treasured sources – the palest ink is better than the longest memory – hence the Latin dictum *quod scriptum manet* ('what is written remains').

From *manere*, the source of *manet*, and meaning 'to remain' or 'stay in a place', we derive immanent, meaning indwelling or pervading. The idea that an intelligent and creative principle is immanent in the universe, but not transcendent (having existence apart from it, *transcendere* being the Latin 'to climb over'), is fundamental to the doctrine of pantheism.

archy
anarchy, autarchy, hierarchy, matriarchy, monarchy, oligarchy and patriarchy – these are all words whose common suffix *archy* derives from the Greek *archein* 'to rule'

Anarchy is the absence of government – it is disorder (*a – an* before a vowel – is a Greek prefix that negatives a word).

Autarchy is rule by a single person (*autos* is 'self' in Greek). A different word, autarky, from *autos* and the Greek *arkein* 'to suffice', is used to refer to a system or policy of economic self-sufficiency. Autarkic economies, such as that of Spain under Franco, have historically stagnated.

Hierarchy is rule by priests (*hieros* means 'sacred' in Greek). In time hierarchy has come to mean the group of priests who rule the Church – the bishops – and also the pyramidal structure through which organizations are usually managed.

Matriarchy is rule by a woman or mother (*mater* is 'mother' in Latin and in Doric Greek).

Monarchy is rule by a king or queen, emperor or empress, or high noble (*monos* in Greek means 'alone' or 'single').

Oligarchy is rule by a small group (*oligos* means 'few' in Greek).

hieratic
means of or relating to priests. Sacerdotal, derived from the Latin *sacerdos, sacerdotis* 'priest', is a synonym. Hieroglyphic is used to describe a kind of writing using picture symbols, especially as found in ancient Egyptian temples – *glyphein* is the Greek 'to carve'. A hierophant – the *phant* formation derives from the Greek *phainein* 'to show' – is someone who interprets or explains mysteries.

Patriarchy is rule by a man or father (*patēr* is 'father' in Greek and in Latin).

arctic
of or relating to the Arctic

The Arctic refers to the regions north of the Arctic Circle, the imaginary circle round the earth parallel to the equator, at latitude 66.32°N. It derives from the Greek *arktikos* 'northern', itself derived from the fact that it relates to the constellation of the Bear (Greek *arktos*). The Antarctic (from the Greek *anti* 'against', here 'opposite', and Arctic) refers to the regions south of the Antarctic Circle, at latitude 66.32°S – Antarctica, the continent surrounding the South Pole, and its seas.

argumentum ad hominem
a point directed against the man rather than his argument

Argumentum is the Latin 'proof'; *ad* means 'to', 'for' or, as here, 'against'; *hominem* is a form of *homo, hominis* 'man'. In logic an *argumentum ad hominem* is a fallacy because it fails to address the points made by the other person and instead attacks his or her character or background. Nonetheless since it plays on the hearers' prejudices it is often effective.

Two ancient orators excelled in the use of this technique – Demosthenes, the Athenian, in his speeches against King Philip of Macedon (called, therefore, the philippics) and Cicero, the Roman, against many opponents, legal and political, for example his philippics modelled on Demosthenes, delivered against Mark Antony.

asinine
of or like an ass

Asinus is the Latin 'ass'. Asinine is usually applied in a pejorative sense.

A range of English words derive from the Latin names for common animals.

Apis 'bee' gives apiary (beehive) and apiarist (beekeeper); honey, the sweet viscid or viscous (*viscosus* is the Latin 'sticky') fluid made by bees is *mel, mellis* in Latin, from which we derive mellifluous or mellifluent – *fluere* is the Latin 'to flow' – for smooth, sweet sounds or utterances.

Aquila 'eagle' gives aquiline. The Roman nose is famously aquiline.

Avis 'bird' gives avian (as well as aviary and aviation). The Latin poet Juvenal, famous for his *Satires* that attacked the corruption of Roman society, coined the expression *rara avis* 'rare bird'. A still-quoted maxim of his is *mens sana in corpore sano* (Latin, 'a healthy mind in a healthy body'). Certain birds are associated with the classical divinities. Zeus, whose symbol was the eagle, once turned himself into a swan in order to ravish the lovely Leda as she strolled along the river Eurotas. Oliver St John Gogarty, whom Joyce used as the model for '[s]tately, plump Buck Mulligan' in *Ulysses*, has a poem 'Leda and the Swan', which closes with Leda's mother's reaction when Leda tells her she's pregnant:

> Of the tales that daughters
> Tell their poor old mothers,
> Which by all accounts are
> Often very odd;
> Leda's was a story
> Stranger than all others.
> What was there to say but:
> Glory be to God?

They say Leda later laid an egg out of which Helen of Troy was hatched. The owl was the symbol of Pallas Athene, the tutelary goddess of Athens (the Latin *tutela* means 'guardian'), and appeared on Athenian coins. The peacock was the symbol of Juno, the wife of Jupiter – hence the title of Sean O'Casey's play *Juno and the Paycock*. Geese were also sacred to Juno. The Romans loved to tell the story of how, one night during the Gaulish siege of the Capitol in Rome in 390 BC, a scaling party of Gauls was about to surprise the sleeping garrison when the sacred geese of Juno raised the alarm with their unholy honking.

numismata
is the Greek 'coins' – hence numismatics, through the French *numismatique*, the study or collection of coins and medals

Junoesque
may be applied to a beautiful woman who, like Juno, has a regal bearing. It may have a connotation of jealousy (owing to Jupiter's numerous infatuations)

Bos, bovis 'cow' gives bovine.

Canis 'dog' gives canine. Dentists call the four teeth shaped to rend food the canines. They call the twelve broad-faced teeth in man used for grinding food the molars (*mola* is the Latin 'millstone').

Caper, capris 'goat' gives caprine (goat-like), caprice (a sudden, unpredictable change of attitude or behaviour), capricious (changeable like a goat) and Capricorn (a constellation and a sign of the zodiac, represented as a horned goat, *cornu* being the Latin 'horn'; from *cornu* we also derive the Italian *corno* for the peculiar cocked hat worn by the doges, tricorn(e) for a cocked hat with opposing brims caught in three places – the Latin prefix *tri* means 'three' – and unicorn for the mythical animal, *unus* being the Latin 'one').

Corvus 'crow' gives corvine.

Equus 'horse' gives equine and equestrian (as

opposed to pedestrian, meaning someone on foot – *pes, pedis* is the Latin 'foot'); *caballus* is another Latin word for 'horse', which by a common exchange of v for b gives cavalry, cavalcade, cavalier and, through the French *cheval* ('horse', itself derived from *caballus*), chevalier and chivalry.

Feles 'cat' gives feline.

Leo, leonis 'lion' gives leonine. In popular fiction American senators frequently sport silver manes and are described as leonine.

Lupus 'wolf' gives lupine. The Roman playwright Plautus said, '*Homo homini lupus*' (Latin, 'Man is a wolf to man'). Freud quoted this in his pessimistic essay 'Civilization and Its Discontents', published as the Nazis were poised to seize control in Germany. Freud himself found refuge from the Nazis in London in June 1938 and died just at the outbreak of World War II in September 1939. His four sisters tragically experienced the aptness of the dictum – they all died in concentration camps. Incidentally, Terence, who succeeded Plautus as Rome's leading comic playwright, gave us the expression *quot homines, tot sententiae* (Latin, 'there are as many opinions as there are men').

Lykos is the Greek 'wolf'; lycanthropy – *anthrōpos* is 'man' – is the power to change oneself into a wolf, or a madness in which the patient thinks he is a wolf; a lycanthropist is a werewolf (the Old English *wer*, like the Latin *vir*, means 'man'). Plato and a number of other classical authors tell us that there was an altar on Mount Lycaeon in Arcadia where human sacrifice was offered. Anyone who ate the human flesh turned into a lycanthropist.

Mus 'mouse' gives muscular (because the Romans fancied that a muscle was a little mouse running up and down under the skin; *musculus* is the Latin 'little mouse', *ulus* being a suffix indicating a diminutive form; thus minuscule means very small, *minus* being 'less', and homunculus means a small man or dwarf, *homo* being 'man').

Ovis 'sheep' gives ovine (resembling a sheep).

Porcus 'pig' gives porcine. From it we also derive pork through the French *porc*. When the Normans conquered England in 1066 AD, the language of the manor (French *manoir*) came to predominate in culinary matters – *culina* is the Latin 'kitchen'. Thus Anglophones

vir
gives us virile, virility and virilism (the abnormal development in a woman of male secondary sex characteristics). *Puer* is the Latin 'boy'. From it we derive puerile (immature, childish) and puerperal (relating to childbirth, as in puerperal fever)

porcine
connotes both abnormally fat and gross. Obese from the Latin *ob* 'completely' and *edere, edesum* 'to eat' denotes abnormally fat (corpulent from the Latin *corpus* 'body' denotes fat). Doctors use the term adipose for fatty, from the Latin *adeps, adipis* 'soft fat', as in adipose tissue. Archaeologists who dig up representations of the ancient Earth goddess may describe them as steatopygous – in plain language fat-arsed – *stear, steatos* being the Greek 'fat' and *pygē* 'buttock'. Art historians may refer to Rubens's penchant for steatopygous models (penchant means a decided taste from the French *pencher* 'to incline'). He found them callipygous (or callipygian) – *kallos* is the Greek 'beautiful'

Anglophone
means a speaker of English, *Anglo* deriving from the Latin *Angli* 'English' and *phone* deriving from the Greek *phōnē* 'sound' or 'voice'; a Francophone is a speaker of French, *Franco* deriving from the Latin *Francus* 'Frank'. A monoglot is someone who speaks only one language, *monos* being the Greek 'alone' or 'single' and *glotta* being 'tongue'. A polyglot is someone who has a command of many languages, *poly* being the Greek 'many'

amphibian/amphibious
may be used to describe military forces carried in vehicles that can move both on land and on water

serve pork, beef (French *boeuf*) or mutton (French *mouton*) rather than pig, cow or sheep for dinner (French *dîner* 'to dine').

Serpens, serpentis 'snake' gives serpentine. (*Herpeton* is the Greek 'snake' so herpetology is the study of reptiles and amphibians – animals that can live both on land and in water, *amphi* being the Greek 'on both sides' and *bios* being 'life'; herpes, the type of skin diseases to which cold sores and shingles belong, is so called because it seems to creep under the skin like a snake.)

Simia 'ape' gives simian. Darwinism may be connoted by a reference to our simian ancestors.

Taurus 'bull' gives taurine.

Ursus 'bear' gives ursine. Ursula (little female bear) is an affectionate name for a girl.

Vulpes 'fox' gives vulpine: 'Caravaggio's agitated night [in 'The Taking of Christ'] is bathed in an icy moonlight that glints off the centurions' armour and Judas' [*sic*] vulpine eyes.' (*NYRB*, 7 October 1999) *Sic* is the Latin 'thus'; placed between square brackets in a quotation it indicates that the writer considers the preceding word, while from the original, is incorrect in some respect. Here the broken grammatical rule is that the possessive singular is indicated by 's unless the last syllable begins and ends in s, in which case the apostrophe alone suffices – thus Judas's kiss and Moses' death.

assassinate
to kill treacherously

The word is derived from groups called the Assassins, who terrorized parts of Persia and Syria in the eleventh century. They got their name from their practice of taking hashish (cannabis) before they attacked. The word usually connotes a deadly attack on a person of some authority. George Bernard Shaw in *The Rejected Statement* observed: 'Assassination is the extreme form of censorship.'

astronaut
a space-traveller

juggernaut
an inexorable destroying force, is unrelated to the Greek *nautēs*. From Sanskrit *Jagannatha* 'lord of the world', it was an incarnation of Vishnu beneath the car of whose idol at Puri devotees were thought to immolate themselves

Astron is the Greek 'star'; *nautēs* is 'sailor'. An astronaut explores the stars. The Russians call their space-travellers cosmonauts (*cosmos* is the Greek 'universe'). Both words are formed by analogy with argonaut. The *Argo* was the ship in which the Greek hero Jason sailed to find the golden fleece. His companions were therefore called the Argonauts. The saga of Jason and the Argonauts was one of the most famous stories of exploration of the ancient world. The fleece – that of a golden ram – hung upon an oak-tree guarded by a huge, loathsome monster. Helped by the Princess Medea, who had fallen head-over-heels in love with him and who resourcefully mesmerized the dragon and then drugged him, Jason stole the fleece and quickly made off with it in the *Argo*.

Lyncaeus was the most keen-eyed of the Argonauts. In the early decades of the seventeenth century the first modern scientific academy was established in Rome; it was called the Academy of the Linceans after both Lyncaeus and the lynx, which was believed to be the animal with the most acute vision. Galileo, who laid the foundations of modern science, was a Lincean.

asylum
a place of refuge

A is a Greek prefix that negatives a word; *sulon* is 'right of seizure'. The ancient Greeks set aside certain places, such as temples, where fugitives, whatever their crime, could claim sanctuary. Up to quite recent times the word was applied to psychiatric hospitals (lunatic asylums) and homes for handicapped people. It now usually crops up in the media in terms of someone fleeing a repressive regime and seeking asylum in another country.

Sanctuary derives from the Latin *sanctuarium* 'holy place'. Under medieval Church law a fugitive from justice or a debtor was immune from arrest if he or she gained access to a church or other sacred place. In *The Hunchback of Notre Dame*, the film based on Victor Hugo's novel about medieval Paris, *Notre Dame de Paris*, Quasimodo snatches the gypsy girl Esmeralda from the square in front of the cathedral where she is being prepared for public execution and carries her off to the cathedral, crying 'Sanctuary! Sanctuary!'

Robespierre and many of the leaders of the French Revolution were Deists. They turned Notre Dame into a temple of Reason, then into a temple to the Supreme Being, and finally into a store for food. The stonework fell into disrepair. Hugo's novel, published in 1831, gave an impetus (a thrust, *impetus* means 'attack' in Latin) to the movement to restore the building. Between 1845 and 1864 the cathedral was restored to its pristine condition (*pristinus* is the Latin 'original' or 'former').

atavism
a reversion to primitive behaviour

Avus is the Latin 'grandfather', *atavus* is 'great-great-great-grandfather', i.e. ancestor. Psychologists believe that beneath the veneer of civilization there lurks in every one of us a set of responses – atavistic responses – genetically transmitted from ancient times awaiting the stimulus of exceptional circumstances such as extreme danger.

Avunculus, from which we derive avuncular, as in 'He had an avuncular manner,' is the Latin 'uncle'. The *unculus* suffix denotes a diminutive form of the word it is attached to – in this case *avus*. *Avunculus* literally means 'little grandfather'. The English uncle comes from the French *oncle*, which comes from the Latin *avunculus*.

atom
in general, the smallest particle of matter

A is a Greek prefix that negatives a word; *tom* comes from *temnein* 'to cut'. An atom is that which cannot be cut further. The Greek philosopher Democritus, who coined the word, developed an atomic theory 2500 years ago: atoms were the basic building blocks of both body and soul. The story is told that Democritus put out his own eyes so that he could devote himself more fully to philosophical contemplation. He was accused of insanity and the great doctor Hippocrates (who enunciated the famous Hippocratic oath that doctors have ever since accepted as their basic code) was sent to examine his disorder. The physician did so and afterwards declared that Democritus was not mad but his accusers were. Atomism was never a dominant Greek position – Aristotle rejected it.

Modern physics is based on atomic theory, which was revived by the French physicist Pierre Gassendi, who also coined the word molecule. Newton in his *Opticks* assured us that matter consists of 'solid, massy, hard, impenetrable movable particles ... so very hard as never to wear or break in pieces'. However, scientists discovered that what they called atoms could be split – they discovered a subatomic world. Subatomic is etymological nonsense (because it presupposes that that which cannot be cut further can be cut further). Scientists save the concept by defining an atom as the smallest subdivision of an element that retains the chemical properties of the element. At the subatomic level we find the densest part of the atom – the nucleus, derived from *nux*, *nucis*, the Latin 'nut'. Sociologists use the term nuclear, derived from nucleus. They call the family consisting of man, woman and child(ren) the nuclear family. They call the family consisting of the

Hippocrates
was renowned as a physician in fifth-century BC Greece and a large corpus of medical literature is ascribed to him but little is known for certain about him. The Greeks had a god of healing called Asclepius. A son of Apollo, he had two daughters Hygeia ('health', hence hygiene) and Panacea. Many temples were dedicated to him and often developed into sacred hospitals. His symbol, a snake twined around a staff, features in the logo of the World Health Organization (WHO) and in those of some modern hospitals (hospital derives from the Latin *hospes, hospitis* 'guest'; and so does hospitality).

Galen, another Greek doctor, gained a towering reputation in second-century Rome. Born in Pergamum, he was a prolific writer. He came to dominate the whole subsequent Western medical tradition. He promoted the idea we have of Hippocrates as the father of medicine and laid the basis for the modern concept of a *scientia aeterna* – a science in which all scientists share and in

nuclear family and blood relations the extended family.

Tomē, transliterated *tomy* as a suffix in English, means 'a cutting'. Anatomy, from the Greek *ana* 'up' and *tomē*, is the art of dissecting a body or the science of the structure of the body (based on dissection, from the Latin *dis* 'asunder' and *secare* 'to cut'; vivisection, the act of carrying out surgical operations on living animals for the purposes of physiological experimentation, derives from the Latin *vivus* 'alive' or 'living' and *secare*).

A dichotomy is a division into two parts or classifications – *dikha* is the Greek 'in two' – and has a connotation of a sharp distinction or even opposition. Thus, 'There was a dichotomy between the economies of the north and the south, one being industrial, the other pastoral.'

Ek (transliterated into English as *ec*) is a Greek prefix meaning 'out': *ectomy*, a suffix meaning 'a cutting out', occurs in surgery, e.g. appendectomy (a cutting out of the appendix), hysterectomy (a cutting out of the womb; *hystera* is the Greek 'womb' and *uterus* is its Latin equivalent; hysteria is a state of giddy emotionalism, first named as such by nineteenth-century doctors), mastectomy (a cutting out of the breast – *mastos* is 'breast' in Greek) and colectomy (a cutting out of the colon or part of it – *kolon* is Greek for the end part of the large intestine).

Itis is a Greek suffix indicating 'disease' or 'inflammation' – hence appendicitis, mastitis, hepatitis (*hēpar, hēpatos* is the Greek 'liver'), laryngitis (*larynx, laryngos* is the Greek 'upper part of the windpipe') and iritis (*iris, iridos* is the Greek 'rainbow' or, as here, 'the coloured part of the eye'; iridescent means displaying a shimmering spectrum of colours).

Algos is the Greek 'pain', hence neuralgia (a pain along a nerve – *neuron* is the Greek 'nerve') and nostalgia (originally homesickness – *nostos* is the Greek 'return home'). An analgesic is a painkiller; an anodyne is also a painkiller (*odynē* is another Greek word for 'pain').

which all agree. Classical therapeutics (*therapeuein* is the Greek 'to take care of' or 'to heal') employed dietetics (from *diaita* 'mode of living' or 'diet') that focused on the patient's whole way of life, including diet, pharmaceuticals (*pharmakon* is 'drug') and surgery (originally from *chirurgeon*, itself from *cheir* 'hand' and *ergon* 'work')

aureole
halo

Aureole, from the Latin *aureola*, was the gold disc round the head of an emperor or saint in a picture, employed to indicate their glory. The convention developed from the Roman practice of fixing a metal ring to the head of a statue of a god or emperor to keep birds from sitting on it and fouling it. It might be observed

aural
meaning pertaining to the ear, comes from the Latin *auris* 'ear'. *Os, oris* is the Latin 'mouth' – hence oral. *Nasus* is the Latin 'nose' – hence nasal. *Oculus* is the Latin 'eye' – hence ocular, oculist and monocle (*monos* is the Greek 'alone' or 'single'). *Stoma, stomatos* is the Greek 'mouth' – hence stomatology (the study of the mouth). *Ous, otos* is the Greek 'ear' – hence otic (pertaining to the ear) and otology (study of the ear). *Rhis, rhinos* is the Greek 'nose' – hence rhinologist (a nose specialist) and rhinoceros (*keras* is the Greek 'horn'). *Ophthalmos* is the Greek 'eye' – hence ophthalmic (pertaining to the eye) and ophthalmology (the study of the eye)

that following parturition the nipples of women become aureoled (parturition derives from the Latin *parturire, parturitum* 'to have brought forth'). Halo comes from *halos,* the word the Greeks used for the same disc. A disc was originally a circular plate (a *discus*) thrown by Greek athletes and is now applied to any flat thin circular figure, including the sun, moon and planets, which present in the sky as discoid.

Aurum is the Latin 'gold', from which aureole ultimately derives; auriferous (*ferre* is the Latin 'to bear') may be applied to a deposit that yields gold. The word aura, meaning a supposed subtle emanation, as in, 'She had an aura of graciousness,' derives from the Latin *aura* 'breeze'.

The word aural, meaning pertaining to the ear, comes from the Latin *auris* 'ear'.

Nimbus, from the Latin *nimbus* 'dark grey rain-bearing cloud', is also used both as a synonym for 'halo' and for the general emanation of light from a saint or deity in a painting or other graphic representation. In his famous painting of the triumphant Napoleon on a rearing horse, Jacques-Louis David seeks to apotheosize the French emperor by nimbusing his figure.

auspices
patronage

The future, although often referred to as foreseeable, is not foreseeable. People nonetheless seek reassurance about the future, especially when they are about to embark on some great enterprise. In ancient times they looked for signs from the gods, who were believed to control everything.

The kings of Rome had the power to consult the gods by means of *auspicia* (plural form of *auspicium*, literally 'bird-watchings', derived from *avis*, the Latin 'bird' and *spicere* 'to observe'). Typically, the king would go in the middle of the night to a high place, usually a hill, accompanied by an augur, a professional interpreter of signs. They would pitch a tent (*tabernaculum*) there. At daybreak the king would observe the pattern of the flight of birds across a preselected tract of sky called a *templum*. The augur interpreted these signs (*omen, ominis* is the Latin 'sign', from which we derive ominous) declaring them to be either good omens (auspicious) or bad omens (inauspicious).

Auspices were taken before any major proceeding. Action followed only when the auspices (that is, the gods) were favourable. To proceed under unfavourable auspices would be deemed sacrilegious. (In 249 BC the consul Claudius the Fair found, when he went to take the auspices before a naval battle off Sicily, that the sacred chickens would not take their feed. He brusquely took them up in his hands saying, 'If they won't eat, they'll drink!' and threw them into the sea. He fought the battle in defiance of the auspices and lost it.) When the *auspicia* were duly observed, the augur declared them *inaugurata* and the battle or other action began. Thus inaugurate is a solemn, even portentous, word for commence, which in turn is a solemn and often portentous word for begin: 'Uncle Tom commenced shuffling the cards before he inaugurated the poker session.' Portentous, meaning pompous, also means ominous because it derives from the Latin *portentum* 'sign', 'omen' or 'portent'.

Originally, therefore, certain activities were carried out under the auspices of the gods. Auspices, which has in this usage the same meaning as aegis, has suffered the same degeneration: nowadays a concert may be held under the auspices of a musical society.

Roman temples were so called because they were often built on hills where auspices had been taken, the word for the tract of sky being observed, *templum*, having been transferred to the building. Furthermore their shape was said to mirror the shape of the tent set up the night before the auspices were taken. *Templum* also gives us template (any mould or model from which other forms are reproduced).

Roman augury also sometimes involved the examination of the internal organs of birds and other animals for signs. A priest who carried out the examination was called a haruspex (probably from the Latin *hira* 'gut' and *specere* 'to look at'). There were various ways of determining whether a sign was good or bad – for instance, anything from the left-hand side would be regarded as unlucky or sinister (*sinister* is the Latin for the left hand, in contrast to the favoured right hand – *dexter* – from which we derive dextrous meaning adroit, and dexterity).

The Romans also resorted to prophecy and astrology. Their most famous source of prescience (foreknowledge, from the Latin *pre* 'before' and *scire* 'to know'; someone with a facility to anticipate what will

temple
For Jews the Temple in Jerusalem was the only place where sacrificial worship was permitted. With the destruction of the Temple in 70 AD animal sacrifice ceased. In their synagogues (*syn* is the Greek 'with' or 'together' and *agōgē* is 'a bringing') they studied the *Torah* (Hebrew, the 'Mosaic law') and prayed. Among Christian places of worship are basilica, cathedral, church and chapel. A basilica (a church with special privileges) derives its name from the word for a royal palace (*basileus* is the Greek 'king'). A chapel (a place of worship inferior to a church and attached to a house or institution) derives from the French *chapelle*, originally the reliquarium the French kings had made for St Martin's cape (*capella* in Latin), which they carried into battle as a talisman (something thought to have magical or protective powers, from the Arabic *tilsam*)

organ
Organon is the Greek 'tool', which was applied to those parts of the body that carried out a particular function – thus the eye is the organ of sight, the nose is the organ of smell and the stomach is the organ of digestion. An organization is a unit made up of various organs. An organism may be animate or inanimate. A living organism is any living plant or animal, including bacteria and viruses. Organic means relating to or derived from living plants and animals, and is distinguished from mineral, which is inorganic. Psychiatrists use organic to distinguish diseases arising from physical or chemical causes from those arising from purely psychological disorders

happen is said to be prescient) was the Cumaean Sibyl, a prophetess who lived in a cave, whose prophecies in written form – the famous Sibylline verses – were long revered by the Romans. Astrology, the study of the stars based on the view that the movements of the stars determined human affairs, was an eastern influence (*astēr*, *astros* is the Greek 'star'; the *logy* suffix derives from *logos* 'word', 'reason' or 'account'; it was not until the sixteenth century that astrology was distinguished from astronomy, the scientific study of the stars – *nomos* is 'law', here in the sense of a control, and astronomy literally means the laws of the stars; because of the distances involved in astronomy, astronomical is sometimes used to mean immense).

science/scientific derives from the Latin *scire* 'to know' and denotes any systematically formulated body of knowledge. The word scientist was put into circulation by the polymath William Whewell in 1840. A polymath is someone of great and varied knowledge (from the Greek *polus* 'many' and *mathanein* 'to learn')

auto-da-fé
the public burning to death of people condemned as heretics by the Inquisition

This Portuguese expression means literally 'act of the faith' (in Spanish *auto de fe*). The Inquisition was established in 1233 by Pope Gregory IX to prosecute the crusade against the Cathars. It was later deployed in other parts of Europe – against the Waldensians, the Knights Templar, the *conversos* in Spain (Jewish families who had converted to Catholicism but whose sincerity was suspect), witches and Protestants. The Spaniards brought it to Latin America.

In the imperial Roman legal code death by fire was the punishment prescribed for parricide, sacrilege, arson, sorcery (the practice of magic, from the Latin *sors*, *sortis* 'lot') and treason. When Roman law was revived in Bologna in the twelfth century, that law provided a precedent for dealing with heretics.

Autos-da-fé were conducted as great public spectacles. In his book *Reformation* Diarmaid MacCulloch tells us:

> The *auto-da-fé* has been described as 'a mimesis of the Last Judgement' … all human society was represented standing before God, from the King (often physically present in a royal box) to the humblest of his subjects. Repentant prisoners represented to spectators repentance in that part of sinful humanity reconciled to God, while the fate of unrepentant blasphemers, sexual deviants or Judaizers represented the damned in the fires of hell.

mimesis from the Greek *mimeisthai* 'to imitate', occurs famously in Aristotle's *Poetics* where tragedy is said to be an imitative representation (*mimēsis*) of an action that deserves serious attention. From *mimeisthai* we also get mimetic, mime, mimic, pantomime

The 'Great Auto' of 1649 in Mexico City was announced in advance by trumpets and drums sounded throughout the country; crowds began to arrive in the city two weeks before the event. (Spectacle derives from the Latin *spectare* 'to observe', itself derived from *specere, spectum* 'to look at'.)

avant-garde
the innovators in any art form at any period

Avant is the French 'ahead', *garde* is 'guard'. The term, originally the military vanguard, is applied to those artists whose ideas or techniques are markedly experimental or in advance of those generally accepted. Thus:

> From realism to surrealism and from modernism to postmodernism, Sade has to some degree inspired nearly every movement of the French avant-garde.
> –Robert Darnton, *NYRB*, 14 January 1999

In painting, the emergence of the avant-garde can be traced to 1863. In May that year the Emperor Napoleon III visited the Salon in Paris, the official showplace of each year's new French art, before its formal opening. He was taken aback by the dull academicism of the display and asked to see the paintings that had been refused exhibition. Among these was Edouard Manet's early masterpiece 'Le déjeuner sur l'herbe', which was acclaimed by the Impressionists, whom he decisively influenced. The Emperor insisted that a new *salon* should be opened – a Salon des Refusés ('Hall of the Rejected'). Thereafter, the annual exhibitions of the work of progressive artists became a striking feature of the French art world.

B

bacchanalia
feasts in honour of Bacchus or, more generally, drunken revels

to intoxicate
from the Greek *toxikon* 'arrow-poison', is to make drunk (or crapulent, crapulous from the Greek *kraipalē* 'drunkenness') or to make excessively elated. Toxic means poisonous and toxicity is the state of being poisonous. A toxin is a specific poison of organic origin. Toxicology is the science of poisons (the suffix *ology* means 'study of'). Inebriate, from the Latin *ebrius* 'drunk', is a synonym for intoxicate. The British prime minister Benjamin Disraeli famously used the word when he described his Liberal opponent Gladstone as 'a sophisticated rhetorician inebriated with the exuberance of his own verbosity'

Bacchus, also known as Dionysus, was the Greek god of fertility and wine, and so licentiousness (excessive indulgence in animal passion, from the Latin *licere* 'to be allowed') and drunkenness were associated with bacchanalia (also called Dionysia). Dionysus was represented as an ivy-wreathed figure bearing a drinking-bowl and surrounded by a merry troop of satyrs and maenads. A satyr (Greek *saturos*) was thought of as a wild naked man with certain caprine features such as hooves and horns, unflaggingly lustful and hotly intoxicated. (Satyriasis, from *saturos*, is a neurotic condition in men in which they feel compelled to have sex with as many women as possible but are unable to have lasting relationships with them. It corresponds to nymphomania in women.) Maenads (from the Greek *mainas*, *mainados* 'raving') were women possessed by the spirit of Dionysus and therefore ecstatic (from the Greek *ek* 'out' and *histanai* 'to make to stand' – possessed by a divine spirit that leaves one standing outside oneself) or enthused (from the Greek *en* 'in' and *theos* 'god' – possessed by a god). The maenads were also known as bacchantes.

Dionysus once became very angry with Orpheus because he honoured Apollo rather than him. He set the bacchantes against the great musician: they tore Orpheus limb from limb and threw his head into a river where it floated down to the sea, still singing. In *The Birth of Tragedy* Nietzsche made a famous distinction between the two strains to be found in the Greek spirit. The dark, unbridled, violent strain he called Dionysian while the serene, rational, controlled strain he called Apollonian.

In the Graeco-Roman world there was, in addition to the worship of the Olympian gods, a wide range of cults centred on local or foreign deities. Some of these were mystery cults, that is to say, cults into which the worshipper had to be initiated (*mystēs* is the Greek 'initiate'; a mystagogue is someone who initiates others, *agōgos* being the Greek 'leader'; a mystery was originally a secret doctrine or ritual known only to the initiated, and was also known as an orgy – Greek *orgia*). The worship of Bacchus, an Olympian, was also a mystery cult and its character and great popularity gave the term orgy its sense of an uninhibited bout of group indulgence in sex and drink.

In ancient Rome each December they celebrated the Saturnalia, a feast lasting as long as a week in honour of Saturn, the ancient god of agriculture, and chief of the Roman gods until he was deposed by his son Jupiter. It was an orgy of eating, drinking and merrymaking – the precursor of Christmas. Saturn has a continuing presence in Saturday.

bandwagon
the movement towards a person or set of ideas gaining popular support

A bandwagon was a highly decorated wagon carrying a band of musicians, used in America especially to draw crowds in a circus parade. In modern political parlance, to jump (or climb) on the bandwagon means to throw in one's lot with a politician or political party enjoying surging support in the streets, in the media and in the opinion polls.

bankrupt
financially ruined, insolvent

Essentially a banker makes his or her living by paying a lower interest on deposits than he or she charges on loans. Modern banking began in northern Italy in the Middle Ages when goldsmiths (who often were money-lenders) found that the receipts they gave people who deposited their valuables with them were being used as currency. They realized that they could issue receipts (or notes) to a greater value than the valuables they held (and make interest on them) because people tended to leave valuables on deposit for long periods – the bankers held them securely – and that the only limit on their capacity to create money was their ability to redeem the notes with valuables whenever the notes were presented back to them. Before long they were seeking to control that last condition by paying interest on deposits.

currency
derives from the Latin *currere* 'to run', from which we also derive concur, occur and recur, and describes the notes and coins accepted as the medium of exchange at any particular time – that run from one person to another. The word is also applied generally. Anything in circulation – an idea, a story – may be said to be current or to have currency

The system worked so long as bankers were solvent – capable of meeting their financial obligations, from the Latin *solvere, solutum* 'to free [from debt]'. However, there were obvious temptations for money-lenders to lend too much, so local authorities began to control them. In Florence, the city authorities issued licences that allowed those who held them to set up a bench (*banca* in Italian – hence bank and banker) in the square to trade in money. If a money-lender got into financial difficulties his licence (permission, from the Latin *licet* 'it is allowed') was withdrawn and the bailiffs descended on his place of business and broke his bench so that everyone could see he was *bancarotta* (*rotta* is the Italian 'broken' from the Latin *rumpere, ruptum* 'to break') – bankrupt.

barbarian
an abusive term applied originally to foreigners but now to any brutish person

barba
is the Latin 'beard', from which we derive barber and rebarbative (repellent), but not barbarian

The ancient Greeks, though politically divided into numerous small city-states, were united by a common culture, and especially by the Greek language. The languages of other peoples seemed harsh to them – they felt strangers were saying 'Bar! Bar!' all the time. Hence the words barbarous and barbarian.

Imperialists adopted the words because they implied a gratifying cultural superiority and provided a justification for attacks on cultures perceived to be inferior. Another example of this syndrome was the Nazis' concept of *Untermenschen* 'subhumans' (*unter* is the German 'under', *Menschen* is 'people'); they applied this term to the peoples of eastern Europe whose lands they wanted to rob to provide *Lebensraum* 'living space' for Germans.

baroque
the bold, dramatic, vigorous style in architecture that flourished from the late sixteenth to the early eighteenth century in Europe. Baroque is also applied to contemporary art, such as painting and music

The word, derived from the Portuguese *barroco* 'imperfectly shaped pearl', was originally pejorative and sought to connote grotesque. Those who first used it wished to criticize baroque architects for borrowing basic forms from the classical ruins but combining them in novel, non-classical ways. Because the style became successful the word lost its negative sense. Baroque art seeks verisimilitude so as to capture the substantiality of both the natural and the supernatural worlds. It was used as an ideological instrument by both ecclesiastical and secular authorities.

In the history of art two styles are interposed between the Gothic and the Baroque – the Renaissance and the Mannerist. The style that followed the baroque is called rococo. In contrast, it is delicate, playful, florid. It developed in Louis XV's France and spread through Europe. The word seems to have been coined by one of Jacques-Louis David's students by combining rocaille, from the French *roc* 'rock', which meant decorative rock or shell work, and baroque.

bedlam
a noisy, confined place or situation; uproar

Bedlam is a corruption of Bethlehem. The priory of St Mary of Bethlehem in London became an asylum for lunatics called Bethlehem Royal Hospital, where the inmates notoriously were put on display for public entertainment. The first Bethlem Hospital was near what is now Liverpool Street station in London. The hospital later moved to what is now the Imperial War Museum. The present Bethlem is located in Kent.

belle époque, la
the beautiful period

Belle is the feminine form of *beau*, the French 'beautiful' or 'fine'; *époque* is 'epoch' or 'period'. The French applied the term to the period around 1900, which they found agreeable and carefree (*sans souci*). The period ended with the outbreak of World War I. It is not clear when exactly after the end of the Second Empire in 1870 that it began but we know it took about twenty years for the Third Republic to create the wealth that ushered in the period. It comprehended (embraced, from the Latin *cum* 'with' and *prehendere* 'to seize'), but was not coextensive with, the Gay Nineties, the *fin de siècle* (French, 'end of century') decadence and the Edwardian period (from the British King Edward VII).

The *belle époque* connotes art nouveau, the artistic movement called after a Paris shop, which brought curvilinear (*curvus* is the Latin 'crooked' or 'bent') decoration to architecture and artefacts. It is characterized by *douceur de vivre* (French, 'sweetness of living') or *joie de vivre* (French, 'joy of living'). *Belle époque* (plural *belles époques*) may be employed generically.

ben trovato
happily invented if untrue (of a story)

An Italian expression: *ben* means 'well'; *trovato* means 'found'. Apocryphal stories about politicians are often *ben trovato*; indeed verisimilitude is the quality that gives them currency.

bicameral
having two legislative chambers

Bi is derived from *bis*, the Latin 'twice' (thus a bicycle is a two-wheeler); *camera* is 'room' or 'chamber'.

Legislative bodies nowadays are either unicameral, i.e. having one house, as in Denmark, or bicameral, as in the USA where Congress consists of the House of Representatives and the Senate.

Bicameralism has its origins in the fact that the feudal system culminated in the creation across Europe of powerful dynasties that gradually established their royal power. Initially that power was seen to rest on two powerful corporate groups – the Church, represented by bishops and abbots (who in England came to be called the Lords Spiritual), and the aristocracy (who in

senate
derives from the Latin *senatus*, the Roman Council of Elders, itself derived from *senex*, *senis* 'old man' (thus endorsing the traditional equation of old age and wisdom). *Senex* also gives us senile and senility. Endorse derives from the Latin *in* 'on' and *dorsum* 'back' – one acknowledges the authenticity of a cheque or other document by

signing it on the back. From *dorsum* we also derive dorsal: a dorsal fin is found on the back of a fish

spiritual
Spiritus is the Latin 'breath'. A breath is something that moves unseen and so *spiritus* came to be used to describe the soul; spiritual relates to things of the soul and therefore of religion. Temporal derives from the Latin *tempus, temporis* 'time' and means relating to time and therefore to things of this life

the Fourth Estate
means the mass media. The phrase was coined by the Irish orator Edmund Burke. Speaking in the British House of Commons, he observed that there were three estates in parliament; then, referring to the newspaper reporters' gallery, he declared, 'Yonder sits the Fourth Estate, more important than them all!'

England came to be called the Lords Temporal). Kings consulted these groups in parliament either separately as in France, where the clergy were the First Estate and the aristocracy the Second, or together as in England, where the two groups met as the House of Lords. Subsequently a Third Estate was discerned – the substantial farmers and business people in towns and cities. These met separately in parliament in France as the Third Estate and in England as the House of Commons (the lower house). Thus France had a tricameral (the Latin *tri* indicates 'three') legislature before the Revolution and England a bicameral one.

Constitutionalists have long argued the issue whether a legislature should have an upper house. The great constitutional lawyer of the French Revolution, the Abbé Sieyès, was vehemently opposed: 'If a second chamber dissents from the first, it is mischievous; if it agrees, it is superfluous.' However, George Washington felt that an upper house was needed to act as a check on the lower house. To Thomas Jefferson, who once protested to him against the establishment of a two-house legislature, Washington posed the question, 'Why do you pour coffee into your saucer?' 'To cool it,' replied Jefferson. 'Even so,' said Washington, 'we pour legislation into the senatorial saucer to cool it.' The function of providing calm deliberation and deep analysis of national issues is an important one, but it can be and often is carried out by a committee of a unicameral legislature. The idea of an upper house as a check on the supposed impetuosity of the people's representatives in the lower house seems to play to the ancient classical prejudice against democracy as readily degenerating to mob rule; and, of course, in a unitary state it may be seen as a vestige of the medieval privilege of powerful people having a separate legislative say.

With the development of democracy in the nineteenth century, effectively legislative power passed to the so-called lower house and the rationale for having an upper house in a unitary state became weak, so much so that three-quarters of unitary states are now unicameral.

The rationale for having a bicameral legislature in a federal state was always strong because, as in the USA, a house of representatives could represent the people and a senate the states, and each house could be given pre-eminence in certain areas of legislative interest. Of the twenty-two federal states in the world eighteen are bicameral.

bilateral
between two parties

Bi is derived from the Latin *bis* 'twice'; *latus, lateris* is 'side'. Bilateral is frequently used in the context of foreign affairs where trade or other agreements between two states are called bilateral. Agreements between three states are called trilateral (*tri* is the Latin 'three'; bipartite means relating to two parts and tripartite means relating to three, *pars, partis* being 'part').

Multilateral agreements involve more than two parties (*multus* is the Latin 'many').

Unilateral means one-sided (*unus* is 'one' in Latin). Examples of its use are a unilateral declaration of independence, unilateral disarmament.

blackshirt
a member of the Italian Fascist Party before and during World War II

Giuseppe Garibaldi was one of the leading figures in the struggle to unify Italy (the Risorgimento, from the Italian *risorgere* 'to rise again'). He conquered Sicily and Naples with his famous redshirts – a volunteer army (the Thousand) which, lacking the uniforms of a regular army, he dressed in cheaply available red shirts. Brewer's *Dictionary of Phrase and Fable* suggests that Garibaldi first adopted the red shirt when he took command of a merchantman in Baltimore – in the nineteenth century American sailors habitually wore red shirts just as British sailors wore blue ones. A more recent source (Lucy Hughes Hallett, *Heroes*) says that in the 1840s Garibaldi was in Uruguay leading an Italian legion in support of the liberal government in a civil war. The government had no uniforms for their volunteers so they requisitioned a stock of red overalls due to have been shipped to Buenos Aires for the slaughterhouse workers. Belted around the waist they were passed off as military tunics (from the Latin *tunica*). When he returned to Italy to lead his incredibly popular crusade to unify his country, red shirts became the distinctive dress of Garibaldi's followers. The adulation of the redshirts led in time to the fascist vogue for coloured shirts – black shirts in Mussolini's Italy, brown shirts in Nazi Germany and blue shirts in Falangist Spain.

The Falange derived its name from the Greek *phalanx, phalangos* 'a body of heavy-armed foot-lancers closely ranked', who, behind a wall of overlapping shields protecting their heads and sides, could withstand cavalry charges or spears hurled at long range. It was a highly successful tactical innovation in warfare in classical times. The word has come to be applied to any closely packed mass of disciplined people.

missile
derives from the Latin *mittere*, *missum* 'to send'; hence also mission, emission (e is the Latin 'out'), emissary, transmission (*trans* is the Latin 'across') and missionary. Projectile is another word for a missile, from the Latin *pro* 'forward' and *jacere*, *jectum* 'to throw'. A ballista (from the Greek *ballein* 'to throw') was an ancient siege catapault. From it we derive ballistics, the study of the flight of projectiles under various conditions

In corroboration of Alphonse Karr's maxim *Plus ça change, plus c'est la même chose* (French, 'The more things change, the more they stay the same'), the word recurs in modern warfare. Aircraft carriers are particularly vulnerable to attacks by missiles. The US Navy has developed a defence that consists of a metal shield that goes around a ship and over a ship, created by rapid-fire guns. They call it the Phalanx Anti-Missile System.

A Phalangist is a member of a Lebanese Christian paramilitary group founded in 1936 and originally based on the ideas of the Spanish Falange.

blarney
honeyed talk meant to deceive

Blarney is said to have come into the English language this way. Blarney is a village in County Cork in Ireland. During the time of Queen Elizabeth I, the Lord of Blarney was Cormac MacDermot MacCarthy (his name captures a moment when the patronymic MacDermot, that is son – *mac* in Irish – of Dermot, was being used together with the emergent surname MacCarthy to name a single person). He found himself under intense pressure from the English government, which was then moving towards the total conquest of Ireland, to renounce the Gaelic system by which he held his titles and acquired his privileges and to accept tenure (*tenere* is the Latin 'to hold') of his lands from the English Crown. Blarney gave the impression that he would concur with the policy but from day to day put off doing anything about it 'with fair words and soft speech'. Finally, Elizabeth became exasperated. 'This is all Blarney!' she declared. 'What he says he never means.' Blarney Castle is today famous for a magic stone that has the traditional power to confer eloquence on all who kiss it.

Elizabeth I, who never married, was known as the Virgin Queen. The US state of Virginia is called after her. *Virgo, virginis* is the Latin 'virgin'; *parthenos* is its Greek equivalent. The Parthenon, the great temple on the acropolis in Athens, is called after the virgin goddess, Athene Parthenos – also known as Pallas Athene;

parthenogenesis refers to virgin birth, *genesis* being the Greek 'birth' or 'origin' – hence the first book of the Bible describing the creation of the world is called Genesis.

English borrows quite a number of colourful words from Irish. The following are some other examples. Galore derives from the Irish *go leor* 'aplenty'. Shanty, as in shanty town (an area of decrepit or ramshackle housing) derives from the Irish *seantigh* 'old house' (although also arguably from the French *chantier* 'timber yard'). Whiskey derives from the Irish *uisce beatha* 'water of life'. Slogan derives from the Irish *sluaghairm* 'war cry' (literally the cry – *gairm* – of the host – *slua*). Slew as in a slew of troubles also derives from *slua* 'host' or 'crowd'. Smithereens, as in 'She let the cup fall and it broke into smithereens,' derives from the Irish *smidiríní* 'little pieces'. Kibosh, as in the song 'Belgium put the kibosh on the Kaiser', is said to be the way New York Poles rendered the Irish expression *caidhp bháis* ('death-cap'), which they heard their Irish neighbours using. To put the kibosh on something is to give it a mortal blow, for, before the burial of an uncoffined Irish famine victim, the relatives covered the face of the dead person with a cloth – a *caidhp bháis*.

The humorous five-line verse-form called a limerick derives from the Irish city of Limerick where in the late eighteenth century limericks in Gaelic were especially popular.

The Gaels, whose language is called Gaelic or Irish, were a Celtic-speaking people who invaded Ireland from the European continent several hundred years before Christ. They established a polity (a system of government, from the Greek *politeia*) that lasted two millennia. After St Patrick brought Christianity and writing to Ireland in the fifth century, Irish monks and the learned classes (the *aos dána* in Irish), stimulated by contact with Christian and classical literature, engaged in a creative transmission in writing of the Gaelic sagas and poetry, and thereby began a literary tradition in Irish that continues to the present day. Ireland has the longest continuous literary experience in Europe after Greece and Rome.

literary
like literal, literate, illiterate, alliteration (the occurence of the same letter or sound at the beginning of adjacent or closely connected words) and literature, derives from the Latin *littera* 'letter'. Littoral, meaning relating to the shore of a sea or lake, derives from the Latin *litus, litoris* 'shore'

blitzkrieg/blitz
a sudden, overwhelming attack

Blitz is the German 'lightning' and *Krieg* is 'war'. The term originally described the combination of rapid panzer (tank) and air attacks that characterized the

German successes in the opening stages of World War II. Nowadays an advertising agency may plan a blitz on television for a client's product.

bohemian
a person of loose and unconventional habits, or an artist or writer; or pertaining to such

Bohémien is the word the French use for a gypsy because they believed those wandering folk came from Bohemia in the Czech Republic, named after a Celtic people, the Boii, who also live on in Bologna. (The English word gypsy comes from Egyptian because the English thought they came from Egypt.) As outsiders, living on a few basic skills and their wits, gypsies were poorly regarded by the settled communities among whom they moved.

The word bohemian came to embrace writers and artists. In Paris in the mid-nineteenth century there was a large population of struggling young artists and writers who sought to extract a living by working for the myriad, ephemeral magazines being published there. These so-called 'water drinkers' (because they could not afford wine) of the Latin Quarter (the riverside quarter between the Seine and the Luxembourg Gardens containing the Sorbonne, from whose Latin-speaking scholars in medieval times it took its name) and their female companions led the life of the gypsies (*la vie de Bohème*), a phenomenon made famous in a series of articles written in the mid-1840s by Henri Mürger and later published as a novel, *Scènes de la Vie de Bohème*. Thus Gustave Flaubert, author of *Madame Bovary* and *L'Education sentimentale*, when asked whether he was proud to be a Frenchman, could joke, 'The question doesn't arise. I am an artist – so Bohemia is my native country.' At the end of the century the bohemians and their loves were apotheosized in Giacomo Puccini's *La Bohème*.

myriad
means an immense number. It comes from the Greek *myrias, myriados* 'ten thousand'

bona fide
sincere(ly)

Bonus is the Latin 'good'; *fides* is 'faith' or 'trust'. *Bona fide* means 'in good faith'. If a dealer were to offer you a new car for €100, you might rightly wonder if it were a bona fide offer.

Bona fides means 'good faith [in the sense of genuineness]': 'As president of the Plutocratic Party you were perfectly right to question the bona fides of a man who, having spent many decades trying to organize the lumpenproletariat, now offers his services to the Party's public relations department.'

Mala fide means 'in bad faith'; *malus* being 'bad' in

Latin, from which we derive a large range of words such as maladministration (bad management), maladroit (clumsy), malaria (with the Greek *aer* 'air'), malefactor (criminal, with Latin *facere, factum* 'to do'), malice and malignant.

bourgeoisie
the middle class

Bourgeois is the French 'townsman' from *bourg* (German *Burg*) 'town' or 'city', e.g. Strasbourg. Townspeople typically lived by trade and by providing professional and other services. The term bourgeoisie came to mean that class who came in the social scale between the peasants and artisans (the lower class), and the landowners and aristocrats (the upper class). While the bourgeoisie connoted conservative and materialistic, some people viewed the class as parsimonious and philistine, others as cultured and respectable. Indeed the terms *haute bourgeoisie* (*haut* is the French 'high') and *petite bourgeoisie* (*petit* is the French 'small' or 'petty') were employed to capture that difference. Marx used the term to describe those who were not proletarians. The bourgeoisie, according to Marx, were those who owned the means of production (land, raw materials and machinery). They exploited the workers and controlled the state whose constitution was framed to maintain their control.

History, according to Marx, was climaxing in a violent struggle between the proletarians and the bourgeoisie – the class struggle – which the proletarians were bound to win because of the laws governing the economy: the fierce competitiveness of the capitalist system would inexorably concentrate the means of production in fewer and fewer hands so that capitalists would progressively eliminate themselves, even if the proletarians did not precipitate the process by a revolution.

history
derives from the Greek *historia* 'what has been learned by inquiry' and means a record of past events. Between history and prehistory scholars insert protohistory (*prōtos* is the Greek 'first') to indicate a period when a region is referred to only sporadically in written records and before it is served by proper histories. The fifth-century BC Greek Herodotus is known as the Father of History – it was Cicero who first hailed him as such.

Histrionic is unrelated to history. It means theatrical and derives from *histrio, histrionis*, the Latin 'actor'. Thespian is another word for actor, from Thespis, a sixth-century BC Greek who was thought to have invented tragedy

bowdlerize
expurgate a book in editing it

Thomas Bowdler published an edition of Shakespeare's works in 1818 from which he had removed anything that might bring a blush to a maiden's cheek. Consequently the word has a pejorative connotation of excessive delicacy. In eighteenth-century France a special edition of the classics was prepared *ad usum Delphini* (Latin, 'for the use of the Dauphin') and that expression is also used as pertaining to an expurgated work.

Expurgate derives from the Latin *ex* 'from' and *purgare* 'to purge'; the latter Latin verb also gives us

Purgatory
Theology also required the existence of limbo as the abode of infants dying without baptism and the just who died before Christ. It derives from the medieval Latin *in limbo* 'on the borders [of hell]' and gives us a word for a dark indeterminate place or condition

Purgatory, a place or state in which, in Roman Catholic eschatology, souls after death are purified from venial sins. Venial derives from the Latin *venialis* 'pardonable'; venial sins are distinguished from mortal ones (from the Latin *mortalis* 'causing death' of the soul, *mors, mortis* being the Latin 'death'). Venal, from the Latin *venalis* 'for sale', is applied to a corruptly mercenary person. Dauphin, which was applied to the eldest son of the King of France, derives from the Latin *delphinus* 'dolphin', which itself derives from the Greek *delphis, delphinos*. The name was originally the surname of the counts d'Albon (Latin *Delphinus*) who ceded their province to the French king in 1349. They had dolphins in their crest and these were adopted by the dauphin in his. Delphic, as applied to the Greek god Apollo, derives from Delphi, the name of the village in Greece where his oracle resided, and not from *delphis*.

boycott
a non-violent means of coercing someone by combining to cut him or her off from social and business contacts

In Ireland in 1880 at the height of the struggle against landlordism, Captain Boycott, a land agent of Lord Erne, refused to reduce rents by a quarter following a bad harvest. His tenants were outraged. They ostracized him: no labourer would work for him, no servant would cook for him, no one would pay him rent. Six policemen had to be assigned to guard him. When he brought in workers from the north-east of the country to save his crops, a large body of troops had to stand by to guard them. After six months Boycott left his home, Lough Mask House, near Ballinrobe, County Mayo, for England with his family.

This form of coercion – called boycott after the egregious captain – was then applied successfully against tenants who made a bid for farms from which the occupants had been evicted.

Brechtian
in the manner of the German dramatist Bertolt Brecht

Brecht is a major figure in modern drama. He swung away from the naturalism that dominated European theatre after Ibsen and that sought, through carefully articulated realistic scenes, to draw the spectator subjectively into the action. Brecht strove to develop an epic theatre in which the play consisted of a series of loosely connected scenes through which the spectator was invited to consider objectively the social and political complexity of real situations.

epic
derives from the Greek *epos* 'song'. Epics were originally long, narrative poems about a hero or band of heroes. A saga is a long prose narrative of the achievements of a

In the 1920s and 1930s Brecht collaborated as librettist with the German composer Kurt Weill. Their best-known work is *The Threepenny Opera*, a modernization of John Gay's *The Beggar's Opera*; it was made into a film several times and features the hit song 'Mack the Knife'.

Brecht, as a communist (though not a member of the Communist Party), had to flee Nazi Germany. He returned in 1949 and settled in East Berlin. Some of his plays, e.g. *The Preventible Rise of Arturo Ui*, attack both Hitlerism and capitalism. His great period was between 1937 and 1948 when he wrote *The Life of Galileo*, *The Good Woman of Setzuan*, *Mother Courage* and *The Caucasian Chalk Circle*.

family or king, of the kind written in medieval times in Scandinavia (*saga* is Old Norse for 'narrative')

Brussels
the centre of the European Community

The headquarters of the European Council and the European Commission are both in the Belgian capital and so Brussels is used in the media to describe thinking on policy at the highest level in the European Union, just as Washington is used to describe thinking on policy at the highest level in the US government. Such usages are examples of metonymy, a trope (a figure of speech, from the Greek *tropos* 'turn') much favoured by journalists (literally people who work for dailies, from the Latin *diurnalis* 'daily' through the French *jour* 'day') because it can provide a vivid image for something amorphous or abstract. The Hill for Capitol Hill in Washington, the seat of the US legislature, is another example. Metonymy is effectively the same as synechdoche, a trope in which a part is named for the whole or the whole is named for a part (from the Greek *syn* 'with' or 'together' and *ekdechesthai* 'to receive').

budget
the financial statement made in parliament at the beginning of each year by a minister of finance

In Britain, where the usage originated, it is customary for the chancellor of the exchequer to bring his yearly financial proposals in a leather bag to the House of Commons. *Bougette* is the Old French 'bag', hence budget.

Expenditure is of two kinds, current and capital. Current expenditure is the money a government spends from day to day on purchases of goods and services or on transfer payments (such as pensions and children's allowances). Capital expenditure is the money it spends on investment goods – roads, hospitals, ships, school buildings and the like – and on capital transfers (such as grants and loans to industry). The estimates provide separately for both kinds of expenditure.

Governments get the money they need from sales

of goods or services but mostly from taxation and from borrowing at home and abroad.

problem
derives from the Greek *problēma*, which itself is related to *proballein* 'to throw forwards', *pro* indicating 'forwards' and *ballein* 'to throw'

Multi-annual budgets, that is, budgets that project income and expenditure over a number of years (usually three) is an attempt to deal with the problem that the assessment of how effective certain expenditures are must be made over a number of years. Multi-annual budgets, however, are extremely difficult to prepare in volatile economic conditions (*volare, volatum* is the Latin 'to fly'). They are based on national plans that project over a number of years not only budgetary developments but also developments in various sectors of the economy.

A current budget deficit occurs when a finance minister provides in the coming year for a greater amount of current expenditure than he or she expects in income. The deficits are met by borrowing (*deficere* is the Latin 'to fail'), which it is anticipated will be repaid out of growth in the economy.

A mini-budget is a number of fiscal changes to either the income or the expenditure components of the budget, or to both, e.g. increased tax on gas, introduced some time after the budget, to correct budgetary performance (*mini* is a Latin particle meaning 'small').

C

cabal
a secret faction

Cabala, the medieval Latin word from which cabal derives, itself derives from *qabbālā*, a Hebrew word meaning 'tradition', and denotes instruction about the mystical significance of certain combinations of numbers, words and letters that Jewish rabbis studied. Something cabbalistic might also be called hermetic or Orphic. The use of the word cabal for a group of intriguers entered English by way of the French *cabale*. It was famously used to describe Charles II's group of advisers in the early 1670s – Clifford, Arlington, Buckingham, Ashley, Lauderdale – from the first letters of whose names could coincidentally be derived the acronym CABAL. This cabal is the origin of the cabinet in the British system of government.

cabinet, the
the government

Cabinet is the diminutive of the French *cabin*, which derives from the late Latin *capanna* and means a 'little or inner room'; by transference it means an inner group. States choose to exercise the executive powers of government through either a cabinet or a presidential system. In a cabinet system, the government – the prime minister and his ministers collectively – is responsible for its actions to parliament. (The principle of collective cabinet responsibility was embraced by the cabinet of George III because that monarch would take individual members of the cabinet aside after a meeting and question them assiduously about who proposed what and who said what, thus exposing individual members to external pressure and undermining group solidarity.)

solidarity
means oneness of interests and derives from the Latin *solidus* 'solid'. Something solid is resistant to change and contrasts with what is fluid (or liquid) or gaseous (gas was coined by J.B. van Helmont, by analogy with chaos)

In the US the heads of the twelve major executive departments (for example the secretary of state) are appointed by the president with the consent of the Senate. They are known as the cabinet when they act in a body to advise the president.

Some presidents use their cabinets extensively. Some deal with the various members separately. Others rely on groups of personal advisers (the informality of this arrangement has led to such advisers being called the kitchen cabinet). A head of government in a cabinet system who dominates the cabinet to such an extent that its role becomes *de facto* advisory rather than executive is said to have a presidential style.

In the European Commission each commissioner has a small group of advisers, called his or her cabinet, to help him or her with his or her functions. In this context the word is given a French pronunciation (cabinay) because it derives from the practice in French government. The chief adviser is known as the *chef de cabinet.*

cache
a hidden store

Cacher is the French 'to hide'. It can relate to a hidden store of arms or treasure.

cancer
any type of malignant growth or tumour

tumour
Tumere is the Latin 'to swell'. From it we derive tumour (a swelling, especially a new growth of cells in the body without inflammation), tumid (swollen or, applied to expression, inflated, bombastic), tumescence (the process of becoming swollen), and tumulus (a burial mound – a swelling on the earth). Tomb derives from a related word

Cancer is the Latin 'crab': cancer is a tumour that was thought to creep like a crab. Carcinoma, from the Greek *karkinos* 'crab' and *oma*, a suffix indicating 'tumour', is a synonym. A melanoma (*melas*, *melanos* is the Greek 'black') is a malignant tumour in the skin. A substance that causes cancer may be described as carcinogenic, the *genic* suffix indicating 'causing', from the Greek *genēs* 'born'. Tumours may be benign or malign. A specialist concerned to study and treat tumours is called an oncologist, *onkos* being the Greek 'tumour'.

Cancer (the Crab) is also the name of a constellation (a group of stars, *stella* being the Latin 'star', as seen from the earth and the solar system) in the northern hemisphere. The ancients believed that the sun turned back at the solstices. *Tropos* is the Greek 'turn'; *tropikos*, from which we derive tropical, means 'relating to a turn'. The tropic of Cancer is the line of latitude at about 23.27°N of the equator and the tropic of Capricorn is the line of latitude at about 23.27°S. The belt of the earth between the two lines is called the tropics (or the Torrid Zone, *torridus* being the Latin 'scorched' and *zōnē* the Greek 'girdle' or 'belt').

candidate
one who offers himself or herself for public office or at an examination or election

Candidatus is the Latin 'dressed in white', from *candere* 'to be white', which also gives us candour. Those who offered themselves for a public office or honour in ancient Rome presented themselves dressed in brilliant white to imply that they were without stain.

Candidates went round (Latin *ambire*, *ambitum*) canvassing voters; hence ambition, a strong desire for success. Ambience or ambiance, meaning the atmosphere of a place, and ambient, meaning surrounding as in ambient noise, also derive from *ambire*.

Capitalis is a Latin word meaning 'relating to the chief [principal] thing', derived from *caput, capitis* 'head'. Capital, meaning the stock (including property and equipment) and/or money used in carrying on a business, comes from a shortening of the expression capital stock.

Capitalism has existed wherever an individual produced some good or service and bartered or sold it. Its most colourful agents were those itinerant traders who through the ages hauled goods from a point of supply to distant points of demand (an itinerary is a travel plan, from the Latin *iter, itineris* 'journey'; to iterate or reiterate is to say or do again, from the Latin *iterum* 'again', and an iterative solution to a problem is the repeated application of a formula so that successively closer approximations to a solution are obtained). Up to modern times foreign trade was very modest: in the early part of the fourteenth century the total volume of goods coming into France each year on one of the major trade routes would not fill a modern freight train.

The Industrial Revolution transformed the volume of trade and placed capitalists rather than landowners at the centre of economic activity. It also drew masses of labourers from the countryside into the towns and cities to become wage-earners (proletarians), and so transformed society. This is the phenomenon referred to by the technical term capitalism, which Marx made the object of his analysis.

In the *Wealth of Nations* the great Scottish economist and philosopher Adam Smith examined how the wealth of a country – meaning the wealth available to everyone in a country – might be increased. He concluded that capitalism, operating ideally, was a cornucopia: capitalists increased their own wealth endlessly by producing endlessly, but at the most competitive prices, what everyone wanted. Society, he felt, should organize itself in such a way that capitalism would flourish.

Capitalism requires the right to private property. Since its efficient operation requires the market conditions of free trade, governments should follow *laisser-faire* policies and limit themselves largely to internal and external security and to the refereeing of market operations (by, for example, preventing monopolies and restrictive practices). The freedom capitalists required for themselves had in principle to be extended to everyone – everyone had to be free to become a capitalist – and so

capitalism
an economic system in which the production of goods and the provision of services is undertaken almost entirely by private owners – individuals and firms – who from sales in a free market derive profits for themselves, the wages of their workers, the costs of raw materials and machinery, and compensation for the risk-taking involved in their enterprise. The chief characteristic of the capitalist system is that there is no central determination of either the allocation of resources or the rewards for work

kephalē
is the Greek equivalent of the Latin *caput*. Cephalic means relating to the head. Autocephalous refers to a bishop who is independent of a patriarch (*autos* is the Greek 'self'). An acephalous (*a* is a Greek negative) society is one that has no recognized ruler or leader

freedom is seen as a concomitant of capitalism (hence the expression the free capitalist societies).

Satan
the chief fallen angel, the adversary of God, from the Hebrew *satan* 'adversary'

Industrial capitalism operated in a far from ideal way. The 'dark Satanic mills' (William Blake) produced immense human misery as well as goods. Soon vehement critics arose to attack the whole system – none more powerfully or effectively than Karl Marx. Marx laid down the theoretical basis for the great rival system to capitalism – communism. With the Bolshevik Revolution in Russia in 1917 and the abolition of private property, the communist system began to be put to empirical tests. It failed.

carnal
fleshy; relating to the appetites and passions of the body

Carnal comes from the Latin *caro, carnis* 'flesh' – a word we find nowadays in the dish *chilli con carne* (Spanish, 'chilli with meat') and also in carnival (originally used to describe the feasting and revelry – the fleshly indulgence – that preceded the fast of Lent), carnage (slaughter), carnivorous (flesh-eating, *vorare* being the Latin 'to eat', from which we also derive voracious and voracity; herbivorous means grass- or plant-eating, *herba* being 'grass'; insectivorous means insect-eating, *insectum* being 'insect'), carnation (the flower or the flesh-colour ranging from pink to crimson), Incarnation (the becoming flesh of Christ), and reincarnation (the belief that on the death of the body the soul is born again in a new body).

carpetbagger
a politician seeking office in a locality where he or she has no connections

After the defeat of the Southern states in the American Civil War, 1861–5, there were rich political and commercial pickings for the victors. The resentful Southerners, seeing numerous Yankee adventurers descending on their cities and towns with their travelling-bags, made of carpet-like material, dubbed them carpetbaggers. The term is now used of American politicians who run for office outside their home states.

Yankees or Yanks was a term first applied to the inhabitants of the New England states. In the Civil War it was applied to the Northerners generally. In Europe it came to be applied to all Americans (as in 'The Yanks are Coming' in the George M. Cohan World War I song). The origin of the word is uncertain. It may come from Janke, a diminutive form of the Dutch Jan (John) or Jankaas (literally 'John cheese' – *kaas* is the Dutch 'cheese'). The Dutch were the first settlers in New England – hence New York was originally New Amsterdam.

The eleven Southern Confederate states (Alabama, Arkansas, Florida, Georgia, Louisiana, Mississippi, North Carolina, South Carolina, Tennessee, Texas and Virginia) were popularly referred to as Dixie. The origin of the word is uncertain. It possibly derives from the surname Dixon because the line that separated the slave states from the free states was drawn during the years 1763–7 by two surveyors called Charles Mason and Jeremiah Dixon – the famous Mason–Dixon line.

The heartland of the conservative south-eastern US is known as the Deep South (broadly South Carolina, Georgia, Alabama, Mississippi and Louisiana). In 1925 H.L. Mencken coined the term the Bible Belt for the swathe of territory in the Southern and Midwestern US where the predominant Christian fundamentalists (from the Latin *fundamentum* 'foundation') believed politics should be imbued with understandings derived from the Bible construed literally.

inhabitant
derives from the Latin *habitare* 'to dwell'. A habitat is the natural home of an animal or plant. A denizen, which may refer sometimes to an inhabitant or resident and sometimes to a plant or animal that has become established in a place to which it is not native, derives from the French *denzein*, itself derived from the Latin *de intus* 'from within'

carte blanche
full discretionary power

A French expression meaning literally 'white card', carte blanche is used of a blank paper signed by a person with authority and left to be filled in by the receiver. It gives the receiver a free hand.

Cassandra
someone who expresses gloomy views about the future but is not believed

Cassandra was the daughter of Priam, King of Troy. One day when she was asleep in the temple Apollo appeared and promised her the gift of prophecy if she would make love to him. Cassandra, after accepting the gift, went back on the bargain. Apollo persisted, begging her to give him just one kiss. As she did so he spat into her mouth, thus ensuring no one would ever again believe what she said. So when Cassandra announced at a critical point in the Trojan War that the wooden horse left by the Greeks outside the walls of Troy contained armed men no one believed her.

casus belli
something put forward as a justification for war

Casus is the Latin 'occasion'; *belli* is a form of *bellum* 'war' and means 'of war'. Leaders intent on war often feel a political need to justify an attack before their own people so as to marshal support for the war effort, or before the rest of the world so as to isolate their victim. Thus in September 1939 the Germans arranged for an attack on some of their own installations near the Polish border to provide themselves with a *casus belli*. SS men in Polish Army uniforms carried out the attack and drugged concentration-camp inmates, cynically code-named 'canned goods', were left dying as casualties. The cause of the war was something quite different.

casualty
derives from the Latin *cadere*, *casum* 'to fall' – casualties are the dead and injured in a war or accident; we use fatalities for the dead alone

As far as casualties in battle are concerned, field doctors and their assistants carry out a triage on them, that is to say, they sort them out in categories of dead, dying and wounded to establish priority for treatment (*trier* is the French 'to sort'; triage gained currency during Napoleon's wars). Because such triages tend to be hurried and inexact the word is also applied to the practice of allocating scarce resources on a basis of expedience rather than moral principles or the needs of the recipients.

A belligerent is someone who wages war (*gerere* is the Latin 'to wage'). It is also used to describe the characteristics of such a person.

character(istics)
derives from the Greek *kharaktēr* 'stamp' – hence the meanings ranging from 'letter' to 'the set of qualities and habits that differentiates one person from another'

A bellicose person is also aggressive but usually in speech or gesture (*bellicosus* is the Latin 'warlike').

Antebellum means of or during the period before a war (*ante* is the Latin 'before'), especially the American Civil War: 'There are many examples of antebellum architecture in Charleston.'

catastrophe
a sudden calamity

Kata is the Greek 'down'; *strophē* is 'turning'. A catastrophe is a downturning (of the wheel of fortune). In Greek tragedy the catastrophe was the crucial turning-point in the plot.

A cataclysm is a violent upheaval that is worse than a catastrophe (*kataclusmos,* literally meaning 'downpour', is the word used in the Greek version of the Bible for the Flood; *diluvium* is the Latin 'flood' and *ante* is 'before' – antediluvian therefore means before the Flood or very old-fashioned, as in 'The office procedures were antediluvian: every Friday afternoon the supervisor stood at his desk while the clerks queued to receive their wages.')

A disaster is a calamity (*dis* is a Latin prefix meaning 'bad'; *astēr* is the Greek 'star' – a disaster is an action carried out under an unlucky star; *dys* is the corresponding Greek prefix to the Latin *dis*: dysfunctional pertains to the impaired or abnormal functioning of an organ or system and dyslexic pertains to an impaired ability to read, not caused by low intelligence, *lexic* being derived from the Greek *lexia* 'speech').

an asterisk
(from *astēr*) is a star-shaped character used in printing. An asteroid (from the Greek *asteroeidēs* 'starlike') is any of the numerous small celestial bodies that move around the sun

A tragedy is an unhappy story or turn of events, usually involving death. *Tragōidia* is the Greek 'goat-song' or 'goat-ode'. Drama originated in ancient Greece when groups of men joined together in a chorus to sing poetry; they wore goat-skins, possibly with the head on top (a feature later formalized in the persona or actor's mask). Drama was born when one member of the chorus stepped forward and began to contest the story being told by the chorus. He was called the protagonist (*prōtos* is 'first' in Greek; *agōnistēs* is 'combatant' – hence the modern meaning of protagonist as champion or advocate). Later a second member of the chorus stepped forward to argue with the protagonist. He was known as the antagonist (*anti* is the Greek 'against' – hence the modern meaning of antagonist as opponent). Later other actors entered into the dialogue. Eventually the whole story was delivered in action and dialogue, and the chorus disappeared.

The earliest dramas presented grave and solemn stories – they were tragedies. The tragedy was often brought on by an act of hubris leading to a crisis that ended in a catastrophe. Tragedies aimed at having a cathartic effect. *Catharsis* is a Greek word meaning a 'cleansing' or 'purification'. The philosopher Aristotle in his *Poetics* defines tragedy:

> Tragedy is an imitative representation of an action that deserves serious attention, that is complete in itself, that is large in range. It uses language enriched by a variety of artistic devices appropriate to the various parts of the play. It is presented in terms of action not narration. By means of pity and fear it brings about the purgation [catharsis] of those emotions.

In contrast to a tragedy, a comedy is pleasant, humorous or ribald (*kōmos* is the Greek 'revel'; ribald derives from the French *ribauld* 'licentious').

A melodrama is a play or film characterized by extravagant action and emotion. Originally a melodrama was a dramatic presentation with words and music (*melos* is the Greek 'music', from which we derive melody) which, like opera, arose in Italy at the end of the sixteenth century in an attempt to revive classical tragedy with its characteristic choric element. In melodrama the actors spoke their words against a musical background. In nineteenth-century France it lost its

modern
derives from the Latin *modernus* 'pertaining to just now', which is itself derived from *modo* 'just now'; however, scholars also use the word to describe one of the three great periods into which, broadly speaking, human experience can be divided – ancient, medieval and modern; in that context modern may denote anything relating to the sixteenth/seventeenth century onwards

catharsis
is used as a modern psychological term to describe the purging of the psyche that occurs when, through psychoanalysis, repressed thoughts and emotions are brought to consciousness for resolution

musical element and acquired its overwrought, sensational, even Grand Guignolish features.

caucus
an inner group (either formal or informal) that seeks to determine how a larger political group or party will act

The ending *us* in caucus would suggest a Latin origin but the word was coined in America. One explanation of its etymology is as follows. A short time before the Revolution there, the caulkers of Boston (caulkers were men who waterproofed boats and ships; caulk is pronounced cawk) had a dispute with some British soldiers in which a number of civilians were killed. Meetings were later held at the caulkers' house (caulk-house) to decide on what further action should be taken against the soldiers.

In the US caucus describes a meeting of party leaders and activists; caucuses are sometimes used for the selection of party election candidates. In Canada caucus is used to describe a whole parliamentary party, for example the Liberal caucus, rather than an inner group.

Parliamentary party describes those members of a political party who are members of parliament.

Caudillo, El
the leader

El is the masculine form of 'the' in Spanish – thus El Greco (The Greek) is an epithet for, and not the name of, the great painter; *caudillo* is the Spanish 'leader' derived from the Latin *capitellum*, the diminutive form of *caput, capitis* 'head'. In September 1936 General Francisco Franco was appointed head of the unified command of the armed forces of nationalist Spain and hailed as Generalísimo. The other generals in the junta that appointed him were not all agreed that in addition he should have civilian powers. The draft decree finally accepted by the generals spoke of him as assuming 'all the powers of the Spanish state'. Franco immediately presented himself as Jefe del Estado (head of state).

The blueshirted fascist Falangists, who admired the German dictator, Der Führer (leader) Adolf Hitler and the Italian dictator, Il Duce (leader) Benito Mussolini, assented to the appointment but hailed Franco not as El Jefe but as El Caudillo. Historically, *caudillo* was used to describe El Cid and the medieval warrior-kings who sought to roll back the Moorish conquest of Spain. The title connoted that Franco was the protagonist of traditionalist Spain against alien communism. To maintain the support of the monarchists who wished to see a king restored as head of state, the wily general maintained a certain ambiguity as to whether he was head of government or head of state, and if either, for how long. When the Spanish Civil War ended, Franco continued to serve as El Caudillo.

In 1947 Spain legally became a monarchy but it was not until 1969 that Franco named Juan Carlos as his successor as head of state. It was a further six years before Franco died. When Juan Carlos I was installed as King of Spain in 1975, he reintroduced democracy.

caveat emptor
let the buyer beware

Caveat is a form of the Latin *cavere* 'to beware'; *emptor* is 'buyer'. *Caveat emptor* is the traditional seller's charter. However, modern consumer protection legislation has placed an onus (*onus, oneris* is 'burden' in Latin – from which we also get onerous and exonerate) on the seller to carry a higher degree of responsibility than before for enabling the buyer to evaluate the goods or service offered for sale. A caveat is a warning. In the expression 'I would like to enter [or put in] a caveat,' a lawyer formally indicates that no step should be taken in a particular matter without giving him or her due notice.

Emptor derives from the Latin *emere, emtum* 'to buy', from which we derive redeem, redeemer and Redemption (the Christian doctrine that mankind has been delivered from sin – bought back – through the Incarnation, sufferings, death and resurrection of Christ).

Emporium means a large shop with a wide variety of merchandise, or a centre of commerce ('Venice was for long the emporium of the East.') It derives from the Greek *emporos* 'merchant' and *ium*, a Latin suffix indicating 'place'.

Vendor from the Latin *vendere* 'to sell' is seller.

merchant
derives from the French *marchand* 'trader' – hence also merchandise; mercantile means relating to trade, from the Latin *mercari* 'to trade'

cenotaph
a monument to a person whose body lies elsewhere

Kenos, transliterated *cenos,* is the Greek 'empty'; *taphos* is 'tomb'.

A sarcophagus is a stone coffin, usually an elaborately carved one. The most famous sarcophagus of modern times is probably that of Napoleon in Les Invalides in Paris. *Sarx, sarcos* is the Greek 'flesh', *phagein* is 'to eat'. The Greeks made coffins of a limestone thought to consume the flesh of corpses. Anthropophagi are cannibals, *anthrōpos* being 'man' in Greek – and were known as such to the ancient Greeks. In medicine a phagocyte – *kytos*, transliterated *cytos*, is 'vessel' – is a white-blood corpuscle that engulfs bacteria and other

medicine
derives from the Latin *medicus* 'physician', itself derived from *mederi* 'to heal'

harmful particles: 'Stimulate the phagocytes. Drugs are a delusion.' (George Bernard Shaw, *The Doctor's Dilemma*)

A mausoleum is a magnificent tomb. Mausolos was a wealthy fourth-century BC Persian satrap who set out to build a tomb for himself in Halicarnassus that would be (as it did become) a wonder of the world. The expense of building the mausoleum was so great that a Greek philosopher, on seeing it, exclaimed, 'How much money turned into stones!' The *eum* Latin suffix indicates 'place' – compare museum. Considerable remains of the tomb are displayed in the British Museum. The most famous modern mausoleum is probably the Lenin Mausoleum in Red Square in Moscow where Lenin's embalmed body is displayed.

census
an official counting of the population under various statistical headings

Censere is the Latin 'to estimate' or 'to tax'. In Rome a census, with the registers of people and property derived from it, was originally an aid to determining citizenship, liability for military service, and taxation. A census aims at a complete enumeration of the population. The major instrument used in taking the census is the census form filled out by each householder.

The results of the census, set forth in volumes dealing with such topics as population (by area, sex and conjugal condition), housing and transport, are of great value to officials in the public service who must plan the provision of services. A planning team may contain a demographer. Demography is concerned with the study of population statistics (*dēmos* is the Greek 'people'; *graphein* is 'to write').

conjugal
means relating to marriage from the Latin *con* 'with' and *jugum* 'yoke' – as the Romans saw it a married couple were yoked together. To subjugate is to conquer – the Romans made their captives pass under (Latin *sub*) a yoke

The most famous census in history was that conducted by the Romans in Palestine that brought Joseph and Mary to Bethlehem.

The two officials in Rome who carried out a census were called censors. Because they had the power to exclude unworthy persons from the list of citizens, it seemed natural that over the course of time they should be given the duties of ensuring that the public and private life of every citizen conformed to the *mos maiorum* (*mos* is the Latin 'custom'; *maiorum* is 'of our ancestors') – the 'traditional standards'. The office of censor became the most revered and the most dreaded in the Roman state. It is from this aspect of their functions that we derive our ideas of censor, censorship and censure.

ceteris paribus
other things being equal

Ceteris is a form of the Latin *ceteri* and means 'other things'; *paribus* is a form of *par, paris* 'equal'. The expression is used to isolate the condition that will decide an issue when other conditions are even. Thus, 'The appointment of a member of the board of a public body is a function of the minister to whom the body reports. Where a number of well-qualified people are available, the minister will appoint, *ceteris paribus*, a supporter of the government.'

Et cetera (etc.) means 'and so on' (*et* is the Latin 'and'; *cetera* is a form of *ceteri*).

When people or things are equal, they may be said to be on a par or comparable (the prefix *com* is derived from the Latin *cum* 'with'). When they are not equal, there is a disparity between them or they are disparate (*dis* is a Latin prefix that negatives a word). Industrial disputes sometimes hinge on whether one group of workers should get parity with another (i.e. the same wages and conditions).

peer
for an equal or, in Britain, for a member of the House of Lords, derives from the Latin *par, paris*. Lord (a master or a feudal ruler) derives from the Middle English *lovered* 'guardian of the bread' (from in turn the Old English *hlaf* 'bread' and *ward* 'keeper')

The expression *primus inter pares* 'first among equals' is used by many Christians to denote the position of Peter among the Apostles and therefore of the Pope among bishops. By extension it is applied to anyone in a group of equals to whom the others accord a moral authority. (*Primus* means 'first' in Latin; *inter* is 'among'.) However, Catholics maintain that the Pope's position is one of primacy in authority as well as in honour. The expression was used originally to describe the Emperor Augustus's position in the state after he had restored peace to the Roman empire (to maintain the formality that he had restored the Republic).

doyen
for the senior member of a group, profession or society – 'he was the doyen of American political commentators' – derives, like dean, from the Latin *decanus* 'the leader of a group of ten' (Latin *decem*). Doyenne is the feminine form

charisma
the exceptional quality of a person or of the office he or she holds that makes the person impressive and inspirational to others

Charisma is the Greek 'grace' or 'gift'. It was used in the early Church to denote the spiritual gifts of the Holy Spirit, such as the gifts of tongues, prophecy and healing. In modern times the charismatic movement, a largely non-denominational religious movement, is based on a belief in those gifts. The German sociologist Max Weber carried the word over into secular usage. He pointed out that charisma could flow either from the individual or from the office (such as king or judge) the individual held. The word is now often associated with magnetic leaders such as John F. Kennedy, Charles de Gaulle and Martin Luther King Junior.

chauvinist
a person who is excessively patriotic

Nicolas Chauvin was a simple-minded French soldier who had served in Napoleon's army. Content with his modest military honours and small pension, he retained an unshakeable pride in the defeated emperor and the glory of French arms. In modern times the term male chauvinist is applied to men who resist the claims of women to equality with men.

In Britain in the 1880s the term jingoism came into use to describe the same attitude as chauvinism. It was derived from the phrase 'by jingo' in a popular song supporting aggressive moves by Britain against Russia:

> We don't want to fight, but, by jingo if we do,
> We've got the ships, we've got the men, we've got the money too.

chim(a)era
a wild unrealistic notion

accidental
means occurring by chance, or unintentionally, and usually describes something unfortunate, from the Latin *ad* – *ac* before c – 'to' and *cadere* 'to fall'. However, in philosophy, the qualities we ascribe to a person or thing may be either essential or accidental – the distinction goes back to Aristotle. Being able to float and being stable are essential qualities of a ship; having a casino on board is not – it is accidental

After accidentally killing his brother, the Greek hero Bellerophon left his native Corinth and sought the protection of Proteus, the King of Tiryns. The wife of Proteus fell in love with him but he rejected her advances. In revenge she sought to have him killed by claiming he had raped her. Bellerophon was given the task of slaying the Chimaera, a she-monster with a lion's head, a goat's body and a serpent's tail, who shot flames from her mouth, incinerating anyone who came near. A seer told Bellerophon that he must catch the winged horse Pegasus to help him. Bellerophon tracked the horse down to the pool of Pirene, tamed him, leaped on his back and sped off to find the Chimaera. The monster was unable to cope with Bellerophon's aerial assault and, to the amazement of the locals, Bellerophon killed her.

After the Battle of Waterloo in 1815, Napoleon fled to Rochefort and surrendered to the British – to Captain Maitland of the *Bellerophon*.

chron
anachronism, chronic, chronicle, chronology, chronometer and synchronize – these are all words whose common element *chron* derives from the Greek *chronos* 'time'

An anachronism is something out of harmony with the time referred to (*ana* is the Greek 'backwards'): 'Robert E. Lee could easily have saved the South if he had used tanks.'

Chronic means lingering, or inveterate, for example chronic asthma. Someone who chronically reverts to crime is called a recidivist (*recidivus* 'falling back' derives from the Latin *re* 'again' and *cadere* 'to fall').

A chronicle is a narrative of events in the order they occur: 'Case-studies are a valuable teaching resource. Each one provides not only a chronicle of a real-life problem but also a close analysis of why things happened the way they did.'

A chronology is a table of events with dates: 'The defence attorney suggested there must be something wrong in the chronology prepared by the District Attorney's office. The defendant could not have entered the premises at 8.30 pm, grabbed what was in the till and then taken the last train to Rochester. The last train to Rochester left the station at 8.00 pm.'

A chronometer is a clock designed to achieve great accuracy in all conditions (*metron* is 'measure' in Greek). The word was coined by the English horologist or horologer Jeremy Thacker in 1714.

an horologist
is a clockmaker. *Hora* is the Latin 'hour'. Horology (*hora* and the Greek *logos*, here 'telling') is the art or science of making timepieces. Horoscope (*hora* and *scope*, from the Greek *skopein* 'to look at') is the prediction of a person's future by comparing zodiacal data for the time of birth with data from the period under consideration

To synchronize is to occur at the same time or to make to occur at the same time (*sun* is the Greek 'with'). It occurs frequently in thrillers and war movies: 'Let's synchronize our watches.' In linguistics, synchronic applies to the study of language as one finds it at a particular time and is opposed to diachronic (through time, *dia* being the Greek 'through'), which applies to the study of language as it has evolved. Sociologists and anthropologists also find this dichotomy useful.

Tempus, temporis is the Latin 'time', from which we derive: contemporary (relating to the same time, often misused to mean modern present-day), extemporize (speak or perform without planning), tempo (the rapidity of movement in music), temporal (relating to the things of this life), temporary (lasting only for a time), and temporize (avoid committing oneself, playing for time).

Ciceronian

in the manner of the Roman statesman Cicero

Cicero was one of the most brilliant and successful orators that ever lived – only the Athenian Demosthenes can be compared with him. His writings, in their style and content, had an immense influence on European literature and history. In popularizing Greek philosophy ('I merely supply the words, and I have plenty of those'), he coined many words that we still use, such as essence (Latin *essentia*), moral (Latin *moralis*), and quality (Latin *qualitas*). During the Renaissance he was regarded as the exemplar of the rounded man – Renaissance man or *uomo universale* (Italian, 'universal man') – which became the ideal of that movement, someone multi-talented, articulate and persuasive, universally cultured and, through his virtue, promoting the common good. The first secular book, printed in 1465,

an exemplar
is a person or thing to be copied or imitated – a model, from the Latin *exemplum* 'example'. Exemplary means fit for imitation, or serving as a warning as in 'exemplary punishment', or typical or representative as in 'an action exemplary of his conduct'

was his *De Officiis*. The American and French revolutionaries drew in particular on his *De Legibus* and *De Republica* for their exposition of human rights and the brotherhood of man (derived from Cicero's endorsement of the Stoic idea that all men share a spark of divinity that makes them brothers). Ciceronian describes an eloquent, erudite rhetorical style or stylish writing marked by antitheses and long periods. A cicerone (from Cicero) is someone who guides and informs sightseers. The word originated in eighteenth-century Italy, where the function was carried out by eloquent and learned antiquarians (people who study antiquities, *antiquus* being the Latin 'ancient').

cide

deicide, fratricide, genocide, homicide, infanticide, matricide, parricide, patricide, regicide, suicide and tyrannicide – these are all words whose common suffix *cide* derives from the Latin *caedere* 'to kill'. Each word may refer to the act of killing or to the person who kills

Deicide refers to the killing of a god, a charge formerly made by Christians against the Jews (*deus, dei* refers to 'god' in Latin; from it we also derive deity, deify and deist).

Fratricide refers to the killing of one's own brother (*frater, fratris* is the Latin 'brother').

Genocide refers to the killing of a race (*genos* is the Greek 'race'). The lawyer Raphael Lemkin, a Polish Jew, coined the term in 1944 for what Churchill had called a 'crime without a name'. In 1948, the UN defined it as 'a criminal act ... with the intention of destroying ... an ethnic, national or religious group ... targeted as such'.

Homicide refers to the killing of a man or woman (*homo, hominis* means 'man', and by extension 'human being', in Latin).

Infanticide refers to the killing of a newborn child (*infans, infantis* is the Latin 'newborn child'; *in* is a Latin prefix that negatives a word, *fans* is 'speaking' from *fari, fatum* 'to say': an infant is a child that does not yet speak).

fari

gives us fate, fame, famous, fable, fabulous and ineffable (unutterable, indescribable, too sacred to be uttered): *in* being a Latin negative prefix, e – *ef* before a word beginning with f – meaning 'out', and *fable*, a formation meaning 'capable of being said'

Matricide refers to the killing of one's own mother (*mater, matris* is the Latin 'mother').

Parricide, derived from the Latin *parricida*, refers to the killing of one's own father or other near relative or someone whose person is held sacred; it may also apply to someone guilty of treason against the fatherland. (The *parr* element may be related to the Latin *pater* 'father' – *patria* is the Latin 'fatherland' – and the Greek *peos* 'kinsman'.) In ancient Rome a parricide was sewn into a sack with a dog, a cock, an ape and a viper, and thrown into the river to drown; later the sentence was to be burned alive.

Patricide refers to the killing of one's own father specifically (*pater, patris* is the Latin 'father').

Regicide refers to the killing of a king (*rex, regis* is the Latin 'king').

Suicide refers to the killing of oneself (*sui* is a form of the Latin *se* 'self').

Tyrannicide refers to the killing of a tyrant (*turannos* is the Greek 'tyrant').

civil service
the departments and offices directly controlled by members of the government and the offices attached to the other constitutional organs of State

Civis is the Latin 'citizen', from which we also derive civic and civics. In political science the civil service is distinguished from the military service (*miles, militis* is the Latin 'soldier'). While the origins of the civil service are traced to those court servants and clerks who helped kings with their civil, i.e. non-military, business, the term civil service originated with the British East India Company (which was eventually succeeded by the Raj) to allow it to distinguish its non-military servants from its military servants. The term was given currency in Britain by Macaulay, though as late as the 1870s ministers and officials in Britain tended to refer to public offices or public establishments rather than to the civil service. The civil service consists mostly of the officials who work in the offices of the central government. By analogy, the term public service is used to embrace all those who are remunerated from the public purse. It includes the civil service but also such workers as those in local authorities, hospitals and the police service (the police are the organized civil force of a state responsible for maintaining law and order, derived from the Greek *politeia* 'administration' and introduced to English in the fifteenth century through the French *police*).

civil society
the network of institutions that links the individual and his or her family to the institutions of the State

In the *Philosophy of Right* Hegel categorized the institutions of modern society as the family, civil society and the State. Civil society is the panoply of non-State organizations through which citizens seek freely to create the conditions in which they can best live, work and play. They usually seek to do so by working apart from State institutions, sometimes in concert with them, but always in a democracy fundamentally in support of them. The churches, trades unions, employers' organizations, the media, the banks, political parties and other major interest groups are important elements of the network. People concerned to gauge the strength of civil society in a particular country would seek to measure the health of those organizations as well as the social conditions they aim to create:

create
means to make out of nothing, from the Latin *creare, creatum* 'to create'. A creationist, the opposite of an evolutionist, believes that everything that exists has its existence as a result of acts of God. From create we also derive creature, creation and creative

> Strong civil societies exist in those places where the citizens trust each other; where they are inclined to keep their bargains; where they are not inclined to cheat strangers, or to give and take bribes; and where they encourage good citizenship in one another by unofficial means.
>
> –Alan Ryan, *NYRB*, 10 August 2000

In the aftermath of the fall of communism, which sought to substitute the party apparatus for civil society, the concept has regained currency among political pundits.

classic
of the highest rank, especially in art or literature

Classis is the Latin 'assembly', 'group' or 'class'; to classify is to put items in groups that have some characteristic in common. Classical pertains to something first class. It is applied particularly to anything that is related to or characteristic of the ancient Greeks and Romans or their civilization. In art, there is a major dichotomy between classical and romantic. A *locus classicus* (*locus* is the Latin 'place', *classicus* is 'classic') is any passage or epigram in a book or play that provides an excellent exposition of a recurrent human situation. Hamlet's soliloquy 'To be or not to be' is a *locus classicus* for suicide. The Greek *taxis* means 'rank'; taxonomy means the act or principles of ranking or classifying. The Swedish botanist Linnaeus established the binomial system of classification of flora and fauna that characterizes modern biological nomenclature. Binomial, derived from the Latin prefix *bi* 'two' and *nomen, nominis* 'name', means referring to two names (or terms): binomial classification employs two Latin names for each subject, one of which indicates the genus and the other the species. *Felis cattus* names the domestic cat. A typology (*tupos* is the Greek 'type', which also gives us typical) is any system for classifying.

clerical
relating to the clergy or to the work of clerks in an office

Klēros is the Greek 'lot' and *klērikos*, from which cleric, clerical and clergy derive, means 'chosen by lot'. In the early Christian Church, leaders were chosen by lot. That was how Matthias was selected to replace Judas as one of the Twelve – 'the lot fell upon Matthias'. *Klēros* therefore originally indicated the gratuitous favour of God. With increasing institutionalization *klērikos*, derived from it, came to denote ecclesiastical office and to connote authority. Thus cleric came to be used to describe those set apart from the people (*laos* in Greek – hence lay and laity) to serve as ministers of the sacraments. Because during the medieval period only clerics, broadly speaking, were able to read, write and do sums, clerk came to mean someone engaged in office work. In France, clerk in the form *clerc* has also taken on the meaning of writer or intellectual. *La Trahison des Clercs* ('The treachery of the intellectuals') by Julien Benda, which was published in 1927, is a famous diatribe against intellectuals for their espousal of belligerent nationalisms that eventually led to the hideous carnage in the trenches in World War I.

Professionals now use the term lay to characterize people who are outside their own profession. A profession is an occupation requiring special training in the liberal arts or sciences. Law, theology and medicine are the three learned professions (the Latin *professio*, *professionis* 'public acknowledgment' originally applied to the taking of vows by a candidate entering a religious order). George Bernard Shaw observed, 'All professions are conspiracies against the laity.' (*The Doctor's Dilemma*)

The Latin for 'lot' is *sors*, *sortis*. It was a common practice in the Roman world to seek to ascertain the future – the will of the gods – by drawing lots (*sortes*) from an urn, the lots being usually wooden tablets or counters with various words or messages written on them, depending on the issues upon which certitude was sought. Because of the vatic character imputed to the work of Virgil, lines from his poems were often used. Such lots were called *sortes Virgilianae*. The practice arose later of randomly opening a page of a book by Virgil or of the Bible and taking the word or line upon which the eye first fell as indicative of the future. The practice of divination by drawing lots is called sortilege, from *sors* and *legere* 'to select'.

After the conversion of the Roman Emperor Constantine in the fourth century AD, Christianity became the state religion and the authority of clerics in temporal affairs developed. After the fall of the Roman empire, the clergy, in combination with strong local

vatic
derives from the Latin *vates* 'divinely inspired poet' and has a connotation of prophetic. Virgil's fourth *Eclogue* was read by Christians as anticipating a messiah (from the Hebrew *mashiach* 'anointed'; *christos* is the Greek 'anointed'). The most famous line in Latin poetry comes from Virgil's *Aeneid*: *Sunt lacrimae rerum et mentem mortalia tangent* ('Tears are to human sorrow given, hearts feel for mankind' – translated grandiloquently and loosely by Sir Charles Bowen; grandiloquent means inflated or pompous, from the Latin *grandis* 'great', which also gives us grandiose and grandeur, and *loqui* 'to speak')

leaders, brought order and a degree of stability out of the chaos of the Dark Ages and helped in the development of the feudal system. (*Chaos* is a Greek word meaning the primal state of the world, the formless void before the creation of the universe – the cosmos: 'In the beginning there was chaos, vast and dark …' [Hesiod, *Theogony*]; chaotic is the adjective derived from it.)

theogony
means the origin and descent of the gods, *theos* being the Greek 'god' and *gony* a suffix indicating 'origin'

symbiotic
means mutually beneficial, literally pertaining to living with – *sym* is derived from the Greek *sun* 'with' and *biotic*, from *bios* 'life'

The relationship that developed between Church and State, though often subject to great strain, was, broadly speaking, symbiotic. However, a general questioning of authority, both secular and ecclesiastical, was a characteristic of the humanist tradition that became marked during the French Enlightenment (the period between the death of Louis XIV in 1715 and the French Revolution in 1789). Thereafter, kings were deposed and, throughout Europe in the eighteenth and nineteenth centuries, anticlericalism (*anti* is the Greek 'against') was a notable feature of civic culture.

In modern times, with the effective separation of Church and State, anticlericalism is seldom more than the expression of the disaffection of individuals with elements of Church policy or practice.

coalition
a temporary union of diverse parties to achieve a common aim, e.g. government

Coalescere, from which coalition is derived, is the Latin 'to grow together'. Coalitions divide broadly into three types: where the largest party conjoins with a smaller one to form a majority against the rest, where two or more parties conjoin to form a majority against the largest party, or where the two largest parties conjoin to create a dominant majority – sometimes referred to as a grand coalition.

codicil
a supplementary clause or clauses in a will

Codicillus is the diminutive form of *codex, codicis,* the Latin 'manuscript in book form' (from which we get code by a transference of the name of the medium – the manuscript book – to the matter it often carried, laws or regulations). It was in the second century AD that the Romans changed from their use of volumes (or scrolls) to the more convenient book form. A codicil alters a will in certain particulars. To be effective it must be signed and witnessed just as a will must.

Codification, from *codex* and a form of the Latin *facere* 'to make', is a process that brings all the laws together in a systematic way by using the underlying principles (from the Latin *principium* 'beginning', 'basic tenet'). The most famous codification in ancient times was made by the Emperor Justinian. His codification was entitled *Corpus Juris Civilis* ('the body of civil law'). It brought together all the laws made by him and previous emperors, omitting laws that had fallen into desuetude (Latin *desuetudo* 'disuse') and seeking to make the laws consistent. Codification has the practical aim of making the courts more efficient. In modern times the *Code Napoléon*, promulgated between 1804 and 1810, famously codified French civil law.

Justinian also produced excerpts from the writings and opinions of distinguished lawyers in fifty books, which were called the *Digesta* (from the Latin *digerere* 'to divide'). Digest in time came to name a periodical that summarizes current events.

corpus
is the Latin 'body', used in English to mean the complete works by an author or on a subject or in a language, as in 'the corpus of Greek literature'. The French *oeuvre*, from the Latin *opus, operis* 'work', is also used for the complete output of an author or artist

cohort
a large group of people

Cohors, cohortis is the Latin for 'a large formation of Roman soldiers' (it was one tenth of a legion). The word still appears in writing about military affairs but it is more commonly used nowadays by statisticans, sociologists, economists and actuaries, for whom a cohort is an age cohort – any group of people born in a single year. In the plural, cohorts, it may mean followers: 'Mussolini and his cohorts'.

actuary
an expert in statistics who calculates insurance risks and premiums (*actuarius* is the Latin 'bookkeeper')

collage
an art form in which compositions are made by pasting disparate elements on a common ground

Kolla is the Greek 'gum', from which the French *coller* 'to stick' is derived. The elements might be photographs, advertisements, other pieces of print, or material such as cloth or straw. The juxtaposition of the elements may be used to shock or humour (to juxtapose is to place side by side, *juxta* being the Latin 'next to' and *ponere, positum* the Latin 'to place'). *Papier collé* (French, 'glued paper') is a variety of collage in which pieces of decorative paper are used in a picture, usually to create an abstract design. The form was invented by the French painter Georges Braque in 1913.

Montage is a technique for using ready-made images to make a new composition by assembling them and mounting them together (French *monter* is 'to mount').

A pastiche (from the Italian *pasticcio* 'piecrust' and therefore something blended) is applied to a picture or piece of music drawn from or imitating a variety of sources. It is also applied to a work of art that imitates the style of another artist or period, for example a pastiche of baroque painting.

comme il faut
as it should be

This French phrase literally means 'as it should be'. Balzac in *History of the Thirteen* has a street-seller claim that marabou feathers (the marabou is a kind of stork) give to women's coiffure *quelque chose de vague, d'ossianique et de très comme il faut* ('something airy, Ossianic and very much as it should be').

Ossianic is derived from Ossian (in Irish Oisín), a legendary Iron Age Irish hero and bard who became widely celebrated at the end of the eighteenth century when the Scottish poet and translator James Macpherson, who wanted to provide Scotland with an epic based on Gaelic sources, published *The Works of Ossian* (largely his own composition). This became a contributor to the Romantic movement because of its popularity with European writers such as Goethe and Schiller, and with Napoleon.

Iron Age
Archaeologists name ancient periods of human experience after the material used for tools and weapons – Stone Age, Bronze Age, Iron Age. By analogy Nuclear Age is applied to the period from 1945

Ossian's son was called Oscar. That name also became prominent in modern times with the accession of Oscar I to the throne of Sweden and Norway in 1844. Born in Paris, he was the son of Charles XIV of Sweden, formerly one of Napoleon's marshals, Jean-Baptiste Bernadotte, and the celestial Desirée Clary, a descendant of Irish emigrés in France. The name became celebrated in literature with Oscar Wilde, whose mother, steeped in the romanticism of Irish folklore, had written to a Scottish friend: 'He is to be called Oscar Fingal Wilde. Is not that grand, misty, Ossianic?' It entered the popular vocabulary with the naming of the awards of the Academy of Motion Picture Arts and Sciences in Hollywood. An official on seeing the first statuette was supposed to have said it reminded him of his Uncle Oscar, a corn-grower. By a happy chance *oscar* in Irish means 'champion'.

vocabulary
derives from the Latin *vocare, vocatum* 'to call' and indicates either a selective or an exhaustive list of the words of a language. Lexicon, from *lexis* 'word', is its Greek-based equivalent

communism
a body of ideas that envisages the abolition of private property, its replacement by communal ownership and the establishment of a classless society where there are neither rulers nor ruled

Communis is the Latin 'common'. In its root sense the term communist may be applied to any society that holds all property in common, e.g. the early Christian Church. As a modern political term communism emerged in the middle of the nineteenth century. Marx and Engels used it to describe their manifesto: they saw communism as a working-class movement and socialism as a middle-class movement (as, in effect, a projection of liberalism beyond the political and into the social and economic areas of life). In 1918, following the Russian Revolution, the Russian Social Democratic

Labour Party (the Bolsheviks) changed its name to the Communist Party of the Soviet Union. Subsequently the term communist came to distinguish revolutionary socialists from democratic socialists. Like socialism, communism lays stress on the group rather than the individual. It might be described as an extreme form of socialism. However, Karl Marx, the great German Jewish prophet of modern communism distinguished communism from socialism, which he defined as the penultimate stage in the progress towards communism. His system is called Marxism.

Socialism envisages a State that owns and distributes equitably the communal wealth. Marx envisaged communism as arriving with the disappearance of the State ('the withering away of the State'). Under communism everyone would achieve full human emancipation.

Marx, of course, was only one among a number of thinkers who throughout history have constructed utopias. What distinguishes Marx's ideal society is that he worked out a brilliant model, based on his particular form of economic, social and political analysis, which made the realization of communism inevitable. (Marx, therefore, denied that his system was utopian; it was, he insisted, the only scientific one.)

Moreover, great numbers of people throughout the world have, until recently, found his thinking either so compelling that they accepted communism as an inspiring programme for life or so popular that they used it as a vehicle for revolution to further their ambitions.

Marx believed that one could explain everything about a society by analysing the way economic forces influence and shape its social, religious, legal, political, and cultural aspects. Social change, he maintained, entails change both at the level of consciousness and at the economic level. (He encouraged the development of workers' study groups to develop true understanding and to generate in workers a desire for change.)

When he looked at contemporary society he saw that the changes in production and exchange wrought by capitalism were momentous. Factory production was dividing society into two classes – the proletarian masses living in poverty and the bourgeoisie, the owners of the means of production, living in affluence. Because goods were exchanged (i.e. sold) in a free market there was intense competition. Entrepreneurs (from the

analysis
derives from the Greek *ana*, here meaning 'again', and *lusis* 'a setting free' – to analyse something is to break it up, physically or mentally, into its elements. The word was coined by the Irish-born scientist Robert Boyle, sometimes called the Father of Chemistry, to describe the process by which one determined the composition of substances. Synthesis, the opposite of analysis, derives from the Greek *sun* 'with' and *thesis* 'a placing'. To synthesize is to bring various elements together to form a whole. Synthetic describes something artificial. The German philosopher G.W. Leibnitz established a famous distinction between analytical and synthetic statements (see philosophy). Catalysis is a chemical interaction caused between two substances by the presence of a third that undergoes no change. The unchanging substance is called a catalyst. Catalyst is often used of someone whose presence allows understanding, agreement or other interactions to occur in a group. Catalysis derives from the Greek *kata* 'down' and *lusis*

French for businessmen) would inevitably seek a competitive edge by exploiting their workers (helped by the law that at the time forbade combinations of workers, i.e. trades unions) or by using labour-saving machines (which would depress wages further by making more workers pursue less work). As a result, a deadly class struggle would ensue. The means of production, in the dog-eat-dog conditions of the market, would be steadily concentrated in fewer and fewer hands. Periodic recessions would convulse society further. Finally, the proletarians would rise up and 'expropriate the expropriators' (*proprietas* is the Latin 'property'; *ex* is 'from' or 'away' – to expropriate is to take property away from, to dispossess).

irony/ironically
means the expression of one's meaning by the use of terms with an opposite meaning, or the fact that an action or condition is the opposite to what one would have expected. Irony derives from the Latin *ironia*, which in turn is derived from the Greek *eirōneia*, the practice of an *eirōn*, a 'dissembler'. It is in this original sense that we use the expression Socratic irony. Socrates loved to pretend he was ignorant because that allowed him to question people closely and fundamentally and so either confute them or lead them to understandings other than the ones they had setting out. Socrates saw himself as a midwife to men's thoughts and described his dialectical *modus operandi* as maieutic – relating to a midwife (Greek *maia*)

Ironically, the proletariat, from their experience of working in factories, would be socialized, that is, they would become very conscious of the value of working together. They would seize the means of production, produce goods to meet the needs of society rather than the market, and in the first instance arrange for equitable distribution through a State apparatus. In this way they would achieve socialism. After some experience of socialism, Marx believed, everyone would work together voluntarily for the common good. There would be no need for a State with all its laws and procedures designed to control people. The State would wither away under the glow of a red sun.

Marx elaborated his system in his monumental work of 2500 pages, *Das Kapital,* written in the British Museum over a period of eighteen years when he lived with his family in great poverty in London. So towering was his genius that now no one can think about history or economics or society without using Marx's categories: he caused a paradigm shift.

Marx was not, however, a successful revolutionary. He died thirty-four years before a revolution inspired by his ideas was achieved by Lenin and his Bolsheviks in industrially backward Russia. Lenin had to make certain adjustments to Marxism (hence the expression Marxist–Leninist) to deal with the actual conditions he faced. Later communist revolutions in other countries, e.g. China and Cuba, led to further adjustments to Marxism. As for capitalism, it has shown itself to be far more resilient and subtle than Marx's analysis allowed.

complex
intricate, involved

Plectere, plexum is the Latin 'to braid'; *com* derives from *cum* 'with'. A cognate (meaning related, from the Latin *co* 'with' and *natus* 'born') word is complicated (from *cum* and *plicare, plicatum* the Latin 'to fold'), which also gives us complicity and accomplice. The opposite of complex is simple, from the Latin *simplex*. Simplistic is used to characterize the over-simplification of complex problems.

Jung introduced complex into psychology to describe a group of interconnected conscious and unconscious ideas and feelings that exert an effect on behaviour. There are two complexes in Freudian psychoanalysis – the Oedipus (and related Electra) complex and the castration complex. Alfred Adler introduced the term inferiority complex (more properly inferiority feeling) to describe the feelings of resentment felt at being inferior. He used it to explain conditions ranging from petulance at imagined slights to shyness and timidity. It has become a popular term for a profound sense of inadequacy.

compos mentis
of sound mind

Compos is the Latin 'in possession of'; *mens, mentis* is 'mind', from which we derive mental, mentation (mental activity) and demented.

conservatism
a body of political beliefs that stresses the importance of maintaining the traditional values and institutions, opposes radical political change, and favours gradual and peaceful reform as the means of coping with necessary change

Con is derived from the Latin *cum* 'with'; *servare, servatum* is 'to keep'. To conserve is to keep intact. Conservatives are characterized by a disposition to maintain the status quo and resist change. In this broad sense we may refer to a conservative person, a conservative Church, the conservative wing of the Chinese Communist Party. Because modern life is marked by great economic, social, cultural and technological change, conservative tends to have pejorative connotations. Change per se is not exclusively either good or bad. It is illogical, therefore, to use the term conservative in an invariably pejorative sense.

Radical is the opposite of conservative. The radical believes that human advance can be guaranteed by fundamental change in social structures and processes. The conservative believes human nature remains the same throughout history and that every social system is threatened by the selfishness, conceit and deceitfulness of the individual. Politically, the conservative and the radical are diametrically opposed. The radical seeks major changes in order to guarantee a better future. The conservative recoils from the dangers inherent in sudden large-scale social change; moreover, he or she believes there is no guarantee of a better future. The support attracted by conservative parties in different countries at different times suggests that great numbers of people may find the conservative perspective the more realistic one.

However, conservatism is often regarded as simply a cluster of beliefs, attitudes and practices promoted by the privileged to maintain their own positions. The masses are seen to be lulled into acquiescence by equality before the law (a major condition for peace in society) and the comforts of social stability. A traditional paternalistic culture bonds them to the great national institutions, typically, as in Britain, to Crown, country and Church, and to the local institutions that individuals are born into and that sustain them throughout their lives such as the family, the local authorities, the local church and the local constabulary.

tradition(al)
the process by which beliefs and customs are passed on from one generation to another (*tradere, traditum* is the Latin 'to hand on'; a traditionalist is someone who adheres to tradition; to extradite is to hand someone over for trial or punishment to a foreign government – *ex* is the Latin 'from' or 'direct from', e.g. ex-works)

The classic conservative model of society as organic is provided by Plutarch in the fable of the belly (repeated by Shakespeare in *Coriolanus*). The poor people of Rome, squeezed ruthlessly by the moneylenders and finding no solace from the Senate, which supported the interests of the rich, refused to defend Rome against the Sabines and marched *en masse* (French, 'in a mass') to a hill three miles outside the city. The frightened Senate sent emissaries to persuade the people to come back. Their chief spokesman, Menenius Agrippa, ended his appeal with a fable.

'Once upon a time,' he said, 'all the parts of the body revolted against the belly. "You just sit there enjoying yourself," they snorted, "while the rest of us sweat and slave to keep your gross appetite satisfied!" But the belly simply laughed at them for their naïveté. "You see", the belly said, "it's true I receive all the body's nourishment but I send it out again and distribute it to every organ, thus giving each the strength to play its part in achieving the common good." ... The Senate, my fellow-countrymen, plays the same part as the belly: it studies the various proposals for state action and decides what to do, and the fruits of those decisions are shared by you all.' The people were eventually convinced and returned to work for their city.

Modern European conservatism was articulated initially in the struggle that developed in the late part of the seventeenth century between the aristocracy and the bourgeoisie. The aristocratic party – the landowners and their dependent tenant farmers and farm labourers, supported by the clergy – struggled to maintain the traditional medieval system. The bourgeoisie – industrialists, merchants, shopkeepers, tradesmen and bankers with their dependent lower classes of clerks and workers – sought to destroy the privileges of the aristocracy and do away with feudal restraints on production and trade.

Liberalism, based on the writings of the English philosopher John Locke and developed by the French philosophers of the eighteenth century, with its stress on the equality and freedom of the individual, was the natural ideology of the bourgeoisie. Liberalism became the dominant ideology of the nineteenth century: right-wing and reactionary became pejorative terms liberals applied to conservatives.

In the twentieth and twenty-first centuries conservatives have defined their position further in the struggle against socialism. They oppose centralized planning of the economy and the nationalization of industry. They favour free enterprise and the disciplines of a free market. They favour less government rather than more government. They seek to curtail the welfare state and to place on individuals much of the onus of providing for the contingencies of life.

The Conservative Party in Britain developed from the Tory Party of the late seventeenth, eighteenth and early nineteenth centuries (tories was a name derived from the Gaelic *toraí* meaning 'pursuer' or 'raider' for those dispossessed Irish Catholic landowners who took to the hills and woods and raided the new Cromwellian settlers; it was later transferred to the group in England that refused to concur in the exclusion of James II from the throne).

The Tories supported divine right, hereditary succession, and the royal prerogative; above all, they supported the Anglican Church – hence the observation of Agnes Maude Royden that the Anglican Church is 'the Tory Party at prayer'. They broke eventually with James II, therefore, because he was seen to favour Catholicism. The Tories, who represented the landowners, were

medieval
means pertaining to the Middle Ages (c.5th to 15th century; c. is the shortened form of *circa*, Latin 'around' or 'about') between the ancient and the modern worlds and derives from *medius*, the Latin 'middle', and *aevum* 'age'. Primeval means belonging to the first (*primus* is the Latin 'first') and therefore earliest age or ages of the world. People are said to be coeval if they were born on the same date. Era is a series of years reckoned from a particular point, e.g. the Napoleonic era, the era of the miniskirt (*aera* is a Latin word meaning 'number'). An epoch is a time so remarkable that it marks the beginning of an era in history – the launch of the first sputnik was an epoch-making event (*epokhē* is the Greek 'stoppage'). An aeon is a vast period in the history of the universe (*aeon* is a Latin word derived from the Greek *aion)*

contingencies
are chance happenings, literally 'things that touch with you', from the Latin particle *con* 'with' and *tingere/tangere*, the Latin 'to touch'. A contingency plan is one concerned to deal with possible but unlikely events that may disrupt a primary plan. Philosophers distinguish between necessary and contingent statements. A necessary statement must be true: 'A heptagon has more sides than a square.' A contingent statement *may* be true and *may* be false: 'This building will last a thousand years.'

James
is Jacobus in Latin. Jacobite refers to an adherent of James II of England and his descendants. Jacobean means of or characteristic of the period of James I of England – thus Ben Johnson is hailed as a genius of the Jacobean stage. Jacques, the most common name in France, is the French James. The jacquerie means rebellious French peasants (from a fourteenth-century revolt). A jack was a medieval defensive coat and a jacket – a diminutive of it – is a short coat, both almost certainly derived from Jacques. A Jacobin was originally a French Dominican monk; their monastery was that of St Jacques in Paris. The radical revolutionary Jacobins were so called from their meeting in a hall of the Jacobin convent in Paris. (The Parisian poor extreme republicans were known as the *sans culottes* – French *sans* 'without' and *culotte* 'knee-breeches')

opposed by the Whigs, who represented the moneyed interests of the towns and cities. (Whig is probably derived from *whiggamore*, the word for a Scottish rebel of the seventeenth century.) The Whigs sought to subordinate the power of the king to the will of parliament – hence they were led in the direction of electoral reform.

British conservatives look towards Edmund Burke, the Irish orator and statesman, as the thinker who provided the first – and classical – exposition of conservatism in his speeches and writings. It was his dictum 'We must reform in order to preserve' that rescued conservatism from the sterility of opposing all change.

Following the Whig Reform Act of 1832, which began the transformation of the electoral system, the Tories called themselves the Conservative Party. The Conservatives split over the repeal of the Corn Laws, which protected home-grown corn from cheap imports, in 1846. The Peelites supported repeal and, in an alliance with the Whigs, formed the Liberal Party. The Liberals also split when their leader Gladstone espoused Home Rule for Ireland. Some joined with the Conservatives in 1886 to create the Conservative and Unionist Party.

After World War I support in Britain for the great Liberal Party collapsed and the Conservatives stood as the major opponent of the ascendant socialist Labour Party.

constitution
the fundamental or basic law of a State

Constituere is the Latin 'to make to stand'. A constitution is a basic law upon which all other laws and all the institutions of a State rest. A constitution may be usefully thought of as a contract between the people and their rulers. It states what powers the rulers may exercise and establishes the institutions through which they shall do so; it defines the relationship between those institutions; it states, if it is a democratic constitution, the basic duties the citizens must perform to enjoy the benefits of democratic government; and it lists the rights citizens have to protect them from unconstitutional actions the State and its servants may seek to take against them. It also indicates procedures for changing the constitution, such as by referendum. A constitution acts as a control by the citizens on the possible abuse of power by those who govern. It also serves as the source of the authority of those who govern.

conurbation
the process by which villages, towns and cities, through continuous growth, join together and form a physical, but not a political, entity; or the result of that process

Urbs, urbis is the Latin 'city'; *con* is derived from *cum* 'with'; conurbation literally means forming a city with. It typically consists of towns or villages merging with the suburbs of a cental city. The term was first used by Patrick Geddes in *Cities in Evolution* in 1915.

About a fifth of the people of the United States live in the conurbation that stretches from Boston to Washington DC.

cornucopia
a superabundance

Cornu is the Latin 'horn' and *copia* is 'plenty'. *Cornucopiae* or *cornu copiae*, transliterated cornucopia in English, means horn of plenty. Zeus was the chief of the Greek gods. (In primitive times he was the sky god – that is why, when it began to rain, the Greeks would say bleakly, *Zeus huei* – 'Zeus is pissing'.) When Zeus was an infant, his mother hid him away from his father Cronus. Cronus, to avoid a prophecy that he would be usurped by one of his own children, was wont to eat his newborn offspring. His story evokes (literally calls forth – from the Latin *e* 'out' or 'forth' and *vocare* 'to call') the atavistic horror of cannibalism (cannibalism derives from the Spanish *Caníbal*, which itself derives from Carib via Caribal). A princess called Amalthea fed Zeus with goat's milk. Zeus was so grateful that he broke off one of the goat's horns and gave it to her, vowing that whoever owned it would always have an abundance of everything he or she desired. Incidentially, the aegis also came from this goat.

Leader writers in our newspapers will occasionally regret that the government does not possess a cornucopia and that, therefore, whatever benefits it distributes it must pay for from taxes.

cosmopolitan
a citizen of the world

Cosmos is the Greek 'universe'; *polis* is 'city-state' and *politēs* means 'citizen of a city-state'. The cosmopolitan is not bound by his or her nationality: his or her interests and loyalty extend to the whole world. Modern technology is fostering cosmopolitanism by turning the world into a global village (*globus* is the Latin 'ball' or 'sphere'; *sphaira*, from which we derive sphere, is the Greek 'globe'). Combined with the deregulation of markets, communications technology is creating the phenomenon of globalization – the process that enables financial and investment markets to operate at a global level.

coterminous
having the same extent

The Latin *terminus* means 'boundary': coterminous literally means having the same boundaries as, *co* being derived from the Latin *cum* 'with'. *Terminus ad quem* is the Latin 'the boundary [in the sense of end] to which' – the aim of a person or organization. *Terminus a quo* is the Latin 'the end from which' – the starting point. The *terminus ad quem* of a private business may be an annual $1 million profit. The *terminus a quo* may be a parent's suburban garage. Terminus is also used for the final stop of a bus or railway route. Terminal (as in terminal cancer), terminate and exterminate also connote finality.

Term, derived from *terminus*, in its broadest sense means any word or expression. Terminology means the body of specialized words relating to a particular subject. A term of art is a word or phrase to which a definite and precise sense is given by the practitioners of a particular art or science.

Co occurs widely in conjunction with nouns such as co-author, co-pilot, co-founder and co-education; verbs such as coexist, coincide, coagulate and co-produce; adjectives such as coextensive, coercive, collaborative and cooperative.

coup d'état
a sudden usurpation of State authority and power, usually by the army or elements of it

Coup is the French 'blow' or 'stroke'; *d'état* means 'of state' in French. A *coup d'état* is now used almost invariably of the actions of a group who bring about a change of government by force or who attempt to do so. A *putsch* (a Swiss-German word for 'push') means a sudden revolutionary outbreak or a *coup d'état*; those participating in it are called putschists.

A *coup de grâce* is a deadly and merciful blow delivered to someone who has already been mortally struck (*grâce* is the French 'grace').

A *coup de théâtre* is a dramatic turn of events such as might occur in a play.

A *coup de foudre* is a sudden and amazing action or event (*foudre* is the French 'lightning').

A *coup de main* is an attack that achieves complete surprise (*main*, from the Latin *manus*, is the French 'hand').

cracy
aristocracy, autocracy, bureaucracy, democracy, gerontocracy, kleptocracy,

Aristocracy is a privileged class, or rule by that class (*aristos* means 'best' or 'noble' in Greek). In ancient Greece when the cities became prosperous, the rich families – they called themselves *aristoi* 'the best people' –

took over control from the city king, who as a war-leader had been critical in the bad times, through the device of annually elected presidents. The *aristoi* referred contemptuously to the mass of the people as *hoi polloi* 'the many'.

Autocracy is literally self-rule; the word autocrat means one who rules in his own interest (*autos* means 'self' in Greek). Among the long list of proud titles renounced by Nicholas II, the last czar of Russia, on his abdication in 1917 was Autocrat of all the Russias. Czar, the pre-eminent title, came to be adopted in the following way. Ever since the fall of Constantinople, called Tsargrad (the city of Caesar) by the Russians, in 1453, Muscovite propaganda had promoted Russia as 'the third Rome'. In 1472 the Grand Duke of Muscovy Ivan III married Zoë, the niece of the last Byzantine emperor and Ivan's metropolitan hailed him as 'the new Emperor of the new Constantinople in Moscow'. He used the title czar which, adopted by Ivan the Terrible in 1547, became the official title of the head of the Russian empire. To underpin their 'Roman' claims the Russians also adopted as their imperial symbol the double-headed eagle that the Byzantine empire had itself adopted, under the dynasty of the Palaeologi, as a symbol of their succession to the Roman empire in both the east and the west.

Bureaucracy is rule by public officials (*bureau* means 'office' in French) or, more usually, the slow and often unnecessarily complicated procedures – the red tape – thought to characterize the work of public bodies. The sociologist Max Weber, observing that any continuing, large-scale, complex operation required a bureaucracy for its efficient administration, identified the following features of a bureaucracy: it was hierarchial, impersonal, continuous and expert.

Democracy is rule by the people (*dēmos* means 'people' in Greek). See headline note.

Gerontocracy is rule by old men (*gerōn*, *gerontos* is 'old man' in Greek). Spartan government had a gerontocratic feature – a *gerousia* consisting of twenty-eight elders, all at least sixty years old, and two kings. Plato's last work, *The Laws*, envisages a 'nocturnal council' of old men, all passion spent, working tirelessly for the good of the State. In the 1970s and early 1980s most of the Russian leaders, survivors from the revolutionary period, were old men and the Russian government was

meritocracy, phallocracy, plutocracy, technocracy, thalassocracy, theocracy and timocracy – these are all words whose common suffix *cracy* derives from the Greek *cratia* 'power'

empire
derives from the Latin *imperium* 'rule', from which we also derive imperial and imperious

red tape
means the bureaucracy associated with the civil service. Red tape was traditionally used to bind legal and official documents

often described as gerontocratic. The same held true of the Chinese rulers in and beyond the same period. Geriatric means an elderly person in need of care, from the Greek *geras* 'old age' and *iatric* from *iatros* 'healer'. Geriatric is also used as an adjective, e.g. geriatric services, meaning services for the elderly. A geriatrician is a doctor who specializes in the care of the elderly. A psycho-geriatrician is a psychiatrist who specializes in the mental health of the elderly.

Kleptocracy is rule by thieves (*kleptein* is the Greek 'to steal'). Kleptocrats is applied to a clique that uses its control of government to plunder a State's resources.

In a meritocracy (*meritum* is the Latin 'a thing deserved'; emeritus, as in professor emeritus, means retired but retaining one's title on an honorary basis) people gain positions by reason of their ability rather than such adventitious conditions as where they were born, where they went to school, what contacts they have (adventitious means coming from outside – *adventus* is the Latin 'a coming'; in botany a part that grows in an abnormal position, such as a root that grows from the stem, is said to be adventitious).

Phallocracy is a word coined by feminists to denote the predominance of men in government and public affairs simply because they are men. *Phallus* is the Latin equivalent of *phallos*, the Greek for 'penis' – both words are used in English for the male organ. Phallic, as in phallic symbol, is derived from *phallos*. Priapus, the Graeco-Roman god of gardens and fertility generally, was represented with a tremendous phallus – tremendous literally means 'that is to be trembled at', from the Latin *tremere* 'to quake'. Priapic may be used as a synonym for phallic but it has a connotation of indefatigability: 'He [James Boswell, Dr Samuel Johnson's biographer] was no longer a priapic simpleton, but a figure of furious and even Romantic contradictions.' (Richard Holmes, *NYRB*, 20 September 2001)

phalluses or phalli
were carried by the maenads at Dionysia as symbols of reproductive power. Unlike the god Pan, the god Dionysus was never represented as ithyphallic (*ithys* is the Greek 'straight' and here 'erect')

Plutocracy is rule by rich people (*ploutos* means 'wealth' in Greek). It is used in a general rather than a technical sense for people who, by reason of their wealth, exert great political power: 'Although his mother was the daughter of an Ontario whiskey distiller and bank president, Acheson did not belong to the plutocracy or even strictly to fashionable society, much admired and sought-after by the cognoscenti though he mostly was.' (Roy Jenkins, *Portraits and Miniatures*)

A technocracy is government by technical experts (*technē* is the Greek 'craft', which also gives us technique, technical and technology). Modern societies, increasingly dependent on the development of technology, tend to be technocratic because more and more decisions tend to be made by technical experts.

A thalassocracy is a seapower (*thalassa* is the Greek 'sea'). The Athenian empire, the historic Venetian Republic, the seventeenth-century Dutch and the eighteenth- and nineteenth-century British empires, all of which exercised power through the prowess of their sailors, are sometimes referred to as thalassocracies. *Pelagos* is another Greek word for 'sea'. An archipelago is a group of islands. Archipelago should mean the chief sea, *arch* being a Greek prefix meaning 'chief', 'principal' or 'first', but it is believed to be a mistranslation of *Aigaion pelagos* 'the Aegean Sea', which is studded with islands. Marine biologists use pelagic for fish that live in the upper waters of open sea; pelagic whaling is the pursuit of cetaceans (whales, from the Greek *kētos*) in the oceans. Ocean comes from Oceanus, the god of the great river the Greeks once believed flowed round the flat earth. Another Greek word for sea is *pontos*. The *Hellespont* ('Helle's Sea', Helle being a legendary young girl who drowned there) is the name the Greeks gave the Dardanelles.

Theocracy is literally rule by God (*theos* means 'god' in Greek). The word is applied to rule by men who claim to speak for God or who claim divine authority for their actions and decisions. A society ruled by a religious leader, such as Iran under the Ayatollah Khomeini, might be described as theocratic. More loosely, the term is applied to a state in which the doctrines of a particular religion pervade law and government.

A timocracy is a form of government in which property is a prerequisite of holding office or one in which ambition or the desire of honour is the ruling principle (*timē* is the Greek 'honour').

In Byzantium God or Christ were often referred to as Pantocrator ('almighty', from the Greek *panto* 'all' and *crator*, a form of *cratia*; note that crater – the bowl-shaped opening at the top or the side of a volcano – derives from the Greek *krater* 'mixing bowl').

miniature
for something small or in small scale is derived from the fact that scribes often embellished texts with little drawings done in red lead (Latin *minium*). A vignette (literally a little vine from the French *vigne* 'vine') was originally a small illustration at the beginning or end of a book or chapter, and derives from the frequency with which the motif of the vine was used to embellish a text. Cameo (from the Italian *cameo*) is a brooch or ring with a profile head carved in relief, from which we get cameo in the sense of a small role or scene in a play or film. If the design is incised rather than in relief the artefact is called an intaglio (from the Italian *intagliare* 'to engrave')

credo
a statement of basic beliefs

Credo is the Latin 'I believe'. In order to preserve its unity the early Church drew up a statement of the basic beliefs every Christian was expected to subscribe to. The first word of the statement in Latin is *Credo*. Credo is now used to describe any formal statement of beliefs. Thus, 'The equality of men and women, the necessity of a rigorously progressive taxation system, and the need to replace multi-seat constituencies with single-seat constituencies – these were elements of his political credo.'

Creed, meaning a particular religion, is also derived from *credo*.

Credible means worthy of belief, for example, a credible story.

Credulous means given to believing on insufficient grounds – a naïve person is credulous.

A person's credentials are statements or actions that establish a reason for trusting him or her.

A *del credere* (Italian, 'of trust') agent, in addition to getting orders, guarantees that the buyer will pay for the goods.

Credit in all its senses also derives from *credere*.

crisis
a decisive point, a turning-point, a time of danger

Crisis comes from the Latin *crisis*, derived from the Greek *krisis* 'judgment', itself from the Greek *krinein* 'to judge' or 'to decide'. Just as a judgment determines the outcome of a case, so the moment that decided the outcome of an experience came to be called the crisis.

Before the use of antibiotics, fevers, especially pneumonia (inflammation of one or both lungs – *pneumōn* is the Greek 'lung' – in which the air sacs become filled with liquid, which renders them useless for breathing; double pneumonia is where both lungs are affected), typically reached a high point of intensity – a crisis – after which the patient either recovered or died. Some connotations of the word are derived from that context.

The words critic, critical, criticism and critique (a measured review) are used by academics in a neutral sense because judgment may be favourable or unfavourable. But critic, critical and criticism in popular speech have negative connotations – thus, 'He was very critical of the standard of service in the hotel.' Critical is also used to mean pertaining to a crisis: 'The situation was critical. He had no food or fuel and winter was setting in.'

antibiotic
Anti is the Greek 'against'; *bios* is 'life', from which biotic, pertaining to life, derives; antibiotic, literally inimical to life, refers to substances that either kill bacteria and are bactericidal (the *cidal* suffix is from the Latin *caedere* 'to kill') or prevent them from growing but do not destroy them and are bacteriostatic (the *static* suffix is from the Greek *statikos* 'bringing to a standstill'). Selman Waksman, a Ukrainian who became a naturalized American, coined the word antibiotic in 1941 after having discovered streptomycin (from the Greek *streptos* 'twisted' and *mykēs* 'fungus')

Criterion, meaning the standard by which something is judged, also derives from *krinein*. In a democracy each citizen must decide in a general election whether to support the government or not. The work of government is complex. To decide how effectively a government has worked one needs to apply a number of criteria (plural form) to measure its performance on the economy, on welfare, on culture, on security, on foreign affairs, and so on. To apply the criteria one must know what the government has done in those areas, what resources it had and what difficulties it faced. For this knowledge the citizen relies largely on the mass media. Having made these assessments the citizen must make a summative judgment (*summare, summatum* is the Latin 'to add up') and cast his or her vote. The quality of government depends greatly on the criteria applied by those whom the government knows to be most influential. In a democracy that ought to mean the electorate.

crusade
an aggressive campaign against some evil, real or imaginary

Crux, crucis is the Latin 'cross'. The Crusades were a series of holy wars conducted between 1096 AD and 1270 AD by the Christian kings and nobility of Europe, ostensibly to free the holy places in Palestine from the Moslems. The Christian warriors wore the cross as their emblem.

A Moslem holy war is called a jihad.

crypto
secret

Kruptos is the Greek 'hidden'. Combined with the name of a group and transliterated in the form *crypto*, it denotes a secret sympathizer, e.g. crypto-communist, crypto-fascist.

The Spartans had a secret institution called the *krupteia* that young men in Sparta had to work with as part of their training. The *krupteia* carried out the duties of both police and spies. It was the duty of young Spartans in the *krupteia* to spy out potential troublemakers among the subject race, the Helots, whom they then proceeded to murder secretly. To justify this conduct, Spartan officials called *ephors*, on entering office, always declared unconditional war on the Helots.

Cryptic means secret, mysterious.

cui bono?
to whose benefit?

Cui is a form of *quis*, the Latin 'who'; *bono* is a form of *bonus* 'good'. *Cui bono?* literally means 'to whom for a good?' The phrase occurs first in Cicero's writing. *Cui bono?* is a test applied by the worldly-wise to help them understand what would otherwise seem daft. Thus, if a councillor proposes that the council should buy umbrellas to issue to tourists during the summer one could find, by asking who benefits, that the councillor is the first cousin of an umbrella manufacturer.

cum laude
with praise

Cum is the Latin 'with'; *laus, laudis* is 'praise' (hence, for example, laudatory remarks). The expression is used in relation to university degrees that may be conferred in rising levels *cum laude, magna cum laude* ('with great praise' – *magnus* is 'great') or *summa cum laude* ('with the highest praise' – *summus* is 'highest', from which we also derive summit).

cuneiform
wedge-shaped

Mesopotamia, the cradle of civilization, lay between two rivers, the Tigris and the Euphrates, and was almost coextensive with modern Iraq. The name means the between-the-rivers country, *meso* being a Greek prefix meaning 'between', *potamos* being 'river' and *ia* being a suffix indicating 'country'. In the fourth millennium BC the city was invented there and in the third, writing. The characters employed in the writing were wedge-shaped – hence the term cuneiform to describe the writing, *cuneus* being the Latin 'wedge'. Ur was an important city in ancient Mesopotamia, founded in the fourth millennium BC. According to Genesis it was the birthplace of Abraham (Ur of the Chaldees).

The cuneiform literature, which predated the Old Testament, contained stories about the creation of the world that closely paralleled some passages in the Bible.

curriculum
a course of studies

Curriculum, a course or race, is derived from Latin *currere* 'to run'. The curriculum is the course of studies for a school or other educational institution.

A syllabus (plural syllabi or syllabuses), from a misprint made in 1470 of the Greek word *sittyba* 'book label', outlines the contents of each subject on a curriculum just as a book label outlined the contents of a book.

A curriculum vitae is a document outlining the salient features of one's life and usually accompanies a job application (*vitae* is a form of *vita*, the Latin 'life', meaning 'of life', which also gives us vital and vitality).

salient
derives from the Latin *salire* 'to leap' and refers to something projecting, prominent, or striking. A salient is an outward-pointing angle in a line of defence

cynic
someone who characteristically takes a mordantly pessimistic view of other people's motives and actions

Kunikos (which transliterates into English as cynical) is a Greek word meaning 'dog-like'. It was first applied to a philosopher called Diogenes, who was born in Sinope, a Greek colony on the Black Sea (the *Pontus Euxeinos* or Euxine Sea). One of his aims was to expose the falseness of current conventions. So he acted unconventionally. He lived the life of a tramp, sleeping in a tub, and begging for food; he performed his bodily functions with a breathtaking lack of ceremony – hence his nickname.

Diogenes was a wit and a showman. When Alexander the Great visited him he asked him to name his wish and he would grant it. Diogenes replied, 'I wish you would stand out of my sunlight.' On hearing this Alexander turned to his aides and said, 'Were I not Alexander, I would wish to be Diogenes.' On another occasion Diogenes went out in broad daylight with a lighted lamp 'in search of one honest man'.

Diogenes and his followers – the Cynics – were distinguished more by their way of life than by a worked-out system of thought. They aimed to be self-sufficient. They considered asceticism (from the Greek *askēsis*, meaning 'training' or 'exercise') to be necessary for moral excellence because it develops resistance to the pressures of pleasure and pain. The Cynics preached the universal brotherhood of man. Indeed Diogenes made a famous claim to be 'a citizen of the world' – a cosmopolitan. That was an unthinkable idea up to then in the Greek city-states, whose stability and cohesion depended on their being tightly exclusive communities. So Diogenes might be described as the first anarchist.

Nowadays we use the word cynicism in a pejorative sense to indicate the attitude of someone who sarcastically doubts the sincerity or good intentions of other people. However, we should resist attempts by people who seek to brand true statements, pithily expressed but unpalatable to them, as cynical (*palatum* is the Latin 'the roof of the mouth'; something palatable may be swallowed with relish by either the mouth or the mind).

D

d(a)edal
skilful or intricate

A term used in literary criticism, it derives from Daedalus, an Athenian legendary for his inventiveness and his skill in all the arts – it was he who devised the labyrinth in which King Minos of Crete kept the Minotaur. Minos controlled the seas around Crete with a huge navy. When Daedalus fell foul of Minos and sought to escape, he was faced with a tough problem indeed. He solved it by making a pair of wings for himself and for his son Icarus, threading together the quill feathers and holding the smaller ones in place with wax. He warned Icarus: 'Don't soar too high in case the sun melts the wax and don't swoop too low in case the sea wets the feathers.' They both tied on the wings and flew out over the sea. Unfortunately Icarus, delighting in flight, ignored his father's warning and began soaring towards the sun. Soon, when Daedalus looked over his shoulder, he could no longer see Icarus. But on the waves below scattered feathers floated. Daedalus, as the cunning artificer (inventive designer and craftsman, from the Latin *ars*, *artis* 'art' and a form of *facere* 'to make') along with the Greek *logos* 'word' gives us logodaedaly, the practice of crafty and tricksy word-use.

sun
in Latin is *sol, solis* – hence solar and solstice (the time when the sun reaches its maximum distance from the equator – the summer solstice around 21 June and the winter solstice around 21 December). Apollo, represented as an extremely handsome young man, was the Greek sun-god. He was also called Phoebus. He stood for reason, physical beauty, moderation, the music of the lyre, and law and order

James Joyce chose Daedalus (in the form of Dedalus) for the surname of Stephen in *A Portrait of the Artist as a Young Man* and *Ulysses*.

decentralize
to undo the concentration of power in a single centre

Centrum is the Latin 'centre' – it was originally the stationary foot of a compass around which the other foot revolved to describe a circle. It is itself derived from the Greek *kentron* 'goad' or 'spike'. The Latin prefix *de* negatives a word.

The development of industry led to the growth of towns and cities at the expense of the countryside. Capital cities in particular benefited (*caput, capitis* is the Latin 'head', from which we derive capital as well as decapitation). In addition, the development of communications led to the drawing of political power from the countryside, towns and cities to the capital. As the decision-making system gets clogged, decisions are not taken or, if taken, are not implemented. People get irritated, and call for decentralization.

To truly decentralize you need to do more than

simply disperse parts of the central government around the state – you need to take powers from central departments and give them to lesser bodies such as regional or local authorities. The litmus test of decentralization is: have powers been devolved or not?

From centre we derive epicentre. The epicentre of an earthquake or underground explosion is the point on the earth's surface above where the movement originated (the Greek *epi* here means 'above'). The point on the earth's surface below where an explosion occurs in the air is called ground zero.

litmus
is a soluble powder obtained from certain lichens that turns red under acid conditions and blue under basic conditions, used as the classic test of acidity (from the Latin *acidus* 'sour' or 'sharp', a term first used by Francis Bacon)

decorum
correct behaviour in polite society

Decorus is the Latin 'seemly' or 'elegant'.

The following words ending in *um* are also taken directly from the Latin.

A desideratum is a thing lacked and wanted (*desiderare* is the Latin 'to desire'): 'Many might think that secrecy of the ballot, proportionality in party results and national geographic representation are desiderata [plural] of any electoral system.'

A factotum is someone employed to do all sorts of work (from the Latin *fac* 'do' and *totum* 'everything').

A modicum is a small amount (from the Latin *modicus* 'moderate').

Momentum is the impetus of a body resulting from its motion (from the Latin *momentum*, itself derived from *movere, motum* 'to move', which also gives us motion, motivation, motive, motor and moment).

Pabulum, from the Latin *pascere* 'to feed', means food. It is now often used in the sense of insipid intellectual fare (insipid derives from the Latin negative prefix *in* and *sapidus* 'full of flavour').

A sanctum is a sacred or holy place (*sanctus* is the Latin 'holy') and by extension a room or place of total privacy, as in inner sanctum. Something regarded as very sacred or inviolable is said to be sacrosanct (from the Latin *sacro* 'by sacred rite' and *sanctus*).

A simulacrum is a material image of a deity, person or thing. It now often connotes something that merely has the form or appearance of a certain thing, without possessing its substance or proper qualities (*simulare* is the Latin 'to make like').

A vade-mecum is a guidebook (from the Latin *vade* 'go' and *mecum* 'with me').

de jure
by law (legal right)

De is the Latin 'by' or 'from'; *jure* is a form of *jus, juris* 'law'. The expression is often used in contrast to *de facto* meaning in reality (*facto* is a form of the Latin *facere* 'to do' meaning 'a thing done' or 'a reality'): '*De jure* Tibet may belong to the Tibetans but *de facto* it belongs to the Chinese.'

delegate
representative

De is a Latin particle here meaning 'away'; *legare* is 'to send with a commission'. *Legatus* was originally a Roman general's lieutenant – *Labieno legato* ('Labienus being his lieutenant') is a recurrent phrase in Caesar's *Gallic War*. The word also came to be used of Rome's ambassadors. It persists in legation (a diplomatic mission) and papal legate (a Pope's representative). In common usage delegate and representative are treated as synonymous but political scientists distinguish them: a delegate is assigned to act on behalf of a group in a manner specified by it, i.e. in accordance with the mandate given to him or her (thus the delegate of a trades-union branch to the union's congress votes as instructed by the branch); a representative acts on behalf of a group but his or her actions are not predetermined – he or she is expected to use his or her own judgment.

It was the great parliamentarian Edmund Burke who first made the distinction when he insisted that he was the representative of the electors of his constituency, Bristol, not their delegate: 'Your representative owes you, not his industry only, but his judgement; and he betrays, instead of serving you, if he sacrifices it to your opinion.'

A plenipotentiary is a representative who acts with full authority (*plenus* is the Latin 'full', from which we get plenty, plenitude, plenary and plenum; *potentia* is the Latin 'power', from which we get potent, potentate and potential, meaning possible but not yet actual).

Gallic War
Caesar's account famously begins, *Gallia est omnis divisa in partes tres* (Latin, 'The whole of Gaul is divided into three parts'). Gallic derives from the Latin *Gallicus* 'Gaulish'. Gallican (pertaining to France) is applied to the nineteenth-century national and independent tendency in the Catholic Church in France. The opposing position of unqualified subjection to the authority of the Pope was called ultramontanist, from the Latin *ultra* 'beyond' and *mons, montis* 'mountain' (the mountains referred to here being the Alps)

Delphic
pertaining to prophecy, particularly of an ambiguous kind

One of the most famous and numinous (conveying a sense of the presence of a god, from the Latin *numen, numinis* 'divine majesty') shrines in ancient Greece was that of the handsome, athletic god Apollo at Delphi. Here great and humble people alike sought advice about the future. They would first make a sacrifice, pay offerings and go through rituals aimed at creating awe and reverence. Then they would be brought to a vestibule (*vestibulum* is the Latin 'entrance hall') where a priestess sat upon a tripod (a three-legged stool, from the Greek *treis, tria* 'three' and *pous, podos* 'foot') that stood astride the supposed navel (the centre) of the world, while round about curled the mildly hallucinogenic fumes of burning laurel leaves. Falling into a kind of fit or trance, she would utter wild and swirling words. Before they left, the priests would hand them the substance of her remarks written out in verse.

the Delphic navel
called *omphalos* in Greek, was an egg-shaped stone with two images on it representing the two eagles sent by Zeus, one from the east and one from the west, which met at Delphi, thus proving it to be the centre of the world. Omphaloid means navel-like. Umbilicus, from the Latin *umbo* 'shield boss', is another word for navel. Umbilical, as in umbilical cord, is the adjective derived from it

Very often the advice turned out excellently (the priests, after all, knew more than anybody else about what was going on because they met people from all over Greece and indeed from outside Greece). If it proved to be wrong, the priests could usually point out that the oracle's words meant something quite different, if you had had the sense to see that.

oracle
an agent of divine revelation or a prophecy itself, derives from the Latin *orare* 'to speak' or 'to pray'

A famous example of this ambiguity concerned Croesus, the fabulously wealthy King of Lydia. When he asked the oracle whether he should make war on the growing power of Persia, he was told that if he did, he would destroy a mighty empire. Thus heartened, he attacked Persia and was defeated. The oracle explained later that Croesus had destroyed a great empire – his own. The oracle's most profound general exhortations were carved into the stone of the temple at Delphi: 'Know thyself!' and 'Nothing in excess!'

Modern governments and businesses spend a good deal of money trying to predict (from the Latin *pre* 'before' and *dicere, dictum* 'to say') events. One forecasting technique they use is called the Delphi method. It involves inviting a number of prominent people in a particular area of activity, e.g. tourism, to write down what they think is going to happen, and formulating a forecast by a judicious synthesis of their views (judicious means according to sound judgment, from *judex, judicis*, the Latin 'judge').

demagogue

a political agitator who skilfully works on the prejudices of the mob

Dēmos is the Greek 'people'; *agein* is the Greek 'to lead'. The Athenian Menestheus is said to have been the first man to cultivate the arts of the demagogue: he set the masses in a ferment with the accusations he brought against Theseus, the city's founder and first ruler. Another demagogue in ancient Athens was Cleon the tanner. He did much to give the word its pejorative connotation of facile crowd manipulation (*facilis* is the Latin 'easy'). A populist (from the Latin *populus* 'people') is someone who believes that the common people and their concerns should predominate in government. Leading populists often turn out to be demagogues.

Huey Long was one of the most famous demagogues thrown up by the American Depression. He became governor of Louisiana. Difficult to classify because of his contradictory policies, he was variously described as dictatorial, liberal, fascist, leftist, democratic, idealistic and corrupt. He himself liked to pretend he was too different to be classified. On one occasion as he dozed on a bed, a group of journalists in the room fell to analysing him. Huey suddenly roused himself and brought the discussion to an end, saying: 'Oh hell! Say that I'm *sui generis* and let it go at that!'

depression
as used here describes a reduced level of trade and prosperity (*de* is the Latin 'down' and *premere, pressum* is 'to press'); a recession (*re* is the Latin 'back' and *cedere, cessum* is 'to go') describes the same conditions when they are expected to be short-term. US president Harry Truman sought to distinguish them: 'It's a recession when your neighbour loses his job; it's a depression when you lose your own.' Technically a recession follows two consecutive quarters of negative growth

Demiurge
the maker of the universe

Demiurge derives from the Greek *dēmos* 'people' and *ergon* 'work'. The Greeks used the term in two senses – either to name certain senior officials or as a term for a craftsman (someone who makes things out of various materials). It was in the latter sense that Plato used it for the maker of the universe. The Demiurge did not make the cosmos *ex nihilo* (Latin, 'from nothing') as the Judaeo-Christian God did, but from the chaotic materials available to him. He was good but his materials were good and bad – that is why we encounter a mixture of good and bad in the world. Gnosticism (from the Greek *gignōskein* 'to know'), an eclectic belief system that combined Plato's idea of the Demiurge with Orphic mysticism, Christian doctrine and certain Eastern influences, popularized the word.

A dramaturge (from *drama*, the late Latin 'play', itself derived from the Greek *dran* 'to do' and *ergon*) is a dramatist or a play-doctor attached to a theatre. Dramaturgy is the art and technique of the stage. In classical Greek dramaturgy the pre-eminent names are Aeschylus (*Oedipus, Seven Against Thebes, Persians*), Sophocles (*Electra, Oedipus Tyrannus, Antigone*) and Euripides (*Medea, Trojan Women, Iphigenia at Aulis*) for tragedy, and Aristophanes (*Birds, Clouds, Wasps*) for comedy. Incidentally, we get the term Cloud-Cuckoo-Land, often without capitals, for a far-off never-never land from Aristophanes's *Birds* – it was a realm built by the birds to separate the gods from mankind. Aristophanes's coinage was *Nephelococcygia* from the Greek

agnostic
from the Greek *a* 'not' and gnostic, refers to a person who maintains that in regard to any particular question – especially regarding the existence of God – the answer cannot be known with certainty. It was coined in 1869 by T.H. Huxley, the leading exponent of Darwin's theory of evolution

gnosis
meaning 'knowledge', from *gignōskein*, occurs as a suffix in the medical terms prognosis, a prediction of the outcome of a disorder (*pro* is the Greek 'before'), and diagnosis, the opinion reached after an examination of symptoms (*dia* is the Greek 'through')

nephelē 'cloud', *coccyx, coccygos* 'cuckoo', and the suffix *ia* indicating 'country'.

Nebula, related to the Greek *nephelē,* is the Latin 'cloud'. The term is used in astronomy for a diffuse cloud of particles and gases. Nebulous means vague. Thus, 'The reasons given by the defendant for his being found with a smoking gun near the body were nebulous.'

A thaumaturge (from *thauma* the Greek 'miracle' and *ergon*) is a miracle-worker.

Liturgy (from the Greek *leit* 'people' and *ergon*) was originally a duty placed on rich men in Athens to undertake some activity for the state at their own expense, such as maintaining for a year a trireme (a warship with three banks of oars, from the Latin *tri* 'three' and *remus* 'oar') or hosting a public banquet. It was later adopted by the Church for the rules governing public as distinct from private worship.

coccyx
is also a term used by doctors for the protruding termination of the spine in humans because the ancients thought it resembled the bill of a cuckoo. Darwinians recognize it as a vestigial tail (vestigium is the Latin 'footprint')

democracy
'… government of the people, by the people, and for the people' –Abraham Lincoln

A state where the government derives its authority from the people is a democracy – a word meaning rule by the people, derived from the Greek *dēmos* 'people' and *kratein* 'to rule'.

In the past, few governments were democratic. Rulers derived their power from immemorial custom (the way it always was), from the actual power and wealth they commanded or from religious laws. The forms of government usually found were monarchies, autocracies, oligarchies or theocracies. Democracies flourished only occasionally, for example in ancient Athens, and even there with a very limited (from the Latin *limes, limitis* 'boundary') franchise.

In modern times the American and French revolutions undermined immemorial custom as a source of authority by providing a contemporary alternative – the people. The French revolutionaries, moreover, also weakened religion as a plausible source of governmental authority. They executed a king who claimed authority not only from immemorial custom but also from God (through the principle of the divine right of kings, namely, that a king's authority derived from God). Thus the people alone remain as the obvious source of authority. Without the people's endorsement of some set of beliefs that bind the State together, would-be rulers must resort to force. Naturally most governments go out of their way to claim they are democratic rather than tyrannical.

Democracy is not an exact term because people use it in different senses. In the Greek city-states the citizens came together in one place and voted on public issues. They made their decisions by a majority. Such democracy is called direct democracy. Modern states are believed to be too big and complex to make direct democracy possible (though in Switzerland the people are consulted on proposed legislation several times a year; moreover the Internet may facilitate – make easy, from the Latin *facilis* 'easy' – such consultation everywhere). Instead of deciding issues for themselves people elect representatives to act on their behalf. Such indirect democracy is called representative democracy. It is the predominant form, moderated in some states by occasional referendums.

freedom
Negative freedom is the condition brought about by minimum interference by government in the lives of the citizens (liberals and conservatives espouse this view of freedom). Positive freedom is the condition brought about by a government that acts to create the authentic conditions for human growth and development (socialists espouse this view of freedom)

The ideas of freedom (positive or negative) and equality have become core values of democracy. Since democracies are based on majority rule, freedom (in either sense) and equality can often be at risk. Indeed, many democracies in ancient times quickly degenerated to mob rule. To promote political freedom and equality, therefore, most democracies guarantee basic rights to all citizens in their constitutions. (It is common experience, however, that the citizens must press their government to honour the guarantee.) Such democracies are called constitutional democracies.

Many people, for example socialists, believe the actual degree of freedom and equality enjoyed by a citizen is related to such factors as his or her income and education. They feel, therefore, that democracies should go further and aim to bring about a society where every citizen is broadly equal to his or her fellows economically and socially. States that have laws to bring about political, economic and social freedom and equality are known as social democracies.

The communist countries maintained they pursued the real democracy of economic and social equality; their critics pointed out that the dictatorship of the proletariat (effectively the dictatorship of the leaders of the Communist Party) precluded democracy because it denied the citizens the right to democratic activity. The communist critique of Western systems of government was that under cover of democracy the masses were economically and socially exploited.

Against that the defenders of Western democracy adduced (cited as evidence, from the Latin *adducere* 'to lead to') the vast apparatus of the welfare system.

an apparatus
is the equipment for doing something, from the Latin *apparare, apparatum* 'to make ready'. *Apparat*, derived from apparatus, is a Russian word for 'the Communist Party machine': an *apparatchik* was a member of the *apparat*

Because democracy means so many different things people sometimes get involved in a protracted and confusing argument about whether a particular state is democratic or not. The fact is that some governments elected by a majority of the people act in an extremely authoritarian manner. It is much more productive to think of democracy as a quality that exists to varying degrees in different countries at different times.

Thinking of democracy in this way, one can readily appreciate why people tend to acquiesce in authoritarian government in time of war or deep economic recession, that is, when physical or economic survival is at stake, when simple and speedy decisions are required. At other times, when there is the opportunity for reflection and consultation, one tends to find greater participation in decisions – or at least the demand for it. One also appreciates that the degree of democracy in a state depends fundamentally on the commitment of the citizens to freedom and justice for one and all.

People who have power usually wish to be free of any supervision of their use of it: decisions they make may be revealed as foolish or unfair. Or worse. Because they derive their power from a popular constitution they invariably proclaim the virtues of democracy. However, if they wish to limit the quality of democracy they have many means of doing so. They may create a sense of crisis and thereby a demand for strong non-participative government. They may restrict the flow of information or cloud it with misinformation. They may buy the support of powerful interest groups by allowing them privileges. Given human nature, it is realistic to suppose that all rulers, however well-intentioned, will fail to meet the democratic ideal.

The quality of democracy at any particular time must largely depend on the interest the people take in how rulers use the powers they, the people, have delegated to them. As John Philpot Curran, Irish lawyer and politician, famously declared: 'The condition upon which God hath given liberty to man is eternal vigilance.'

denote
indicate what is being spoken of

Denotare, denotatum is the Latin 'to indicate by a sign'. A distinction is made between what a word denotes and what it connotes. The denotation of a word is the thing, idea or concept referred to. The word rat denotes any of the larger animals of the genus *Mus*. The connotations of a word are the family of meanings, literal or metaphorical, associated with its use. The word rat connotes such meanings as four-legged, tailed, living, dirty, sneaky and disloyal (*connotare, connotatum* is the Latin 'to indicate with' or 'in addition').

The distinction between denote and connote, which was first made by the English philosopher J.S. Mill, is important to a writer. He or she may have a choice of words to denote the meaning he or she wishes to convey. Thus yellow is the colour of the rainbow between orange and green and may be denoted by a range of words in addition to yellow itself, such as primrose, buttercup, lemon, golden, saffron, crocus and jaundiced. The connotations of each of these words will determine the *mot juste* (French, *mot* is 'word'; *juste* is 'exact'): 'The boxer in the yellow shorts' is one thing; 'The boxer in the buttercup shorts' is something else.

colour
derives from the Latin *color, coloris* 'colour'. White light is dispersed by a prism (from the Greek *prizein* 'to saw') into a spectrum (from the Latin *specere, spectum* 'to look at') of seven colours ranging from the longest to the shortest wavelength: violet, indigo, blue, green, yellow, orange and red. *Chrōma* is the Greek 'colour', from which we derive chromatic (relating to colour), chromatics and chromatology (both mean the science of colour), monochrome (single-coloured, *mono* being the Greek 'alone' or 'single'), polychrome (multicoloured, *poly* being the Greek 'many') and achromatic (without colour, *a* being a Greek negative particle)

dénouement
the final resolution of a play or complicated situation

Dénouer is the French 'to unknot', derived from *de*, a Latin particle that negatives a word, and the Latin *nodare* 'to knot'. To refer to the final dénouement is tautologous.

de novo
afresh

De is the Latin 'from' or 'by'; *novo* is a form of *novus* 'new'. The expression denotes a fresh start: 'Let us forget about what happened in the past and build up our relationship *de novo*.'

determinism
a belief that the movement of everything in the universe is fixed in advance

Terminus is the Latin 'boundary' or 'destination'; *determinare* means 'to set the destination in advance', 'to ordain' or 'to determine'. When modern scientists renewed the exploration of why things in the world act the way they do, they unfolded a whole range of causes and effects; and as they began to see everything fitting into a system they conceived the world as a kind of machine, a predetermined instrument like a clock. This kind of thinking is called scientific determinism. They then began to apply the idea to human society – their study of the economic system suggested economic determinism, their study of the way people were ranked in society suggested social determinism.

Marx developed an elaborate form of historical determinism by combining economic and social determinism to explain how the forces of production (the way people meet their material needs), the stages of history and the evolution of social consciousness (law, religion, morality) develop. But he also spoke of the conscious direction of these events by men, though, he averred, we cannot overleap 'the natural phases of evolution'. Men can read the signs wrongly, and indeed Marx did so himself. Still, his analysis has helped us understand how economic factors mould our personal, social and political lives.

deus ex machina
a totally unexpected intervention that resolves a difficult situation

Deus is the Latin 'god'; *ex* is 'from'; *machina* is 'machine'.

European drama was invented by the Greeks, imitated by the Romans, and passed on to us. Not all ancient playwrights were as fastidious (exceedingly delicate and demanding, from the Latin *fastidiosus* 'easily disgusted' and therefore hard to please) as the Greek tragedians Aeschylus and Sophocles, in terms of their art. Many, including Euripides, sometimes allowed their plots to become so complicated that only the arrival on stage of a god, conveyed through the air by a machine, could resolve the situation. Many a modern playwright and film director has relied on a *deus ex machina* in the form of a rich aunt or the US cavalry.

diaphanous
transparent

Dia is the Greek 'through'; *phainein*, from which the *phanous* formation derives, is 'to show'. An ekdysiast (from *ekduein* 'to strip'), a facetious word for a stripper coined by H.L. Mencken, may shed increasingly diaphanous clothes. Transparent derives from the Latin *trans* 'through' and *parere* 'to appear' and means easy to see through. Translucent, derived from *trans* and the Latin *lucere* 'to shine', means semi-transparent, that is, allows light to pass through partially.

facetious
derives from the Latin *facetiae* 'jests'

dictator
a non-monarchial absolute ruler

Dicere, *dictum* is the Latin 'to say', from which dictator is ultimately derived. A dictator declares what is to be done. In times of great crisis the Romans would appoint a dictator for a six-month period to assume all the powers of the state. A despot (from the Greek *despotēs* 'master') may be a dictator or an absolute monarch such as the czar of Russia was. A benevolent despot is one who rules paternalistically (*pater* is the Latin 'father') with care for the interests of his subjects, as opposed to a tyrant (from the Greek *tyrannos*, also meaning 'master'): an absolute, non-dynastic ruler who cares only for his own interests.

A *diktat* (German, 'something dictated') is a brutal order or harsh statement that must be accepted without discussion.

A ukase, from the Russian *ukaz*, was an edict of the czar.

didactic
intended to instruct

Didaskein is the Greek 'to teach'. An autodidact is someone who is self-taught (*autos* is 'self').

Docere, doctum is the Latin 'to teach'. From it we derive doctor and document.

dinosaur
any extinct terrestrial reptile of the orders Saurischia and Ornithischia

fossil
from the Latin *fossilis* 'dug up', itself derived from *fodere, fossum* 'to dig', means a relic or remnant of a plant or animal that existed in a previous geological age. A fossil may occur in mineralized form as a cast or impression or as a frozen, perfectly preserved organism. *Fossum* also gives us fosse (a ditch or moat)

Dinosaur derives from the Greek *deinos* 'terrible' and *sauros* 'lizard'. The word was coined in 1842 by the English comparative anatomist Richard Owen to describe a newly recognized group of giant reptiles that had been discovered in fossil deposits during the previous twenty years.

Every new science requires a new nomenclature to establish its taxonomy. In this difficult area scientists latched on to physical peculiarities. Thus, pterodactyl is any extinct flying reptile (any ornithischian dinosaur – from the Greek *ornos, ornithos* 'bird'; hence also ornithology) having membranous wings supported on an elongated fourth digit (*pteron* is the Greek 'wing' and *daktulos* is 'finger'; helicopter derives from the Greek *helix, helikos* 'spiral' and *pter*). The pterodactyl was first identified and named by Baron Georges Cuvier, the French zoologist and geologist regarded as the father of comparative anatomy and palaeontology (*palaios* is the Greek 'old' and *onto* is a particle derived from *ōn, ontos* 'being'; palaeontology, literally the study of old beings, is the study of fossils to determine the structure and evolution of extinct animals and plants).

doctrinaire
pertaining to someone who applies principles rigidly without making allowances for circumstances

Doctrina is the Latin 'doctrine' – literally knowledge imparted by teaching – derived from *docere, doctum* 'to teach'. To indoctrinate is to teach a set of doctrines until they are completely accepted by the person being indoctrinated. To use advanced and intensive psychological techniques to indoctrinate is to brainwash. During the Korean War the North Koreans brainwashed captured American soldiers so that they publicly and voluntarily repudiated their homeland and its values.

Doctrines may be religious, political, scientific, etc. The Monroe Doctrine is probably the most famous use of the term in politics. In 1823 the American president James Monroe said of the European powers, 'we should consider any attempt on their part to extend their system to any portion of this hemisphere as dangerous to our peace and safety'. This policy position was first referred to as the Monroe Doctrine in 1848. A policy is described as a doctrine when it is strategically important to a party that has the power to uphold it. A set of doctrines may form an ideology. An ideologist (or ideologue) who insists on applying doctrine irrespective of practical considerations would be described as doctrinaire. Those in government in Britain during the period of the Irish Famine were doctrinaire *laisser-faire* economists and refused to intervene in the economy to avert the consequences of the potato blight. They believed that the provision of free or cheap food would make it impossible to bring into being an effective market which, they thought, was the only long-term solution to the shortage.

Monrovia
(a Latinized form of Monroe's name) is the capital of Liberia (land of the free, *liber* being the Latin 'free' and *ia* a suffix indicating 'country'), the west African settlement founded by freed African-American slaves in 1820, which became an independent republic in 1847

laisser-faire
to let happen – these two French words mean 'to allow' and 'to do' respectively; an alternative form *laissez-faire* is also used

dolce far niente
pleasant idleness

In this Italian expression *dolce* means 'sweet', *far* 'to do' and *niente* 'nothing'. *Dolce* derives from the Latin *dulcis* 'sweet', which gives us dulcet, as in dulcet tones. A form of it occurs in two famous quotations from Horace: *dulce est desipere in loco* ('it is pleasant to act the fool on occasion') and *Dulce et decorum est / Pro patria mori* ('It is a sweet and honourable thing to die for one's country'). Wilfred Owen used *Dulce et Decorum Est* as the title of a poem that branded Horace's sonorous line as 'the old Lie' (*sonor* is the Latin 'sound', which also gives us sonar and sonata).

The word fainéant meaning do-nothing is taken to derive from the French *faire* 'to do' and *néant* 'nothing' and was famously applied to the later Merovingian kings of France who allowed their high officials to govern the country in their place. In modern usage it connotes indolence and procrastination:

> Hailsham began as the front runner [in the 1963 race to be the Tory leader], or at least the most noisy one.

indolence
means disliking effort or lazy, from *in*, a Latin negative prefix, and *dolens*, *dolentis* 'causing distress'

procrastination
means putting off doing something until some future time – a notable characteristic of Hamlet – from the Latin *pro* 'onward' and *crastinus* 'of tomorrow'

> When he began to fade Macleod believed that he himself might emerge between the fainéant Butler and the too rumbustious Hailsham.
>
> –Roy Jenkins, *Portraits and Miniatures*

draconian
a description for an exceptionally harsh law or government measure

Draco was an Athenian law-giver – his was the first written Athenian code – who imposed the death penalty for a breach of any of his laws and so his name became a byword for severity. A later Greek described this code as 'writ in blood'.

The rule of law, that is to say that the law must be obeyed by all citizens and be applied equally to all citizens in a manner that ensures them a fair trial, was one of the greatest concepts of the Greeks: for it they declared themselves prepared to die. 'The people should fight for the Law as if for their city-wall,' the philosopher Heraclitus proclaimed. The rule of law secures order in society, the essential context for civilized living. However, it was the Romans rather than the Greeks who created the legal system whose concepts and practices still illuminate the practice of law in the modern world (*lumen, luminis* is the Latin 'light' – hence luminous and luminary; to illuminate is to light up a place or a mind; illuminati are any group that believes it has special enlightenment, especially on religious matters). The Romans wrote down their laws and judgments, codified the laws, and helped the law evolve by using past judgments as precedents (from the Latin *praecedere* 'to go before'). The predominance of Latinisms in legal discourse attests to the prevailing relevance and pervasive influence of Roman law.

lux, lucis
is another Latin word for 'light', from which we derive lucid, pellucid (meaning very clear, as in pellucid prose), translucent and Lucifer (the light-bearer, *ferre* being the Latin 'to carry')

dynasty
a succession of hereditary rulers

Dunamis is the Greek 'power', from which dynasty is derived (as well as dynamite, dynamic and dynamo). Aristotle used the term to mean government vested in a few privileged families. Dynastic rule provides for orderly succession, normally from father to eldest son, and therefore political stability, but it provides no proof against incompetent rulers. Hereditary derives from the Latin *heres, heredis* 'heir'.

Dynasty may be used nowadays in relation to a family that over a number of generations has won political office at the polls (a political dynasty) or that has maintained itself in the front ranks of business (a commercial dynasty).

E

eccentric
departing from convention in an odd, even bizarre way

Ek is the Greek 'away from' and *kentron* is 'centre'. Eccentric may also refer to circles that do not have a common centre, i.e. that are not concentric (*con* is a form of the Latin *cum* 'with').

Caligula was one of the most eccentric of the Roman emperors. He succeeded Tiberius in 37 AD. As his short reign progressed, he became increasingly unhinged and tyrannical. Because he was related to Julius Caesar and Augustus, both of whom had been apotheosized, he became convinced he himself was a god. He built a bridge from his palace on the Palatine to the Capitoline to enable him to consult more easily with Jupiter in his temple there. He built a marble stable for his favourite horse, Incitatus, and adorned him with a jewelled collar. Rumour had it that he intended to make the horse a consul. The imperial coffers, exhausted by his extravagance, were replenished by bequests from patricians who had been encouraged to show their (and their families') affection for the emperor by writing him into their wills before committing suicide. Caligula was assassinated by a member of his staff whom he had insulted. Commentators today sometimes greet an egregious public appointment with the assertion, 'Not since Caligula made his horse a consul has there been such an appointment.'

Idiosyncratic may serve as a synonym for eccentric. The *idio* form derives from the Greek *idios* 'private, separate', and *syncratic* derives from the Greek *sun* 'with' and *kerannunai* 'to mingle'. Idiosyncratic, then, means relating to what makes a person different. Applied to behaviour it means bizarre. Doctors also apply it to patients who have an abnormal reaction to particular foods or drugs – an idiosyncratic reaction.

The eighteenth-century Irish landlord George Robert Fitzgerald was undoubtedly idiosyncratic. He kept a pet bear that he treated as a boon companion and took with him everywhere, even in stagecoaches. Once, Fitzgerald's lawyer, who was travelling through the night with him in his carriage, discovered when dawn broke over the hills that the 'gentleman' beside him, swathed in a blue travelling cloak, had a face covered in fur and a big red tongue lolling over fiercesome

Caesar
was originally the family name of the Julian clan (a group of people interrelated by ancestry or marriage, from the Irish *clann* 'family') at Rome. Its most famous member was Julius Caesar. Octavian (the future Augustus), as the adopted son of Julius Caesar, assumed the name. He handed it on to his successors – it was even used by those emperors who did not belong to the Julian clan. Kaiser is the German version of Caesar, Czar (or Tsar or Tzar) the Russian. Caesarean section is a surgical incision to deliver a baby, so called because Julius Caesar (*caedere, caesum* is the Latin 'to cut') was believed to have been thus delivered. Shakespeare refers to such an operation in *Macbeth*: 'Macduff was from his mother's womb untimely ripp'd'

idiosyncrasies
are any quirky forms of behaviour, such as drinking black coffee with lemon, using exclusively a quill to sign contracts or insisting on an armed guard to make a modest lodgement in the bank. Idiom also derives from *idios* and refers to linguistic usage that is grammatical and natural to native speakers of a language. Idiopathic from *idios* and *patheia* the Greek 'suffering' applies to any disease of unknown cause. An idiot, from the Greek *idiōtēs* 'private person', acquired the sense of fool from its contrast with the Greek ideal of the citizen – a person with a lively concern for public affairs

teeth. When the bear kissed the lawyer on Fitzgerald's command, the poor fellow leapt from the carriage and dashed for safety.

eclectic
selecting elements that please you from various philosophies or arts

Eclegein is the Greek 'to select'. A person may be eclectic in art, for instance, by drawing upon a wide range of styles or by selecting for study a limited range such as the Pre-Raphaelites, the Impressionists and the Dadaists. Art forms are so numerous that one's taste is more likely to be eclectic than catholic (embracing everything, universal, from the Greek *catholicus* – *kata* 'throughout' and *holos* 'the whole'). So-called *à la carte* (French, 'from the bill of fare') Christians are eclectic.

The fusing of various attractive elements of different systems of belief into a harmonious whole is also called syncretism. Early Christianity had to define itself against a strong, syncretic tendency current throughout the Roman empire that was most virulently (*virulentus* is the Latin 'full of poison') expressed in Gnosticism. The word derives from the Greek *synkretismos* 'confederation' and apparently was originally applied to Cretan (Kretan) communities, *syn* being the Greek *sun* 'with'.

holistic
from *holos*, is applied in medicine to describe consideration of the complete person, physically and psychologically, in the treatment of disease

economy
the system by which goods and services are produced and allocated among consumers

Oikos is the Greek 'house' and *nomos* is the Greek 'law' (*nomy* indicates the science or the laws governing a certain field of knowledge). The Greek *oikonomia* (transliterated into Latin as *oeconomia* and into English as economy) originally described the ruling or management of a household. The word may now be applied to the management of the material resources of an individual, a community, a locality (the local economy), a region (the mid-west economy) or a country (the national economy); it may also be applied globally (the international economy, the world economy). When the media refer to the economy, they usually mean the national economy. Since thrift is one of the great virtues pursued in household management, the word economical means in common usage thrifty, parsimonious or efficient.

Economics is the scientific study of the economy. It is divided into macroeconomics and microeconomics. Economics has been called 'the dismal science' (Thomas Carlyle, *Latter Day Pamphlets*) because it was seen as seeking to cope with Malthus's view that humanity was condemned to a losing battle between

nomy
also gives us astronomy, agronomy and gastronomy (the art of good eating, *gastēr*, *gastros* being the Greek 'stomach')

economical
Robert Armstrong, head of the British civil service from 1981 to 1987, once sought to defend an official letter: 'It contains a misleading impression, not a lie. It was being economical with the truth.'

population growth and food supply, as population rises in geometrical progression and food supply rises in arithmetical progression. (A geometric progression is a sequence of numbers, each of which differs from the succeeding one by a constant ratio. An example is 1, 2, 4, 8, 16, where the succeeding number is twice that of the preceding one. An arithmetic – *arithmein* is the Greek 'to count' – progression is a sequence of numbers, each term of which differs from the succeeding term by the addition of a constant amount. An example is 3, 6, 9, 12, 15, 18, where the constant amount is three.) Economists are experts in economics.

National economies are of three kinds. In free-market economies, the government plays very little part in the production, exchange and consumption of goods and services. In command (or dirigiste, from the French *diriger* 'to direct') economies, the government, through a planning system, determines production and allocates resources. In mixed economies, market forces play a large part but the government intervenes extensively.

Gross Domestic Product (GDP) measures the output of the factors of production located in the domestic economy regardless of who owns them. In essence the GDP is the total value of a country's annual output of goods and services. Gross National Product (GNP) is GDP adjusted for income flowing out to non-nationals and flowing in to nationals. It identifies the output, income and expenditure of a country's nationals in a year.

domestic
derives from the Latin *domus* 'house'; it may refer to the home of an individual and contrast, like the word private, with public; it may also refer to the national home, and in that sense contrast, like the word national, with foreign

annual
derives from the Latin *annus* 'year', which also gives us anniversary and annuity. *Annus mirabilis* is a year of notable events, whether disasters or wonders, *mirabilis* being the Latin 'wonderful'

GDP and GNP are often used as benchmarks against which to measure certain activities such as public sector expenditure (the total spending controlled by the public service).

When goods and services are produced and not declared for tax purposes, they will not be counted in GDP or GNP. This unrecorded production of goods and services constitutes the black economy (sometimes called the shadow economy).

education
the long process whereby people develop the attitudes, knowledge and skills that their society feels they should have to function

Educare, educatum is the Latin 'to rear' or 'to develop' (and is to be distinguished from *educere* 'to lead out'). Education is distinguished from training, which is concerned simply to transfer skills and competencies (and is usually a relatively short process).

Education is characterized by the approach taken

productively; a perennial opposing view defines education as the moral and intellectual development of persons towards truth, goodness and beauty for their own sakes rather than for society

by educators in either of two ways. A liberal education is one in which knowledge is pursued for its own sake (liberal derives from the Latin *liber* 'free' – a liberal education was the kind people in medieval times thought appropriate to a freeman, a gentleman rather than a craftsman or servant). A utilitarian education is one that is pursued for the sake of practical advantages (utilitarian derives from the Latin *utilis* 'useful').

e.g.
for example

The abbreviation e.g. is from the Latin expression *exempli gratia*. *Gratia* means 'for the sake of', *exempli* means 'example'. The MGM motto *ars gratia artis* means 'art for the sake of art' (*ars, artis* is the Latin 'art'). Artificial literally means made by art (the *ficial* ending derives from the Latin *facere, factum* 'to make'). An artefact/artifact is something man-made, the *fact* suffix being derived from *facere* and contrasts with the French *art trouvé*, a natural object found lying about that looks like an artefact (*trouver* is the French 'to find'). The German *Ersatz* means 'replacement' and is sometimes used in English to mean artificial in a decidedly pejorative sense. During World War II the Germans, cut off from external supplies of certain materials, produced a wide range of ersatz goods, such as rubber, coffee, tea and sugar, which did not always satisfy the consumers' expectations.

egoism
the moral disposition to be concerned solely with one's own interests

Ego means 'I' in Latin. Egoism or egotism means self-centredness. Leaders may be egotistic or egocentric (self-centred) or even egomaniacal (*mania* means 'madness' in Greek). In Freudian psychology the mind consists of the ego (representing reason and common sense, the part of the mind that has been modified by the direct influence of the external world), the id (representing the automatic – from the Greek *automatos* 'acting independently' – instinctual responses to pleasure and pain, *id* being the Latin impersonal 'it') and the superego (or conscience that seeks to control both the id and the ego, *super* being the Latin 'above'). Ego is now used in popular speech for self-image as in 'His ego took a bruising on the quiz show. They asked him what two and two was and he said twenty-two.'

Alter ego means one's other self (*alter* is the Latin 'other', from which we derive alternative). It is used of friends so close that in any given situation one can be relied upon to act in the same way as the other would.

Doppelgänger is a German word meaning 'one's double' (literally 'one's double goer') manifesting in a natural way as a physical lookalike or in a sinister way as a wraith. The use of a doppelgänger is a common device in German fiction.

élitist
favouring a select group for social and particularly political privileges; it has the connotation of applying standards that can be attained only by the few

Élite is the French 'chosen', derived from the Latin *eligere, electum* 'to select', from which we also get elect, election, electoral and electorate. An élite is a minority within a group that exercises preponderant influence over the group (*pre* is a Latin particle here meaning 'surpassingly'; *ponderare, ponderatum* is the Latin 'to weigh').

A ruling élite is the minority in a state that holds most of the public offices. People may enter the élite through such advantages as their birth and the social connections thereby established, the schools they go to, their ability or the positions their wealth wins for them.

Probably most people regard élites as snobbish and anti-egalitarian – élitism and élitist are usually pejorative terms; others regard élites either as the natural product of man's tendency to associate with people of like tastes and talents or as a means of asserting standards of excellence in a society (not necessarily standards of moral excellence but standards of excellence in whatever activities a society places value on: thus an élite army corps is so identified not because it is exceptionally good morally but because it is exceptionally good at killing).

éminence grise
a minor functionary who exercises great hidden power through being the confidant of a powerful figure

Cardinal Richelieu, as minister to Louis XIII for eighteen years, was practically the master of France. His private secretary and alter ego was a Capuchin priest Père Joseph. Père Joseph's skills, devotion and energy made him effectively the French foreign minister. His secretiveness gave him a sinister aura.

Éminence is the French mode of addressing a cardinal. Because of his great influence with the scarlet-robed Richelieu, Père Joseph was nicknamed L'Éminence grise ('The Grey Eminence'), grey being the colour of the Capuchin habit.

eminent
means above others in rank or distinguished, from the Latin *minere* 'to stand' and e 'out'. Prominent means to stand out from one's surroundings, *pro* being the Latin 'forward'. One may be prominent but not necessarily eminent

A modern use of the term occurs in Paul Preston's *Franco*:

> On the table was an extremely realistic paper presented by Admiral Moreno, which had been drawn

up by the naval staff – including his chief of operations, Franco's future *éminence grise*, the dour and plodding Captain Luis Carrero Blanco.

empirical
pertaining to knowledge derived from experience

Empeirikos is the Greek 'from experience'. To experience is to articulate for oneself the meaning of a real-life situation whether it be an action, a relationship (such as marriage), a walk in the mountains or a kiss. Here, for example in the experience of a kiss or falling in love, what is stressed is the newness of experience, that is, it reshapes our thoughts and feelings in such a way that we see the world anew. That element is true of all genuine experience even if it is not always manifest to us. In that sense experiencing is synonymous with knowing and learning.

Experience, like knowledge, can be true or false, though we tend to regard experience as always true. The experienced person is one who, through living and acting in a particular area of human life, and reflecting on it, has acquired understanding and knowledge of that area, and is capable of articulating it to others. The experienced person is usually regarded as a wise person. However, it is worth recalling what was said of the Bourbons when Charles X abdicated and fled Paris in 1830: 'They experienced everything and learned nothing.'

The word empiricism – the doctrine that all knowledge of matters of fact derives from experience – has a special meaning in the history of philosophy and the attempt to explain knowledge. The empiricists believed that what we know are the impressions or sense data that objects leave on our senses, and that consequently we have no direct knowledge of the external world (*data* is the plural form of *datum,* the Latin 'a thing given'). We can only know the external world, therefore, through inference from these impressions or sense data. What we know about the world is nothing more than complexes of these impressions or sense data. Thus table is a word we use to refer to a complex of impressions like hardness, colour, shape and size. It does not refer to the real table at all. In other words, our sensations, instead of being knowledge of the real thing, are barriers between us and things.

Statements of fact, then, are inferences, from our impressions, to the real world. Empiricists consequently have always had a problem with the connection between thought (language) and reality. This is called the problem of verification, of how, if we know only our impressions, we establish the truth of what are called factual propositions (*verus* is the Latin 'true'; to verify is to establish the truth about something). The empiricist account of knowledge locks the knower inside himself or herself. Solipsism, that is, self-enclosedness, leads to the problem of how we know other persons or things.

solipsism
derives from the Latin *solus* 'alone' and *ipse* 'self'. A solecism is a grammatical error and is derived from the Greek *soloikismos* 'speaking like the citizens of Soloi', that is, incorrectly; Soloi was a colony of Athens; the Athenians, sophisticated and chic, were inclined to sneer at their ruder countrymen

Among the greatest empiricist philosophers were the Englishman John Locke and the Scot David Hume. The Irishman George Berkeley, Bishop of Cloyne, after whom the University of California at Berkeley is called, has traditionally been ranked among the empiricists. However, modern research suggests Berkeley should be classified with the Cartesians, the followers of the French mathematician and philosopher René Descartes, the founder of modern rationalist philosophy, who enunciated the famous principle *cogito ergo sum* ('I think therefore I am'). Much of current British philosophy might be arguably viewed as a refined version of empirical thinking.

encyclical
a circular letter sent by the Pope to all Catholic bishops dealing authoritatively but not necessarily infallibly with religious and social issues; the term is used in other Christian churches too

Kyklos is the Greek 'circle': an encyclical is sent round in a circle among the faithful. Probably the most famous encyclical of modern times is Pope Paul VI's *Humanae Vitae* (issued in 1968), which condemned artificial forms of birth control (encyclicals, usually written in Latin, take their titles from their first few words – *humanae vitae* means 'of human life' in Latin).

An encyclopaedia is a book, often in many volumes, dealing with all of human knowledge or segments of it in articles that are usually ordered alphabetically. The word, which came into use in the sixteenth century, derives from the Greek *paideia* 'education' and *enkyklios* 'circular' (in the round or general as opposed to specialized). The most famous example is the *Encylopédie* published between 1751 and 1772 under the direction of the French rationalist philosophers d'Alembert and Diderot.

ephemeral
lasting for a short time

Epi – *eph* before a vowel or a word beginning with h – is the Greek 'upon' or 'at'; *hēmera* is 'day'. In Greek tragedy the gods – the immortals – often address men as *ephēmeroi* – 'beings of a day'. A writer's juvenilia (writings done in his or her youth, from *juvenis* the Latin 'young', from which we also derive juvenile) are usually ephemeral. Newspapers, periodicals and notes are referred to as ephemera (the plural of the Greek *ephēmeron*, 'a thing of no lasting value'): 'Every relic and jotting [of the novelist Marguerite Duras] is now being collected, which is fine for biographers, but these ephemera are also published as if they were unknown fragments of the Upanishads.' (Olivier Todd, *LRB*) *Hēmera* lurks in the title of Boccaccio's *Decameron*, a book made up of stories, like Chaucer's *The Canterbury Tales*, told on successive days (in the case of the *Decameron* ten days – *deka* is the Greek 'ten').

the Upanishads
are rare theosophic or philosophic writings in Sanskrit, the ancient Indo-European literary language of India

epigraphy
the study of inscriptions written on durable materials such as stone, metal, wood and earthenware

Epi is a Greek prefix meaning 'upon' and *graphein* is 'to write'. Such an inscription itself is called an epigraph (a word that may also be applied to a motto, or a pithy statement appearing at the beginning of a book or of each chapter of a book). Evidence of man's past is mostly archaeological, literary or epigraphic. One of the most famous epigraphs occurs on the Rosetta stone, an ancient Egyptian monumental stone found near the town of Rosetta by one of Napoleon's engineers in 1799 during the French occupation of Egypt. The stone has three parallel texts in hieroglyphic, demotic Egyptian and Greek. The French archaeologist Jean-François Champollion was able to decipher the hitherto impenetrable hieroglyphics thanks to his knowledge of Greek and Coptic, which he correctly believed was close to demotic Egyptian, and to the fact that the hieroglyphic text had two cartouches, one of which, he knew from the Greek text, contained the name Cleopatra and the other the name Ptolemy. This in turn led to the translation of ancient Egyptian texts such as *The Book of the Dead,* and to Champollion's being hailed as the father of Egyptology.

In the nineteenth century the Englishman Henry Rawlinson deciphered Assyrian cuneiform from a trilingual epigraph on a rock face in Behistun in Persia.

An epigram (*gramma* is the Greek 'writing' or 'letter') is a self-contained witty statement, such as Oscar Wilde's definition of a cynic in *Lady Windermere's Fan*: 'a man who knows the price of everything and the value of nothing'. It may also describe a short satirical poem.

An epitaph is an inscription on a tomb (*taphos* in Greek). One of the most celebrated epitaphs was that

a monument
is anything that preserves the memory of a person or event (from the Latin *monere* 'to remind'). The epitaph of Christopher Wren in St Paul's Cathedral, London, reads *Si monumentum requiris, circumspice* (Latin, 'If you seek a monument, look about you'). He was the architect

a cartouche
is an ornamental panel in the shape of a scroll; in Egyptian hieroglyphs it is an oblong panel enclosing characters conveying a divine or royal name. It derives from the Italian *cartoccio*, which itself is derived from the Latin *charta* 'paper' or 'card'

cipher
from the Old French *cifre*, was used for the Arabic numerical invention zero. It now denotes a code or secret message in writing that uses letters transposed according to a key; to decipher is to decode, the Latin prefix *de* indicating the removal or reversal of something

to the handful of Spartans cut down defending the pass of Thermopylae (Hot Gates, *thermos* being Greek 'hot' and *pulai* 'gates') against the invading Persian masses of King Xerxes:

> Go, stranger, to Sparta tell
> That here, obeying her, we fell.

It is the normal character of epitaphs to be sombre. But some are ironic. An epitaph in Athens to a Cretan merchant read:

> Here Broticus of Cretan Gortyn lies
> He came not for this but merchandise.

An epithet, from *epi* and the Greek *tithenai* 'to put', is a descriptive word or phrase added to or used instead of a person's name – thus Ivan the Terrible and El Greco. The word occurs famously in *Tamburlaine* by Christopher Marlowe:

> Ah, fair Zenocrate! – divine Zenocrate!
> Fair is too foul an epithet for thee.

thermos
gives us a range of words, such as thermos (flask), thermal, thermometer, thermostat, thermodynamics and thermonuclear

pulai
is the plural of *pulē* 'gate'. The pylorus from *pulē* and *ouros*, the Greek 'guardian', is the small circular opening at the base of the stomach that allows the passage of partially digested food into the small intestine. Pylon, from the Greek *pulōn* 'gateway', is used by engineers to describe a supporting structure and by doctors to name an artificial leg – a support for the thigh

eponymous
pertaining to someone who gives his or her name to something, e.g. a place, people, book, play, film

Epi is the Greek 'upon' or 'at'; *onoma* is 'name'. We might say that at the end of *Hamlet* the eponymous hero dies of a wound from a poisoned sword or that Pallas Athene, who sprang fully armed from the head of Zeus, is the eponymous goddess of Athens.

esoteric
not generally intelligible

Aristotle set up a school in Athens in a grove sacred to Apollo Lyceus, which came to be known as the Lyceum (from Lyceus, *eum* being a Latin suffix that indicates 'place'). Because Aristotle liked to instruct his students while walking about the grove, they became known as the Peripatetics and Aristotelian philosophy was sometimes referred to as Peripatetic. Aristotle was wont to give two kinds of lectures – popular and advanced, the latter being accessible only to those who belonged to his inner circle. The popular ones were for exoterics (outsiders – *exo* is the Greek 'outside') and the advanced ones were for esoterics (insiders – *eso* is the Greek 'within').

Arcane, abstruse and recondite are synonyms for esoteric. Arcane derives from the Latin *arcanus* 'relating to a chest' and therefore to something concealed. The Latin *arca* 'chest' also gives us Ark (of the Covenant). Abstruse derives from the Latin *abs* 'away

peripatetic
comes from the Greek *peri* 'around' and *pateein* 'to walk'; peripatetic, meaning going from place to place on one's business, is still used; a peripatetic person may give the impression of being ubiquitous – *ubique* is the Latin 'everywhere'

lecture
derives from the Latin *legere*, *lectum* 'to read'. Legend, also from *legere*, meaning a popular story handed down from previous times but not verifiable, is derived from the medieval Latin *legenda* 'passages to be read' because they dealt with the lives of the saints

from' and *trudere, trusum* 'to push' – what is abstruse is thrust away and concealed. Recondite derives from the Latin *re* 'away' and *condere, conditum* 'to conceal' and means obscure.

esprit de l'escalier
a retort thought of too late to be delivered

The expression is ascribed to the encyclopaedist Denis Diderot although only the idea and not the words are found in his *Paradoxe sur le comédien*. It imports the regret a wit might experience who thinks on his way downstairs (*escalier* is the French 'stairs') of the retort he should have made in the drawing room.

establishment, the
those who control, or influence those who control, a country

matrix
means womb and derives from *mater* the Latin 'mother'; by extension matrix means that within which something is embedded

The modern usage of the word is traced back to the *Spectator* of September 1955 where Henry Fairlie wrote in his regular column: 'By the "Establishment" I do not mean only the centres of official power though they are certainly a part of it – but rather the whole matrix of official and social relations within which power is exercised.' Establishment, derived from the Latin *stare* 'to stand', means setting up on a firm foundation. The people who maintain a state would include politicians, senior public servants, media owners, leaders of trades unions and other major interest groups. The establishment is an informal concept and therefore one cannot define precisely who belongs to it. It has a conservative connotation and those who belong to it would contrast with radicals, iconoclasts and revolutionaries (depending on how conservative the society is). The term may also be applied to any organized segment of society – for example the medical establishment, the cycling establishment.

ethnic
pertaining to race

exodus
means a going out, from the Greek *ex* 'out' and *hodos* 'way' and is applied most famously to the departure of the Israelites from Egypt led by Moses. The scattering of the Jewish people following their unsuccessful revolts in Palestine against the Romans in the first and second centuries AD is called the Jewish diaspora (derived from the Greek *dia* 'through' or 'across' and *spora* 'scattering')

Ethnos is the Greek 'a people', the equivalent of the Latin *natio, nationis*. The flood of emigration that followed the Great Famine in Ireland in the middle of the nineteenth century – an exodus sometimes referred to as the Irish diaspora – has resulted in the existence of large numbers of people (perhaps as many as sixty million) of Irish ethnic origin in Britain, the US, Canada, Australia and New Zealand.

Ethnology is the study of the origins, distinctive characteristics, and interrelationships of the various peoples that make up the human race (*ology* here means 'study of', from *logos*, the Greek 'word', 'reason' or 'account'). It is a branch of anthropology, the study of man (*anthrōpos* is the Greek 'man'), itself distinguished from zoology, the study of animals (*zōion* is 'animal') and botany, the study of plants; anthropology, zoology and botany comprise biology, the study of living organisms, *bios* being the Greek 'life'.

eu
eugenics, eulogy, euphemism, euphony, euphoria and euthanasia – the common prefix *eu* means 'well' in Greek

Eugenics means the science of producing fine offspring, applied particularly in livestock breeding, especially horse breeding. The term, coined in 1883 by Darwin's cousin Francis Galton, became notorious when Nazi Germany applied it as a policy for the breeding of humans (*genikos* means 'concerning stock or race' in Greek). *In vitro* fertilization (*vitrum* is the Latin 'glass', from which we also derive vitreous for something related to, or resembling, glass) occurs in a test-tube. To clone is to produce a group of organisms or cells of the same genetic constitution that is descended from a common ancestor by asexual (*a* is a Greek negative particle) reproduction (*klōn* is the Greek 'twig', 'shoot').

policy
a general rule for systems or organizations, from the Greek *politeia* 'government' or 'administration'

A eulogy is a speech or article in praise of someone (*logos* is the Greek 'word', 'reason' or 'account'); it tends to be formal, often delivered at a funeral. An encomium, from *enkōmion*, is also a speech in praise of someone – usually a living person – and so is a panegyric, from *panēgurikos* '[a speech] fit for a national assembly' (*pan* is 'all', *aguris* is 'assembly').

A euphemism is a mild expression for something harsh or distasteful. A speaker would be euphemistic if he or she were to characterize a raving lunatic as 'somewhat odd' (*phēmē* is the Greek 'speech').

Euphony is a pleasing sound (*phōnē* is 'voice' or 'sound' in Greek). Cacophony is its antonym (*kakos* is 'bad').

Euphoria is a state of great delight (*phoria* is 'feeling' in Greek).

Euthanasia is the act of bringing about an easeful death, notorious for being a policy of Nazi Germany towards old unproductive people, the physically and mentally handicapped, and the sexually deviant (*thanatos* is 'death' in Greek).

European
pertaining to Europe

The word Europe is Greek in origin. Robert Graves in *The Greek Myths* tells us it may mean broad-face (*europē*), which is a synonym for the full moon and a title of the moon-goddess Demeter. It may also mean good for willows (*eu-ropē*) and therefore well-watered.

The eponymous Europa was a beautiful Phoenician princess. Zeus, in the form of a white bull, seduced her and carried her off over the sea to Crete where she bore him three sons, one of whom was Minos. The Greeks came to apply her name to their territories to the west of the Aegean Sea.

Geographically Europe is a peninsula of Asia. When one seeks to define it as a continent one finds that its eastern boundary can be fixed only arbitrarily (in a manner that leaves it subject to personal whims, from the Latin *arbiter* 'referee'). Historically there was little concern among politicians with Europe *per se*. The Roman empire embraced much of Europe as provinces. When the Roman empire became Christian the Church's geographical concern readily extended to both the western empire centred on Rome and the eastern empire centred on Constantinople (the 'city' – Greek *polis* – of Constantine). A broader concern was expressed in the Greek term the *Oikoumene* – 'the whole inhabited world', *oikein* being the Greek 'to inhabit' – and in the use of the term ecumenical, derived from it to describe the world councils of the early Church. In that context the Roman empire and the world were almost coterminous.

With the fall of the Roman empire in the west and the rise of Islam, the term Christendom (*dom* is an Old English suffix indicating a 'state' or 'condition' – note also freedom and serfdom) came to be used for those parts of the world that were Christian – predominantly the Byzantine empire and Western Europe; its use also indicates the seminal role played by Christianity in what we understand as European civilization.

seminal
in its extended use, as here, means original and influential and is derived from the Latin *semen, seminis*, the thick whitish fluid containing spermatozoa that is ejaculated from the male reproductive organ to fertilize the female *ovum* (Latin 'egg', plural *ova*; hence oval and ovary). *Semen* also gives us seminary, seminar, inseminate and disseminate. Sperm from the late Latin *sperma*, itself derived from the Greek *speirein* 'to sow', is a synonym for semen. Panspermia (*pan* is the Greek 'all') is a theory proposed in the 1970s by Fred Hoyle and Chandra

In *A History of Europe* Norman Davies points out that Europe gradually replaced the earlier concept of Christendom in a complex intellectual process lasting from the fourteenth to the eighteenth centuries:

> The decisive period, however, was reached in the decades on either side of 1700 after generations of religious conflict. In that early phase of the Enlightenment it became an embarrassment for the divided community of nations to be reminded of their common Christian identity; and 'Europe' filled the need for a designation with more neutral connotations.

The eastern boundary of this Europe was not clear. In medieval times it was thought to begin on the Don, following a tradition going back to the second-century Greek geographer Ptolemy. With the rise of the Russian empire in the eighteenth century the matter received renewed attention: a Swedish officer in the Russian service called Strahlenberg suggested that the boundary should be pushed back from the Don to the Urals. The concept of Europe from the Atlantic to the Urals was born.

Wickramasinghe that the building blocks of life may exist throughout the cosmos and could be carried to planets such as the earth by comets or drifting interstellar dust particles

In the nineteenth century the rise of Prussia created a concern with Mitteleuropa (Central Europe, *mittel* being the German 'middle'). Mitteleuropeans were regarded as either charming for their culture and manners or sinister for their politico-commercial ambitions.

In the twentieth century, following World War II and the beginning of the Cold War, Europe presented politically as Western Europe, with its free enterprise, liberal democratic societies, and Eastern Europe (the Soviet bloc countries), with its centrally planned, economically stagnant, communist societies. The success of the European Union, established by the Treaty of Rome in 1957 as the European Economic Community, tended to give the concept of modern Europe its content, a process accelerated by the fall of communism and the application of the former Eastern European countries to join the Union. Western and Eastern are now politically inactive epithets for Europe.

accelerate
means speed up from the Latin *celer* 'swift' which also gives us celerity (speed)

The term Europe still seeks coherence in the geographic and political spheres. The same holds true in the cultural sphere. In Europe's general encounter with Islam and in the specific encounters of its imperial powers with countries of the East, a sense of European cultural unity was created among intellectuals by the perceived dichotomy between a mystical Orient and a rational, realistic Occident. The reality for the peoples of Europe however is one of cultural diversity. Europe's different languages are the obvious marks of that diversity. The search for a common language reveals the centripetal pull of the very idea of Europe. In the eighteenth century Europe's élites embraced French – in 1714 French replaced Latin for the first time as the *lingua franca* of diplomacy in the Treaty of Rastadt and in 1774 even the Russians and the Turks used French for the text of a treaty they had agreed. In today's Europe English presents as the language most likely to move into general use:

campanilismo
(Italian, from *campana* 'bell') and the French *l'esprit de clocher* (from *cloche* 'bell') both refer to the view from the church tower and mean parochial or narrow-minded

> Could not English serve as a lingua franca today just as French did two centuries ago? It need not obliterate other languages. There is plenty of room for other varieties of culture to flourish between the extremes of cosmopolitanism and *campanilismo.*
>
> –Robert Darnton, *NYRB*, 28 February 2002

evolution
the theory that plants and animals have achieved their present forms through a process of gradual change over long periods, in which the mechanism of natural selection confers reproductive advantage on those organisms that acquire favourable genetic mutations

With the publication of *On the Origin of Species* in 1859 Charles Darwin provided a theory, later called Darwinism, of how plants and animals have evolved (from the Latin *evolvere, evolutum* 'to unroll'). In the struggle for existence in nature – 'Nature, red in tooth and claw' as Tennyson characterizes her – those hereditary variants that equip an organism to deal with the demands of the environment – that are the fittest – will be preserved and become the prevailing type. New species develop where changes in the environment require adaptations in the organisms. Such adaptations take long periods. The fossil record confirms this.

Darwin
once said, 'Linnaeus and Cuvier have been my two gods, but they were mere schoolboys to old Aristotle.' In *Wisdom of the West* the British philosopher Bertrand Russell tells us that contributions by Aristotle to marine biology were not surpassed until the nineteenth century

Darwin did not know the principles of heredity. His contemporary Gregor Mendel, an Augustinian monk and botanist from Moravia, became the founder of the science of genetics (heredity; genetics is derived from the Greek *genēs* 'born', which also gives us gene, a unit of heredity composed of DNA) when he developed his theory of organic inheritance from experiments on the hybridization of green peas (the Latin *hibrida* means 'offspring of a mixed union'). At the beginning of the twentieth century Darwin's and Mendel's theories were combined to give us neo-Darwinism. Neo-Darwinism is the central unifying theory in biology.

The name of the French naturalist Jean Baptiste Lamarck occurs in the discussion of evolution: he developed the false theory that characteristics acquired in the course of a lifetime – the stretch of a giraffe's neck, say – are passed on directly to the next generation. A modern form of the theory – Lysenkoism, from the Russian geneticist T.D. Lysenko – was adopted as official Soviet policy from the mid-1930s to the mid-1960s, with deleterious effects on Russian agriculture, on the ideological grounds that Darwinian genetic mutation (from the Latin *mutare, mutatum* 'to change'), being random, ran counter to the determinism of

Marx's dialectical materialism.

The English philosopher Herbert Spencer popularized the term evolution and coined the phrase 'the survival of the fittest'. He became the father of social Darwinism by applying Darwin's biological ideas to society: history is the story of the evolution of the fittest groups in the human stock. The concept became notorious when it was applied to justify social inequality, imperialism and racism.

Darwinism presents a direct challenge to creationists. Other religious believers are able to accept it provided God's direct intervention in the creation of man is allowed.

Spencer
was a friend of George Eliot. The latter might be described as a philosopher *manqué* (French 'having missed' and therefore 'unfulfilled' or 'would-be') because her lover G.H. Lewes persuaded her to give up the study of metaphysics and take up fiction writing. We find her reflections on the human condition therefore in such forms as 'Human converse … is not always rigidly sincere.' (*Adam Bede*)

ex cathedra
with absolute authority

Ex is the Latin 'from'; *kathedra* means 'chair' in Greek. The *cathedra* (the Latin transliteration of *kathedra*, with a stress on the first syllable) was the chair or pulpit from which a lecture was given and therefore it came to mean the place from which authoritative statements were made. The doctrine of papal infallibility states that when a Pope speaks *ex cathedra* (from the chair of Peter) on matters of faith or morals, to be held by all the faithful, he is speaking infallibly (not liable to error – *in* is a Latin prefix that negatives a word, *fallere* is the Latin 'to deceive', from which we also derive fallacy and fallacious).

A cathedral (with a stress on the second syllable) is a church where a bishop has his seat. The word church is itself derived from the Greek *kurios* 'master' or 'lord', the name the early Christians used for Christ – hence the Greek expression *Kyrie eleison* ('Lord, have mercy') in the Latin Mass. *Kuriakon* ('the Lord's house', *on* being a Greek suffix indicating 'place') was the word they used for their meeting-place. It came to English in the form cirice. The pronunciation tradition in southern England was to sound a c before a vowel as ch. Cirice came to be pronounced 'chiriche' and later church. The pronunciation tradition in northern England was to sound a c before a vowel as k. Cirice there came to be pronounced as 'kirike' and later kirk.

bishop
derives from the Greek *episkopos* 'overseer', from which we also derive episcopal. A bishop's see (or diocese) derives from the Latin *sedes* 'seat', itself derived from *sedere* 'to sit'; hence also sedentary, as in a sedentary job

exchequer
the national treasury

Scaccarium is the Latin 'chessboard', from which we get chequered. In medieval times the Court of Exchequer in England was charged with looking after the king's revenues and was so called because a chequered cloth was laid on the table of the court. Its various columns were assigned to thousands, hundreds, scores and tens of pounds, and to shillings and to pence; with the use of various types of counters, it provided a simple accounting display unit for a virtually innumerate society.

existentialism
a modern, mainly German and French, philosophical movement that concentrates on the existence rather than the essence of the individual, who, being free and responsible, makes himself what he is by the experiences he chooses or fails to choose

The Danish philosopher Søren Kierkegaard (the English form of the surname is Churchwarden) reacted to the high abstraction of Hegelianism and insisted on the paramount importance of the subjective, personal dimension of human life – the existential. The dichotomy drawn between essence and existence highlights the fact that the pursuit of the essential is necessarily a process of abstraction from the concrete realities that face the individual, and therefore involves removal from the ground upon which the individual can make the highest human moral judgments – those that are freely made and for which he or she takes full responsibility.

At the existential level the individual confronts reality alone; he or she must freely choose those values that truly fulfil him or her. Kierkegaard was a Christian, but alienated from the institutional Church. For him the angst created by a realization that the individual's life is prone to dissipation and destruction underlined the need for a leap of faith by embracing a Christ-like life. However, most of the existentialists who followed Kierkegaard – Nietzsche, Heidegger and Sartre, for example – were atheists seeking an authentic life in a meaningless world. Heidegger's thinking led him to a cosy accommodation with Nazism, Sartre's led him to embrace the scientific certitude of Marxism: 'I have said – and I repeat – that the only valid interpretation of human history is historical materialism.' (However, for communists existentialism was anti-collectivist because it declared that man as an individual – not society or history – was responsible for defining his own life. Stalin, communism's *pontifex maximus*, branded existentialism a reactionary bourgeois philosophy.)

prone
from the Latin *pronus* 'bent forward' means either lying with one's forehead to the ground or in a transferred sense inclined to do something. Supine from the Latin *supinus* means either lying on one's back or in a transferred sense lethargic

ex officio
by reason of one's office

Ex is the Latin 'from'; *officio* is a form of *officium* meaning 'public position' – hence office, official and officious. The expression is used in relation to membership of certain institutions or committees and denotes that a certain person is a member by reason of the office he or she holds.

ex parte
from one side only

Ex is the Latin 'from'; *pars, partis* is 'part'. *Ex parte* is an expression that means giving only one side of a matter, being partial or one-sided. In law, *ex parte* describes an application by one side in a judicial proceeding without formal notice having been given to the other side of the intention to make the application.

Because the courts are bound to follow the rules of natural justice, one of which is that a person has a right to be heard in his own defence (the rule in Latin is *audi alteram partem* 'hear the other side'), a court will not, on an application made *ex parte*, determine finally any contested issue between persons. Orders made *ex parte* generally relate to preliminary or procedural matters arising before proceedings are commenced, for example an application for leave to serve a summons on a person resident outside the jurisdiction of the state or to substitute service of a document by post for personal service. Sometimes a judge may issue temporary orders *ex parte* when, for example, quick action is required in a case of domestic violence.

The other great rule of natural justice is that the judge should be impartial (the rule in Latin is *nemo judex in causa sua* 'no one may be a judge in his own case', that is, where his or her own interest is involved).

extempore
without preparation, on the spur of the moment

Ex is the Latin 'from'; *tempus, temporis* is 'time'. The expression is used of public speaking. Someone who successfully speaks extempore is admired because the feat is so difficult.

extravert/extrovert
a person more concerned with the external world than with inner feelings

It was Jung who introduced the typology of extravert and introvert to differentiate the two broad psychological types into which people may be divided. The common ending *vert* derives from the Latin *vertere, versum* 'to turn'; *extra* is 'outside' or 'beyond' (hence extraordinary and extraterrestrial, for example) and *intro* is 'inwardly' or 'within' (hence introspection and introduce, for example). The introvert, Jung said, 'holds aloof from external happenings, does not join in, has a distinct dislike of society as soon as he finds himself among too many people'.

F

Fabianism
the strategy of the Fabian Society, founded by British socialists in 1884, to seek social and political change peacefully and gradually rather than through revolution

Fabian is derived from the Latin name Fabius. When the Carthaginian general Hannibal crossed the Alps with his elephants and invaded Italy, he trounced the Roman armies sent against him. The Romans then appointed Q. Fabius Maximus as dictator. He stubbornly refused to hazard his troops in a pitched battle with Hannibal. He resorted to skirmishes and guerilla tactics to contain the Carthaginians. Indeed his impatient Roman critics nicknamed him Cunctator (The Ditherer). The policy, however, worked. Hannibal's strength was gradually dissipated and he left Italy in 203 BC without having attained his objectives.

fait accompli
an accomplished fact

Fait is the French 'fact'; *accomplir* is 'to do' or 'to accomplish'. Thus, 'By the time his warning got through to the government the rebel takeover of the television station was a *fait accompli*.'

fanatic
someone who is excessively enthusiastic about a leader, a movement or even an activity – a fan

Fanum is the Latin 'temple'. Fanatics were originally religious enthusiasts – they were *fanaticus*, i.e. inspired by a deity of some kind. The word profane derives from *pro*, a Latin prefix meaning 'before', and *fanum* – a profane thing is something that is before, i.e. outside, the temple. In its weak sense profane is equivalent to secular; in its strong sense it means blasphemous.

fascism
the aggressive, dictatorial, totalitarian, nationalistic, right-wing movements associated especially with Hitler and Mussolini

The *fasces* were a bundle of rods tied around an axe that was carried before a Roman consul as a symbol of his authority to punish and to execute. Mussolini, who dreamt of restoring Italy to greatness, harked back to Roman times and used the fasces as a symbol for his movement: the bound bundle of rods represented the strength a society derived from uniting around an authoritarian political leader (the axe).

The other dictators and extreme right-wing leaders who appeared in other countries later, for example Hitler in Germany, Mosley in Britain, Quisling in Norway, Franco in Spain, were also called fascists. Fascism was a heady mix of nationalism, socialism, and pseudo-scientific theories on race, mass psychology, violence and discipline. It appealed to ordinary people frightened by widespread unemployment and world recession because

quisling
is used for a traitor who collaborates with an occupying enemy power, derived from Vidkun Quisling, the Norwegian fascist leader who headed a puppet government following the Nazi occupation of Norway in 1940

it gave hope, a glimpse of glory, and for some time it improved the physical conditions of the masses.

Fascism found its most powerful expression in Germany where it was called national socialism (in German *National Sozialismus*, hence Nazi), but German socialists and communists rejected it. Being anti-communist, it attracted support from the conservatives and right-wing elements (the German conservatives thought they could control the Nazis with the help of the army and its traditionalist officers). It was anti-democratic and illiberal (it did not tolerate any ideas other than those of the leader). It was totalitarian – it demanded a total commitment to the State on the part of the citizens, this being seen as a condition for their own welfare (*totus* means 'all' in Latin).

Though the original fascists have disappeared, fascist is still sometimes loosely used to abuse anyone opposed to left-wing or liberal positions. Totalitarian was popularized by Mussolini in his speeches in the 1920s when he often referred to *lo stato totalitario* (Italian, 'the totalitarian state'). Totalitarianism sought to rebuff any claims on the individual that might be made by ideologies or international movements such as communism, and subordinated regional, local and personal claims to those of the State. After World War II and the beginning of the Cold War the Western democratic powers employed it as a pejorative term for both fascism and communism that connoted a more thoroughgoing tyranny than that of any earlier period.

fate
destiny

Fata is a form of the Latin *fari* 'to speak' meaning 'the things that have been spoken [about a person by an oracle]', and therefore his or her destiny. The Fates (Latin *Fata*) were personified as the three goddesses of fate. The Greeks named them as Clotho, who assigns each man and each woman his or her lot at birth, to be rich or poor, healthy or weak; Lachesis, who spins the thread of life; and Atropos, who cuts it at the end 'with th' abhorred shears' (as Milton says in *Lycidas*).

The idea that a person's life and death are determined at the moment of birth fascinated and depressed the Greeks and gave them one of their greatest literary themes. Thus Oedipus, destined to kill his father and marry his mother, does so in spite of the extraordinary efforts of his parents and himself to escape that fate;

Trojan
is someone who works, fights etc. extremely hard or courageously; or a citizen or inhabitant of Troy (also called Ilium, from which we derive *Iliad*, the epic dealing with the siege of Troy). Paris, the son of Priam, King of Troy, fell in love with Helen, the beautiful wife of the Greek Prince Menelaus, and carried her off to Troy. The Greeks gathered a great fleet and pursued the lovers. Thus Helen's became 'the face that launch'd a thousand ships' (Christopher Marlowe, *Doctor Faustus*)

and in Homer's *Iliad* Achilles knows that if he stays on at Troy he will die young but become famous whereas if he returns home he will live to a ripe old age but die obscure. (He stays on and is killed by a Trojan arrow that strikes the only vulnerable part of him, his right heel; for when he was born his mother, the goddess Thetis, in order to make him immortal, had dipped every bit of him in the river Styx except the heel by which she held him – a fateful oversight.)

If their belief in fate is strong, people tend to become fatalistic, that is, passive. 'Whatever will be, will be' is how the popular song expresses it; 'There's a divinity that shapes our ends / Rough-hew them how we will' is how Shakespeare expresses it in *Hamlet*. Fate is associated with death, the most awesome feature of one's destiny; and so we describe an accident in which someone is killed as fatal and the person killed as a fatality.

Faustian
relating to Faust who sold his soul to the devil in exchange for knowledge and power

mantic
meaning relating to divination or prophesying, also derives from *manteia*

Georg Faust (Doctor Faustus) was a sixteenth-century German astrologer and necromancer (someone who seeks to call up the dead, particularly to find out about the future, from the Greek *nekros* 'corpse' and *manteia* 'soothsaying' or 'predicting'; a necropolis, city of the dead, is a cemetery, *polis* being 'city'; necrosis is the death of one or more cells in the body, often within a localized area, when blood supply to that part is interrupted, *osis* being a suffix indicating 'state'; necrophilia is sexual attraction for dead bodies, *philia* being 'love'; necrophobia is an abnormal fear of death or dead bodies, *phobia* being a suffix indicating 'fear of'). Towards the end of his life Faust would boast that his powers came from a pact he had made with the Devil (the Latin *pactum* is an agreement between two or more parties for mutual or common advantage). After his death, rumours of his damnation spread like wildfire.

Faust became famous when a resourceful publisher issued a cautionary tome (a large weighty book, from the Latin *tomus* 'a section of a larger work', itself from the Greek *temnein* 'to cut' – see atom) about his career which became a *succès fou*. Faust is presented as a monstrous egotist (to the Devil: 'Why shouldst thou sit and I stand?') who quickly exhausts his special powers – the Devil for instance once gave Faust a cloak that could convey him anywhere he wished – and is terrifyingly damned. The Devil is named Mephistopheles or Mephisto – hence Mephistophelean or Mephistophelian.

Faust made his first appearance in art in Marlowe's play *Doctor Faustus*. The two-part verse tragedy *Faust* by Johann Wolfgang von Goethe – his masterpiece – inspired operas by Charles François Gounod and Hector Berlioz. In 1947 *Doktor Faustus*, the novel by Thomas Mann, appeared.

A Faustian bargain is one where trifling short-term benefits are accepted in exchange for a terrible long-term cost.

Hector
was the name of the eldest son of Priam, King of Troy, and his wife Hecuba. The greatest champion of the Trojans, he slew Patroclus, the friend of the Greek champion Achilles who, in revenge, slew Hector and dragged his body behind his chariot around the walls of Troy. To hector (from Hector as a challenging bully) is to bully or torment by teasing

federation
a union of a number of states or associations

Foedus, foederis is the Latin 'treaty'. When a number of states that wish to retain their identity to some degree come together for a long-term common purpose and subscribe to a treaty or constitution providing for a central authority, they may be described as either a confederation or a federation. They are distinguished by the fact that the central authority of a confederation is far weaker than that of a federation. In a confederation the central authority acts only indirectly on the citizens through the governments of the component states. In a federation the central authority (the federal government) acts directly on the citizens in regard to matters ascribed to it in the constitution, while the governments of the individual states act directly on the citizens in regard to those matters ascribed to them. The United States of America, whose Latin motto *E pluribus unum* means 'From many one', is the paramount example of a federation. It has a written constitution that provides for a central government – the federal government – and state governments for each of the fifty states. The federal and state governments have all got a separate legislature, executive and judiciary. The federal government acts directly on the citizens in specified matters.

In modern times groups of states that have conjoined have tended to form federations rather than confederations. Thus Switzerland describes itself as a confederation (*Confederatio Helvetica* – hence CH on Swiss car-plates, *Helvetia* being the Latin 'Switzerland') but since 1848 it has been a federation. The German Federal Republic, Russia, Canada, Australia and India are also federations.

About one-eighth of the states in the world have

both federal and state governments. States with a single government – the other (and predominant) type of state to a federal one – are known as unitary states (*unus* is the Latin 'one'). A unitary state usually has local or regional authorities but these are totally subordinate to the national government.

fellow traveller
a non-communist who sympathized with communism

The term came into vogue in the 1930s in Britain to describe people intellectually sympathetic to the Russian communists and therefore quasi-communist (*quasi* is the Latin 'as if'; as a combining form it means 'almost but not really'). George Bernard Shaw, the Irish-born Fabian who returned enthusiastically from his visits to Russia, was accused of being a fellow traveller. So were many Americans during the course of Senator Joe McCarthy's notorious anti-communist witch-hunt in the US in the 1950s. The term was coined by Leon Trotsky, the father of the Red Army and brilliant communist ideologue, to describe those Russian authors who accepted the 1917 Revolution but not the rationale proposed to justify it. Deported from Russia in 1929, he was assassinated in Mexico by a Stalinist agent who struck him in the cranium (brainpan, from the Greek *kranion*) with an ice pick. Trotsky believed that the Revolution could not be sustained in economically backward Russia unless it fomented world revolution (and thereby released the dynamic of class warfare in the large bourgeois states). Trotskyites sought immediate worldwide revolution. Stalin in contrast enunciated (stated precisely, from the Latin *nuntiare, nuntiatum* 'to announce') the policy of 'socialism in one country'.

capitalist roader
was used by Chinese communists as a synonym for fellow traveller

feminism
a movement aimed at promoting the rights of women

Femina is the Latin 'woman'. The suffragettes or the suffragists at the beginning of the twentieth century campaigned to secure equal political rights for women (*suffragium* is the Latin 'vote') – the right to vote and the right to stand for election. Feminism today is also concerned with attaining economic and social equality. It had its origins in the radical politics of the 1960s when various minorities, for example the African-Americans, sought to liberate themselves from legal discrimination and deleterious (*dēlētērios* is the Greek 'hurtful') stereotyping. Women began to appreciate the economic and social disabilities from which they suffered. They began to campaign to liberate themselves – hence Women's Lib.

gender equality
may be based on the equality of intellect: 'The mind has no sex.' (Poulain de la Barne) or on the equality of souls – thus Charlotte Brontë has Jane Eyre challenge Rochester: 'I have as much soul as you … I am not talking to you now through the medium of

Consciousness-raising (CR) groups and courses in assertiveness helped women psychologically in sustaining their campaign. Subsequently some advances have been made in marriage and employment law and stereotyping is being tackled in schools through, among other measures, the elimination of sexism in texts. The hard sociological reality, however, is that the majority of positions in the middle and top ranks of business and public administration are held by men. Women experience restrictions or discrimination that create a hidden barrier to promotion – the so-called glass ceiling.

custom, conventionalities, nor even of mortal flesh; it is my spirit that addresses your spirit.'

feudalism
the basis of political organization in Europe from about the eighth century to the late Middle Ages, when the modern state began to emerge

In the Dark Ages – the period of social disintegration and intellectual darkness that descended upon Europe after the fall of the western Roman empire in the late fifth century and lasted beyond the tenth – the disappearance of a central power required that the order necessary for survival should be established and maintained by local lords. Thus began the seigneurial or manorial system under which, in return for protection, the ordinary people in a district became sharecroppers, called serfs, who gave the lord part of their produce, worked his lands, paid for the use of his mill to grind their wheat, obeyed his rules, and even acquiesced in the notorious *droit de seigneur* whereby the lord claimed the right to deflower a serf's bride on her wedding night – a right also known as *lex primae noctis* (Latin, 'the law of the first night').

seigneurial
comes through the French *seigneur* 'lord' from the Latin *senior* 'older man'. The Italian *signor* and the Spanish *señor* also derive from *senior*. *Junior* is the Latin 'younger man'

In the Roman world there had been a highly developed system in which a powerful man called a *patronus* had a number of *clientes* ('clients') to whom he extended benefits and favours such as food and money, and who in turn supported him politically and socially. The size and quality of a patron's *clientela* ('clientele') redounded to his political and social status. The seigneurial system probably grew out of this. Curiously, we find clientelism as a feature of modern democracy, where public representatives treat their constituents as clients whose interests they champion *vis-à-vis* (French, 'face-to-face with') the bureaucracy.

patronus
means protector, derived from the Latin *pater* 'father', which also gives us patron, patronage and *padrone*, the Italian 'boss'

Feudalism developed in the eighth century as a superstructure on the seigneurial system. It was concerned to regulate the relations between the more powerful people. A lord would make grants of land to powerful lesser figures who became his vassals and served him in turn militarily, politically and financially (feudal, derived from the Latin *feudalis* 'pertaining to a fee', captures this reciprocity). A lesser lord might become the vassal (*vassalus* is the late Latin 'servant') of a greater lord until eventually kings become the vassals of greater kings. The term of this process was the establishment of the monarchial dynasties whose possessions formed the core of the modern European states.

Monarchs found themselves at the apex of a hierarchical aristocratic system. Early monarchies were squirearchies – government through squires or large landowners, the *archy* suffix indicating 'rule', from the Greek *archein* 'to rule'.

squire
derives from esquire, which ultimately derives from the Latin *scutarius* 'shield-bearer'; a squire was the attendant and shield-bearer of a medieval knight who was often subsequently knighted himself; it then came to mean the main landowner in a rural community. Charles Dickens in *The Chimes* captured the rigid social stratification of a squirearchy in the parson's prayer: 'O let us love our occupations, / Bless the squire and his relations, / Live upon our daily rations, / And always know our proper stations.'

The feudal serf lived precariously, which comes from the Latin *prex, precis* 'prayer', *precarius* being the Latin 'obtained by begging': to be precarious was to be completely dependent on another's will. A serf was *adscriptus glaebae* (Latin, 'tied to the land'; *glaeba* means 'a piece of cultivated land' and survives in English as glebe, a portion of land that is part of a clergyman's benefice or living).

Commentators today describe certain contemporary non-industrialized, agricultural countries controlled by large landowners as feudal societies. Feudalism was formally abolished in France in the Revolution of 1789 and in Russia in 1861.

Marx saw feudalism as a stage between slavery and bourgeois capitalism and his doctrine of dialectical materialism required history to observe such a progression.

Following the second Congress of the Russian Socialist Democratic Party in 1903, the party split into two groups – the Bolsheviks (the majority, from the Russsian *bolshe* 'more') under Lenin who believed Russia could progress directly from feudalism to communism and the Mensheviks (the minority, from *menshe* the Russian 'less') who believed Russia must first gradually achieve bourgeois capitalism. Lenin seized power in 1917 and imposed communism and the Mensheviks sank into oblivion.

fiat
a magisterial command

Fiat is a form of the Latin *fieri* and means 'Let it be done!'

It derives from God's magisterial (*magister* is the Latin 'master') command in Genesis, the first book of the Bible: *Fiat lux*! (Latin, 'Let there be light!'). Thus,

> On Monday, Reagan told the United Nations that the United States would continue to fight for democracy in Nicaragua, as it would all over the world, including in South Africa. The sentiment was admirable, but democracy can seldom be imposed by American fiat.
>
> –*The Sunday Times*, 27 September 1987

sentiment
means feeling. Sentimentalists are people governed more by feelings than reason (*sentire* is the Latin 'to feel')

The word also occurs in the Latin maxim *fiat justitia et ruant coeli* ('let justice be done even though the heavens collapse'; *coelum* is the Latin 'heaven', from which we derive celestial).

Fiat, the Italian car-maker, derives its name not from the Latin but from the acronym from *Fabbrica Italiana Automobili Torino* ('Italian Automobile Factory Turin').

fifth columnist
a secret supporter of the enemy operating from within

The Spanish Civil War broke out in July 1936. In October of that year the nationalists under General Mola were poised to seize Madrid. When asked by a group of foreign journalists which of his four columns would take the city Mola replied that it would be that fifth column of secret nationalist supporters already within the capital. Madrid held out until the end of the war in March 1939.

filibuster
to obstruct legislation by making interminable speeches during the debate on it

An American political term, filibuster comes from the French *filibustier*, a corruption of the English freebooter, a piratical adventurer. Filibusters were common practice in the US Senate where, until comparatively recently, debate was unlimited. It was a favourite tactic in the 1960s by which senators from the South thwarted the attempts of the majority to introduce civil rights legislation. Since 1975 a filibuster can be ended by a vote of three-fifths of the full Senate.

fiscal rectitude
the management of the public finances in a strictly prudent manner

Fiscus is the Latin 'money chest'. It originally signified a wicker basket such as the Romans used to store and carry about large sums of money. In imperial times it came to be applied to the emperor's treasury and therefore to that of the state. Fiscal, derived from *fiscus*, refers to the public purse – the exchequer. Confiscate – *con* is the Latin 'with' – is literally to make part of the exchequer and means to seize for the public treasury. *Rectitudo, rectitudinis* is the Latin 'straightness' or 'rightness'.

focus
the central point, the point on which attention centres

Focus is the Latin 'hearth'. The fireplace is a natural centre in any home but the hearth was sacred to the Romans because it was dedicated to their household gods – the

Lares and Penates. The focus of the Roman state – the altar of the goddess Vesta in the Roman forum – contained the eternal flame, tended by the Vestal Virgins. If the fire went out it was considered ominous for the state and the Vestal responsible was whipped.

A person or thing that is a focus of attention, especially by reason of brilliance or beauty, may be called a cynosure (from the Greek *Kunosoura*, transliterated into Latin as *Cynosura*, the constellation of Ursa Minor, from *kuōn* 'dog' and *oura* 'tail').

forensic
pertaining to the courts of law

Forensis is the Latin 'relating to the forum' (where among other things the Romans held their courts of law).

Forensic evidence is physical evidence that has been subjected to scientific analysis, such as fingerprints, fibres, guns, and DNA.

A forensic expert is someone who produces forensic evidence (like the state pathologist).

Forensic medicine is that scientific study of the human body that allows the development of forensic evidence on such issues as cause and time of death, contact with certain substances and fingerprints.

fortune
whatever comes by chance

Fortuna was an Italian goddess identified in classical times with chance or luck. She was represented holding a cornucopia, the symbol of endless wealth, and a rudder, a symbol of change. Her temple in the village of Palestrina outside Rome was one of the largest in the ancient world. In the original cult she signified fertility, increase and plenty, so fortune tended to mean most commonly good fortune. It also came to mean the result of good fortune – prosperity or wealth. The rather godless Julius Caesar attributed many of his successes to the working of Fortuna; Napoleon, when asked to approve the promotion of an officer to field rank, always put the question 'Is he lucky?'; and throughout history the reputation of some generals for being lucky and others for being unlucky has itself been a factor in the outcome of battles.

promotion
derives from the Latin prefix *pro* 'forward' and *movere*, *motum* 'to move'

The Roman orator Cicero, in his famous speech *Pro Lege Manilia*, considered a general or leader needed four qualities – knowledge (*scientia*), moral excellence (*virtus*), prestige (*auctoritas*) and good luck (*fortuna*).

For the Greeks, luck was a central force in human affairs. They believed they could control it by craft or technique – hence their adage 'luck loves craft'. Machiavelli also regarded the ability to control fortune as a sign of the great statesman. Unlucky people are said to be unfortunate (*un* is a Latin negative prefix) or to have suffered misfortune (*mis* is a Latin prefix indicating 'bad').

forum
a place where, or medium in which, discussion may take place

Forum is the Latin 'marketplace'. Every Roman town had its forum where citizens met not only to buy and sell but also to talk about public affairs and to listen to addresses from lawyers engaged in law cases or from politicians campaigning. In Rome the latter spoke from the *rostra*. A *rostrum* (singular form) was the beak of a ship.

In the first Punic (Carthaginian) War the Romans went to sea for the first time and defeated the Carthaginians, one of the great thalassocracies of ancient times. They were so proud of this that they set up the *rostra* of the captured ships in the forum in Rome to adorn the platforms for the speakers there. Subsequently the platform itself came to be called a rostrum.

The *rostrum* of a Roman ship consisted of a beam to which were attached sharp and pointed irons such as an iron cast of the head of a ram. It projected just above the keel of a warship and was used to sink another ship by ramming and breaking in its sides. The beam of wood attached to the mast and used to spread out a square sail to catch the wind was called the *antenna* (plural *antennae* or *antennas*) – hence our use of that word as a synonym for an aerial, which receives or emits radio signals, and as a description of the feelers on insects.

Our use of the term forum allows us to say something like 'Television is not a good forum for serious philosophical discussion.'

fresco
a painting using water-colours on wet plaster

A wall-painting or mural (*murus* is the Latin 'wall'; extramural – *extra* is 'outside' or 'beyond' – is used for studies that are connected to a university or college but not part of its normal courses or programme) is a painting executed on a wall or ceiling as part of a scheme of decoration. A fresco (from the Italian *fresco* 'fresh') is a wall-painting that allows the colours to penetrate the surface so that the painting lasts far longer than one on dry plaster (provided there is no dampness).

Freudian
relating to the

Freud was born in 1856 in Freiberg, Moravia, of Jewish parents who went to live in Vienna when he was three.

psychoanalytic thought and practice of Sigmund Freud

Freud lived and worked in that city all his life except for the last year when he fled to London.

Freud became a doctor whose early interest centred on the problems of neurosis as opposed to organic diseases of the nervous (from the Latin *nervus* 'nerve') system. Neurosis, from the Greek *neuron* 'nerve', is a relatively mild mental disorder, characterized by symptoms such as hysteria, anxiety, depression or obsessive behaviour. A neurotic is someone afflicted with a neurosis and tends to be emotionally unstable or unusually anxious. Before Freud academic psychology had been content to observe and describe behaviour; Freud saw the need to explain it. The theories he developed revolutionized our way of looking at ourselves and permeated our language.

Freud was a determinist and insisted on the scientific character of his theories. These displayed intellectual brilliance and ingenuity but the clinical research upon which they were based was so exiguous that the psychoanalytic movement showed from the beginning schismatic tendencies.

To explain all the phenomena of the mental world Freud postulated two basic instincts within people – Eros (the Greek 'love'), the instinct that sought positive, binding relationships and Thanatos ('death'), the death instinct or death wish that sought to undo connections and destroy. He saw the evolution of civilization as a struggle between Eros and Thanatos.

Among the other concepts developed by Freud in his exploration of the aetiology (the causes or the study of the causes, *aitia* being the Greek 'cause') of neuroses (plural form) are: sublimation, id, ego, superego, Oedipus complex, castration complex, repression, Freudian slips, the unconscious, dream symbolism and libido (psychic energy emanating from the id, from the Latin *libido, libidinis* 'sexual desire', from which we also derive libidinous).

energy
is a transliteration of the Greek *energeia* which is derived from *en* 'in' and *ergon* 'work'. Ergonomics is the study of the worker in the workplace with a view to creating conditions in which he or she can work most efficiently. Ergatocracy is rule by workers (*ergatēs* is the Greek 'worker'). Metallurgy, the art of working metals, derives from the Greek *metallon* 'metal' and *ourgia* 'working'. A malleable metal is one that can be shaped under pressure or blows without breaking (*malleus* is the Latin 'hammer'). Synergy, from the Greek *sun* 'with' and *ergos*, denotes the extra power that develops when people or groups work productively together

the Furies
spirits of punishment, called Erinyes by the Greeks, who avenged wrongs done to kindred, especially murder within the family or clan

In Greek myth Orestes was the son of Agamemnon and Clytemnestra. When Clytemnestra and her lover Aegisthus murdered Agamemnon, Orestes, who was only ten at the time, was spirited away by his nurse to avoid being killed himself. When he became a man he visited the Delphic oracle to enquire whether or not he should avenge his father's death. He was told that if he neglected to do so he would become a pariah. So he secretly returned to Mycenae, bent on killing Aegisthus and his own mother.

He gained entry to the palace and succeeded in despatching Aegisthus with his sword. When he rounded on his mother, Clytemnestra tried to soften his heart by baring her breast and appealing to his filial feeling (*filius* is the Latin 'son', which also gives us filiate and affiliate). Orestes, however, beheaded her with a stroke of his sword and she fell beside the body of her lover.

That night the fearful Erinyes (the Furies) appeared, swinging their scourges, and attacked the matricide. Orestes set out for Delphi but they pursued him there. When he went into exile they continued to torment him, so much so that he went mad. They persisted, even though he performed many cleansing rituals and offered the holocaust of a black ram to the gods. Finally, he came to Athens. There, in a trial in which the god Apollo defended him and the eldest of the Erinyes led for the prosecution, he was acquitted. The Erinyes gave up their pursuit of him.

The philosopher Heraclitus said of the Furies that even if the sun were to leave his course they would find him out. According to some they represented the ghost of a slain person while to others they were actual curses that had become personified. They were as real to the Greeks as the banshee was to the Irish. Their abode was in Erebus beyond the river Styx in Hades and so their power to punish reached beyond the grave. To avoid giving them offence they were often called the Eumenides (the Gracious Ones) just as the treacherous Black Sea was euphemistically called the *Pontus Euxeinos* ('Sea Friendly to Strangers') so as to not ruffle the god of that dreaded waterway.

The banshee, from the Irish *bean sí* 'fairy woman' or 'woman of the Otherworld', is a preternatural female death-messenger. Something that acts in accordance with the laws of nature is natural; something that cannot be explained by natural laws but that proceeds from a divine source is said to be supernatural (*super* is the Latin 'above'); something that cannot be explained by natural laws but that proceeds from an occult (magical, mystical, from the Latin *occultus* 'concealed') source is said to be preternatural (from the Latin *praeter* 'beyond').

Styx
In Greek myth, the ghosts of the dead descended to the underworld and made their way to the Styx where they paid Charon to ferry them across (that is why the Greeks placed a coin in the mouth of the dead). If they were good, they were sent to the delightful Elysian Fields (French *Champs Elysées*); if they were evil, they were sent down deeper into Tartarus for punishment; if they were neither good nor evil, they were sent to the Asphodel Meadows to join the throngs of torpid (*torpidus* is the Latin 'numb' or 'lethargic'), aimless dead. Sometimes the gods had the souls of heroes and good men taken after death to the *Hesperides* ('Islands of the Blessed'). Stygian describes something dark and gloomy like the Styx (gen. *Stygios*)

The Eumenides
is the title of one of the tragedies in Aeschylus's *Oresteian* (relating to Orestes and his family) trilogy

G

gamy
bigamy, monogamy and polygamy – these are all words whose common suffix *gamy* derives from the Greek *gamos* 'marriage'

Bigamy is the crime of being married to two people at the same time (*bi* is the Latin 'two'). Monogamous means having one wife or husband (*monos* is the Greek 'alone' or 'single'). Polygamous means having more than one husband or wife at the same time (*polus* is the Greek 'many'). There are two forms of polygamy – polyandry, meaning having more than one husband (*anēr, andros* is the Greek 'man' or 'husband'); and polygyny, having more than one wife (*gynē* is the Greek 'woman' or 'wife', from which we also derive gynaecology).

geo
geocentred, geodesic, geography, geology, geometry, geopolitics – these are all words whose common prefix *geo* derives from the Greek *gē* 'earth'

the Milky Way
is the Galaxy, from the Greek *gala, galaktos* 'milk'; a galaxy (with lower case g) is any luminous band of stars stretching across the skies. *Lac, lactis* is the Latin 'milk', from which we derive lactose (milk-sugar) and lactic acid

Geocentred is applied to the thinking of those cosmologists who believed the universe was centred on the earth (whereas the earth is heliocentric – centred on the sun – and the sun is a peripheral star of the Milky Way; *hēlios* is the Greek 'sun', from which we also derive helium, the light gas that abounds in the sun's atmosphere; peripheral means on the circumference and therefore not of central importance, from the Greek *peri* 'around' and *pherein* 'to bear'; circumference is its Latin equivalent, *circum* being the Latin 'around' and *ferre* 'to bear').

Geodesic means concerned with measuring curved surfaces such as the earth (*daiein* is the Greek 'to divide').

Geography is the study of the earth's surface and atmosphere (*graphein* is the Greek 'to write').

Geology is the study of the earth's physical composition (*ology* here means 'study of', from the Greek *logos* 'word', 'reason' or 'account').

Geometry is the branch of mathematics concerned with the properties and relations of lines, surfaces and solids in space, so called because it was developed as an aid for man's measurement of the earth (*metria* is the Greek 'measuring', from which we also derive metre).

Geopolitics is the study of politics, especially international relations, as influenced by geographical factors, such as lack of access to the sea (*politikos* is the Greek 'relating to the affairs of the state').

Two other words derived from *gē* in quite common use are apogee and perigee. The movement of the planets in relation to the earth is elliptical. When a planet is at its furthest point from the earth it is said to be at its apogee (*apo* is the Greek 'far from'). When it is at its nearest point it is said to be at its perigee (*peri* is the Greek 'near'). Apogee is also used in a transferred sense to mean the highest point or zenith.

gerrymander
when ruling politicians draw or re-draw electoral districts in such a way as to favour their supporters and so distort the outcome of elections, they are said to gerrymander

In 1812 when Elbridge Gerry was governor of Massachusetts, the state legislature divided Essex County into two districts with boundaries so drawn as to give the maximum advantage to the ruling Republican Party. Normally boundaries follow natural features such as rivers and mountains, but in this case they frequently reached out oddly to include certain isolated homesteads. Looking at a map of one of the districts, someone said 'Hey, that looks like a salamander!'(a kind of lizard). Someone else rejoined: 'I'll tell you what it is – it's a *gerry*mander!'

ghetto
a run-down, impoverished part of a city whose inhabitants are forced to live there either because of their poverty or race

Borghetto is an Italian word meaning 'little borough' (*borgo* is 'borough'), from which some say the word ghetto derives. Others say it comes from *getto,* the name of the foundry in Venice where a ghetto was established in the sixteenth century. It was originally used in reference to the area of a European city to which Jews were confined. It is now used of any poor district of a city.

glamour
charm and allure

Gramma is the Greek for 'letter of the alphabet' and grammar pertains to the rules of language, a study that developed when language was written (put into letters). In medieval times grammar came to be identified with Latin. Indeed grammar schools were originally set up to teach Latin. Because Latin was mysterious to the uneducated, grammar came to mean magic. In Scotland grammar was pronounced glammar (the substitution of l for r is quite common; it is known to phonetists as lallation, which is derived from the Latin *lallare, lallatum* 'to sing a lullaby'). Glammar came into English as glamour and shifted in meaning to a magical beauty attaching to a person or thing, and then to its meaning today.

phonetists
or phoneticians – experts in phonetics, the science that studies speech processes, *phōnē* being the Greek 'sound' or 'voice'

glasnost
the policy of openness in Gorbachev's USSR

Glasnost is the Russian 'openness'. It characterized the style of government of Mikhail Gorbachev – an openness to ideas, including the revision of modern Russian history; greater freedom, including the release of at least some nonconformists from prison – political prisoners, dissidents, refuseniks; greater freedom of expression in the media; greater freedom of movement between the Soviet Union and the rest of the world, including the emigration of Soviet Jews to Israel. A concomitant policy, *perestroika* ('restructuring'), sought reforms of the economy that would produce the kind of consumer wealth that characterized the Western, non-communist countries. *Glasnost* and *perestroika* sought to change the arthritic bureaucracy that developed under the gerontocracy of Leonid Brezhnev, Yuri Andropov and Konstantin Chernenko.

G-men
government men – armed federal (that is employed by the US government rather than a state government) detectives who in the 1930s combated violent crime under the leadership of J. Edgar Hoover

In September 1933 George Kelly – public enemy number one, commonly known as Machine-Gun Kelly from his favourite piece of protection – was captured by federal agents in Memphis, Tennessee. He had been on a spending spree in Mexico with his wife Kate after pulling off a successful job, and both of them were relaxing in bed in a rented bungalow. Suddenly law officers burst into the room. Kelly reached for his machine-gun but realizing that double-barrelled shotguns were trained not only on him but also on Kate, he surrendered. 'Don't shoot, G-men!' he yelled, thus coining what became an American colloquialism widely known from its use in gangster movies. (A colloquialism is a word or phrase appropriate to informal conversation, from the Latin *cum* – *col* before l – 'with' and *loqui* 'talk'; a colloquium is an informal gathering for discussion; a colloquy is a formal conference.)

Gordian knot
a person is said to cut the Gordian knot if, when faced with an intricate problem or task, he or she solves it by decisive force or by evading the conditions

Some time before 300 BC, when Alexander the Great was conquering Asia, he came to the city of Gordium. There he was told of a local curiosity – a chariot in the palace of the former kings bound to its yoke by a knot of cornel-bark no man had ever been able to undo. The day before he left the city, Alexander went up to the palace and, surrounded by his friends, tried to loosen the knot. No matter how much he pulled, the knot remained stubbornly tight. He began to fret because if he failed, he would lose face with his men. So, drawing his sword, he slashed the knot in half and claimed, correctly, that the knot was loosened (if not untied).

Gothic
the style of architecture and art that prevailed in

As the Dark Ages drew to a close and stone-roofed churches began to be built, architects drew their inspiration from what they knew of the forms the Romans had used. That style came to be called Romanesque. Romanesque churches, with their firm unbroken walls and towers, gave an impression of massive strength. In the middle of the twelfth century certain technical advances, in particular the method of vaulting a church by means of crosswise arches, allowed cathedrals to address the skies with the soaring vaulted roofs and celestial spires that typify the Gothic style.

Western Europe from the twelfth to the sixteenth centuries

The Italian Renaissance architects, with their predilection for the classic style, coined Gothic as a pejorative term, wrongly supposing the style to be that of the Goths, the north European barbarians who had helped to bring down Rome. Between the late eighteenth and late nineteenth centuries there occurred a renewal of interest in Gothic architecture – the Gothic Revival – which was an aspect of Romanticism. In Britain and Ireland Augustus Pugin was a leader of the movement – he collaborated on the design of the Palace of Westminster, which was begun in 1836. In Germany Wagner's patron Ludwig II of Bavaria promoted the movement in an extravagant building programme.

to collaborate
is to work with, from the Latin *cum* – *col* before l – 'with' and *laborare* 'to work'

extravagant
means ostentatious, showy or excessively costly, from the Latin *extra* 'beyond' and *vagari* 'to wander'

Gothic is also used to name the family of typefaces associated with German script. See also Gothic(k), under novel.

Götterdämmerung
the twilight of the gods

Götter is the plural of *Gott*, the German 'god'; *Dämmerung* means 'twilight' (strictly, the half-light before either dusk or dawn). In the German *Nibelungenlied*, Valhalla (the Hall of the Slain) was the great hall where Wotan and the other gods and goddesses sat with the slain heroes carried thither by the Valkyrie – the maidens who served Wotan and rode over battlefields to claim dead heroes and bring them to Valhalla, *köri* being the Old Norse 'to choose'. In the end Valhalla is consumed by fire and the power of the gods fades. Richard Wagner based his *Ring* cycle of operas – a tetralogy – on that epic: the last of the operas, *Götterdämmerung*, ends in the death of the hero, Siegfried, and the destruction of Valhalla by fire.

twilight
derives from the Old English *twi* 'half' and light. Crepuscular, from the Latin *crepusculum* 'dusk', means relating to twilight. *Vesper* is the Latin 'evening', from which we derive vesperal (pertaining to the evening). *Dies* is the Latin 'day', from which we derive diurnal (happening during the day). *Nox, noctis* is the Latin 'night', from which we derive nocturnal (happening during the night). Matuta is the Roman goddess of dawn, from which we derive matutinal (happening during the morning), matinee and matins (the first of the canonical hours of prayer)

Adolf Hitler, in his heyday as dictator of Germany, was received with great ceremony each year when he visited Bayreuth in Bavaria to see Wagner's operas performed there. The destruction of Germany at the end of World War II and Hitler's own death in the bunker in Berlin as the Russian armies closed in are sometimes described by historians as the *Götterdämmerung.*

government
the group of people who exercise the executive power of the State

Kubernaein is the Greek 'to steer', from which government derives. The government steers the ship of State. In business the chief executive and his or her management team have the executive (implementing) power; the board has the policy-making power. In political contexts the government has the executive power and parliament has the policy-making (legislative) power.

The Latin equivalent of *kubernaein* is *gubernare,* from which we derive govern and governor. A helmsman in Latin is *gubernator* – from it we derive gubernatorial as in the gubernatorial elections in the US, i.e. the elections for state governors.

A helmsman, in Greek *kubernētēs,* transliterates into *cybernētēs*. Cybernetics is the study of automatic communication and control in functions of living bodies and in mechanical electronic systems such as computers – in simple terms the study of self-steering systems. Cyberphobia is an irrational fear of computers (*phobia* is the Greek 'fear').

Grand Guignol
something designed to horrify

grotesque
derives from the Old Italian *grotta* 'cave' and referred originally to the bizarre shapes of rock found in caves

Le Grand Guignol was a small theatre in Montmartre, Paris, founded in 1897, which specialized in short horror plays. Guignol, the name of the chief puppet in French puppet shows, derives from the French *guigner* 'to wink'. Grand Guignol connotes something sensational, grotesque, macabre, hyperbolic. Grand Guignolesque, Grand Guignolish, Grand Guignolism and guignolesque are derivatives from it. (Practice in regard to capitalization and italicization varies.)

graph
autograph, biography, calligraphy, cardiograph, cartography, electroencephalograph, graphic, graphology, hagiography, heliograph, mammograph, monograph, orthography, photograph, seismograph, telegraph and topography – these are all words whose common component *graph* derives

Autograph means a person's signature (*autos* is 'self' in Greek).

Biography means an account of a person's life (*bios* is 'life' in Greek). An autobiography is a person's account of his or her own life. *The Confessions* by Saint Augustine is the first autobiography we have. With its intellectual brilliance, its wonderful humanity and frankness – 'Lord make me chaste, but not yet' – it is regarded as a classic of the genre.

Calligraphy is beautiful handwriting (*kallos* is 'beauty' in Greek).

A cardiograph is a record of the electrical impulses that drive the heart to beat (*cardia* is 'heart' in Greek).

Cor, cordis is the Latin 'heart', from which we derive cordial.

Cartography means map-drawing (*carte* is the French 'chart').

An electroencephalograph (EEG) is a means of reading the electrical activity generated in the brain, usually through electrodes placed on the scalp, useful in the diagnosis of epilepsy and other cerebral disorders. *Enkephalon* is 'brain' in Greek; encephalitis is inflammation of the brain, *itis* being a Greek suffix indicating 'inflammation'. Hydrocephaly describes an excessive accumulation of fluid within the ventricles (chambers, the Latin *ventriculus* being a diminutive of *venter, ventris* 'belly') of the brain, resulting in the displacement of normal tissue; *hydro* is a Greek prefix indicating 'water' from *hudōr* 'water'. Anencephalic means born with no brain or only a partial one, *a* – *an* before a vowel – indicating a negative.

Graphic may be used to describe the arts of writing, printing, drawing, painting, etching, engraving. It is also used in the general sense of vivid.

Graphology is the study of handwriting (*ology* here means 'study of' from *logos*, the Greek 'word', 'reason' or 'account'): 'The graphologist who studied the ransom note concluded it was written by a one-legged sailor with a hacking cough.'

A hagiography is the biography of a saint. In secular usage, it may refer to a gushing, uncritical biography of a public figure (*hagios* is the Greek 'holy').

Heliography is a means of transmitting messages by reflecting sunlight on mirrors (*hēlios* is the Greek 'sun').

A mammograph is the record of a breast scan (*mamma* is 'breast' in Latin).

A monograph is a treatise on a single subject or class of subjects (*monos* means 'alone' or 'single' in Greek).

Orthography is a writing system or a spelling considered to be correct (*orthos* is the Greek 'straight' or 'right').

A photograph is a picture taken by a camera (*phōs, phōtos* is 'light' in Greek; photosynthesis is the building up of complex components by the chlorophyll in plants using the energy of sunlight – see synthesis on page 71).

A seismograph is an instrument for measuring earthquakes, usually on the Richter scale (*seismos* is

from the Greek *graphein* 'to write'

hydro
is also a prefix in hydroelectric (electricity produced by water-power), hydrography (the mapping of seas and other bodies of water by sounding, charting and study of tides) and hydrogen (a gas – the lightest of all known substances – which combined with oxygen produces water). Hydraulics (from *hudōr* and *aulos*, the Greek 'pipe') is the science or practice of using water or other liquids in pipes to produce motive power. To dehydrate is to lose or cause to lose water (*de* is a Latin negative)

phōs
also gives us phosphorus (an inflammable substance that shines in the dark, *phoros* being the Greek 'bearing'), phosphate (a salt of phosphoric acid), phosphide (a compound of phosphorus and another element), and phosphorescent (shining in the dark)

'shaking' in Greek, from which we also derive seismic).

A telegraph is an apparatus for sending messages or signals over long distances by electricity (*tele* is the Greek 'far').

Topography is the description of a limited geographical area or, by transference, the features of such an area. *Topos* is 'place' in Greek, from which we also derive topic because *ta topica* were the places marked by headings where Greek scholars located references in books; topic came to be transferred to the reference itself. Topos is used in English to refer to a stock theme in literature:

> Bandemundus tells us that Amandus was reluctant to accept the see of Maastricht. A typical hagiographical topos, we might think.
>
> –Richard Fletcher, *The Conversion of Europe*

Topical is used variously – as relating to something of current interest or to a particular locality or, as in a topical ointment, to something applied to a sore on the body.

guerrilla
one who takes part in a war in which the regular military forces are harassed by small bands of irregular forces or, as a descriptive word, pertaining to such warfare

During the French Revolution the most serious counter-revolutionary movement appeared in La Vendée in the west of France. There the people, conservative and Catholic, rose up in rebellion in the winter of 1792 and the spring of 1793. The uniformed troops of the Republic's army found themselves having to deal not with massed enemy forces but with bands of militia that engaged in hit-and-run raids, skirmishes in narrow streets, ambushes in the woods, and such-like tactics. When, fifteen years later, the French generals who had fought in La Vendée found themselves faced with a similar kind of warfare in the Peninsular War in Spain, they referred to it as *la petite guerre* (French, 'little war'), a phrase that became rendered in Spanish as *guerrilla* (*illo, illa* being diminutive suffixes that apply to masculine and feminine words respectively; *cigarillo*, 'small cigar', is another example and so is *peccadillo*, 'small sin', from the Latin *peccare* 'to sin').

Counter derives from the Latin *contra* 'against'. The pros and cons are the arguments for and against (*pro* is the Latin 'for'), which crop up in a controversy (*vertere, versum* is the Latin 'to turn'), which, of course, involves contradiction (*dicere, dictum* is the Latin 'to say').

Athenasius, a fourth-century bishop of Alexandria,

was the orthodox protagonist in the struggle against Arianism, a heresy that denied the divinity of Christ. Arianism was supported by the Roman emperor and the intelligentsia, and Athenasius at one stage found himself standing famously *contra mundum* 'against the world' (*mundus* is the Latin 'world', from which we derive mundane and *demi-mondaine* – literally 'half-world' in French and meaning a woman of the *demi-monde* – those women in the nineteenth century considered to be outside respectable society). Counterfactual history explores what might have been.

guillotine
a machine for inflicting capital punishment by decapitation

Joseph Ignace Guillotin, a French doctor, was one of the 1139 delegates (270 from the nobility, 291 from the clergy, and 578 from the Third Estate) to the fateful meeting of the Estates General in Versailles in 1789. He successfully promoted a law that required that all death sentences be carried out by means of a machine. The intention was to make decapitation, which was a privilege of nobles, available to everyone, and the process of execution as painless as possible. The guillotine came into use in 1792 and became one of the enduring symbols of the Revolution.

privilege
means an advantage enjoyed by one or a few, from the Latin *privus* 'individual' and *lex, legis* 'law'. Sacrilege, the desecration of anything regarded as sacred, has a completely different etymology. It derives from the Latin *sacrilegus* 'temple-robber', from *sacra* 'sacred things' and *legere* 'to take'

Nowadays the word usually arises in a parliamentary context. It is an important function of the government to manage the progress of its legislative programme through parliament. If a government is promoting a particularly urgent piece of legislation, it may 'apply the guillotine', that is it may name a time by which debate on the bill must cease and the vote be taken. The procedure was introduced into the House of Commons in 1882 by the British prime minister, W.E. Gladstone, to deal with the obstructionist (filibustering) tactics of Charles Stewart Parnell, the Irish leader agitating for Home Rule.

The word also occurs nowadays in printing. A guillotine is used to cut a book into its design shape.

For the ancients the Sword of Damocles was the classical image of impending peril. Damocles, a sycophant at the court of Dionysius, the tyrant of Syracuse in Sicily, had extolled as paradisiacal (also paradisiac or paradisaical) the happiness of the tyrant's state so Dionysius, in order to impress on him the contingent nature of that happiness, made Damocles sit at a banquet with a sword suspended over his head by a hair.

H

habeas corpus
an order made by a higher court in response to a complaint that someone is being unlawfully detained

Habeas is a form of *habere* the Latin 'to have', meaning 'let you have'. *Corpus, corporis* is 'body' or 'person', from which we derive corporate, corporation, incorporate, corporeal and corpulent. The phrase means 'Let you produce the person!' The official in whose custody the person is held is ordered to produce the person in court on a named date and certify the grounds on which he or she is being detained. If the court is not satisfied that the person is being held in accordance with the law, it may order the person's immediate release. *Habeas corpus* sets a definite term to the period a person may be incarcerated without a formal charge in court.

head of state
the chief citizen who represents the state

The head of state is either a president or a monarch, although exceptionally a group of officials may perform the function. In some states, e.g. the US, the head of state – the president – is also head of government. In others the offices of head of state and head of government are separate. In constitutional monarchies, such as the UK, it is usual for the monarch and the head of government to be separate officers.

hegemony
leadership of a group of independent states through having effective influence or power over them

unite
to make one, derives from the Latin *unus* 'one', which also gives us unit, unity, disunity, union, disunion and communion

Hēgemōn is the Greek 'leader', from which hegemony is derived. The map of classical Greece presented a patchwork of small independent states such as Athens, Sparta, Corinth and Boeotia. In the face of external threats they needed to unite. So it was under the hegemony of Sparta that they thwarted the designs of the Persian King Xerxes to conquer Greece. When there was no external threat, they fell to warring among themselves. A protracted war (the famous Peloponnesian War, described by Thucydides in one of the most brilliant and earliest pieces of history) conducted by two sets of allies, one under the hegemony of Sparta, the other under the hegemony of Athens, ended in the defeat of Athens. But the Peloponnesian states were so exhausted that they quickly fell under the hegemony of King Philip of Macedon whose son Alexander the Great was to lead them on to conquer the world.

In the modern world during the Cold War (that term was introduced to English by George Orwell) the

Western states were under the hegemony of the US and the Eastern bloc countries were under the hegemony of the USSR. The non-aligned states did not acknowledge the hegemony of either superpower. Hegemony is also applied to the leadership of one dominant social class over others.

bloc
from the Old French *bloc* is used for a group of people or countries combined by a common interest or objective

Hellenistic
characteristic of or relating to Greek civilization in the Mediterranean world in the last 400 years BC, broadly speaking

Hellen, a legendary Thessalian king, was recognized as the ancestor of the Greeks (the Hellenes; in modern times the Greek king was styled King of the Hellenes; Hellenic relates to the ancient Greeks and the Greeks of the classical period; philhellenic means loving Greece and its culture – *philein* is the Greek 'to love' – and gained wide currency in the early nineteenth century as indicating support for Greek national independence; Panhellenic means pertaining to all Greece – *pan* is the Greek 'all'). Greek culture spread throughout the Mediterranean area, the centre of the ancient world, following the dazzling conquests of Alexander the Great and the installation of Greek dynasties in the conquered lands. The last of those collapsed with the defeat at Actium in 30 BC of Antony and Cleopatra by Octavian (later to become the Emperor Augustus) and his Roman legions. Thus in the eastern Mediterranean, the Romans inherited a part of the world that had been cosmopolitan for centuries with the Greek language serving in most cities as the *lingua franca* of administration and culture.

Alexander was the son of King Philip of Macedonia. Philip entrusted the education of his son to Greek tutors, among them the philosopher Aristotle. Alexander's favourite book was Homer's *Iliad* – he kept a copy under his pillow along with his dagger. Before he was twenty-one, Alexander inherited the throne. Within thirteen years, he had conquered a large part of the known world. Julius Caesar, who was himself to become the greatest man in the ancient world, was once seen weeping in a temple in Spain. Asked why, he replied, 'At this age Alexander was master of the world and I, I have achieved nothing!' Napoleon considered Alexander the greatest general in history.

On his deathbed, when asked who was to succeed him, Alexander replied, 'The strongest!' In fact, no one man succeeded him – his generals divided the empire among themselves. Ptolemy took over Egypt where he

lingua franca
derives from the Latin *lingua* 'tongue' (hence linguist) and *franca* 'Frankish' and is a term that came into being much later than the Hellenistic period. It means a language used for communication among people of different mother tongues. Thus French was for long the *lingua franca* of diplomacy. The term was first applied to the language based on Italian, Spanish, French, Arabic, Greek and Turkish that developed in the ports of the Mediterranean and was spoken from the time of the Crusades (with their Frankish leaders) to the eighteenth century. The Greek spoken in the Hellenistic and Byzantine periods was called *koinē* ('common') Greek. Demotic means relating to the ordinary people (Greek *dēmos*). A demotic form of language or writing is distinguished from that used at a court or by a ruling caste: 'When the Duke struck his thumb with the hammer his language became decidedly demotic.'

named his capital Alexandria, after Alexander who had built it. Alexandria became the second biggest city in the Roman empire, famous for its wealth and culture and especially for its library, the greatest in the ancient world. (Alexandria is today the second most populous city in Egypt.) On the island of Pharos in the Bay of Alexandria was the lighthouse called the Pharos, which was one of the Seven Wonders of the World. Alexandria under the Ptolemies had a Jewish quarter with its own ethnarch.

ethnarch
ethnic ruler, from the Greek *ethnos* 'nation' and *archein* 'to rule'

It is thought that the long six-iambic verse called an alexandrine derives its name from the fact that a medieval French poet wrote a poem about Alexander the Great, employing such metres. Pope in his *Essay on Criticism* famously employs the metre:

> A needless Alexandrine ends the song,
> That, like a wounded snake, drags its slow length along.

hermetic
esoteric, abstruse

Hermetic derives from Hermes, the herald of the Greek gods, through his identification in Hellenistic times with the Egyptian god Thoth under the name Hermes Trismegistos (thrice-greatest, from the Greek *tris* 'thrice' and *megistos* 'greatest'). The ibis-headed Thoth was the god of science and especially of alchemy. Just as Orpheus had a body of esoteric writings ascribed to him so too Thoth, as Hermes Trismegistos, had a large collection of works ascribed to him – the so-called hermetic books – written in Greek and dealing almost encyclopaedically with the mystical culture of the ancient Egyptians. (Translated into Latin during the Renaissance, they achieved currency into modern times.) The knowledge sealed up in this corpus could be opened up only through scholarly interpretation; *hermēneus*, from Hermes, as tutelary god of speech and writing, is the Greek 'interpreter'; hermeneutics, from *hermēneutikos* 'of or relating to an interpreter' is the science of interpretation – a science that became very important after the Reformation when Protestants, having repudiated the *magisterium* ('the teaching authority', from *magister* the Latin 'master') of the Roman Catholic Church, required scientific rules for interpreting the Bible. Someone expert at explaining or critically interpreting a text, especially a sacred one, is called an exegete (from the Greek *exēgētēs*, another word for 'interpreter'). Exegetes in ancient times were

tri
is a prefix indicating 'three' derived from *tris* or the Latin *tres*. A triad is a set of three. The Holy Trinity is the Christian mystery of the union of three persons – Father, Son and Holy Ghost – in one Godhead. A triptych is a set of three paintings on hinged panels, the Greek *ptux, ptuchos* meaning 'plate'. (A diptych is a pair of paintings on hinged panels, *di* being a prefix indicating 'two', from the Greek *dis* 'twice'.) Sexual activity involving three people is called troilism, probably after the French *trois* 'three'. A tribe – a social division of a people – probably comes from the Latin *tres* because in early times the people of Rome were divided into three tribes

professional interpreters of oracles, omens and dreams (in which role they were called oneirocritics). An exegete through his or her exegetical endeavours produces an exegesis.

Trismegistos, coined as a summative form of *Megistos, Megistos, Megistos*, is solecistic because it seeks to indicate a degree beyond the greatest. It derives from the Egyptian practice of creating a superlative by uttering or writing a positive adjective three times in succession: thus we find that on the Rosetta stone Hermes appears as *Megas, Megas, Megas* ('Great, Great, Great'), that is, Greatest. The practice is found famously in the Latin Mass: *Sanctus! Sanctus! Sanctus!* ... ('Holy! Holy! Holy! Lord God of Hosts') – the *Trisagion* ('Thrice Holy'), *agios* being the Greek 'holy'.

superlative
means highest, from the Latin *super* 'above' and *lativus*, a form of *ferre* 'to carry'. There are three degrees of adjectives – positive, comparative and superlative. Thus grateful, more grateful, most grateful (regular form) and good, better, best (irregular form)

We also encounter hermetic in the expression hermetically sealed, meaning sealed so as to be airtight (related to Hermes through his association as Hermes Trismegistos with alchemy). Swift in *Gulliver's Travels* tells us that the first man Gulliver met when he visited the great academy of Lagado 'had been eight years upon a project for extracting sunbeams out of cucumbers, which were to be put in vials hermetically sealed, and let out to warm the air in raw inclement summers'.

Hermes was also the god of travellers. In Athens it was common to see squared pillars surmounted by a head of Hermes at street corners or in front of houses. These were called *hermae*, in English herms. The term is now applied by sculptors to any piece of stonework that features a head upon a squared pillar. Sculptors use the term stele or stela as the general term for an upright stone slab or cylinder upon which an art form rests (stele derives from the Greek *histanai* 'to stand').

Note that hermit (a person who lives alone away from others, especially a religious ascetic), hermitical and hermitage derive from the Greek *erēmos* 'solitary'.

hetero
heterodox, heterogeneous and heterosexual – these are all words whose common prefix *hetero* means 'other' or 'different' in Greek

Heterodox (or unorthodox) is the opposite of orthodox and means having a different (and therefore wrong!) opinion. (*Doxa* is 'opinion' in Greek; *orthos* is 'straight' or 'right'.) Bishop William Warburton caught the distinction between the terms nicely in a remark to Lord Sandwich: 'Orthodoxy is my doxy; heterodoxy is another man's doxy.'

Heterogeneous is the opposite of homogeneous

and means diverse in character (*genos* means 'kind' in Greek, *homos* means 'same').

Heterosexual is the opposite of homosexual and means attracted to the opposite sex (*sexus* is 'sex' in Latin). A female homosexual is sometimes called a lesbian. Lesbos is a Greek island. Its most famous inhabitant was an inspired erotic, lyric poetess, Sappho. Sappho's fame was such that more than two centuries after her death Plato could hail her as 'the tenth Muse'. The library in Alexandria possessed nine volumes of her verse, each containing as much as 1300 lines. All that now remains is one complete poem (preserved because it was quoted in full by an ancient scholar) and some two hundred fragments. Feminists regard Sappho as the greatest of early Western female writers. Sappho's work is suffused with yearning for young women and most people infer that she was perfervidly homosexual. Lesbian speech and style is therefore sometimes called Sapphic or sapphic. Sappho, however, may not have been an erotomaniac. She may have been leader of a women's chorus that sang in public to honour the goddess Aphrodite.

Sappho
coined bitter-sweet to describe love (*glukupikron* in Greek, literally 'sweet-bitter', from *glukos* 'sweet', which gives us glucose, and *pikros* 'bitter', which occurs in the term picric acid)

suffused
means shot through, from the Latin *sub* – *suf* before f – 'under' and *fundere, fusum* 'to pour'

perfervidly
per – *pel* before l, as in pellucid – is a Latin prefix that intensifies; *fervidus* means 'fervid' or 'intensely passionate'

Hobbesian
relating to the philosopher Thomas Hobbes

Hobbes was one of the most influential of English philosophers. He took a pessimistic view of the condition of man – 'a condition of war of everyone against everyone' – and he famously characterized man's life in the state of nature, that is to say, before states came into being, as 'solitary, poor, nasty, brutish, and short'. In his book *Leviathan* he advances the theory that men, in order to escape the nightmare of continual strife, band together and delegate their individual powers to a central authority called a sovereign. The sovereign is like a giant man made up of ordinary men – a leviathan – and has absolute power in all spheres of life.

Leviathan is a Hebrew word that occurs in the Book of Job in the Old Testament and describes a crocodile – a terrifying monster. The word *behemoth* occurs in the same book and describes a hippopotamus. Both leviathan and behemoth may be used to describe a gigantic creature. Mammoth, which is also used to mean gigantic, derives from the Russian *mammot,* the name for an extinct species of elephant, the remains of which were originally yielded up by the Siberian snows.

Crocodile comes from the Greek *krokodeilos*

Hobbes
On his deathbed he declared, 'I am about to take my last voyage, a great leap in the dark.'

'lizard'. It is distinguished from the alligator, a mainly American reptile (some are also found in China) with a broader snout. Alligator comes from the Spanish *el lagarto* (Latin *lacertus*) 'the lizard' – the Spanish being the first Europeans to encounter it. English words seldom end in a or o. When southern English people come to pronounce words with such endings, where the word that follows begins with a vowel, they can feel the need to tack an r to the ends of them – thus they tend to pronounce India and Africa as Indiar and Africar. When they anglicized *el legarto* they stuck an r on his tail. This propensity (from the Latin *propensus* 'inclined to') is known to phonetics as rhotic, rho being the Greek r.

honoris causa
honorary

Honoris is a form of *honor*, the Latin 'honour'; *causa* means 'for the sake of'. Each year our universities seek to honour people who have contributed to the good of the community in an outstanding, often non-academic, way by conferring degrees on them *honoris causa*.

hubris
overweening pride

Hubris was an important concept in Greek life and literature: it was a preoccupation of tragedians and historians. The Greeks believed that any insolent or wanton act would inevitably bring destruction to the person who has committed the act of hubris. Those who commit hubris were perceived to derive pleasure from the belief that by hurting others they are shown to be superior to them. The young and the rich were thought to be hubristic in tendency. The Greeks believed the invasion of Greece by the Persian King Xerxes was an act of hubris and bound to fail. We might say Hitler's attack on Russia was an act of hubris.

humanist
someone concerned with human beings and their interests exclusive of any supernatural dimension

Humanus is a Latin word derived from *homo* 'human being' – human means pertaining to the nature of man. Humane means having the feelings proper to a human being. A humanist was originally a student during the Renaissance period who devoted himself or herself to the study of the ancient classical texts. These were pagan so a student of them was seen as pursuing a secular interest in human nature. Gradually the term humanist came to be applied to anyone who placed human interests and the mind of man above everything else.

Renaissance, from the Latin *re* 'again' and *nasci* 'to

Renaissance
is a French word. The fourteenth-century Italian poet Petrarch admired the poetic achievements of his compatriot Dante so much that he declared they represented a rebirth (Italian *renascita*) of poetry, being as good as anything written in ancient Rome. Nineteenth-century French scholars took over the term to describe the cultural phenomenon that the humanists represented

be born', means revival or rebirth. It was the Italians who developed the notion at the end of the fourteenth century. They were aware that in the distant past Italy, with Rome as her capital, had been the centre of the civilized world but that the invading barbarians had destroyed that world and its art, science and scholarship. They conceived of a revival of the great Roman tradition. The highest praise they could give their artists was to say that their work was as good as that of the ancients. Italy's wealth, especially that of Florence, gave an impetus to a movement in classical scholarship, architecture, art and science that, spreading throughout Europe, marked the waning of the Middle Ages and the rise of the modern world.

The forms employed by Renaissance architects, being classical, are recurrent architectural references. A pediment is a structure in the shape of an isosceles triangle – having two sides of equal length, *isos* being the Greek 'equal' and *skelos* being the Greek 'leg' – crowning the front of a Greek building; it was later applied to any similar structure over a door, window or niche. Its etymology is obscure; it does not derive from the Latin *pes*, *pedis* 'foot' nor is it related to impediment, a hindrance, which is derived from the Latin *impedimenta*, 'the baggage and equipment carried by an army'; it may be a corrupt form of pyramid (as viewed in two dimensions).

A pilaster, from the Latin *pila* 'pillar', is a square column, partly built into, partly projecting from, a wall.

An arch, from the Latin *arcus* 'bow', is an upwardly curving structure capable of bearing a superimposed structure.

A column, Latin *columna*, is a long round body used as a support or decoration. The Greeks developed three main kinds of classical column – Doric, Ionic and Corinthian – most readily identified from their capitals. The Doric, the oldest and severest style, has no decoration except for a round moulding on its capital. The Ionic has spiral forms (volutes). The Corinthian has a flourish of acanthus leaves.

The part of a classical temple above the columns is called the entablature, from the Latin *tabula* 'table'. The entablature had an architrave, a frieze and a cornice. The architrave, from the Greek prefix *archi* 'chief' and the Latin *trabs* 'beam', was the beam resting immediately on the columns. (Architrave is now also used for a moulding around a doorway or a window opening.) The frieze was the horizontal band above the architrave that was normally decorated with sculptures (frieze in this usage ultimately derived from Phrygia, once renowned for its embroidery in gold; frieze, with a different etymology, means a heavy woollen fabric.) The cornice, from the Greek *korōne* 'crown', was the projecting moulding that topped the frieze.

cornice
is also an overhanging ridge of snow formed by the wind on the edge of a mountain ridge or cliff. In the form corniche it describes a coastal road, especially one built into the face of a cliff

humour
the quality of being funny; also temper or mood

Humour derives from the late Latin *humor* 'moistness'. Medieval physicians, taking their line from Galen, believed that the human temperament was determined by the proportion in which the various humours (bodily fluids) existed in the individual. They conceived of four humours – blood, phlegm, yellow bile and black bile. Where the blood (Latin *sanguis*) predominated, the individual was of a courageous, optimistic disposition – sanguine. Where phlegm predominated, he or she was, in a negative perspective, lethargic – phlegmatic – and in a positive perspective, imperturbable. Where yellow bile, the bitter secretion of the gall bladder, predominated, he or she was irascible – choleric (*cholē* is the Greek 'bile'; from it we also derive cholera, the highly infectious and deadly disease characterized by bilious vomiting). Where black bile predominated, he or she was depressed, in a black humour – melancholy (melancholy comes from the Greek *melas*, *melanos* 'black' and *cholē*). The spleen (Greek *splēn*) was once thought to be the seat of the emotions and splenetic, derived from it, has come to mean spiteful or irritable.

lethargic
derives from the Greek *lēthē* 'oblivion' (itself derived from the Latin *oblivio, oblivionis* 'forgetfulness'). Lethe was the name the Greeks gave to a river in Hades that caused sleepiness and gradual forgetfulness in those who drank its waters. In *Hamlet* Shakespeare refers memorably to 'the weeds that grow fat on Lethe's wharf'. (Note that lethal derives from the Latin *letum* 'death', itself derived from the root form of *delere, deletum* 'to blot out', 'to destroy' – hence delete)

From this understanding flow the expressions ill-humoured and good-humoured. The variousness of humour led to its being equated with caprice or whim, and from there it shifted to funniness.

Sometimes one's humour is taken to derive from one's digestion (*pepsis* in Greek; peptic means of or relating to digestion). An irritable person may be said to be dyspeptic (*dys* is a Greek prefix indicating 'bad'), a jovial person may be said to be eupeptic (*eu* is a Greek prefix indicating 'good'). The Scottish historian Thomas Carlyle described Augustus, King of Poland, who fathered 354 illegitimate children, as 'the ever-cheerful man of sin', 'gay eupeptic Son of Belial' (a demon often mentioned in apocalyptic literature).

Carlyle
also famously characterized Robespierre as 'the seagreen Incorruptible'. Seagreen or aquamarine (*aqua* is the Latin 'water' and *marine* derives from *mare* 'sea') is bluish green, the colour of Robespierre's coat, and connotes a cold elemental dispassion

Modern medicine has identified numerous bodily fluids that affect and modulate our temper and behaviour, notably hormones. A hormone is a chemical substance produced in an endocrine gland and transported in the blood to a certain tissue on which it exerts a specific effect (hormone derives from the Greek *horman* 'to stir up'). An endocrine gland is any of the glands that secrete hormones directly into the bloodstream. They include the pituitary, pineal, thyroid, parathyroid, adrenal (hence adrenaline), testis (hence testosterone) and ovary.

endocrine
derives from the Greek prefix *endo* 'within' and *krinein* 'to separate'; an exocrine gland, from the Greek *exo* 'outside' and *krinein*, is a gland such as a salivary or sweat gland that secretes its product through a duct on an internal or external surface of the body

hurricane
a severe, often destructive storm especially in the West Indies; a wind with a velocity of 118 kph (73 mph) or more

Tropical revolving storms occur on nearly all the equatorial oceans of the world. They usually form about 5° north or south of the equator (the great geographical circle dividing the northern and southern hemispheres of the earth, from the Latin *aequare, aequatum* 'to make equal'), moving westwards for a time before whirling either north or south. When they occur in the Caribbean, North Atlantic and Pacific south of the equator they are called hurricanes (from the Spanish *huracán*, itself derived from a Caribbean word). When they occur in the Indian Ocean they are called cyclones (from the Greek *kuklos*, transliterated *cyclos*, 'circle'). In the Chinese seas and in the North Pacific they are called typhoons (possibly from the Chinese *tai fung* 'big wind').

hypo
hypocrisy, hypodermic, hypoteneuse and hypothermia – these are all words whose common prefix *hypo* means 'under' in Greek

Hypocrisy is the act of pretending to be better than one really is (*hypocritēs* is the Greek 'actor'). Pharisaical is a synonym for hypocritical, derived from the Pharisees, an ancient Jewish sect excoriated in the Gospels for their self-righteousness and hypocrisy. (Excoriate is to flay and by extension to censure severely, from the Latin *ex* 'from' and *corium* 'hide'.)

Hypodermic is used of a needle for injecting under the skin (*derma* is the Greek 'skin'). Since some drug addicts inject themselves with a hypodermic needle the slang term to hype has come into use to mean to overstimulate; thus to hype a film or a book is to promote it beyond its true worth.

The hypoteneuse, from the Greek *hyperteinein* 'to stretch under', is the line opposite the right angle of a right-angled triangle (which was drawn by the Greeks with the right angle above and the hypoteneuse below).

Hypothermia means subnormal body temperature, a condition that often leads to the death of elderly people in winter as, in simple terms, their weak hearts strain to pump warm blood to their extremities (*thermē* means 'heat' in Greek).

Hyper is the Greek 'above' – the opposite of *hypo* – from which we get hyperbole, an extravagant expression (*ballein* is the Greek 'to throw'; a hyperbole, then, is an overshooting); hypermarket, a store bigger and more extensive in its range of goods than a supermarket; hypercritical, excessively critical; hyperactive, excessively active; and hypersensitive, excessively sensitive.

winter
is *hiems* in Latin hence hiemal (wintry); *autumnus* is the Latin 'autumn' hence autumnal; *aestas, aestatis* is the Latin 'summer' hence aestival, in America estival (relating to summer); *ver, veris* is 'spring' in Latin hence vernal (relating to spring)

hypothesis
a supposition made as a basis for reasoning in the hope of discovering some truth from it

Hypo is the Greek 'under'; *thesis* is 'that which stands'. A hypothesis is a foundation for reasoning. The concept is very important in science, which proceeds through subjecting hypotheses (plural) to scientific tests.

A hypothetical question is one which sets forth a set of conditions and asks the person addressed what he or she would do, or how he or she would react, if the conditions were realized. Media people frequently put hypothetical questions to politicians (so as to give their readers, listeners or viewers a fix on the future). Politicians usually respond by simply saying: 'That's a hypothetical question!' (because they don't wish to have their hands tied).

I

iconoclast
one who attacks old cherished images, ideas or practices

Eikōn is the Greek 'image', from which icon is derived; *klaein* is the Greek 'to break'. The Byzantine empire was centred on Byzantium (Constantinople, now Istanbul). It lasted from 330 AD when Byzantium was officially dedicated as the capital of the Roman empire to 1453 when the city fell. One of the features of the Christianity that developed there was an extraordinary, possibly superstitious, devotion to icons – holy images, statues, and emblems. In the eighth century the Emperor Leo III began a crusade against this practice, which lasted 120 years and involved vast destruction.

The iconoclasts were only partly motivated by religious zeal. The devotion to the icons was promoted by the monasteries. These were steadily extending the amount of property they owned and, since they were exempt from income tax, they were increasingly limiting the emperor's revenues. The attacks on them reduced their wealth and influence.

In secular usage, a mordant revisionist historian might be described as iconoclastic (*mordere* is the Latin 'to bite', from which the French *mordre*, the immediate source of mordant, derives). Lytton Strachey, who in his *Eminent Victorians* debunked such revered figures as Florence Nightingale and Cardinal Manning, was an iconoclast.

Iconography, from *eikōn* and *graphein* 'to write', refers to the symbols used in a piece of art or in an art movement or in relation to a particular art subject.

Aniconic means relating to a symbol for something that does not present a resemblance of it (from *a* – *an* before a vowel – a Greek negative particle, and *icon*). Aniconism is the worship of an object that represents a god without being an image of him.

superstition
is irrational belief usually based on ignorance or fear and characterized by obsessive reverence for omens, oracles, charms and the like. It derives from the Latin *superstitio* 'dread of the supernatural'. That word is said to derive from *superstare* 'to be brought to a standstill in amazement at something' but the etymology is not certain

revisionist
someone who reviews a settled account of an historical period with the intention of changing people's view of it (*re* is a Latin prefix meaning 'again' and *visere* is an intensive form of *videre* the Latin 'to look at')

i.e.
that is

I.e. is an abbreviation of the Latin expression *id est*: *id* means 'that'; *est* means 'is'.

imprimatur
official permission to print; formal assent

Imprimatur is the Latin 'Let it be printed!' Following the development of printing in Europe, the Roman Catholic Church established a formal system of censorship. Manuscripts (things written by hand: *manus* is the Latin 'hand'; *script* derives from *scribere, scriptum* 'to write'; a typescript is a text produced by a typewriter) were submitted to ecclesiastical censors who, if they found the texts unobjectionable, certified them with the Latin *nihil obstat* ('nothing hinders') and passed them to a higher authority, such as a bishop, who gave them his imprimatur.

ecclesiastical
derives from the Greek *ek* 'out' and *kaleein* 'to call'. An *ecclēsia* was an assembly called out of the world – the Church. Ecclesiology is the science relating to the Church

Church censors were not noted for their whimsy. However, in France before the Revolution a son of the playwright Crèbillon was an official literary censor. One of his evaluations is renowned: 'By order of Monsignor the Chancellor I have read the work by Mr Mahomet entitled *The Koran* and have found in it nothing contrary either to religion or to morality. Signed: Crèbillon fils.'

In secular usage, imprimatur means sanction: 'The chief of staff would never have issued such a statement without the president's imprimatur.'

in absentia
in the absence of someone

The phrase is usually used in a legal context: 'The court tried him *in absentia* and condemned him to death.' *In* is the Latin 'in'; *absentia* is 'a state of being away'. In *The Hostage,* the Irish playwright Brendan Behan captured a certain weakness in the procedure: 'When I came back to Dublin, I was courtmartialled [by the IRA] in my absence and sentenced to death in my absence, so I said they could shoot me in my absence.'

in camera
in private

In is the Latin 'in'; *camera* is 'vault' and therefore a private room. The expression *in camera* is used in a legal context. Where evidence may unfairly jeopardize the good name or prospects of someone, a judge may decide to hear it *in camera* – in his private chamber or in court with the press and public excluded. Certain proceedings, such as private family matters, may be held *in camera*.

Camarilla is a diminutive form of the Spanish *camara* 'room' and means 'little room'. It is also applied to a body of secret intriguers, a cabal, especially historically a court party against legitimate ministers.

The German *Kammer* 'room', in combination with *Wunder* 'wonder', gives us *Wunderkammer* for a room full of curiosa (curiosities, from the Latin *curiosus*) or exotica (literally things brought in from abroad: *exo* is a Greek prefix indicating 'outside', the *a* ending indicates 'things' – thus also, for example, Americana, Africana, arcana, erotica, esoterica). *Wunder* in combination with

arcana
'The mental gymnastics required to leap with the author among the arcana are too demanding.' (Norman Davies, *NYRB*, 18 April 1996)

Kind 'child' gives us *Wunderkind* 'child prodigy'. The German plural of *Kind* is *Kinder* – hence *Kinder, Küche, Kirche* ('children, kitchen, church'), the proverbial concerns of the conformist German housewife. *Kinder* in combination with *Garten*, the German 'garden', gives us kindergarten, a word coined by F.W.A. Froebel for an infant school organized in accordance with his educational principles, but now applied generally.

inchoate
just beginning

The Latin *inchoare, inchoatum* is 'to make a beginning'; incipient (from the Latin *incipere* 'to begin'), nascent, embryonic (relating to the beginning of germination from the Greek *en* – *em* before b – 'in' and *bruein* 'to swell'), elementary and rudimentary (from the Latin *rudis* 'unformed') are synonyms: 'The objective was clear but the plan to achieve it was inchoate.'

in flagrante delicto
(caught) in the act

In is the Latin 'in'; *flagrante* means 'blazing'; *delicto* is a form of *delictum*, which means 'crime'. *In flagrante delicto* literally means 'while the crime is blazing'.

Delicti is a form of *delictum* meaning 'of the crime'. Lawyers use the term *corpus delicti*, literally 'the body [*corpus*] of the crime', for the body of facts that constitute an offence.

inflation
a process whereby prices rise and money drops in value

Inflare, inflatum is the Latin 'to blow into', 'to inflate'. There are three basic reasons for a rise in the prices of goods and services. Firstly, if consumers have a great deal of money and suppliers have a small amount of goods and services, a situation arises in which too much money chases too few goods: the suppliers raise their prices. Secondly, if the costs of production such as wages, oil and energy rise, producers will put up their prices in order to get back the money to cover the increased costs. Thirdly, if a government finances any part of its deficit by borrowing directly from a Central Bank, it increases the money supply and thereby fuels inflation by having too much money chasing too few goods.

The opposite of inflation is deflation – *de* is a Latin prefix meaning 'from'. Stagflation is where inflation is combined with stagnant or decreasing output and employment.

infrastructure
the support system underpinning any activity

Infra is the Latin 'below'; *struere, structum* is 'to build'. The word occurs in public affairs, mostly in the context of industrial development. Industry needs a certain infrastructure to function properly. There must, for example, be a transport system to bring in raw materials and bring out finished goods, a water supply (large amounts of water are used in many industrial processes), a telecommunications system and an energy supply. Many government agencies, especially the local authorities, are involved in providing and maintaining the infrastructure required by industry.

Apart from this physical infrastructure there is the need for a social infrastructure – a framework of law and order, an educational system, a financial system, etc.

in loco parentis
in place of a parent

In is the Latin 'in'; *loco* is a form of *locus* 'place'; *parentis* is a form of *parens* 'parent'. The expression is used in legal and educational contexts, for example when someone who acts in the place of a parent – say a teacher – is deemed to have responsibility for a child similar to that which a parent has.

Locus standi means 'recognized status', literally 'a place on which to stand'. Thus the courts operate completely independently of the government in accordance with the doctrine of the separation of powers. Nonetheless it is conceivable that a citizen might appeal to a minister for justice to have a decision made against him or her in the courts changed. In such a case a minister would refuse to intervene, saying he or she had no *locus standi* in the matter.

intelligence
the capacity for understanding

The Latin *intelligentia*, from which intelligence derives, itself derives from *intellegere* 'to discern', 'to understand', from *inter* – *intel* before l – 'between' and *legere* 'to choose'. Psychometrics (from the Greek *psychē* 'mind' and *metron* 'measure') is concerned with applying tests to measure mental states or processes including intelligence.

As far as the existence of animal intelligence is concerned we have testimony in a book called *The Tailor and Ansty* by Eric Cross which, though innocent of the scientific rigour of a Pavlovian experiment, nonetheless carries a graphic conviction.

The book presents the thoughts of a remarkable old couple who lived in a tiny cottage on the mountain road up to Gougane Barra lake in County Cork in Ireland.

Here is the Tailor's story in support of his view that a sow is a very intelligent animal:

> I was on the road to this side of Turendubh. There is a pool there at the side of the road, and a 'johnny the bog' [a crane] had caught an eel in the pond and was swallowing him. The 'johnny the bog' is a strange kind of bird. He has only a straight gut. Well, he was swallowing the eel and he wasn't making much of a hand at the business, for the eel ran straight through him, and the 'johnny the bog' kept swallowing him and losing him again. John Jerry had a sow at the time and she was always on the side of the road. She came along and stood for a while and watched the 'johnny the bog' go through the performance several times. Then she made a grab for the eel herself and swallowed him and clapped her backside up against the wall!

gut
is *viscus, visceris* in Latin; its plural form *viscera* is a synonym for guts; visceral is applied to feelings proceeding from intuition or instinct rather than the mind. *Enteron* is the Greek 'intestine'; enteritis is a pain in the gut, *itis* being a Greek suffix indicating 'inflamation' and dysentery is an infection of the gut marked by severe diarrhoea (*dys* is a Greek prefix indicating 'bad')

The bucolic ingenuousness of *The Tailor and Ansty* led to its being banned, under the conservative censorship of the time, as being 'in its general tendency indecent' – and secured it considerable sales outside Ireland. Ingenuous, meaning naïve or frank, derives from the Latin *ingenuus*, 'freeborn' or 'virtuous'. Disingenuous (*dis* is a Latin negative) means insincere or lacking candour. *Ingénue* (feminine of the French *ingénu* 'ingenuous') refers to a naïve young woman.

intelligentsia, the
the class in society that aspires to intellectual activity; those possessing culture and a capacity to discuss public affairs at an elevated level

The term, from the Russian *intelligentsiya*, itself from the Latin *intelligentia,* came into use in pre-revolutionary Russia. The intelligentsia, in effect the educated bourgeois, were a prime target for the extreme socialists. The Latin *intelligentia* derives from the Latin *intelligere, intellectum* 'to discern', 'to understand', which also gives us intellectual: the intellectuals is a synonym for the intelligentsia. When they are discussing cultural matters the intelligentsia/intellectuals may be referred to as the *cognoscenti*, the plural of the obsolete Italian *cognoscente* (modern *conoscente*) for someone with an expert knowledge of an area, especially the fine arts (the *i* suffix is the Italian plural). *Cognoscente* derives from the Latin *cognoscere* 'to know' as does connoisseur, a well-informed judge in the field of the arts, through the Old French *conoiseor*. A savant (from the French *savoir* 'to know') is a man of great learning. A pundit is an expert (from the Hindi *pandit* 'learned person'). A guru is a

Hindu or Sikh religious teacher who gives personal spiritual guidance to his disciples, extended to mean an expert (from the Sanskrit *guruh* 'weighty'). The literati are literary or scholarly people (from the Latin *littera* 'letter'). A *littérateur* (from the French, itself from the Latin *litterator* 'grammarian') is a professional writer.

Since the Dreyfus affair the term intellectual in France has taken on the connotation of a writer or artist who plays an active part in the political struggles of his or her age. Alfred Dreyfus, a Jewish French army officer, was falsely imprisoned for treason in 1894 and was only rehabilitated (restored to his former position, from the Latin *re* 'again' and *habilitas, habilitatis* 'skill' or 'ability') in 1906 after an intense campaign begun by Emile Zola in his famous letter to *L'Aurore*: *'J'accuse'* (French, 'I accuse'). The tradition of *l'ecrivain engagé* (French, 'the politically engaged writer') was notably continued by the existentialist Jean-Paul Sartre. The term intellectual is not ideologically defined although many French intellectuals, like Sartre, were leftist.

aurore
is the French 'dawn' from the Latin *aurora*. Aurora is used in English for the atmospheric phenomenon of streamers of light that move across the sky in polar regions; aurora borealis describes the northern lights, borealis being derived from *Boreas*, the Greek 'north wind'. *Ēōs* is the Greek equivalent of the Latin *aurora* and gives us *eo* as a prefix for early, for example in eohippus the earliest horse (*hippos* is the Greek 'horse') and eolithic for the early part of the Stone Age (*lithos* is the Greek 'stone')

interdict
prohibit

Interdictum is the Latin 'a thing forbidden'. Certain Roman judges had the power to settle disputes by either ordering or forbidding something. These decisions were called *interdicta* ('interdictions').

In canon law an area may be placed under interdict, that is the people living in the area may be forbidden the sacraments. It is a communal penalty aimed at forcing a Christian community to live up to what the authorities perceive as its religious duties.

interest groups
voluntary associations of people who promote a special interest or cluster of interests that they share, especially through representations to government

Interest, a form of the Latin *interesse* 'to be among', means a concern. Interest groups, also called pressure groups, range from powerful national or international associations to small local organizations, for example a local tourism body.

The major national interest groups have permanent offices and staffs. They provide research and information services, negotiate on behalf of their members, lobby ministers and government departments, provide spokespersons for the media, and represent their group internationally.

Political scientists distinguish between special interest groups, which are marshalled by a single interest (for example road haulage) and general interest groups, which are marshalled by a wide spectrum of interests (for example a church).

Interest groups are politically important by reason of either their numerical strength (the number of potential voters they represent) or their strategic strength (their ability to obstruct the flow to the community of key goods or services). It is a major task of government to serve the public interest, that is, the interest of the community as a whole, and to protect it from damage by interest groups.

interpolate
insert a comment or passage into a text or conversation and thereby alter and occasionally falsify it

The Latin *interpolare, interpolatum* means 'to give a new appearance to' and derives from *inter* 'among' or 'between' and *polire* 'to polish'. In establishing the authenticity of a document it is essential to ensure that no interpolations have been made. Authenticity derives from the Latin *authenticus* 'coming from the author', itself derived from the Greek *authentēs* 'one who acts independently', *auto* being 'self' and *hentēs* 'doer'. It has a special meaning for existentialists who regard as authentic the individual who responds to the *Angst* (German) or *angoisse* (French) – 'the anxiety' – that he or she is alone in the world by reflecting on his or her goals and values, and embracing them bravely.

The term to extrapolate was formed to describe the opposite of interpolate: to remove a passage from a document. Mathematicians use it for the calculation, based on the known terms of a series, of other terms outside of them, whether preceding or following them. This sense is extended generally:

> We are informed about the ideas of that section of the literate who wrote as well as read – or at least of some of them – but it is clearly illegitimate to extrapolate from the elite to the masses, the literate to the illiterate, even though the two worlds are not entirely separable, and the written word influenced the ideas of those who only spoke.
>
> –E.J. Hobsbawm, *Nations and Nationalism Since 1780*

interregnum
an interval between two reigns; more generally, a period of discontinuity in government or control of an organization

Inter is the Latin 'among' or 'between'; *regnum* is 'kingdom' or 'reign'. Early Rome was ruled by kings. Succession to the throne was not hereditary but proceeded from the election of a patrician (a noble) by his peers. When a king died, the patricians elected an *interrex* (*rex, regis* is the Latin 'king' – hence regal) to conduct the election of a successor.

Interregnum is now most likely to occur in a general sense: 'The chief executive died in November and his successor was not appointed until the following July. During the interregnum the boardroom was a hotbed of intrigue.'

The history of ancient Rome divides into three broad periods: the period of the kings from the reputed foundation of the city in 753 BC to the expulsion of the kings in 510 BC, the republican period from 510 BC to the appointment of Octavius as *princeps* ('first citizen') in 27 BC, and the imperial period from 27 BC to the deposition of the last Roman emperor in the west, Romulus Augustulus, in 476 AD (*Anno Domini* 'in the year of the Lord', *annus* being the Latin 'year' and *dominus* 'lord'; the Romans dated their history *ab urbe condita* 'from the foundation of the city' – hence the acronym AUC; a sixth-century Scythian monk, Denis Exiguus – Denis the Short – calculated, probably incorrectly, that Jesus was born in 753 AUC and started the Christian era in 754 AUC which he called AD 1; the latter decision is an interesting example of how our thinking is influenced by symbols: Denis could not conceive of the Christian era beginning at 0 because Roman numerology had no sign for zero).

patrician
derives from the Latin *pater, patris* 'father' – hence also paternal and patriarchal. *Frater, fratris* is the Latin 'brother' – hence fraternal and confraternity (a non-biological brotherhood; the *con* particle derives from the Latin *cum* 'with'). *Soror, sororis* is the Latin 'sister' – hence sorority (sisterhood). *Maritus* is the Latin 'husband' – hence marital (of a husband, or between a husband and wife). *Uxor* is the Latin 'wife' – hence uxorious (excessively fond of one's wife)

exiguous
from the Latin *exiguus* means meagre, scanty; it is derived from *exigere* 'to weigh out'

Iron Curtain
the frontier set up by the communist bloc countries after World War II

To maintain his dictatorship Stalin required rigorous control over the movement of people and ideas. The Iron Curtain was one element in his system of control. The origin of the term is uncertain. It was used in the 1930s by Hitler's propaganda minister, Dr Joseph Goebbels, and other anti-Bolshevik German writers. It was popularized by Winston Churchill in a speech he made at Fulton, Missouri, the hometown of president Harry Truman, in March 1946: 'From Stettin in the Baltic to Trieste in the Adriatic an iron curtain has descended upon the Continent.' Churchill was one of the greatest orators of modern times.

Following the victory of Mao Tse Tung and the Communists over the Chinese Nationalists under Chiang Kai-shek in 1949, the tight border control exercised by the Chinese came to be described as the Bamboo Curtain.

orator
is the Latin 'public speaker'. *Rhētor* is its Greek equivalent, so oratory and rhetoric are synonymous (though rhetoric often carries a connotation of being high-flown). A rhetorical question, one that does not expect an answer, is a device used by orators and writers to heighten interest: 'Shall I compare thee to a summer's day?' (Shakespeare, *Sonnets*)

irredentist
someone who advocates the forcible recovery of territories lost by his or her country

Irredenta is the Italian 'unredeemed', derived from the Latin negative *in* – *ir* before r – and *redimere, redemptum* 'to buy back' (from which we also derive Redeemer). Territory may be lost through conquest (as parts of northern Italy were to the Austrians in the nineteenth century) or by partition. Irredentists, who derive their name from an Italian political association prominent in 1878, are also called revanchists (from the French *revancher* 'to take revenge'), a term that became current in France following the Franco-Prussian War of 1870 and the loss of Alsace-Lorraine to Germany.

People who are removed by war or other circumstances from their natural environment may be said to be deracinated (uprooted, *de* is a Latin prefix indicating 'loss' and racinate is derived ultimately from the Latin *radix, radicis* 'root'). The term *déraciné* (French 'rootless') has a connotation of worthlessness for extreme rightists, just as lumpenproletariat has for communists, from its use by the French ultra and anti-Dreyfusard Maurice Barrès in his book *Les Déracinés*.

A person who has lost social standing or status might be called *déclassé* (feminine *declassée*), from the French *déclasser* 'to remove from a class'.

J

jejune
scanty, naive

Jejunus is the Latin 'fasting'. Applied to physical conditions jejune denotes attenuated and insubstantial. Applied to mental conditions it denotes unsophisticated and puerile.

Etiolated refers to a plant that has become white through lack of sunlight (*étioler* is the French 'to become pale'). Used in a transferred sense, it means weak.

Desiccated (*siccus* is the Latin 'dry') means dehydrated. Used in a transferred sense, it means lacking animation.

Effete means no longer capable of reproduction (from *effetus*, the Latin 'exhausted by bearing young'). In a transferred sense, it means worn out, ineffectual.

Epicene means hermaphroditic and derives from the Greek *epikoinos* 'of both genders'. Used in a transferred sense, it means sexless or effeminate.

jeremiad
a long lamentation or complaint

Jeremiah, an Old Testament prophet, was famous for his prophecies of doom and his denunciations of the lifestyle of the people of Judah. Jeremiad is derived from his name. Thus, 'Many African-Americans ... understand that moralizing jeremiads against character flaws in politicians can just as easily be used to discredit Martin Luther King as Bill Clinton.' (*LRB*, July 1999) Where a long lamentation has no connotation of censure it could instead be called a threnody (*thrēnos* is the Greek 'dirge', *oide* is the Greek 'song').

jeunesse dorée
the gilded youth

Jeunesse is the French 'youth'; *dorée* is 'gilded'. Youth is proverbially golden. The expression gained great currency in France following the fall of Robespierre in July 1794 (9 Thermidor in the Revolutionary calendar, from the Greek *thermē* 'heat' and *dōron* 'gift'), because of the leading part in the reaction taken by Paris's bourgeois youth. They rapturously applauded anti-Jacobin plays in the theatres and then poured out onto the streets to raise riot against 'the blood-drinkers'. The expression is applied in a general sense:

the Revolutionary calendar was introduced by the French First Republic in 1793 as part of its dechristianizing campaign and was abandoned by Napoleon in 1805. Calendar derives from the Latin *calendae*, the first day of each of the months of the ancient Roman year, which were proclaimed (Latin *calare*) in the streets because interest on borrowings was due on those days

> At Carthage, though engaged in high-minded study of the classics, our hero [St Augustine] moved along the fringes of the urbane and risqué Manichees and admired, from a safe distance, the punk rage of the

> 'Subversives' ... These are not the *jeunesse dorée* of a late Roman *Brideshead Revisited.*
>
> –*NYRB*, 24 June 1999

judicial review
the power of a supreme court to declare whether any laws, proposed or enacted, or any actions of the government or other State institutions are repugnant to the constitution or not; or the power of a high court to exercise supervisory jurisdiction over inferior courts, tribunals, public bodies and public persons

Judex, judicis is the Latin 'judge'. Judicial review of legislation is a major protection afforded the citizen against any abuse of power by the government. A law declared by the supreme court to be repugnant to the constitution is invalid *ab initio* (repugnant in this context means inconsistent with, derived from the Latin *re* 'against' and *pugnare* 'to fight', from which we also derive pugnacious).

Judicial review of the courts is concerned with the process by which a decision was made and raises issues such as: Was there power to make the decision? Was the procedure in accordance with natural and constitutional justice? It is a protection that reinforces that provided by the appeal system of the courts whereby there is a right of appeal to a higher court for a rehearing (rather than a review).

junk bonds
securities that offer relatively very high rates of interest but receive a low (below investment-grade) rating from Moody's or Standard and Poor's, the two major investment-rating agencies

Junk bonds are not backed by company assets comparable to those of investment-grade bonds or by comparable cash flow. They are also traded in less liquid (less easily convertible to money) markets.

The expression reportedly originated in a conversation between Michael Milken and one of his early clients Meshulam Riklis, when Milken, after studying Riklis's portfolio, remarked, 'Rik, this is junk.' Milken, from a middle-class Jewish family, was determined to be a millionaire. Nicknamed the Junk Bond King, he succeeded to the extent that in 1986 he earned a record $550 million. But in 1990 he was sentenced to ten years' imprisonment for securities fraud and related crimes. He was released after two years.

portfolio
A minister without portfolio is a cabinet minister who does not have responsibility for a department of state

Portfolio, from the Italian *portafoglio*, itself derived from the Latin *portare* 'to carry' and *folio*, a form of *folium* 'leaf' (here of paper), in its primary sense means a case for carrying documents. The meaning may be transferred to the contents of the case, for example an art student's portfolio describes the drawings, paintings or other artefacts relating to a recent project; or to the office that the papers of a government minister relate to, for example the education portfolio; or to the complete investments of an individual or financial institution.

Folio is used variously in relation to the pages of books. Foliage is a synonym for leafage. A defoliant is a chemical sprayed or dusted onto trees to cause their leaves to fall (*de* is a Latin prefix meaning 'removal of').

junta
an oligarchic ruling group, especially in Latin American countries

Junta (pronounced hunta) is a Spanish word derived from the Latin *junctus* 'joined' (from which we also derive junction, injunction, conjunction and adjunct). A junta (also junto) may describe a cabal or conspiracy. The typical Latin American junta consisted of representatives of the various armed forces – the army, navy and air force. The Argentinian junta that unsuccessfully engaged in war with Britain over the Falkland Islands (Las Malvinas) in 1982 was deposed and democratic government reinstalled. The word *junta* was originally used in Spain and Italy to describe an administrative council.

K

Kafkaesque
conveying a feeling of being real and unreal at the same time

concatenation
means a linking together, from the Latin *cum* 'with' and *catena* 'chain'. The following sentence contains the longest concatenation of prepositions in English: 'Come on out from in under that bed!' A heaping together of unconnected things or ideas might be called a congeries, from the Latin *congerere* 'to pile up', or a conglomeration

Franz Kafka was born in Prague, the son of a rich Jewish Czech merchant. He studied law and became a clerk in an insurance office, but his real interest was in writing. After a while he gave up his job and settled down in Berlin to write. A concatenation of circumstances – his bad relations with his father, his unsatisfactory love-life, his poverty – all played on his hypersensitive nature and broke down his health. He died of pulmonary tuberculosis (*pulmo, pulmonis* is the Latin 'lung'). In *The Trial*, which was published the year after he died, the famous Kafkaesque feeling is created through an account of the experiences of a man, simply called K, who is given to understand that he is to be arrested on a charge that no one will specify.

Some people describe their experience of dealing with bureaucracy as Kafkaesque.

Keynesian
embodying the thinking of the British economist, John Maynard Keynes

Keynes (pronounced kanes) was centrally concerned with the issue of how the economy might be managed so as to achieve full employment. He saw the level of total demand (consumption plus investment) as crucial. If total demand was not great enough, he urged governments to intervene to increase it. They might do this by direct action, such as building roads, by indirect action, such as giving entrepreneurs incentives to invest or cutting taxation to stimulate consumption, or by a combination of both. If total demand were running at too high a level (and creating inflation, itself a threat to employment), he felt governments should seek to moderate it by restrictive measures. He also saw that the government might need to stimulate demand for goods and services through the medium of a budget deficit, which would increase total demand by making available the money borrowed to meet the deficit.

kibbutz(im)
Jewish communal society in which the means of production are owned by all, and work and its produce are shared by all

The impoverished Jews of Russia, ghettoized and forbidden to own land, found socialism an attractive ideology. In response to the pogroms of the late nineteenth century there began a movement among them that harnessed their yearning for the traditional pastoral life and a commitment to socialist principles: groups of them would return to Palestine and set up cooperative farming settlements.

They were also determined to abandon the traditional pacifism of the Jews when attacked – they would defend themselves. Defiantly self-sufficient, they worked cooperatively and defended their settlements themselves. (Reinforcing their socialist principles was the fact that the land was so poor it required a collective effort to work it.) The 270 or so kibbutzim – the first was established in 1909 by Jews from Russia – are a notable but numerically small element of Israeli social organization.

The suffix *im* is a Hebrew plural form; hence cherub, cherubim and seraph, seraphim (orders of angels). The Arabic equivalent is *in*; hence fellah, fellahin (Egyptian peasants) and Bedouin (tent-dwelling nomadic Arabs, derived by the French from the Arabic *badawin* 'dwellers in the desert').

Sephardim
is the name given to the Spanish Jews who fled the anti-Semitism of fifteenth-century Castile – *Sefarad* is the Hebrew 'Spain'

angel
derives from the Greek *angelos* 'messenger' or 'bringer of news'. To evangelize is to proclaim the Good News (Greek *eu* – *ev* before a vowel – 'good' and *angelos*) or Gospel (Old English *god* 'good' and *spell* 'story')

kinetic
relating to, characterized by, or caused by, motion

Kinetic is derived from the Greek *kinein* 'to move' and also gives us cine, cineaste, and cinema; kinetic art is art, especially sculpture, that moves or has moving parts.

kudos
acclaim, glory

A person who is acclaimed as the one who crucially contributed to an achievement is said to have received the *kudos* (Greek 'praise') for it. He or she might also be said to have received an accolade for it (*accollare* is the Latin 'to hug', the ceremonial gesture once used to confer knighthood).

L

labour force
the total number of people at work or available for work

Labor, laboris is the Latin 'work' (from which we also derive laborious, elaborate, collaborate and laboratory). A country's capacity to produce goods and services depends partly on the numbers in the labour force and on the skills they possess. The labour force comprises employers, employees, self-employed persons, and all those unemployed.

lacuna
gap

Lacuna means a gap, from the Latin *lacuna* 'pool' or 'cavity': 'This book fills a lacuna in the literature on avant-garde French art.' Hiatus, from the Latin *hiare* 'to gape', is a synonym. Caesura, from *caedere, caesum* 'to cut' is technically a pause, especially for sense, usually near the middle of a verse line but it may be used more generally:

> Ever the polite hostess, Grace once asked a lady writer what she was working on. When the lady writer answered, 'Actually, I'm writing about ... Evil,' Grace was radiant: 'Oh, how I wish', she said without so much as a caesura of a pause, '*I* had thought of that!'
> –Gore Vidal, *NYRB*, 28 February 2002

Notice how even so famously fastidious a writer as Gore Vidal can slip into pleonasm – here in the adjectival use of the phrase 'of a pause'. (The reason is probably the cruel necessity both to use the *mot juste* – caesura rather than, say, lacuna or hiatus – and, in courtesy to the reader, to provide the essential sense of the relatively rare technical term the *mot juste* is.) Phrase from the Greek *phrasis* 'speech' is a group of words forming part of a clause; in music it is a unit of melody. Phraseology is the manner in which words and phrases are used. To paraphrase is to put something into other words to clarify it. Periphrasis is a roundabout way of saying something (*peri* is the Greek 'around'), a circumlocution (from the Latin *circum* 'around' and *locutio, locutionis* 'phrase').

law
rules established by the authority of custom or judges or the legislature and promulgated and

The third power of government (after the legislative and executive powers) is the judicial or judging power (*judex, judicis* is the Latin 'judge'). It is exercised in regard to two kinds of cases, criminal and civil.

In criminal cases (*crimen, criminis* is the Latin

'crime') a man or woman is tried for breaking a law, whether an important or a minor one. The accused may be either convicted or acquitted. If convicted he or she may be given a prison sentence or a fine or both. There is a system of appeals.

In civil cases (*civilis* is the Latin 'pertaining to a citizen') a person (the plaintiff) brings an action against an individual or body (the defendant), for example a private company or the State, to seek damages for injuries done, to enforce a contract, or to get an injunction (a court order to ensure the defendant refrains from some action the plaintiff believes would unlawfully injure the plaintiff or his or her interests). There is a system of appeals.

Where issues arise from the interpretation of the constitution, they are usually settled by a supreme court or a special constitutional court, as specified in the constitution.

Jurisprudence is the science or knowledge of law (*juris* is a form of the Latin *jus* or *ius* and means 'of law'; *prudentia* is the Latin 'knowledge'; in Rome lawyers or jurists were called *juris prudentes* 'men knowledgeable in the law').

Jurisdiction is the power to apply the law or the area to which the power extends, for example within the jurisdiction (*dictio, dictionis* is the Latin 'saying' from *dicere, dictum* 'to say').

The word civil is also employed in naming one of the two international families into which much of the legal world is divided – the civil law and the common law jurisdictions. The division developed in Europe during the period between 1350 and 1600 AD. Civil law, based on the *ius civile* ('the law relating to citizens') of ancient Rome, permeated the jurisdictions of continental Europe, flourishing in the Renaissance enthusiasm for all things Roman. It lays an emphasis on written law, which through careful codification is applied to specific cases. It failed to penetrate the English legal profession (and therefore the jurisdictions of those countries that later came under the sway of British imperialism). In England the national traditional judge-made rules persisted and were applied uniformly by a single body of judges – hence the term common law. Common law lays an emphasis on case-law.

enforced by the State for the common good

left/centre/right
the range of political thought and organizations, conceived as moving in an arc from anarchism at one extreme to right-wing dictatorship at the other

When in June 1789 King Louis XVI of France capitulated to the wishes of the Third Estate (the representatives of the people) and ordered the three estates to meet together in one assembly, the nobles sat on the king's right (the place of honour) and the Third Estate on his left. In subsequent French assemblies and in other continental parliaments in the nineteenth century, the democratic, liberal representatives took seats on the left of the president's chair. From this practice developed such terms as left, extreme left, leftist, left-wing, left of centre, centre, right of centre, rightist, right-wing, extreme right.

The left ranges from anarchists to communists, socialists and social democrats, the right from fascists to conservatives. The centre seeks to draw support from both left and right.

continent(al)
derives from the Latin *terra continens* 'continuous land'. *Terra* also gives us terrain; territory; terrestrial; extraterrestrial; terracotta (literally baked earth, from the Italian *cotta* 'baked'), unglazed brownish-red earthenware; *terra firma*, the solid earth (the Latin *firma* is 'firm'); and *terra incognita*, an unexplored land or region

legislature
institutions of government that make or repeal laws

Lex, legis is the Latin 'law' (from which we also get legal and legislation). The legislature is the law-making body; it can also repeal or amend laws.

leitmotiv
leading theme

Leiten is the German 'to lead'; *Motiv* is 'motif' (from the Latin *movere, motum* 'to move'). Motif is applied generally in art for any distinctive pattern or theme. A leitmotiv was originally a musical device, a kind of musical tag that identifies a particular character or idea and that recurs in the orchestra at appropriate moments, often with subtle alteration, for example to suggest a change of mood from joy to foreboding.

Perhaps the greatest exponent of its use is Richard Wagner, particularly in the *Ring* where leitmotivs – nearly two hundred in all, for the Rhine gold, Wotan, Siegfried's sword Nothung, etc. – are used to bind together the four operas in the cycle (*Rhinegold*, *The Valkyrie*, *Siegfried* and *The Twilight of the Gods* or *Götterdämmerung*). Claude Debussy, however, was not reverential about this aspect of Wagner's art: he observed that the Wagnerian hero comes on and the orchestra presents his calling card. Leitmotiv is now applied generally: 'A leitmotiv of the party's document on finance is the need to reduce foreign borrowing.'

The verbal (from the Latin *verbum* 'word', which also gives us verbiage and verbose) component *leit* also occurs in gauleiter. *Gau* means 'district' in German; *Leiter* means 'leader'. The *Gau* was the regional unit of

orchestra
derives from Greek drama – it was the place in front of the stage where the chorus danced, *orchesthai* being the Greek 'to dance'.

verbose
meaning wordy has a synonym in prolix meaning long-winded, from the Latin *pro* 'forward' and *liqui* 'to flow'. A particularly verbose or prolix person may be said to be suffering from logorrhoea, from the Greek *logos*, here 'word', and *rhoia* 'flow'

the Nazi Party's organization. The party official who headed a *Gau* was called a *Gauleiter*. Because of the demeanour of many of these, gauleiter came to be applied generally to anyone who wielded petty authority in an overbearing manner.

lèse-majesté
the offence of insulting a person of high position

This French expression derives from the Latin *laesa* 'hurt' (from which we also derive lesion for an injury or wound) and *majestas* 'majesty'. The ninth-century Irish neo-platonist scholar John Scottus Eriugena headed the school at the court of the French king Charles the Bald. Once when he was in the group dining and wining with the king, he being at one end of the table and the king at the other, the king could not resist making a pun at John Scottus Eriugena's expense: 'Can anyone tell me the difference between an Irishman [*Scottus* in Latin] and a drunkard [*sottus*]?' John Scottus shot back: '*Mensae mensura.*' (Latin, 'The length of the table.') The company dissolved in laughter – and so did the risk of *lèse-majesté*.

John Scottus Eriugena is to be distinguished from the more famous Franciscan scholar Johannes Duns Scotus who was born in Scotland and from whose name dunce is derived: sixteenth-century humanists used the word to ridicule his followers. Ironically, Duns Scotus was a most subtle philosopher.

liberal arts
all university subjects other than the scientific, technical or professional

The term liberal in relation to education goes back to classical times, the Latin *liber* 'free' suggesting a distinction between the education appropriate to a freeman and a workman. When Samuel Pepys refers to himself in his diary as a man of liberal genius he means he is temperamentally inclined to gentlemanly pursuits and studies. The term liberal arts was employed in the Middle Ages to name the seven subjects that formed the basis of secular learning – arithmetic, astronomy, geometry, music, grammar, rhetoric and logic – upon which rested the supreme art of philosophy. The genius of the Renaissance artists brought about the recognition of painting and sculpture as liberal arts. Arts in the expression arts degree flows from this usage.

The liberal arts embrace the humanities (a distinction derived from the idea that there were three kinds of objects of knowledge: the divine, natural and human) – the study of philosophy, literature (especially the ancient classics), language and the fine arts. *Les beaux arts* (French, 'the fine arts') was coined by Charles Batteaux to distinguish between the useful and the beautiful arts. The fine arts have become established as painting, sculpture, architecture, writing and music.

Liberal studies is a supplementary arts course for students specializing in scientific, technical or professional studies.

architecture
is a hybrid, being both a useful and a beautiful art. In universities it is often located with engineering: you need engineering knowledge and skills to practise it. However, you need aesthetic sensibility and skills to practise it successfully

liberalism
a body of political beliefs that stresses the rights of the individual within the State (as opposed to the rights of the community, which are stressed by socialists) and the development of economic and political institutions that favour the free market in production and distribution

Liber is the Latin 'free'. Liberalism developed in Europe in the late seventeenth century in opposition to the arbitrary, despotic rule then prevalent. It sought to limit the powers of governments over their citizens through such measures as the enactment of written constitutions and bills of rights, and the extension of the franchise. It located the source of authority not in custom and tradition or religious beliefs but in the idea that every man had by nature inalienable rights.

Totalitarianism is therefore anathema to liberals (*anathema* means 'accursed' in Greek; the word was used in the early Church as a solemn denunciation of a person or thing – 'Let him/it be anathema!'). It is difficult to define liberalism because it has taken many different forms at different periods in different countries. However, political liberalism – liberal democracy – asserts the right of individuals to choose their form of government and to participate in the choice of members of the government and in the conduct of public affairs. This derives from a view of man as autonomous, rational and self-interested, and of the State as properly concerned to maximize freedom by, among other things, adopting *laisser-faire* policies in economic affairs. Liberals, then, seek to build the institutions of government in such a way that the freedom of the individual is interfered with as little as possible.

They favour private property and free trade, factors that enable the individual to maintain and extend his or her freedom. Prizing freedom far more than equality, they are not egalitarian (which would require equality of material as well as other benefits) but they do favour equality of opportunity because they see that as a condition for their understanding of freedom in society (egalitarian is derived from the Old French *égal*, itself derived from the Latin *aequalis* 'equal'). Socialists regard the liberals' endorsement of equality of oppor-

libertine
also derives from *liber*. Holding himself free from any moral law, a libertine is a morally dissolute person

maximize
means to achieve or seek to achieve the maximum – the highest point or greatest amount attainable (from *maximus*, the superlative form of *magnus*, the Latin 'great'). Minimum is the lowest point or least amount attainable (from *minimus*, the superlative form of *parvus*, the Latin 'small').

A maximalist is someone who holds out for the maximum of his or her demands and rejects compromise – the Bolsheviks were maximalists. A minimalist is someone who seeks, or is prepared to accept, a minimum; in art a minimalist seeks to

tunity as a hollow assurance that the satisfactions of life are open to everyone – like the Ritz Hotel.

For liberals religion and morality are private matters and have minimal bearing on the economic and political orders. Liberals, therefore, seek to withdraw religion and morality from the public arena into the arena of the private – they call for the separation of Church and State. The modern notion of pluralism flows from this. It asserts that one's moral vision and actions are one's own concern and not that of the State, unless they result in harm to others. Harm is narrowly defined in terms of a threat to life and property. Otherwise liberals advocate as much tolerance as possible and a minimalist approach to legislation, especially in the area of morality, which is interpreted in a narrow sense referring mostly to sexual and related matters. The way we produce and distribute wealth, for example, is rarely seen by liberals as a moral issue.

Critics of the liberal position on morality in public affairs assert that it assumes that large areas of life covered by law and controlled by institutions are morally neutral. All laws and institutions, they say, have a moral dimension: laws are by their nature normative, and institutions operate through policies that are also by their nature normative. Thus, by seeking to exclude moral debate from certain areas of life, liberals, their critics say, are really legitimating the application of their own morality and suppressing that of others. (That is why Marx called liberalism an ideology.)

In the nineteenth century liberals aligned themselves with nationalist movements with a view to enhancing individual freedoms. Nowadays they tend to favour supranational bodies such as the European Union and the United Nations because they see them as providing stronger guarantees of freedom than nation states (*supra* is the Latin 'above').

communicate using the least possible intervention – thus Samuel Beckett is probably the most famous minimalist in modern writing

illiberal
is the opposite of liberal, from the Latin negative *in* – *il* before a word beginning with l. Hence also illegal, illegitimate, illicit, illimitable, illiterate and illogical

lobby
to seek to influence legislators to pass laws favourable to one's own or group interest

Lobia is the late Latin 'portico'. A lobby is the antechamber to a legislative hall and therefore an apt place to waylay legislators.

In Washington DC lobbying is a formally recognized function: there are some 11,000 registered lobbyists who are retained by a plethora of special interest groups, ranging from foreign countries to local trade associations, to bring pressure to bear on legislators (*plēthōra* is the Greek 'fullness' used in English for an excessively large number). Lobby, by extension, may mean a special-interest group – thus the gun lobby is those Americans who organize themselves to prevent any curtailment of the citizen's right to possess firearms.

In Britain the Westminster lobby correspondents are a group of journalists who are given briefings by ministers on controversial issues, attributable by convention only to an anonymous 'reliable source'.

local government
the system of local authorities which carry out a range of functions delegated to them by the legislature

Locus is the Latin 'place', from which we get local as well as locality, location, allocate and dislocate.

Historically, the central government depended on local authorities to carry out certain functions of government in their areas such as the provision of roads, housing, water supply and libraries. (*Liber, libri* is the Latin 'book', from which library derives. The Romans wrote their books on long strips of paper rolled around a stick – they called such a roll a *volumen*, from the Latin *volvere, volutum* 'to roll' – hence our volume and voluminous. A volute, also from *volvere*, means a spiral form such as the spiral scroll that distinguishes Ionic capitals.)

Modern communications allow central government to act directly in areas throughout a state by setting up local offices reporting to it. In addition a number of other state agencies may have local offices in an area. Local authorities, then, are by no means the only public service bodies to be found locally.

lynch law
summary punishment of lawless or suspected persons usually by hanging, carried out by unauthorized people

The sheriff who faces down a mob that wants to lynch his jailed but innocent prisoner is a topos of western movies. Charles Lynch was a Virginian farmer and patriot who, during the American War of Independence, headed an irregular court formed to punish Loyalists.

M

Machiavellian
relating to the principles of Machiavelli or, more generally, a description for a person who is devious, cunning and unscrupulous

Niccolò Machiavelli was born in Florence, the son of a lawyer. When he was twenty-four, the ruling Medici family was driven from the city and Machiavelli got a job with the new republican government as a civil servant. When the Medici regained power in 1512, Machiavelli was jailed and tortured.

On his release he retired and wrote books. The most famous of these was *The Prince*. It established Machiavelli as the father of modern political science – the study of statecraft. Traditionally philosophers had contemplated the perfect State and deduced the qualities of the good prince who should rule it. In contrast Machiavelli adopted the empirical, experimental approach that was to transform the natural sciences. The material of his study, he pointed out, was provided by the lessons of ancient things and the experience of modern ones.

He concluded that there were two attributes necessary for a State to sustain itself. The first was to have at its disposal sufficient force to defend itself against its enemies and to enlarge its boundaries when desirable. The second was to have the internal political cohesion that derives from a balance between the force of consent from below and that of compulsion from above. History provided numerous examples of states that had only the first attribute – despotic empires that turned out to be giants with feet of clay. It also provided examples of states with only the second attribute – the Greek city-states each with its great internal solidarity but also with a fatal weakness of fighting against its neighbours.

How should a ruler act to make his state great? Not by being Christian – gentle, just, compassionate – but by being ruthless, aggressive, proud, Machiavelli says, 'A prince who wishes to maintain his power must know how to do wrong, when necessary.' Deceit is a diplomat's best weapon. Whatever is good for the State is good. A *raison d'état* (French, 'a reason enunciated by a ruler or government as springing from the needs of the State') has a supreme value.

The morality of *The Prince* was so anti-Christian that in time Machiavelli's first name was transferred to Satan: Old Nick.

magnum opus
a masterpiece

Magnum, the neuter form of *magnus*, is the Latin 'great'; *opus*, *operis* is 'work'. The words are usually applied to an artist's crowning achievement. (Opus is also used in numbering musical compositions. A form of it occurs in scholarly footnotes – *op.cit.*, from the Latin *opere citato* 'in the work cited'.) The word masterpiece derived from a practice of the town craft guilds of the Middle Ages. In order to be admitted to a guild and so become a master, a journeyman had to submit his masterpiece to the guild (a journeyman was a hireling, originally someone paid by the day – *journée* is the French 'day' derived from the Latin *diurnus* 'daily'). If the guild were satisfied, the journeyman was admitted to membership.

opera
the plural form of *opus*, is used as a singular noun in English (following the Italian) – opera – to describe a drama presented in music and song

majority
the greater number

Major is the comparative form of *magnus*, the Latin 'great', and means 'greater'. Democracy works on the basis of decision by a majority. The principle is often applied to carry a decision for the course of action that the greatest number of people vote for. Such a majority is a simple majority. In some cases the greatest number may not be an absolute majority. An absolute majority is any number greater than half of the votes. An absolute majority that must reach a specified level beyond 51 per cent, say 60 per cent, is called a qualified majority.

In order to rule comfortably a government usually requires an absolute majority of the seats in parliament. However, for various reasons, a minority government, i.e. where the government does not have an absolute majority, may provide stable government (minority derives from the Latin *minor* 'lesser').

Rule by majority could degenerate to authoritarian or even mob rule. To protect individuals and minorities liberal constitutions provide for the protection of a range of basic, imprescriptible human rights through appeal to the courts. The attitude of someone committed to decision by a majority *simpliciter* (Latin 'simply') or *tout court* (French, 'without qualification') might be called majoritarian.

authoritarian
means characterized by insistence on strict adherence to the rules of some authority. Author derives from the Latin *auctor*, which itself derives from *augere*, *auctum* 'to increase': an author is someone who grows or originates something. From being an originator comes power – authority. *Auteur*, the French 'author', is applied to a film director who imposes his or her signature on films in terms of a distinctive subject, style and form

The word majority is also used in Britain to denote the number of votes by which a successful candidate exceeds those of his or her nearest rival.

The silent majority is an American political concept that denotes the supposed conservative majority of the people in contrast to the vociferous liberals who are thought to command the media (*vox, vocis* is the Latin 'voice', *ferre* is the Latin 'to carry').

malapropism
the unintentional misuse of a word by confusion with one of a similar sound

The word comes from Mrs Malaprop, a character in *The Rivals* by Richard Brinsley Sheridan who had a penchant for such statements as, 'She's as headstrong as an allegory on the banks of the Nile.' Another famous malapropism occurs in *Juno and the Paycock* by Sean O'Casey, 'The whole world's in a state of chassis.'

mandate
the sanction given by the electors to the government to act in accordance with their election manifesto

Mandare, mandatum is the Latin 'to command'; *mandatum* is 'that which has been commanded'. The basic mandate a democratic government receives from the electorate is to govern in the common interest in accordance with the constitution. Endorsement of its election manifesto strengthens a government's capacity to take specific actions. However, if governments find that their manifesto or elements of it cannot be implemented, or if they find that actual conditions demand actions contrary to their manifesto, they feel they have the right to continue in office: they fall back on the basic mandate to govern.

In law a *mandamus* (Latin 'we command') is an order made by a superior court to an inferior tribunal or public official or agency to carry out a specific public duty.

mania
dipsomania, egomania, erotomania, kleptomania, megalomania, monomania, nymphomania and pyromania – these are all words whose common suffix *mania* means 'madness' in Greek

Dipsomania is the condition of the alcoholic (*dipsa* means 'thirst' in Greek).

Egomania is the condition of someone excessively self-centred (*ego* is the Latin 'I').

Erotomania is the condition of someone with abnormally strong sexual desires (Eros, Erotos is the Greek god of love; homoerotic relates to anything designed to arouse sexual desire among persons of the same sex, *homos* being the Greek 'same').

Kleptomania is the condition of someone who cannot resist the impulse to steal (*kleptein* is the Greek 'to steal').

Megalomania is the delusion that one is powerful; it is often applied to a passion for big things (*megalo*, like *mega*, is a Greek prefix meaning 'big').

Monomania is a madness focused on a single object (*monos* is 'single' or 'alone' in Greek).

Nymphomania is used to describe a neurotic condition in women in which they feel compelled to have

nymph
The Greeks called their wood-nymphs dryads (*drys* is the Greek 'oak-tree'). Keats in 'Ode to a Nightingale' addresses his subject pleonastically as 'light-winged Dryad of the trees'. They called their water-nymphs naiads (*naein* is the Greek 'to flow'). Walter Scott in 'The Lady of the Lake' refers to 'the guardian Naiad of the strand'

sexual intercourse with as many men as possible (*nymphē* is the Greek 'bride'; in Greek mythology, a nymph was also one of the female divinities who lived in woods, rivers, mountains, etc.).

mania
is a mental illness characterized by elation and violence. A maniac is someone who suffers from mania (such a person may be described as manic or maniacal). Maniac has come to be used as a denigratory term (*nigrare*, *nigratum* is the Latin 'to blacken') for anyone deemed to be mentally ill. Hypomania (*hypo* is the Greek 'under' or 'below') is the term used to describe the less intense state of euphoria and excessive drive seen in bipolar (having two – *bi* is a Latin prefix indicating 'two' – poles) affective disorder, or manic depression, a condition much more common than true mania. The suffix *mane* denotes 'enthusiast' rather than a mad person – thus a balletomane is a fan of ballet. The suffix *ast* or *aste*, as in enthusiast and cineaste, also indicates 'keen interest'. Aficionado (from the Spanish *aficion* 'affection') means a fan.

Pyromania is the condition of someone who cannot resist starting fires (*pyr* is the Greek 'fire', which also gives us pyre). Pyracanth is a thorny evergreen shrub that fruits in fiery red berries (*akanthos* is the Greek 'thorn'). Pyrotechnics is a display of fireworks (*technikos* means 'skilled' in Greek). Arson, the unlawful act of setting fire to another's property, derives from the Latin *ardere* 'to burn' (from which we also derive ardent). An incendiary is someone who maliciously sets fire to property or foments trouble (*incendere* is the Latin 'to kindle'). Incandescent is glowing white hot, derived from the Latin *candere* 'to glow' and *in*, a particle denoting 'intensity'. To ignite is to set on fire, derived from the Latin 'fire' *ignis* (from which we also derive ignition and igneous). To scintillate is to sparkle (*scintilla* is the Latin 'spark'; used as a noun in English it means a hint or a trace: 'There wasn't a scintilla of evidence to connect him to the crime.')

Manich(a)ean
relating to the dualist syncretic system of religious doctrines taught by the third-century Persian prophet Mani

In philosophy dualism (from the Latin *duo* 'two') seeks to explain the striking dichotomies between good and evil, light and dark, matter and spirit by postulating that the universe has been ruled from its origins by two conflicting powers, one good, the other evil, both existing as equally ultimate first causes. The Manichaeans regarded matter – and therefore the whole material world – as evil. Salvation, meaning release from the material world to the spiritual world, could be achieved only through extreme asceticism. The Cathars (believed to derive from the Greek *katharoi* 'the pure' – see catharsis) or Albigensians (Albi was a town in Languedoc where some of the Cathars lived) of twelfth- and thirteenth-century Provence embraced the dualist doctrine, although professing Christianity, and were persecuted as heretics. They relied on itinerant teachers rather than a Church hierarchy. They embraced simplicity and poverty and were a reproach to the opulence of the higher clergy. That may account for the particular fury of the crusade against them. In modern usage Manichean connotes a sensibility that finds the body and the material world repulsive. Martin

to postulate
is to assume or require, from the Latin *postulare*, *postulatum* 'to ask for'

heretics
are people who hold unorthodox views; heresy derives from the Greek *hairesis* 'a choosing'

in Voltaire's *Candide* is the best-known such Manichean in literature.

Chinese philosophy also recognizes two primary principles – the Yin and the Yang – but they are complementary rather than opposed. The *Yin* (Chinese 'dark') is negative, dark and feminine, the *Yang* (Chinese 'bright') is positive, bright and masculine. Their interaction maintains the harmony of the universe. (Complementary from the Latin *complere* 'to fill up' refers to something which completes or fulfils something else; complimentary also derives from the Latin *complere* but through the Spanish *complir* 'to complete', in the sense of doing what is fitting or polite.)

Dualism is opposed by monism (from the Greek *monos* 'single'). Monism has two major forms: materialism (only the material world is real) and idealism (only the mental or spiritual world is real). Dualism is also opposed by pluralism (there are more than two first causes).

Finally, dualism is applied to modern man's tendency since Descartes to view nature as comprising subjects and the objects outside themselves that they experience:

> The bifurcation of nature into two kinds of entity – mind and matter, subject and object, observer and observed – became a built-in part of Western man's way of looking at the world. To this day it is referred to by philosophers as 'Cartesian [from Descartes] dualism'.
>
> –Bryan Magee, *The Story of Philosophy*

bifurcation
means the forking or division into two parts from the Latin *bi* 'two' and *furca* 'fork'

manifesto
a political party's statement of the policies it will follow if it is elected to govern

Manifesto is an Italian word meaning 'placard' or 'poster'. A manifesto is now usually a document issued before an election that sets forth the policies a party will follow in relation to such issues as the economy, employment, social welfare, housing, education, the environment and taxation. It is a useful document for party workers canvassing at doors and for briefing the media.

The most famous manifesto was the *Communist Manifesto* written by Karl Marx and Friedrich Engels and published in 1848: 'Let the ruling classes tremble at a communist revolution. The proletarians have nothing to lose but their chains. They have a world to win.'

marathon
a race on foot of 42.195 kilometres; any long, tough task

Marathon is a place in Attica twenty-two miles from Athens. Here in September 490 BC about 11,000 Greeks (nearly all of them Athenians) defeated 30,000 Persians and put an end to the attempt by the Persian King Darius to conquer Greece. (His son Xerxes, ten years later leading an even more ambitious assault on Greece, was to go down to even more ignominious defeat at the great sea-battle at Salamis.) When they turned the tide against Darius's forces, the Athenians despatched the fast runner Pheidippides to the then unwalled city where news of the outcome of the battle was anxiously awaited. This heroic run gave English the word marathon. The marathon has been an Olympic event from the start of the modern Olympics.

mass media
newspapers, journals, television, radio and any other instruments of communication with the public

Media is the plural form of the Latin *medium* 'the middle': a medium is literally a thing in the middle – a channel – through which a message is carried from a sender to a receiver. The channels we have for reaching the population – the mass media – are described as either print (predominantly newspapers and magazines) or electronic (predominantly radio, television and the Internet). From medium we also derive mediate and intermediary.

Mass derives from the Latin *massa,* 'a body of matter that can be moulded', which in turn probably derives from the Greek *massein* 'to knead [like dough]'. It came to be applied to the broad bulk of the population, the masses. Saint Augustine refers to the *massa damnata* (Latin, 'the condemned mass') when he means the whole of humanity except those whom God has gratuitously (without obligation, from the Latin *gratia* 'favour') saved.

The masses is a dehumanizing term. The masses have no individuality or subtlety of feeling – they simply exhibit mass reaction. They are the products of an admass culture (the term is J.B. Priestley's) which, promoted by the mass media, secures monetary endorsement of the products and services offered by advertisers to underpin an unthinking consumerist culture. In *The Intellectuals and the Masses* John Carey exposes how the artistic and academic establishments used the masses to justify a disdain for common humanity and the development of an elitist culture that the masses would necessarily find esoteric.

The term critical mass was first applied in nuclear fission to the minimum quantity of radioactive material needed for a chain reaction. It is now applied generally: 'The classic problem for a conspiracy is how to achieve critical mass while maintaining secrecy.'

materialism
the view that nothing exists but matter. (Materialists, therefore, deny the existence of spiritual, i.e. non-material, beings such as God)

Materia is the Latin 'timber' or 'building materials', and the word matter, derived from it, has come to mean the basic constituent of reality. Marx has been described as a materialist philosopher. By that it is meant that he believed man's endeavours to meet the material conditions of existence determined the character of his social and moral relationships. History is the fruit of that process. Hence the Marxist view of history is called historical materialism.

maverick
an American expression meaning unbranded stock, unorthodox

A Texas lawyer, Samuel A. Maverick, took possession of a herd of cattle in payment of a debt in 1845. Not being a cattleman, he took little interest in them – he did not even realize the importance of branding them – and loosed them on an island to multiply naturally. Eight years later he had the herd brought to the mainland. Surprisingly, it seemed not to have increased. What had happened was that numerous cowpokes had roped some of the cattle for themselves – the law of the range allowed anyone to take possession of unbranded cattle. The men who took the cattle came to be called mavererickers and unbranded cattle came to be described as maverick. Transferred to people, maverick connotes someone who is wayward, eccentric – an outsider. Thus a maverick politician is one who does not belong to any party or who, if he or she does, is conspicuously nonconformist.

mesmerize
spellbind, hypnotize

Franz Anton Mesmer was a Viennese physician who developed a theory of animal magnetism (*anima* is the Latin 'breath' or 'spirit'; an animal is a living organism) to explain how one person might exercise power over another from a distance by relying on a special invisible fluid to carry the power just as, according to Newtonian physics, a magnet could attract nails to itself from a distance by relying on aether, an invisible fluid that filled all empty space, to carry the magnetic power.

Mesmer's acolytes achieved great popular success in Paris and London. At their seances (the French *séance* 'a sitting', which was later transferred to afternoon ses-

magnet
derives from the Greek *magnes* 'the Magnesian stone'. Magnesia was an ancient mineral-rich region. In his book about the earth's magnetic fields *De Magnete*, William Gilbert coined the term electric from the Greek *electron* 'amber': electricity was first observed when amber was excited by friction

sions in which mediums seek contact with the dead), they made passes over their subjects and put them into a trance state in which they responded to the mesmerizers' commands, for instance to somnambulate (to walk in one's sleep, from the Latin *somnus* 'sleep', which also gives us somnolent, meaning drowsy, and *ambulare* 'to walk'). Their most spectacular successes were when mesmerized patients underwent surgery painlessly.

acolyte
derives from the Greek *akolouthos* 'follower' and in early Christian usage it indicated someone assigned to assist a priest

The medical establishment condemned the theoretical basis of mesmerism and it came to be viewed as quackery. However, it did provoke notable developments. In the 1840s James Braid, a Scottish surgeon, who, like many others, thought mesmerism a psuedoscience, concentrated on the art of what he called hypnotism (from the Greek *hupnos* 'sleep') and produced the trance-like effect of mesmerism without recourse to any of its theoretical structures, by getting the subject to focus on something monotonous (from the Greek *monos* 'alone' or 'single' and *tonos* 'tension' or 'tone'). Some observers suggest that Braid's hypnotism has led to certain advances in modern cognitive science, particularly in the identification of the autonomous nervous system.

cognitive science
is the scientific study of cognition, the mental act or process whereby we acquire knowledge including perception, intuition and reasoning (*cognoscere, cognitum* is the Latin 'to learn')

The development of anaesthetics (*a* – *an* before a vowel – is a Greek negative and *aisthēsis* is 'feeling') using gas and drugs, which was pioneered by the American dentist Horace Wells when in 1844 he used nitrous oxide (laughing gas) in a tooth extraction, received an impetus from a perceived need to provide a scientific alternative to mesmeric anaesthesia.

Detached from science, mesmerism drifted into a swirling interest in mediums who establish contact with the dead, clairvoyants who foretell events (from the French *clair* 'clear' and *voyance*, itself from the French *voir* 'to see'), telepathy, and theosophism (from the Greek *theos* 'god' and *sophia* 'wisdom': any of various religious or philosophical systems that claim as their basis an intuitive insight into the divine nature).

voyeuristic
which relates to a person who gets sexual excitement from observing someone engaged in intimate actions; it also derives from *voir*

the Theosophical Society
– the context in which theosophy is now usually encountered – was founded in 1875 by the Russian mystic Elena Petrovna Blatavsky, author of *Isis Unveiled* and *The Secret Doctrine*, and Annie Besant, and claimed to be based on the sacred writings of Brahmanism and Buddhism. It denied the existence of a personal god

Psychic research and parapsychology (the study of mental phenomena beyond the scope of normal physical explanation, such as telepathy, *para* being here the Greek 'beyond') display a small continuing scientific interest in mesmeric – paranormal – effects.

metaphysical
pertaining to an area of philosophy that discusses the questions left unasked by the particular sciences – the fundamental questions of life and the nature of reality

Meta is the Greek 'after'; physical derives from *phusis*, transliterated *physis*, the Greek 'nature'. Metaphysical is opposed to the concreteness of the physical: it is highly abstract. Metaphysics (after physics) is so called not because of its nature but simply because an early editor of the books of Aristotle listed his work on these questions after his work on physics. (During the Middle Ages physics was displaced by the term natural philosophy. In the eighteenth century physics once more became the preferred term.)

Dr Samuel Johnson, the lexicographer (from lexicon and the Greek *graphein* 'to write') and *littérateur*, introduced the word into literary criticism when he described certain English seventeenth-century poets such as Donne, Marvell and Herbert as metaphysical poets. They raised profound questions that nature poets do not. The elaborate imagery and ingenious conceits of their verse led to its being described as cerebral (Latin *cerebrum* 'relating to the brain') as opposed to naturalistic.

metric
of or relating to metre or the metrical system

The French revolutionaries seized the opportunity to do away with the chaotic congeries (or conglomeration, a thing composed of heterogeneous elements, from the Latin *conglomerare* 'to pull into a cluster') of traditional weights and measures by introducing a standard measure, the metre (from the Greek *metron* 'measure'), divided or multiplied on the decimal (from the Latin *decem* 'ten') system. In 1791 the French Academy of Sciences defined the metre as one ten millionth of the quadrant (a quarter of the circumference of a circle, *quadrans, quadrantis* being the Latin 'quarter') of the Earth's circumference running from the North Pole through Paris to the equator. The original standard metre made of platinum-iridium is kept in Sèvres near Paris. The official measure is no longer based on an artefact: it is defined by the world body on weights and measures as the distance travelled by light *in vacuo* (Latin, 'in a vacuum') in 1/299 792 458 of a second.

Metric weights and volumes are based on the metre length. A gram (from the Greek *gramma*, 'letter' or 'small weight') is the weight of a cubic centimetre of distilled water. A litre (from *litra*, an old Greek measure) is a volume enclosed by a cube whose side is one tenth of a metre.

metre
In prosody, the study of the art of versification, derived from the Greek *prosōidia* 'a song set to music', a metre is the rhythmic arrangement of syllables in verse

symmetrical
and its opposite, asymmetrical (*a* is a Greek negative prefix), have technical meanings in mathematics and science. In common usage symmetrical means having harmony of form based on a proportionate arrangement of parts

The common prefixes to indicate divisional measures are *deci* (one-tenth), *centi* (one-hundredth, from the Latin *centum* 'hundred'), *milli* (one-thousandth, from the Latin *mille* 'thousand', which also gives us the English mile from the Latin *milia passuum* 'thousand paces'), *micro* (one millionth, from the Greek *mikros* 'small') and *nano* (one thousand millionth, from the Latin *nanus* 'dwarf').

The common prefixes indicating multiples are *deca* (from the Greek *deka* 'ten'), *hecto* (from the Greek *hekaton* 'hundred'), *kilo* (from the Greek *khilioi* 'thousand'), *mega* (a million, from the Greek *megas* 'great') and *giga* (a thousand million from the Greek *gigas* 'giant').

hecto
gives us hectometre, hectogram and hectolitre. An are (from the Latin *area* which is directly adopted into English for 'any expanse of a surface') is 100 square metres. A hectare is 100 ares or 10,000 square metres. A metric ton or tonne (from the Latin *tunna* 'large beer cask') is 1000 kilograms

metropolis
the capital city of a country or region

Mētēr, mētros is the Greek 'mother'; *polis* is the Greek 'city' (strictly city-state). The ancient Greeks were great traders. Cities like Athens and Corinth would occasionally send out groups of their citizens to colonize other parts of the Mediterranean (from the Latin *medius* 'middle' and *terra* 'earth', a term that came into use in the seventh century AD. It was the sea in the middle of the known world; the Romans called it *mare nostrum* 'our sea'.) These would establish trading ports like Naples in Italy. A metropolis was originally the mother city of a Greek colony, i.e. the city from which the colonists came.

The metropolitan area of a city is the area controlled by the city council. Metropolitan applied to France in the term metropolitan France refers to the mother country and therefore excludes overseas territories or colonies. A metropolitan in a Christian hierarchy is the bishop of the chief see of a Church province – it is a concept derived from the Greek city-colony relationship.

micro
microbe, microcomputer, microcosm, microeconomics, microphone and microscope – these are all words whose common prefix *micro* derives from the Greek *micros* 'little'

A microbe is a tiny living being (*bios* is 'life' in Greek).

A microcomputer is a small computer (*computare* is the Latin 'to reckon', 'to calculate').

A microcosm is a representation in miniature of something large. Man, with a body made up of interrelated parts and a spirit within it, has been regarded by some philosophers as a microcosm of the world (*cosmos* is the Greek 'universe' – the ordered world in contrast to chaos; order brings beauty and so we call those preparations applied to enhance the beauty of the body, cosmetics). A microcosm reflects on a small scale a macrocosm (*macros* means 'big' in Greek). Just as the word analogy allows us to extrapolate our understanding of something known into something less known, so microcosm allows us to extrapolate our understanding of something small into something large.

Microeconomics is the study of the economics of small units, e.g. shops, factories, in contrast to macroeconomics, which is concerned with the study of the economics of large aggregates, e.g. total production of the economy.

A microphone is a small apparatus for amplifying the voice (*phōnē* is the Greek 'voice'). The word was coined on analogy with telescope by Narcissus Marsh, who founded the first public library in Ireland, in 'An introductory essay on the doctrine of sounds, containing some proposals for the improvement of accousticks'. A megaphone is a non-powered, conical instrument used to trumpet the voice (*megas* is the Greek 'great'). Megaphone diplomacy is a term applied to countries that use the media to conduct their verbal disputes rather than the normal diplomatic channels, which allow for sophisticated, nuanced dialogue (the French *nuer*, from which nuance is derived, means 'to show light and shade').

A microscope is an instrument for magnifying tiny objects (*skopein* is the Greek 'to look at'). When scientists first examined water and other liquids under the microscope, they were surprised to find what looked like little rods floating in them. They called these microscopic organisms bacteria, the plural form of the Greek *bactērion* 'little stick'. A bacillus (plural bacilli) is an infectious bacterium (the Latin form of *bactērion*). *Bacillus* is the Latin 'little rod'.

aggregate
originally adgregate, is those things brought together or made to flock together; from *ad* the Latin 'to' and *grex, gregis* 'flock'. To segregate is to group apart – *se* is a Latin prefix meaning 'apart' – and a segregationist is someone who favours or practises racial segregation; a congregation is a large number of individuals who voluntarily flock together – *con* is a Latin particle that means 'with'; a gregarious person is a sociable person who likes to be in a flock; an egregious person is someone outside the flock – e is the Latin 'out of' – and therefore exceptional, usually in an outrageous way

stentorian
describes a trumpeting voice and derives from Stentor, a Greek herald who became legendary from Homer's description of him in the *Iliad* as having a brazen voice that could shout as loud as fifty other men. He was killed because he had boasted he could shout as loud as Hermes, the herald of the gods

Minoan
pertaining to prehistoric Crete and its culture

In Greek legend, Minos was a powerful king who maintained a thalassocracy based on Crete. Minoan, which is used to denote the Bronze Age culture of Crete from about 3000 BC to about 1100 BC, derives from his name. Pasiphae, his wife, fell monstrously in love with the Cretan bull. The Minotaur (Minos and *tauros,* the Greek 'bull'), the product of their passion, was a fearsome creature with the body of a man and the head of a bull. The Minotaur was kept at the centre of a maze, called the labyrinth, in the royal palace at Knossos. King

labyrinthine
may be applied to any intricate physical arrangements. It probably

derives from the Greek *labrys*, the double-headed axe that was the great Minoan royal symbol. The term Byzantine may be applied to intricate and tortuous psychological interactions. It derives from the character of the politics of Byzantium (Constantinople, now Istanbul), the centre of the eastern Roman empire (330 AD to 1453)

Attic
Attica was the territory in Greece belonging to Athens. Attic means of or relating to Attica, its inhabitants or the dialect of Greek spoken there. Because of the sophistication of the Athenians, Attic style denotes something classically elegant. Thus the philhellenic Keats in his 'Ode on a Grecian Urn' addresses himself to the best of its kind: 'O Attic shape! Fair attitude! with brede / Of marble men and maidens overwrought.'

Attic salt refers to polished wit. Attic meaning a space or room within the roof of a house is so called because such spaces were based on a feature of Attic architecture

excavate
means dig out, from the Latin *excavare* 'to make hollow'; concave means curving inwards, from *cavus* 'hollow'; convex means curving outwards, from *convexus* 'vaulted', 'rounded'

Minos, every ninth year, exacted a tribute from the Athenians of seven youths and seven maidens, and fed them to the ferocious Minotaur. The Attic hero Theseus made a bargain with Minos that if he entered the labyrinth, reached the centre and killed the Minotaur, and made his way back through the maze, Minos would henceforth forgo his tribute. Everyone who had previously entered the maze had got hopelessly lost. However, Ariadne, Minos's daughter, helped Theseus by giving him a ball of yarn that he tied one end of to the entrance gate and used to reach the centre of the labyrinth. There he killed the Minotaur. He then used the yarn to make his way back to the entrance – and the joyful arms of Ariadne.

Creatures that combine human and animal forms like the Minotaur and the centaur (half-man and half-horse) are said to be therianthropic, *thērion* being the Greek 'beast' or 'mammal' and *anthrōpos* 'man'. Therology (also mammology) is the study of mammals. Theriolatry is the worship of animals (*latreia* is 'worship' in Greek; idolatry derives from the Greek *eidōlon* 'image' – *eidos* means 'shape' or 'form' – and *latreia*). The Mayans, who worshipped the jaguar, were theriolatrous.

Sir Arthur Evans, the British archaeologist who excavated and restored the royal palace of Knossos, coined Minoan to differentiate the period from that of the Mycenaean civilization on the Greek mainland dating from about 1500 BC to about 1000 BC, the remains of which were earlier excavated by the German archaeologist Heinrich Schliemann, immortalized by his discovery of the site of Troy in Asia Minor (the Asian part of Turkey called Anatolia).

model

a simplified representation or description of a system or complex entity, especially one designed to facilitate calculations and predictions

Physicists and other scientists use models as analogies to convey an idea of how something works or to predict what will happen if certain of the elements are changed. Experiments need to be carried out on a model to determine whether it is good or bad; a scientist must choose a model that is right for the job he or she has to do.

Model derives from the Italian *modello*, itself derived from the Latin *modulus*, a diminutive form of *modus* 'measure', 'manner'. It is also used for a representation, usually on a smaller scale, of a device or structure, for a standard to be imitated and, most frequently, for someone who wears apparel to display to potential buyers.

Entity (something having real or distinct existence, a thing) derives from the Latin *entitas*, *entitatis*, itself derived from *ens*, *entis* 'being'. A nonentity (*non* is the Latin 'not') is literally a non-existent thing, used often to indicate an insignificant person or thing.

Calculation derives from the Latin *calculus* 'pebble'. In the ancient world pebbles with geometric designs were often used for counting. In *The Importance of Being Earnest* Wilde sagely observed: 'Indeed, no woman should ever be quite accurate about her age. It looks so calculating.'

modus operandi
manner of working

Modus is the Latin 'manner'; *operandi* is a form of *operare*, *operatum* 'to work' (from which we get operation) and means 'of working'. There are usually many ways of doing a job. The particular scheme habitually employed by someone might be described as his or her *modus operandi*. The expression is often used in police circles where criminals may be identified by their MO (*modus operandi*): 'Before he touches anything, he sits down and makes himself a cup of tea.'

modus vivendi
a means of accommodating to one another

Modus is the Latin 'manner'; *vivendi* is a form of *vivere* 'to live' and means 'of living'.When people on bad terms with one another nonetheless succeed in developing procedures that allow them to cooperate, they are said to have worked out a *modus vivendi*. Hostile (*hostis* is the Latin 'enemy'), but not warring, countries also find that they must work out a *modus vivendi* in order to enjoy the benefits of trade and cultural exchange.

In the modern world, before the fall of communism, the two superpowers, America and the Soviet Union (*super* is the Latin 'above' or 'beyond'), worked out a *modus vivendi* that was characterized by periods of sharp competition and confrontation followed by periods of *détente* (a French word meaning 'relaxation').

mogul
an important person

The Mongolian leader Baber overwhelmed India and established the Mogul empire. Mogul derives from the Persian *Mughul*, properly Mongol. We use mogul to indicate a person of great position and power in an area of activity, for example, a film mogul.

film mogul
The film mogul Samuel Goldwyn was celebrated for his solecisms and malapropisms. When he wanted the film rights to Lillian Hellman's smash hit play *The Little Foxes*, his story editor warned him, 'But Mr Goldwyn, it's a very caustic play.' 'I don't give a damn how much it costs,' Goldwyn snapped, 'buy it!' Caustic, meaning capable of burning or corroding by chemical action – and by extension sarcastic – derives from the Greek *kaiein* 'to burn' (which also gives us holocaust)

Tycoon denotes a businessman of great wealth and power and has a connotation of ruthlessness. It derives from the Japanese *taikun*, which in turn derives from the Chinese *ta* 'great' and *chun* 'ruler'.

Mandarin was the term used in the Chinese empire to denote a high-ranking member of the bureaucracy. It is now used to describe a high-ranking official with extensive influence, for example the mandarins in Whitehall. It may be used of a writer with an elevated style or to describe the style itself, for example mandarin prose.

A Brahmin (plural Brahmin or Brahmins) is the word used for a member of the highest or priestly caste among the Hindus. It is applied in the US to a member of the older New England WASP (an acronym for White Anglo-Saxon Protestant) families and has connotations of intellectual and social snobbery.

monetarist

someone who believes strict control of money supply ensures optimum economic performance and price stability

optimum
derives from the Latin *optimus* 'best'. Note that maximum and optimum are not identical terms. The maximum output of a factory is the amount that could be produced if the machinery were kept constantly in operation. The optimum output, broadly speaking, is the greatest amount that can be produced consonant with maintaining the machinery, the morale of the workers and the rate of profit. An optimist is someone who takes a hopeful view of the future. A pessimist is someone who takes a despondent view of the future (*pessimus* is the Latin 'worst')

There was a temple on the Capitoline Hill in Rome dedicated to Juno Moneta (Juno the Reminder; *monere, monetum* is the Latin 'to advise' or 'to warn', from which we derive monitor, monitory and admonition). Juno, the eponymous goddess of the month of June, was the queenly wife of Jupiter. The protectress of marriage (at Roman marriages the knot in the bride's girdle that the bridegroom had to untie was consecrated to her), she was concerned to remind couples of their vows. Beside the temple there was a mint for striking coins that came to be called the *moneta*. From it we derive money, monetary, monetarist and mint.

While Keynesians argue that governments should intervene in the economy to ensure that the greatest possible employment is created consonant with keeping inflation in check, strict monetarists argue that governments should concentrate on creating conditions in which money flows towards those activities that are most efficiently managed and for whose products or services there is a real (not an artificially contrived) demand.

Monetarists believe in free market conditions. Since governments are concerned more with political than with economic benefits, strict monetarists wish to see governments involved as little as possible in the production of goods and services. They feel, moreover, that governments cannot undertake these tasks efficiently. Monetarists, therefore, favour privatization.

The great prophet of modern monetarism was the American economist Milton Friedman. He largely influenced the economic thinking of British conservative ideologues – hence the Thatcherites' obsession at one point with the control of money supply, and their continual concern about inflation (seen by them as a concomitant of Keynesianism).

When economists speak of the government's monetary policy, they are thinking of its strategic decisions in relation to interest rates and money supply. When they speak of the government's fiscal policy, they are thinking of its strategic decisions in relation to taxes and public expenditure. Within the European Union eurozone monetary policy is now entrusted to the European Central Bank (ECB).

monolithic
like a single massive block of stone or characterized by hugeness and impassivity

Monos is the Greek 'alone' or 'single'; *lithos* is 'stone'. A monolith is a large block of stone or anything that resembles one in appearance. Monolithic is usually applied to large, enduring organizations that present a single, impassive front to outsiders: 'The monolithic Soviet state brooked no internal dissent.'

Megalithic pertains to a huge stone, particularly such as is found in prehistoric monuments (*mega* is derived from *megas*, the Greek 'large'; in physics and in the decimal system it denotes million or a million times, for example megavolt).

monopoly
the exclusive supply of, and therefore trade in, some good or service

Monos is the Greek 'alone' or 'single'; *polein* is 'to sell'. In a free market the price a particular good or service can command is determined by the amount that consumers are willing to pay while buying the total quantity of the good or service on offer (the market clearing price). A monopolist has no competitors and therefore can raise the price by restricting supply or simply by fiat. A trader can create a monopoly by cornering the supply of raw materials or the means of turning them into goods, or both. A duopoly (from the Latin *duo* 'two' and *polein*) describes a situation where two traders control a market. It is also used in a general sense: 'A yes vote [in changing the electoral system in Britain] would remove the system of first-past-the-post that discriminates against third parties and entrenches Britain's Tory–Labour duopoly.' (*The Economist*, 23–29 January 1999) Where a small number of traders, but more than two, find themselves in control of a market they are called an oligopoly (*oligos* is the Greek 'little' or 'few'). Where a group of traders conspire to eliminate competition among themselves by, for instance, fixing prices or sharing markets they are said to be a cartel.

A monopsonist is the opposite of a monopolist. It is a person who, or organization which, is the sole buyer for the goods or services of several sellers (*opsōnein* is the Greek 'to buy'). The grocery trade, increasingly concentrated in a small number of supermarket chains, tends towards monopsony. Monopsony allows the buyer to take unfair advantage of sellers.

cartel
means a trust or syndicate of independent enterprises formed to regulate production, pricing and marketing of goods and services and derives in this sense from the German *Kartell*, which described certain commercial and political combinations in Bismarck's Germany. Cartel and *Kartell* derive from the Latin *charta* 'papyrus leaf' – a card. Antitrust law is a body of legal rules prohibiting cartels and other restrictions of competition

multinationals
large companies with production and marketing operations located in a number of countries

Multus is the Latin 'many'; *natio, nationis* is 'nation'. Some multinationals trade in strategically important goods such as oil, minerals and other natural resources. They enjoy great political influence by reason of their size and the importance of their trade. They can play one country off against another. Their very character allows them to avoid the full scrutiny of any one government. Multinational corporations, on the other hand, bring many advantages to late-industrializing countries. They increase output, exports and employment (though not always enough to silence their critics), they provide demonstration effects in the form of showing the latest production methodology, and they bring new technology and modern management techniques.

municipal
pertaining to a town or city that has the status of a corporation

A member of a Roman colony with the right to vote was called a *municeps* (from the Latin *munia* 'official duties' and *capere* 'to take'). The full gathering of *municipes* (plural form) was called a *municipium*. *Municipalis* is the Latin 'pertaining to a *municipium* [a corporation]'.

museum
a place where artefacts of various kinds are stored and exhibited

The Mousai (Greek, the Muses) were the nine daughters of Zeus and Mnemosyne (Memory), each a goddess of one or other of the arts. The Latin *eum* suffix denotes 'place'. A long poetic convention has poets appealing to their muse to give them inspiration. Inspiration might also be ascribed to a divine afflatus (*afflare, afflatum* is the Latin 'to blow upon') or to a person's guardian spirit – their daemon (or daimon), from the Greek *daimōn*, which is sometimes transliterated into English as demon.

inspiration
To inspire is literally to breathe into (from the Latin *in* 'in' and *spirare* 'to breathe'), to influence, especially with exalted ideas or emotions. To conspire is literally to

breathe together (*con* is the Latin 'with'); conspirators agree secretly to act together for a purpose

Mount Parnassus in central Greece with Delphi on its slopes was dedicated to Apollo and the Muses. Parnassus through this association has come to mean the world of poetry. Between 1866 and 1876 a poetic movement called Parnassianism grew up in France – the review *Le Parnasse contemporain* was a major platform for their work – which was a reaction against Romanticism and its sentimentality. The Parnassians aimed at an austere, formal aestheticism. The Symbolists, who followed them, eschewed the art for art's sake (in Latin *ars gratia artis*) principle of Théophile Gautier that inspired the Parnassians; they also rejected realism as inevitably superficial. They sought to present the underlying complexity of life through the use of symbols.

superficial
pertaining to the surface, *super* being the Latin 'above' and *facies* 'face'; supercilious – *cilium* is 'eyelid' – means displaying what the raised eyebrows may do, arrogance, pride or indifference

The Muses and their arts are: Thalia (comedy), Terpsichore (dance), Clio (history), Euterpe (lyric poetry), Erato (love poetry), Urania (astronomy), Calliope (epic), Melpomene (tragedy), Polymnia (sacred song).

We use the term cliometrician (from Clio and the Greek *metron* 'measure') by analogy with econometrician (a specialist in the analysis of economic data) for a historian who uses statistics and computer analysis.

mutatis mutandis
after making the necessary changes

Mutare, mutatum is the Latin 'to change' (from which we also get mutable, immutable, mutant and mutation). The phrase means 'those things having been changed which ought to be changed'. It is a useful expression for a rule-maker who can deploy it in such a way that he or she does not have to repeat *ad nauseam* a rule that can be applied with small, obvious changes to different categories. Thus, 'The customs regulations for the importation of motor cars apply *mutatis mutandis* to spare parts and accessories.'

myrmidon
follower or henchman

The Myrmidons were a race of people whom Zeus made from a nest of ants. They settled in Thessaly. Achilles, their king, led them against Troy where they distinguished themselves for their fierce, marble-hearted, military prowess. We might say, 'In the thirties Stalin and his myrmidons organized the Great Terror that left him the undisputed master of Soviet Russia.'

N

narcissism
an excessive or erotic interest in one's own physical features or mental endowments

In Greek myth Narcissus was such a beautiful youth that many fell in love with him, both young men and women, but he spurned them all, even Echo. One disappointed lover prayed that Narcissus himself would fall vainly in love, and Nemesis heard and granted his prayer.

One day when he was out hunting, Narcissus came upon a spring, clear as silver, and as he cast himself down beside it to slake his thirst he fell in love with the reflection. He tried to embrace and kiss the youth who confronted him but then, realizing it was his own image, he became infatuated (from the Latin *infatuare, infatuatum* 'to fill with foolish passion', *fatuus* being 'foolish', 'fatuous') and lay there gazing at himself hour after hour, day after day. He ate and drank nothing and slowly wasted away, finally laying down his head on the grass and dying. The flowers with white petals and a yellow centre that grew around the pool are called narcissi (plural).

The term narcissism was used by Näcke in 1899 to describe a sexual perversion in which the subject is in love with himself rather that with someone else. It was later extended to include any form of self-love. Since self-esteem is necessary to psychic health, some degree of narcissism is considered normal. Anthony Storr in *Freud* explains:

> Extreme forms of narcissism are exhibited in the type of schizophrenia in which everything that happens in the world is interpreted by the sufferer as referring to himself; in manic states in which the subject considers himself omnipotent; and in states of depression in which the subject may be hypochondriacally preoccupied with his own state of body and mind to the exclusion of all else.

omnipotent
means all powerful, from the Latin *omnis* 'all' and *potens* 'able'. Omnipresent means present everywhere; omniscient means knowing everything, *scire* being the Latin 'to know'; omnivorous means eating any kind of food indiscriminately, *vorare* being the Latin 'to devour'

Hypochondria is a chronic abnormal anxiety about one's health. In anatomy the hypochondrium is the upper region of the abdomen just below the lowest ribs (*hypo* is 'below' in Greek). It was thought to be the seat of melancholy.

Freud postulated a narcissistic stage of emotional development that precedes any investment of libido in objects other than the self.

Natio, nationis is the Latin 'a people' or 'nation'. The concept of nation is not clearly defined but it is important because nationalism gave rise to the political dogma that every nation should have its own state, and that dogma has been the most dynamic force in political history since the nineteenth century.

State derives from *status* the Latin 'condition', 'way of existing' or 'well-being', which itself is derived from *stare, statum*, the Latin 'to stand'. Thus we speak of the state of the country, the state of the arts, and such. From this, the word came to refer to the social and economic conditions of a group of people. Then in the form *état*, as in *États generaux* in French, and estate in English, it came to refer to the large groupings within a kingdom that were regarded as the pillars of society. Dante contrasts a 'free state' (*stato*) with a tyranny, and we see the word beginning to refer to the form of government or to the people governed. The first clear-cut use of State in our sense is found in Machiavelli's *The Prince* – it occurs in the very first sentence. Machiavelli also talks about Italy's being divided into many states, signifying different centres of 'rule over men' and different forms of rule. He discusses 'matters of state'. For him a State is an organization with the capacity to exercise force within a particular territory over its people and against other such states. The first formal theoretical account of State as a legal structure of force and power and controlled by a government understood as a legally constituted power centre came with Hobbes, who equates the Latin *civitas*, 'union of citizens' or 'commonwealth', and State. Though the word did not find general acceptance in this sense in England until the late nineteenth century, it was so used on the continent of Europe in the eighteenth century and from there transferred to the US where the constituent elements of the federal state were referred to as 'the States'.

The defining characteristics of a modern State were set forth in the Montevideo Convention of 1933 held under the aegis of the League of Nations as: (a) a permanent population; (b) a defined territory; (c) government and (d) capacity to enter into relations with the other states.

A State may embrace a whole people and a whole country, like the French state. (A country is a geographic entity forming part of a continent, which itself

nationalism
a concept used to embrace the reasons why a particular group of people have a particular identity and are called a nation or people (common territory, culture, language or religion are the ones usually advanced)

statistics
meaning tabulations of figures, also derives from the Latin *status* – statistics originally related solely to those of a State – and so does the English status for one's social or professional position

theoretical
A theory about something is an attempt to systematize one's knowledge of it, or speculation about it, so that one can describe its working in accordance with the laws underlying the theory and predict how it will work. Theory derives from the Greek *theōria* 'view', itself derived from *theōreein* 'to be a spectator'. Theatre derives from a related word *theatron*, from *theasthai* 'to behold'. In their etymology one can anticipate the dichotomy between theory and practice (or praxis) from *prassein* the Greek 'to do'

may contain regions such as provinces and counties.) It may embrace a number of countries (or parts of them) and a number of nations. Thus the United Kingdom of Great Britain and Northern Ireland consists of three countries (England, Scotland and Wales) and part of a country (Northern Ireland); it consists of three nations (English, Scottish and Welsh) and part of a nation (Irish). It may embrace a part of a nation and a part of a country, like the Republic of Ireland.

natural resources
any attribute of the natural environment that humans consider to be of value in promoting their welfare

Natura is the Latin 'nature', the physical reality of the world. Resource derives from the Latin *resurgere* 'to rise up' and denotes anything to hand that can meet a need. In some discussions the term natural resources is used in a restricted sense to mean timber and other vegetative products, metals, coal, oil and gas. In other discussions it seems to be a compendious term that even includes people ('our greatest natural resource').

finite
derives from the Latin *finire, finitum* 'to limit' and means limited; infinite means without a limit, *in* being a Latin prefix meaning 'not'; definite, from the Latin *definire, definitum* (the *de* particle is an intensifier here), means clearly defined, exact

In discussion it is probably useful to divide natural resources into those that are renewable and those that are not. Minerals and fuels such as coal, oil and gas are non-renewable. (Coal, oil and gas exhaust themselves in use but most metals can be reused through recycling.) Among the renewable resources are water, soil, forests, fish, wildlife, solar and tidal energy, and air. Non-renewable resources are said to be finite.

Neanderthal
relating to Neanderthal man, primitive

Neandertal is a valley (*Tal* in German) near Düsseldorf, where, in the middle of the nineteenth century, remains of a primitive type of man were uncovered – *Homo neanderthalensis* (the *ensis* suffix is Latin and denotes 'native of'). The evolution of modern man – *Homo sapiens* – is traced from *Homo habilis*, who emerged about two million years ago displaying primitive skills (*habilis* is the Latin 'skilful'), to *Homo erectus* who stood erect (*erectus* is the Latin 'upright') and emerged about one and a half million years ago. Neanderthal man was one of the many subspecies of *Homo erectus*, that did not survive competition with *Homo sapiens* – it died out about thirty thousand years ago. Apart from its technical application neanderthal may be used to connote something primitive: 'For about three years [in Trieste, the great port of the Austro-Hungarian empire] Joyce defined himself as a socialist, and the connection with his apparent rejection of Irish nationalism is clear: Tri-

Homo sapiens
was coined by Linnaeus (Latin 'wise man', *sapiens* being 'wise'); so was mammal (from the Latin *mamma* 'breast') and primate (from the Latin *primus* 'first') for monkeys, apes and man. Linnaeus divided all of nature into three kingdoms – animal, plant (or vegetable) and mineral

estine socialists saw the irredentists who surrounded them as neanderthal reactionaries.' (R.F. Foster, *LRB*, 30 November 2000)

nemesis
retribution

retribution
means punishment as a repayment for evil, derived from the Latin prefix *re* meaning 'back' and *tribuere, tributum* 'to give', from which we also derive tribute, attribute, contribute and distribute

Nemesis was a mysterious Greek goddess personifying retribution, directed principally towards humans who have been presumptuous. The Greek *nemein*, from which nemesis is derived, means 'to give someone his [or her] due'. It can specifically represent divine indignation at undeserved good fortune. In Greek tragedy Nemesis is the goddess who brings down all immoderate good fortune, checks the presumption that attends it and is the punisher of ordinary crime. We might say nowadays of the fall of a spectacularly successful speculator 'His nemesis came in the form of a glut of oil on the spot market.'

The only Greek temple dedicated to Nemesis was in Ramnous in Attica.

neo
a prefix meaning 'new', found in words such as neocolonialism, neolithic and neologism

Neos is the Greek 'new'; *neo* may be combined with any historical movement or idea, e.g. neoclassical, neopagan, neo-Gothic, to mean a new or modern form of it.

Neocolonialism is the process by which a strong country gains or retains economic control over a weak country: it buys and controls the country's natural resources or means of production, usually in alliance with a kleptocratic native regime (*colonia* is the Latin 'colony'). Old-style colonialism was naked expropriation of the natives.

Neolithic means new (i.e. later) Stone Age (*lithos* means 'stone' in Greek). The Stone Age is divided by scholars into three periods – Neolithic (the one closest to us), Mesolithic (the one in the middle, *mesos* means 'middle' in Greek), and Palaeolithic (the one most distant, *palaios* means 'old' in Greek). The periods are not absolute but relative to regions or peoples. The terms Palaeolithic and Neolithic were coined in 1865 by John Lubbock, a wealthy neighbour of Darwin, to distinguish the periods in which chipped flint tools and polished ones were used.

A neologism is a newly coined word (*logos* here means 'word' in Greek), like wordgloss.

Naples derives from its original Greek name *Neapolis* 'new city' – hence Neapolitan, meaning pertaining to Naples (*polis* means 'city', strictly 'city-state', in Greek).

neophyte
a novice, a young inexperienced practitioner

Neos is the Greek 'new'; *phytos* is 'sown' or 'planted'. A neophyte was a new convert to Christianity in the early period. The term is now applied generally to mean a beginner or novice (from the Latin *novus* 'new'):

> At 44 Mr Giovanni Goria is the youngest Prime Minister of his country [Italy] in the post-war period. He is not a political neophyte, however, as he has served as Treasury Minister since 1982, and has earned credit for masterminding economic progress in that time.
> –*The Irish Times*, 8 August 1987

The Latin equivalent of neophyte is *tiro* (also *tyro*).

ne plus ultra
the ultimate achievement or goal, perfection

Plus Ultra was the imperial motto of Charles V, the greatest Hapsburg ruler. It was also the name of the flying boat in which Franco's brother Ramón and Captain Julio Ruiz de Alda, one of the future founders of the Falange, crossed the south Atlantic in 1926

Ne is a Latin negative particle; *plus* is 'more'; *ultra* is 'beyond' (so ultra is used as a synonym for extremist). The expression, supposed to have been inscribed on the Pillars of Hercules, the headlands at the Mediterranean end of the Strait of Gibraltar, was a command: 'Let there be no more [sailing] beyond this!' Beyond was the edge of the world – a belief vigorously promoted by those who were exploiting the distant Atlantic trade and wished to discourage others. Atlantic derives from the Latin *Atlanticus* 'relating to Atlas' (Greek *Atlas, Atlantos*). It lay beyond the Atlas Mountains in north Africa.

The most famous use of the phrase in modern times occurred in a declaration by the Irish leader, Charles Stewart Parnell, in 1886 when he was being pressed by Gladstone to declare whether or not the proposed Home Rule Bill would satisfy utterly Irish nationalist aspirations:

> No man has the right to fix the boundary to the march of a nation. No man has a right to say to his country 'Thus far shalt thou go and no further.' We have never attempted to fix the *ne plus ultra* to the progress of Ireland's nationhood – and we never shall.

nepotism
a practice whereby those in authority advance their relatives in preference to others

Nepos, nepotis is the Latin 'nephew' or 'grandson'. Political patronage is reprehensible because it is unfair. Nepotism is a form of patronage denounced even by those who enjoy other forms of patronage. Some of the Popes, especially the Borgias, were notorious for their nepotism; so was Napoleon who placed his brothers and sisters on the thrones of Europe. Nepotism may proceed from more than a simple desire to enrich relatives: where a ruler's grip is shaky, he or she may use nepotism to secure loyalty in certain strategic offices or localities.

A democracy favours meritocratic processes.

neutrality
a policy, recognized in international law, of taking sides with neither party in a dispute or war

Neuter is the Latin 'neither'. The essence of neutrality is not being involved in wars between other states. A state whose neutrality is legally recognized has a right to have its integrity respected by the warring states. It in return must perform certain primary neutrality duties: it must deny the use of its national territory (including airspace and territorial waters), by force if necessary, to all belligerents; it must give no support to belligerents although normal trade may continue; it must apply impartially the rules of neutrality under international law.

Nietzschean
in the manner of the German philosopher Friedrich Nietzsche

Nietzsche, the son of a Protestant pastor, became an atheist early on in life. His thinking led him to proclaim in *Thus Spake Zarathustra* (1883–5) the death of God ('the greatest recent event'), which for him meant mankind's loss of belief in any supernatural power to guide and sustain human life. The death of God led to meaninglessness and relativity, a condition Nietzsche described as 'the unbearable lightness of being' but it also implied that man was master of himself and of the world. It is a matter of debate as to whether Nietzsche was articulating a new philosophy or exploring the implications of a movement that had already begun, namely radical individualism, a form of humanism that put man at the centre of the world. Nietzsche is sometimes described as a nihilist, that is someone who denies an objective moral order.

nihil
is the Latin 'nothing'; the term nihilism was coined by the Russian novelist Turgenev in 1861 in *Fathers and Sons* to describe young rebels in czarist Russia who, disillusioned with the slow pace of reform, were prepared to use any means to change the prevailing conditions

Nietzsche suggested that man now had the freedom to become an Übermensch (German 'superman'; *super* is the Latin 'above' or 'beyond'). People were of either of two mentalities – masters or slaves, an idea Nietzsche explored in *Thus Spake Zarathustra*. Religion fostered the slave mentality. Freed from the fetters of religion, man must define his own ideas of nobility and will them. He defined will as power – hence the expression 'will to power' or more accurately 'will as power'. The Übermensch, by articulating new ideas for himself, charts new avenues of achievement for all and thereby accomplishes what Nietzsche called the transvaluation (or redefining) of values; that is the eternally recurring task of the great man. Nietzsche, therefore, was not a

religion
from the Latin *religio, religionis*, was related by Cicero to *relegere* 'to go over again in thought' and by other Roman writers to *religare* 'to bind'. In both etymologies it denoted man's response to an awareness of the bonds that bound men to the gods. *Religare* derives from the prefix *re* 'again' and *ligare* 'to bind' which also gives us ligature (either the act of binding or a bond itself) and ligament (the bands of tough fibrous tissue that connect bones or support muscles)

hedonist or amoralist – he simply articulated the idea of man as self-creator, an idea that is dominant in modern culture. Some thinkers argue that the pervasive resentment many people feel at having their moral values defined for them by society as traceable to Nietzsche.

The idea held by some existentialists that human life is meaningless and that man must assume responsibility for his values flows from Nietzsche's individualism and will as power. His ideas about the Übermensch, the master race and the will to power were seized upon by the Nazis and made part of their *Weltanschauung*.

Some scholars believe that the popular linking of Nietzsche with the bestiality of Hitler's regime is justified; others vehemently repudiate such an idea. Bestiality derives from the Latin *bestia* 'beast'; *ad bestias* 'to the beasts' was a capital punishment in imperial Rome; a bestiary was a kind of book popular in the Middle Ages containing material on real and imaginary animals.

bête
(French) like beast derives from the Latin *bestia*. A *bête noire* (plural *bêtes noires*), literally 'black beast', is a person or thing that one finds unbearable

nomenclature
terminology

Nomen, nominis is the Latin 'name', from which we also derive nominal, nominate, nominee, and denomination; *calare* is 'to call', from which the *clature* formation derives. In Roman times a *nomenclator* was a slave who accompanied a candidate for office on his rounds and fed him the names of people he was about to meet so that he could address them like long-lost friends. *Nomenclatura*, the word used to describe this practice, transliterated nomenclature in English, has come to mean a system of names. Thus, 'The nomenclature used in classifying flowers is, as you would expect, colourful. The chrysanthemum – a species to which the corn marigold and ox-eye daisy belong – derives its name from *chrysos*, the Greek "gold" and *anthemon* "flower". The heliotrope is so called because it turns with the sun – *hēlios* is the Greek "sun" and *tropein* "to turn".'

Nomenklatura was a word used for the list of communist officials in the eastern European countries.

the heliotropic myth
is a centuries-old concept of history as a succession of great civilizations moving, like the sun, from east to west. In this context, America is the last empire, the fulfilment of history (or fascinatingly, for those who believe history is cyclical, the precursor of a new heliotropic cycle beginning in the east – *cursor* is the Latin 'runner'; *pre* is 'before': precursor means forerunner)

nouveau riche
someone who has recently become rich

Nouveau is the French 'new' and *riche* is 'rich'. The term (plural *nouveaux riches*) is applied to new money and carries a connotation of vulgar display. A parvenu (feminine parvenue), from the French *parvenir* 'to attain', is someone who, having risen socially or financially, is considered an upstart. An arriviste, from the French *arrivist* 'to arrive' is an unscrupulously ambitious person.

novel
an extended work in prose, usually in the form of a story

anthropomorphically derives from the Greek *anthrōpos* 'man' and *morphē* 'shape'. It relates to the attribution of human form, sensibility or behaviour to a deity, animal or any non-human thing. Cartoonists frequently employ anthropomorphism

Novel derives ultimately from the Latin *novus* 'new': a novel is a fiction that explores in narrative form the actions, thoughts, motives, moral dilemmas or emotional relationships of people (or of any animals or things treated anthropomorphically). It is the only major form of literature not developed fully by the ancient classical Greek and Roman writers, and in that sense it is 'new'.

Don Quixote by Miguel de Cervantes and *Pamela* by Samuel Richardson were the earliest significant works in the genre in Spain and England respectively.

The picaresque novel was developed in Spain. Consisting of separate, loosely connected episodes, it derives its dynamics and social contrast from the employment of a rogue (Spanish *pícaro*) as the servant of several masters. Picaresque means roguish.

The Gothic(k) novel became a popular genre at the end of the eighteenth and the beginning of the nineteenth centuries. Often set in forbidding medieval castles (hence Gothick), it tells of dark passions, macabre encounters with preternatural beings such as revenants (the dead who reappear as ghosts, from the Latin *revenire* 'to come again'), torture, pursuit through winding passageways and the like. The modern horror film owes much to this form.

A *Bildungsroman* (from the German *Bildung* 'education' and *Roman* 'novel') is a novel concerned with a person's formative years and his development as he encounters his society. The example of the genre usually quoted is Goethe's *Wilhelm Meister's Apprenticeship*.

A *roman-à-clef* (plural *romans-à-clef*), literally 'a novel with a key' (French *clef*), is a novel (*roman*) in which real people and places appear under fictitious names.

A *roman-fleuve* (plural *romans-fleuves)* is a novel or series of novels dealing with a family or other group over a number of generations (*fleuve* is the French 'stream').

An antinovel (*anti* is the Greek 'against') is a novel that consciously challenges the conventions, themes, style and sensibility of contemporary novels. It is likely to employ an anti-hero.

A novella is a short novel or a long short story. A novelette is a short novel but has a connotation of being of a sentimental inferior character. To describe a work, such as a history, as novelistic is to suggest that in style or in method of treatment it has the character of a novel.

O

obfuscate
to obscure

Ob is a Latin prefix used here to intensify; *fuscare, fuscatum* is 'to darken': 'In his testimony he did everything he could to obfuscate the facts.' Fuscous means brownish-grey from the Latin *fuscus* 'dark'; subfusc means drab, from *subfuscus* 'dusky'. At some universities, e.g. Oxford, subfusc refers to academic dress.

obiter dictum
an incidental remark

Obiter is the Latin 'by the way' or 'in passing'; *dictum* is 'a thing spoken' which, taken over directly into English, is used for a maxim. *Obiter dictum* is used in a legal context where a judge in arguing a point may give an opinion not essential to the case. *Obiter dicta* (the plural form of *dictum*) are often cited because they are suasory (from *suadere, suasum* the Latin 'to persuade').

obituary
a published announcement of a person's death, often accompanied by a short biography

a moratorium
is an agreed suspension of activity and derives from the Latin *mora* 'delay' and not *mors*

Ob is Latin, here 'down'; *ire, itum* is 'to go'. A funeral is a ceremony (Latin *caerimonia* 'religious rite') at which a dead person is buried or cremated (Latin *cremare, crematum* 'to burn up') and derives from the Latin *funus, funeris* 'funeral', which also gives us funerary, and funereal.

A mortuary (*mors, mortis* is the Latin 'death') is a building in which dead bodies (corpses, from the Latin *corpus* 'body', or cadavers, from the Latin *cadere* 'to fall') are kept before burial or cremation.

A cinerarium is a place where the ashes of the cremated are kept (*cinis, cineris* is the Latin 'ashes'; an incinerator is a furnace for reducing something to ashes).

Mourners are apt to be lachrymose (from *lacrima* the Latin 'tear'); their cries may be plangent (from *plangere* the Latin 'to beat the breast in grief '). If they are excessively mournful they may be thought of as lugubrious (*lugubris* is the Latin 'mournful').

People offer their condolences to the bereaved (*con* is the Latin 'with' and *dolere* is 'to grieve'; dolorous from *dolere* means causing or involving pain or sorrow). They follow the rubric said to have been laid down by the sixth-century BC Spartan Chilon, one of the Seven Sages of Greece: *De mortuis nihil nisi bonum* (Latin, 'About the dead say nothing but good'.)

Death is inevitable (unavoidable, from *in* a Latin

negative particle and *evitare* 'to shun') or ineluctable (from *in* and *eluctari* 'to escape') or inexorable (from *in* and *exorare* 'to entreat'), but when it will occur is uncertain. The Vicomte de Turenne, Louis XIV's favourite general, was struck by a cannonball while preparing to join battle at Sasbach: 'I did not mean to be killed today,' he cried. The American general John Sedgwick, jauntily looking over a parapet during one of the battles of the Civil War, said, 'They couldn't hit an elephant at this dist–'

a parapet
is a low wall running along the edge of a bridge or balcony. It derives from *para* and *petto*. *Para*, from the Latin *parare* 'to shield', indicates something that protects against something else – thus a parasol protects one against the sun (Latin *sol*), and a parachute protects one against a fall (French *chute*) from an aircraft. *Petto* is the Italian 'chest' and derives from the Latin *pectus*, *pectoris*; a Pope may hold the name of a cardinal designate *in petto* (Italian) or *in pectore* (Latin) 'in his breast', that is undisclosed, for a period

Sometimes a writer mediates the reality of death:

> Golden lads and girls all must,
> As chimney-sweepers, come to dust.
> –William Shakespeare, *Cymbeline*

> The grave's a fine and private place,
> But none I think do there embrace.
> –Andrew Marvell, 'To His Coy Mistress'

Sometimes the grave speaks directly, either with classical grace as in the inscription *Et in Arcadia ego* (Latin, 'I too lived in Arcady' or also, possibly, 'I [Death] was even in Arcady') – a detail in Nicolas Poussin's painting 'The Arcadian Shepherds' – or with bleak medieval bluntness: 'As I am you too will be.' The response of the living may be Horace's pagan *Carpe diem!* (Latin, 'Seize the day!') or Donne's empathy with all men: 'No man is an Island, entire of itself; every man is a piece of the Continent, a part of the main ... Any man's death diminishes me, because I am involved in Mankind; and therefore never send to know for whom the bell tolls; it tolls for thee.' (*Devotions*) Or Saint Paul's triumphant apostrophe 'O death, where is thy sting? O grave, where is thy victory?' (1 Cor. 15:55–6).

For the pious, *ubi sunt* (Latin, 'where are ... ?') reflections in poetry intimated the brevity (Latin *brevis* 'short') of life. A skull served as a *memento mori* (Latin, 'remember you must die') and prepared one for the *dies irae* (Latin, 'day of wrath', the dread of judgment day; the words are taken from a thirteenth-century hymn that was part of the Mass for the Dead – the Requiem Mass; *requiem* is the Latin 'rest', 'repose').

In the Middle Ages when plague often brought sudden and widespread death the dance of death (in French the *danse macabre*) was a popular motif in art and literature: the living in their social order are led by a personification of death – often a grinning skeleton – to the grave. The message was clear. All must die and all are equal in death. Macabre is thought to derive from the biblical Maccabean brothers (cruelly put to death by Antiochus Epiphanes) because prayers for the dead occur in 2 Macc. 12:43–6. The motif produced a macabre (gruesome) feeling.

Sometimes little is known about the dead. *Floruit* means 'he [or she] flourished', from the Latin *florere* 'to flower' and is used to indicate the period when a figure whose birth and death dates are unknown was most active, e.g. *fl.* 1835. A lapidary style (*lapis, lapidis* is the Latin 'stone' – it also gives us delapidated) is, because of the labour necessarily involved in engraving in stone, characteristically laconic. The inscription a lady had placed on a headstone in a pets' cemetery to capture both the transience and the snatched delights of the life of her dog read simply: *Fido – floruit et defloruit* (Latin, 'Fido – he flowered and he deflowered').

cemetery
derives by transliteration from the Greek *koimētērion* 'place for sleeping'. The Emperor Justinian I was a workaholic who habitually worked late into the night. He was known in his court in Byzantium as *akoimētos* 'the sleepless', *a* being a Greek negative

objective
pertaining to a statement, proposition or theory that accords with the known facts or is verifiable by some accepted standards

Ob is Latin, here 'against' or 'in the way of '; *jacere* is 'to throw'. An object is something thrown in the way of – perceived – by a knowing subject. It is something there to be known. Consequently, in the theory of knowledge, the knowing subject and known object are mutually related terms. The knowing subject is said to be objective when he or she is focused clearly and fully on the object. The objective person is one who takes great care to have good reasons for what he or she asserts.

Objectivity is a desirable value in all areas of knowledge. It is the condition one needs to achieve to arrive at just judgments. Subjective, on the contrary, connotes a person who does not take great care to have good reasons for what he or she asserts and who consequently makes statements without due reference to facts or verification. Used in this sense – to describe the quality of someone's knowledge – it has a pejorative meaning: there is a suggestion of bias and prejudice (an opinion, especially an unfavourable one, formed on the basis of inadequate facts, from the Latin *prae* 'before' and *judicium* 'trial'). Subjective is also used to connote what is proper or peculiar to a subject, that is, one who is a centre of knowledge and action. Thus the act of knowing is subjective and feeling is subjective. In these uses, the word is not pejorative.

proper
from the Latin *proprius* 'own' means in its primary sense appropriate, confined to one. Peculiar means belonging

In grammar and logic we use the word subject to describe that part of a sentence or proposition that refers to the topic under discussion to which we apply a predicate – that which is asserted of the object referred to by the subject. Thus, in the sentence 'The cat [subject] is lame [predicate]', 'is lame' is predicated (asserted) of the real cat.

We also use the word subject in the same way as we have defined object, e.g. the subject under discussion, but this is a derivative use.

In politics and in community life we use subject to describe those who are under authority, whether it be lawful or unlawful, for example 'a subject people'.

Finally, as a noun, objective means something aimed at.

exclusively to and derives from the Latin *pecus* 'a head of cattle' (wealth): something peculiar to you belongs exclusively to you. The word later extended to include something exclusive to one in the sense of being odd. From *pecus* also comes pecuniary (relating to money) and impecunious (without money, *in* – *im* before b, m, p – being a Latin negative particle)

obscurantist
someone who is opposed to enlightenment

Obscurare, Obscuratum is the Latin 'to cover', which also gives us obscure. People in authority are often obscurantist so as to lessen their own accountability or to preclude others through ignorance from possible courses of action. Governments have often been blamed for being more obscurantist than open and therefore less democratic in practice than they might be. People who do not wish to have their ideas challenged may also resort to obscurantism by, for instance, banning or even burning books.

Odyssey
the Greek epic poem of Homer that tells of the wanderings of Odysseus on his way home following the fall of Troy; more generally (without italics and sometimes without a capital) any long eventful journey

To the Greek poet Homer are attributed the world's two greatest epics – the *Iliad* and the *Odyssey*. The *Iliad* tells of the capture of Troy (also called Ilium) by the Greeks. The *Odyssey* tells of the adventures of Odysseus (known to the Romans as Ulysses) as he made his way from burning Troy to his home on the island of Ithaca.

When Odysseus set off to fight the Trojan War, his wife Penelope stayed behind in their palace. The war lasted ten years and it took Odysseus another ten to return home – he had insulted Poseidon, a powerful god who sent storms to frustrate him.

Back in Ithaca no less than 112 insolent young princes from the neighbouring islands were courting Penelope on the presumption that Odysseus was dead. Each hoped to marry her and take the throne. Penelope, the archetypal chaste and faithful wife, put them off, at first by asserting that Odysseus was still alive and then

Poseidon
When Zeus and his brothers Hades and Poseidon had deposed their father Cronus, they drew lots for the lordship of the sky, the sea and the underworld (having agreed to leave the earth common to all). Zeus became lord of the sky, Hades lord of the underworld and Poseidon lord of the sea. The Romans identified their sea-god Neptune with Poseidon. Both are represented in art carrying a trident. A trident is a three-pronged spear, from the Latin *tres, tria* 'three' and *dens, dentis* 'tooth' (from which we also derive dentist; *odous, odontos* is the Greek word for 'tooth' – hence orthodontist, *orthos* being the Greek 'straight').

The Romans identified their Jupiter (or Jove) with Zeus and their Dis (or Orcus) with Hades

by the ruse of telling them that she would choose one of them as soon as she had finished weaving a shroud for her father-in-law – a task that lasted three years because every night she would secretly undo what she had woven by day. Just when the suitors found out what she was doing and Penelope was being hard-pressed, Odysseus returned disguised as a beggar, gained entry to the banqueting hall, confronted the feasting suitors, and proceeded to slaughter them ruthlessly.

James Joyce used the framework of the *Odyssey* in his telling of the wanderings of Leopold Bloom around Dublin on 16 June 1904 in *Ulysses*, regarded by many critics as the greatest novel of the twentieth century. The penultimate chapter, in which Bloom returns home to Eccles Street, is called 'Ithaca' by literary critics following Joyce's original intent and the final chapter, given over to his wife Molly Bloom's famous stream of consciousness soliloquy, is called 'Penelope'. (A soliloquy, meaning the act of speaking alone or to oneself, is often a speech delivered in a play when an actor is on his own, from the Latin *solus* 'alone' and *loqui* 'to speak'.)

Oedipus complex
one of Sigmund Freud's most famous theories

In Greek legend, when King Laius of Thebes learned from an oracle that any son born of his wife Jocasta would murder him he immediately put Jocasta away but without telling her why. She was very upset and wondered what she could do. So she made Laius drunk and enticed him into her bed. When nine months later Oedipus was born, Laius had the infant's ankles pierced with a nail and ordered that he be exposed to die on the mountain. The name Oedipus means swollen foot and comes from the Greek *pous, podos* 'foot' and *oidein* 'to swell' (doctors use the term oedema, from *oidein*, to describe any swelling in the body caused by the accumulation of fluid in the tissue). But Oedipus was rescued by a shepherd and brought to the palace of Polybus in Corinth where he was reared. By a number of twists of fate, Oedipus murdered his father and married his mother. When their true relationship became known, Jocasta hanged herself and Oedipus blinded himself – thus providing Greek tragedians with one of their most famous themes.

chiropody
is the treatment of the feet and also derives from *pous, podos*. *Chiro* (or *cheiro*), a combining form indicating 'of' or 'by means of the hand', derives from the Greek *kheir* 'hand'

accumulation
Cumulare is the Latin 'to heap'. Accumulation means a heaping up; cumulative means increasing by successive additions; cumulus is a cloud consisting of rounded heaps with a darker horizontal base

Freud resorted to the myth to describe a son's unconscious desire for his mother and hostility to his father – the Oedipus complex. (The adjective derived from Oedipus is oedipal.) Freud posited that a boy enters a phallic phase at the age of three when his interest centres on his penis. This gives rise to feelings of sexual attraction to his mother and of jealousy towards his father. The Oedipus complex ends about the fourth or fifth year, primarily because the boy fears his desire for his mother will lead his father to punish him by castrating him (the castration complex; *castrare, castratum* is the Latin 'to emasculate').

In a similar phase a girl becomes interested in her clitoris. Since this organ appears inferior to the masculine one she develops an envious desire to be like a boy (Freud called this penis envy). Blaming her mother, she becomes attached to her father (the Electra complex: Electra persuaded her brother Orestes to avenge the murder of their father by killing Clytemnestra, their mother, and her lover Aegisthus). What brings this phase to a conclusion is the girl's growing awareness that other men apart from her father can enable her to have a baby and so overcomes her sense of inferiority. Freud saw the phallic phase as the central emotional stage each human being must pass through if he or she is to reach normal adult equilibrium (balance, from the Latin *equi* 'equal' and *libra* 'pound weight').

oid

a suffix indicating 'likeness' or 'similarity' found in such words as anthropoid, humanoid, android, asteroid, factoid, tabloid

Eidos is the Greek 'form'; *oeidēs* (in English *oid*) indicates 'resembling the form of'.

Anthropoid, from the Greek *anthrōpos* 'man' in the sense of mankind, means like man and is applied to primates in a suborder that includes monkeys, apes and man.

Humanoid from the Latin *humanus*, itself derived from *homo* 'man', is applied more narrowly than anthropoid for something like a human being in appearance.

Android, from the Greek *anēr, andros* 'man [as opposed to woman]', means resembling a human being, and is used in science fiction for a robot resembling a human being.

Asteroid, from the Greek *astēr* 'star', *asteroeidēs* 'starlike', means a minor planet.

Factoid, from fact, meaning an event or thing accepted as a fact (from the Latin *facere, factum* 'to make'), although it is not necessarily such, was coined by Norman Mailer for a piece of unreliable information

asteroids
are relatively small rocky objects that orbit the sun. Comets (from the Greek *komētēs* 'long-haired') are blocks of ice containing rocks or metals that also orbit the sun but vaporize on approaching it and develop a long luminous tail.

Meteors (from the Greek *meteōros* 'lofty'), also called shooting or falling stars, are grain-sized particles that burn up on entering the earth's atmosphere. Meteoroids are small celestial bodies thought to be the remains of comets. A meteorite is a stony or metallic object that has fallen to earth. Meteorology is the study of the earth's atmospere. Meteoric, meaning sudden and speedy, may be applied to a person's rapid career or sudden rise to fame

believed to be true because of the way it is presented or repeated in print.

Tabloid, from the Latin *tabula* 'table', is now usually applied to a small format newspaper measuring about 30 x 40 centimetres in contrast to the normal broadsheet measuring about 40 x 60 centimetres. Because of the characteristically informal style and sensational content of tabloids the word may be employed as an epithet connoting dumbed down – the tabloid press, tabloid television. See also omphaloid and sigmoid.

The Greek suffix *ides* 'offspring of' occurs in the name of the great historian Thucydides. In the form *id* it indicates a member of a dynasty, for example Seleucid (Seleucus was one of Alexander the Great's generals; at its zenith the Seleucid dynasty ruled over an area extending from Thrace in the Balkans to India) or a member of a zoological family, e.g. hominid, from the Latin *homo, hominis* 'man', which includes modern man (*Homo sapiens*) and the extinct precursors of man.

ology

a suffix deriving from the Greek *logos* 'word', 'reason' or 'account'. It usually denotes 'study of' but sometimes simply indicates 'saying' or 'discoursing', for example eulogy, tautology, trilogy, phraseology and martyrology

Anthropology means the study of man in the widest sense (*anthrōpos* is the Greek 'man').

Archaeology is the study of human antiquities usually by excavation (*archaios* is the Greek 'chief', 'principal' or 'first', here in the sense of ancient; thus also archaic, archaism).

Biology means the study of physical life (*bios* is the Greek 'life'). It was coined by Lamarck in 1802. Biomorphic (*morphē* is the Greek 'form' or 'shape') is a term used in abstract art to indicate forms derived from organic nature rather than geometry.

Cosmology means the study of the universe (*cosmos* is the Greek 'universe').

Ecology is a branch of biology concerned with the study of living organisms and their relations to their surroundings (*oikos* is the Greek 'house', man's immediate environment; this was extended to the general environment to give a range of words beginning with the prefix *eco*).

Entomology is the study of insects (small invertebrate animals usually having a body divided into segments, from the Latin *insectus* 'cut into'), used by Roman writers to translate the term Aristotle uses – *entom* (*en* is the Greek 'in' and *tom* derives from *temnein* 'to cut' – see also atom). Five-sixths of all animals are insects.

Lepidopterology is the branch of entomology that studies moths and butterflies (insects with scaly wings, *lepis*, *lepidos* being the Greek 'scale', from which we derive leper, and *pteron* the Greek 'wing'). Invertebrate (without a backbone) was coined by Lamarck for the group of species previously called insects and worms and derives from the Latin negative *in* and *vertebrae* 'the bony segments of the spinal [Latin *spina* 'thorn', 'backbone'] column'.

Eschatology is the doctrine of the last or final things – death and judgment (*eschatos* is the Greek 'last').

Scatological is used to describe obscene literature (*skōr*, *skatos* means 'dung' in Greek).

Etymology is the study of how words are formed (*etumos* is the Greek 'true', 'literal' or 'original').

Ideology is a word coined by the French philosopher Destutt de Tracy in 1796 to describe the scientific study of ideas (*idea* in Greek). Napoleon attacked the radical thinking of the Enlightenment (which provided a basis for democratic government) as ideological (by which he meant unrealistic and remote from the concrete realities a man of action like himself had to deal with). The word now connotes the network of ideas that specifies a particular historical-social consciousness. It comes close to Plato's understanding of public opinion as the unconscious consensus about reality. Ideology is important because by imposing the perspectives within which a community views its political, social, economic and cultural realities, it marshals support for the structures that maintain those perspectives – and thus is used as an instrument of power. Marx saw that to change a society you had to attack its ideology. Ideology was, he declared, unscientific – it was simply a set of ideas upon which a group or class bases the theory that justifies the pursuit of its own interest – and could be routed by science. Marx, by stressing the scientific basis of his own system, sought to raise it above the sectionalism of a mere ideology. However, the basis of science is murky (see paradigm) and so nowadays we refer to Marxist ideology without any sense that Marx himself would have seen the reference as oxymoronic.

Martyrology means an official list of martyrs (*martur* is the Greek 'witness [to the faith]').

Methodology means the study of methods (*meta* means 'after' and *hodos* means 'way' in Greek).

eschatology
is not always a preoccupation of those facing death. James Rodgers, when about to be executed by a firing squad in Utah, replied to the question 'Have you any last request?' with the words 'Why, yes – a bullet-proof vest.'

sectionalism
is a narrow concern for the interests of a group, from *secare*, *sectum* 'to cut'. Sectarian, from the same source, means a narrow exclusive concern for a denomination or sect. It has a pejorative connotation

oxymoronic
derives from the Greek *oxys* 'sharp' and *mōros* 'foolish', which also gives us moron. Oxymoron is a trope that combines contradictory terms to form an expressive phrase such as cruel kindness, falsely true. To characterize a particular combination, for example Army Intelligence, as oxymoronic is to be cynical. 'Stalin, as you know, was dismissive of women. Indeed, he believed the very notion of an intelligent woman was an oxymoron.' (Robert Harris, *Archangel*)

Musicology means the study of music (*musikos* is the Greek 'relating to the Muses').

Mythology means either the study of myths or a set of myths, for example Greek mythology (*muthos* is the Greek 'story', 'myth' or 'legend'; in common usage myth has a pejorative connotation of falseness, but scholars also use the word in a positive sense for any allegory that gives an insight into an important aspect of human culture). The word was coined by Plato.

Phraseology (*phrasis* is the Greek 'speech') is either the manner in which words or phrases are used or a set of phrases used by a particular group of people.

Psychology means the study of the mind (*psychē* is the Greek 'mind'). Psychoanalysis (from *psyche* and analysis; psyche is used in English for the human soul or mind) is a method of studying the mind and treating mental and emotional disorders based on revealing and investigating the role of the unconscious mind. Psychiatry is the diagnosis and treatment of diseases of the mind (*iatros* is the Greek 'physician'). A psychosomatic illness is a physical condition arising from psychological distress in which typically there are symptoms but no signs of organic disease (*sōma* is the Greek 'body').

Sociology is the study of human society (*societas* is the Latin 'society').

Technology is either the science of the industrial arts or the means of production (*technē* is the Greek 'craft'; technical means relating to or specializing in industrial, practical or mechanical arts and applied sciences; technique means a practical method, skill or art applied to a particular task).

Trilogy means a set of three related works, especially literary ones. A tetralogy is a set of four related works, especially literary ones. (*Tri* from the Greek *treis* indicates 'three', *tetra* from the Greek *tettares* indicates 'four'.)

Volcanology (also vulcanology) is the study of volcanoes (Vulcan was the Roman god of fire).

Zoology means the study of animals (*zōion* is the Greek 'animal').

Olympian
one of the greater Greek gods; as an adjective, godlike

Olympia was a celebrated sanctuary of Zeus, the chief of the Greek gods. There from prehistoric times until 394 AD, the Panhellenic Olympian Games were held every four years. (They were abolished by the emperor

Theodosius as a relic of paganism; 1500 years later in 1896 they were revived as the modern Olympic Games.) In the world of the ancient Greeks, athletics, from the Greek *athlein* 'to compete for a prize', were a strong cultural tie. They originally took place in a natural stadium (Greek *stadion*), often between two hills whose slopes readily allowed for the emplacement of tiered seats. A pentathlon, from the Greek *pente* 'five' and *athlon* 'contest' was an athletics contest consisting of five different events. (The modern decathlon consists of ten events, *deka* being the Greek 'ten'.) Training took place in a gymnasium (from the Greek *gumnos* 'naked'). The athletes trained and competed naked. Married women were not allowed to watch the games although virgin girls were, perhaps because potential husbands were on display.

Olympian
conveys a sense of lofty detachment: 'He took an Olympian attitude towards debt, and once informed his creditors that he had them on a list and that they would be dealt with in strict rotation as resources became available.' In *King Lear* Shakespeare captures the detachment of the Olympians: 'As flies to wanton boys are we to th' gods; / They kill us for their sport.'

In Olympia there stood possibly the most famous statue ever made – that of Olympian Zeus by Phidias, a chryselephantine masterpiece. One of the Seven Wonders of the World, it was considered a misfortune to die without seeing it. It is now completely lost. Mount Olympus is the name of several mountains that were regarded as the abode of Zeus and the other eleven high gods of Greek mythology – Aphrodite, Apollo, Ares, Artemis, Athene, Demeter, Dionysus, Hephaestus, Hera, Hermes and Poseidon. These gods, featured on the Parthenon frieze, were known as the Olympians. (Olympian is also now used for a competitor in the Olympic Games.)

The Greeks also adored chthonian gods (*chthōn* is the Greek 'earth'), gods of the earth, including *Gē* (or Gaia), Mother Earth herself. Chthonian and chthonic now connote the mysterious primal religious period. Tellus (gen. *Telluris*), also Terra, is the equivalent Roman earth-goddess and telluric is a synonym for chthonian. Ian Gibson in *Federico García Lorca* tells us: 'Lorca himself liked the word "telluric", and was perfectly aware that his was a primitive, mythical vision with deep roots in the ancient cultures and religions of the Mediterranean.'

Gaia
In the 1970s the scientist James Lovelock developed what might be called a modern form of pantheism when he conceived of the Earth and everything on it, including humankind, as interacting like a superorganism, which he called Gaia, to maintain an environment in which it can survive

ombudsman
an official appointed by parliament to investigate complaints by members of

Ombudsman is the Swedish 'advocate' – the Swedes invented the office of ombudsman. Public bodies are staffed with specialists who can appear forbidding to the ordinary citizen approaching with a complaint.

the public about their treatment by a public body

Such a citizen may find he or she can appeal to an administrative tribunal, to a minister, or in extreme cases, to the courts (which can be expensive) or to the ombudsman (whose services are free). The ombudsman has all the powers, though not necessarily the resources, he or she needs to ascertain the basis of a complaint but normally acts only after other administrative remedies have been exhausted. The ombudsman cannot command a remedy. However, his or her prestige, and the fact that he or she lays reports before parliament, usually ensures a remedy.

Orphic
relating to Orpheus or Orphism (a mystery religion of ancient Greece associated with Orpheus); more generally, and sometimes without a capital, mystical or occult

Orphism was an elaborate theology that explained the origin of gods and men and prescribed rituals and practices, including initiation in the orgies of Dionysus, designed to help man to reach a final deliverance from a human to a divine state. The Orphic writers believed in metempsychosis and attributed the lack of consciousness of a previous existence in the reborn to the fact that the soul about to be reincarnated drinks from the Lethe. They embodied their doctrines in poems that were ascribed to Orpheus. The collection of Orphic poems is the closest the Greeks came to a holy book such as the Bible or the Koran.

Orpheus still holds a place in literature and art through one of the most charming of the Greek legends, which is centred on him.

the lyre
from the Greek *lura*, was a musical instrument like a harp. The poetry composed to be sung to its accompaniment was called lyrical. It was distinguished from epic and dramatic verse. It dealt with individual or private emotions and was typically expressive. Pindar and Horace were the lyric poets *par excellence* of Greece and Rome respectively

The most famous musician in Greek legend, he played the lyre so hauntingly that trees and stones danced to his music and wild beasts were tamed by it. When his wife Eurydice died from the sting of a viper, Orpheus was inconsolable. (The contralto Kathleen Ferrier captured Orpheus's grief in her recording of the aria from Gluck's *Orfeo ed Eurydice* 'What is life to me without you?')

Hades
is referred to by his other name, Pluto, in Milton's *Il Penseroso*: 'Or bid the soul of Orpheus sing / Such notes as, warbled to the string, / Drew iron tears down Pluto's cheek.'

Orpheus determined to go down to the underworld and bring Eurydice back. Hades, the heartless (and eponymous) lord of that dark domain, was so charmed by his music that he agreed to let Eurydice return to the upper world provided Orpheus did not look back, as she followed in his steps, until she had emerged into the sunlight. Orpheus was delighted and led the way carefully through the Stygian gloom, playing on his lyre. Eurydice followed, guided by the music. When Orpheus at last reached the light, he could not restrain himself any longer: he turned around to make sure his beloved was following him. But she had not yet stepped into the sunlight, and he lost her forever.

osmosis
in general application, the gradual, unconscious absorption of ideas, attitudes, styles or postures

Osmosis, from the Greek *ōsmos* 'push', was coined in the latter half of the nineteenth century to describe the process by which living cells take up water. The membranes (Latin *membrana* 'the skin covering any part of the body') that surround and protect the cells are semipermeable. The pores (from the Latin *porus*, which also gives us porous) in the membrane permit the passage of water but may restrict the movement of even single molecules. A higher concentration of salts and proteins on one side of the membrane attracts water, by osmotic pressure, restoring osmotic equilibrium.

Applying the word to human behaviour, one might say of someone who, without any training or formal education, has become expert in a particular business, that he or she had learned everything by osmosis.

A minute opening that may allow something to escape is called an interstice (from the Latin *inter* 'between' and *sistere* 'to stand'); a riddle lets small matter fall through its interstices.

The Greek for skin is *derma* and so dermatology is the branch of medicine concerned with the skin. A pachyderm is an animal with a thick skin (*pachys* is the Greek 'thick') and usually refers to an elephant, rhinoceros or hippopotamus. A taxidermist is someone who stuffs skins (from the Greek *taxis* 'arrangement' and *derma*). The epidermis (Greek *epi* 'upon' and *derma*) is the thin protective outer layer of the skin. Tegument or integument, from the Latin *tegumentum* 'a covering', may be used to describe any outer protective layer such as a cuticle, seed coat, rind or shell. A carapace is the hard shell of a turtle, tortoise or crab (from the Spanish *carapacho*).

cell
derives from the Latin *cella*, the rectangular room that was the core of a Roman temple. In medieval times it was applied to the small room of a monk. The English physicist and inventor Robert Hooke, who studied bird feathers and fish scales under the microscope, first employed the word in biology. In viewing a cell or organism scientists may discern a flagellum (plural flagella) – a whiplike outgrowth that helps the cell to move, from the Latin *flagellum* 'little whip', which also gives us flagellation (flogging) and a cilium (plural cilia) – a projecting short thread whose rhythmic beating causes movement of the cell or organism, from the Latin *cilium* 'eyelash'

ostracize
to boycott

Ostrakon is the Greek word for 'a piece of pottery'. To deal with a leader of the people thought likely to subvert the state but against whom there was no evidence, the Athenians introduced a procedure whereby the people could vote to banish anyone for a period of five or ten years by writing his name on a piece of pottery and placing it in a voting urn.

Plutarch tells us about the ostracism of an Athenian

called Aristides the Just. While the votes were being written down, an illiterate countryman handed his piece of pottery to Aristides and asked him to write the name Aristides on it. Taken aback by this, Aristides asked the man what harm Aristides had ever done him. 'None whatever! I don't even know him! I'm just sick and tired of hearing him being called The Just.' When he heard this, Aristides said nothing, but wrote his name on the *ostrakon* and handed it back to the man. He was subsequently ostracized.

quotidian
means recurring daily or commonplace, from the Latin *quotidie* 'daily'

Ostraka (plural) cost nothing and were used in the Graeco-Roman period for the business of quotidian trade, personal notes, tax receipts and school use. Papyrus, the writing material of the ancient Egyptians, made from the papyrus plant, which grew in abundance along the Nile, being a manufactured article, was expensive and therefore used sparingly in the ancient world. Indeed parchment, which is made from the skin of certain animals such as sheep, is said to have been invented in the second century BC when the Egyptians used their monopoly of papyrus to deprive their great rival Pergamum in Asia Minor of supply (parchment is derived from the Greek *pergamene* 'from Pergamum'). Vellum is a high-quality parchment made from calfskin and derives from the same root as veal (the Old French *velin*). Given their cost, papyrus and parchment were sometimes recycled. A manuscript where a text has been erased to make room for another one is called a palimpsest (*palin* – *palim* before a p – is the Greek 'again'; *psestos* is 'rubbed'; a palindrome is a word or phrase whose letters, when taken in reverse order, give the same word or phrase, for example madam, and derives from *palin* and *dromos* 'race' or 'course'). The mass production of paper in rolls in the nineteenth century created a plenteous and therefore cheap supply. Paper, invented by the Chinese, was made from flax fibre; when it was introduced to Europe in the thirteenth century the Europeans called it paper (from the Latin *papyrus*).

P

paean
a song or as nowadays a statement of praise

Originally a paean was a joyous hymn in praise of a god, especially Apollo (as Paian – Healer), sung to enlist the favour of the god before some great event such as a battle, or to give thanks to the god for a favourable outcome such as a victory. Later, paeans were sung in honour of mortals and this led to its modern use: 'The critics greeted his first novel with a paean.'

A dithyramb was a passionate hymn (Greek *humnos* 'song in praise of a god') addressed to Dionysus; a piece of music with wild and boisterous rhythms might be appositely called dithyrambic.

pagan
heathen

Paganus is the Latin 'country dweller'. Christianity spread through the Roman empire from city to city. Eventually, following the conversion of the Emperor Constantine, it became the state religion. The word pagan is derived from the period when Christianity had not yet reached the country districts.

Country dwellers have always been treated contumeliously (*contumelia* is the Latin 'outrage' or 'insult') by town dwellers. The sophisticated Athenians called anyone who was rude and unlettered a Boeotian because the Boeotians were dedicated farmers. When sophisticated New Yorkers refer to hillbillies, they use a term they clearly think carries no hint of the mores of Versailles (*mores,* the plural of *mos, moris,* is the Latin 'manners', used in English to mean the customs or conventions that characterize a particular community). Hillbilly is said to derive from the fact that those Ulster Scots who settled in poor, small farms carved out of the Appalachian hills of the south-eastern US frequently called their eldest sons Billy after their glorious hero King William III of England.

Ulster
from the Irish *Uladh*, is the northernmost of Ireland's four provinces. It was partly planted by Scottish Presbyterians in the seventeenth century. Many of these, who had developed fighting skills in the struggle with the tories, were later employed by the English planters in the Carolinas in their war with the Cherokees. When that war ended the mercenaries found themselves unemployed and therefore poor

When town dwellers describe someone as a boor (from the Old English/modern Dutch *boer* 'farmer') or a rustic (from the Latin *rus, ruris* 'country'), they do not intend to flatter. If they did, they would use the word urbane (from the Latin *urbs, urbis* 'city', from which we also derive urban). If they used bucolic (from the Greek *boukolos* 'cowherd'), the context would determine whether they were doing so pejoratively or positively (as meaning pastoral or Arcadian).

And so 'by a commodious vicus of recirculation', as Joyce says at the beginning of *Finnegans Wake,* we come to *paganus* once more: from it are derived the French *paysan* and the English peasant.

Palladium
a small wooden statue of Athene whose possession by the Trojans guaranteed the security of their city

Palladium derives from the Greek Pallas (gen. *Pallados*), one of the names given to the goddess Athene. It was common for ancient cities to have guardian statues. The Trojan 'Palladium', kept in the citadel of Troy, was the most famous of them all. When Odysseus and Diomedes succeeded in stealing the 'Palladium' and carrying it off to the Greek camp, the fate of Troy was sealed.

Palladium may now be used generally of a tutelary statue. Thus Benedict Anderson writes in the *London Review of Books*: 'One of the rooms, heavily guarded, contains priceless traditional statuary, including the palladium from which Luang Prabang takes its name: a solid-gold Buddha, almost three feet high, said to have been cast in Ceylon in the first century AD.'

Palladium is also used to name one of the platinum metals which, because it is an excellent catalyst, has many practical uses, including in the catalytic converters in cars. It was first isolated in 1803 by the English physicist William Hyde Wollaston, the year after the discovery of the asteroid Pallas, an event that prompted the name for the metal. (The largest asteroid – and the first to be discovered – was named Ceres after the Roman goddess of agriculture and therefore sustainer of life, from whom we also derive cereal for any grass that produces an edible grain, such as wheat, oats or rice.)

edible
is from the Latin *edere* 'to eat'; potable is from the Latin *potare* 'to drink', from which we also get potion

Palladian, an adjective derived from Andrea Palladio, refers to the style of architecture based on the writings and buildings of that great Italian architect and humanist. Palladio (his name alludes to an angelic messenger from Giangiorgio Trissino's epic *Italia liberata dai Goti* – Italian, 'the liberation of Italy from the Goths') believed buildings should reflect rationality in their clarity, order and symmetry. He based his ideas on a study of the extant ancient classical buildings and the writings of the first-century BC Roman architect Vitruvius, who himself relied on Greek models. Palladianism was especially important to British and Irish architecture in the first half of the eighteenth century. The Capitol in Washington, a characteristic piece of Palladian architecture, features classical forms and decorative motifs, including a statue of Ceres that surmounts it.

Pan is very usefully deployed to cluster states within a country or region (Latin *regio, regionis*, from *regere* 'to govern'), for example, pan-German, pan-Arab, pan-European, pan-American, pan-African.

Panacea is a cure-all from *pan* and *akos*, the Greek 'remedy'. Modern life is complex and modern man is faced with complex problems to which, almost certainly, he must find complex solutions. People, however, like simple solutions and so they put pressure on politicians to find a panacea.

Pandaemonium or pandemonium is literally the place of all the demons and therefore any exceedingly noisy, disorderly place or condition (*daemon* is 'guardian spirit' or more generally 'demon' in Greek; *ium* is a Latin suffix indicating 'place').

A pantheon is a temple to all the gods (*theos* is 'god' in Greek and *eon* is a suffix denoting 'place'). It is also used to describe a building dedicated as a memorial to all the great dead who are immortal in memory, like the Pantheon in Paris – or a notional equivalent of it: 'Verdi has a place in the pantheon of Italian nationalism.'

Panorama derives from the Greek *pan* and *horama* 'view'. Panorama, then, means a total 360° view. We usually use the word nowadays to mean a very broad view. Vista comes from the Italian *vista* 'view', which we use in terms of the narrow view seen through an avenue.

pan
a Greek prefix meaning 'all', found in words like panacea, pandaemonium, pantheon and panorama

Verdi
i Verdi means 'the Greens' in Italian; verdant means green in English, from the French *verdoyer* 'to become green'. Verdigris from the Old French *verd de Grèce* 'green of Greece', is a green patina formed on copper by oxidization; a patina is a fine layer on a surface from the Latin *patina* 'dish'. A variant occurs in Shakespeare, *The Merchant of Venice*: 'Look how the floor of heaven / Is thick inlaid with patines of bright gold.'

In Greek legend, one of the Titans, Prometheus, was a great benefactor of mankind – he was said, for instance, to have stolen fire from heaven and given it to men so that they could develop metallurgy and all sorts of useful arts. Moreover, he went to the trouble of imprisoning in a box all the evils that could afflict mankind – old age, sickness, madness, vice, dark passions, hard work, etc. He gave the box to his brother Epimetheus and warned him never to open it. Some time later, Epimetheus married Pandora, the first and most beautiful woman ever created. Though she was beautiful, Pandora was also foolish, capricious, mischievous and idle – a typical woman, the Greeks thought. She itched to know what was in the box. So she opened it – and out flew all the evils that have plagued mankind ever since. (Pandora comes from two Greek words, *pan* 'all'

Pandora's box
a meretricious gift that becomes a source of great and unexpected evil

benefactor
means someone who supports a person or institution (*bene* is the Latin 'well' and *factor* derives from the Latin *facere, factum* 'to do'). Because of Prometheus's impudence Zeus had him bound to a pillar. Every day his liver was eaten by an eagle and every night it was renewed, until Heracles freed him. Prometheus's defiance of the gods captured the romantic imagination and has given him a luminous place in literature and painting as the exemplar of the free creative spirit

and *dōron* 'gift'; compare with Theodore, the gift of God, *theos* being the Greek 'god', and *Thermidor*.)

paparazzo
a press photographer who harasses notable people in order to get snaps of them in unguarded moments. The word usually occurs in the plural, the paparazzi

In his 1960 film *La Dolce Vita* (Italian, 'The Sweet Life' – a life of wealth, idleness and pleasure) the Italian director Federico Fellini satirized the mores of Rome's hedonistic high society (*hēdonē* is the Greek 'pleasure'; hedonists believe pleasure is the greatest good). In the film the scandal-sheet photographer is called Paparazzo. Fellini's scriptwriter took the name from *By the Ionian Sea* by the English writer George Gissing. Coriolano Paparazzo was the owner of the hotel in Catanjaro where the writer had stayed on his travels around the south of Italy. Fellini was inspired to use the device of an intrusive photographer by an incident he had witnessed one day in the late fifties on the Via Veneto in Rome. The Egyptian ex-King Farouk was sitting at a table with a girl when some press photographers approached and goaded the corpulent king sufficiently to make him jump up and overturn his table, and thereby provide the pictures they wanted.

The Italian *i* plural form occurs in graffiti (singular graffito) and in *capo di capi* the Mafia 'boss of bosses', *capo* being the Italian 'head'.

paradigm
an implicit theory or conceptual framework from which other theories or understandings derive their validity

Para is the Greek 'beside'; *deignumi* is 'to show'. In philosophy a paradigm is an image or cluster of images we freely construct in order to reveal the nature of something by seeking correspondences with the image or cluster of images. A paradigm then, is literally something you show beside something else to extend your knowledge of it. A paradigm is purely provisional; it may be true or false, well or badly grounded. Its use points to the open-ended nature of knowledge and its analogical character (the fact that we understand one thing in terms of another). Thus we speak about justice – a moral concept – in terms of order, harmony and unity between parts (none of which are moral concepts as such).

In logic, the primary usage of a word or concept from which our understanding of other usages flows is said to be paradigmatic. Thus we use the word healthy in a wide range of ways – healthy hair, healthy teeth, a healthy respect, a healthy bank balance – but all these usages of healthy derive their meaning from its paradigmatic use in relation to a living body. The first step in debate is to clarify the terms of the proposition – and this entails either the paradigm (implicit theory) out of which we are thinking or the paradigmatic use of the words or concepts we are using, or both. For example, liberals and socialists use a different paradigm of freedom.

In the philosophy of science a paradigm is a set of implicit beliefs assumed to be true (or partly justified), which both influences our selection of theories and the sorts of facts that might verify them. It decides what is to count as a good question or argument, what is or is not relevant, what is significant or insignificant in our thinking about something. It also specifies the practices by which one becomes a member of a particular scientific community, that is, the professional training required. According to some philosophers, all scientific thinking is governed by a paradigm. Unless one accepts that paradigm, one would not be a respectable scientist in the eyes of fellow-scientists. Scientific paradigms are therefore norms governing the work of scientists and admission to the profession, but norms that cannot be justified scientifically. Periodically some creative scientist breaks with the prevailing paradigm and works with hypotheses and theories not justified by it. He is often laughed at by his colleagues and may even be treated as an outcast. But if his hypotheses and theories can be verified (like Einstein's theory of relativity), gradually a new paradigm emerges and becomes the prevailing one (closing down scientific questioning again).

norm
Norma is the Latin 'carpenter's square' – a norm is a standard by which something is measured. A thing is normal when it conforms to the accepted standard. A study is said to be normative when it lays down standards and prescribes what ought to be done. When it simply describes something it is said to be descriptive. Something not normal is abnormal (*ab* is the Latin 'away from')

The conquest of an old paradigm by a new one is called a paradigm shift. It is apparent from this analysis that scientific rationality (the paradigm, as that term is used in logic, of rationality today) is not as rational as it appears. All hypotheses and theories are themselves grounded on beliefs and hunches that cannot be justified by the same sort of rational argument as the theories they spawn. Scientific thinking is ultimately based on non-scientific thinking.

paradox
a seemingly absurd or self-contradictory statement that is or may be true

The Greek *paradoxos*, from *para* indicating 'contrary' and *doxa* 'opinion', relates to an opinion that conflicts with common belief. Socrates's remark that no one ever knowingly does wrong is paradoxical because it goes against our common belief that people often do things they know they shouldn't. One of the most famous of ancient paradoxes came in the form: Epimenides the Cretan said all Cretans are liars. Was he telling the truth?

In his novel *Catch-22* Joseph Heller set up a famous paradoxical situation in which a person is frustrated by a paradoxical rule or set of circumstances that preclude any attempt to escape from them. In the flyer's code Catch-22 'specified that a concern for one's safety in the face of dangers that were real and immediate was the process of a rational mind. Orr was crazy and could be grounded. All he had to do was ask; and as soon as he did, he would no longer be crazy and would have to fly more missions.'

Antinomy (from the Greek *anti* 'against' and *nomos* 'law') is a synonym for paradox and indicates a contradiction within a law. Antinomian in the more basic sense of against the law is applied to a doctrine that holds that faith and the dispensation of grace cannot be expressed truly through regulations only. In its radical form it releases Christians from the obligation of adhering to any moral law, and was suppressed as heresy.

parameter
a boundary or limit

Para here means 'beside' in Greek; *metron* is 'measure' (from which we also derive metre). The term is derived from geometry: when a circle must be so drawn that it does not intersect a line, i.e. does not go beyond it, the line is called a parameter. In public affairs the term is used to define the boundaries within which an issue is to be resolved. In science it has a range of technical meanings.

pariah
an outcast

The word is from Hindi and derives from *parai* 'large drum' such as was beaten at festivals by low caste servants. The Hindu population was divided into classes ranging from the Brahmin, the highest, to the Dalit, the lowest – the pariahs or untouchables, who carried out all the menial tasks. In democratic politics it is rather important not to allow yourself to become a pariah.

pari passu
in equal steps or comparable stages

concomitant
means accompanying (*con* is the Latin 'with'; *comes,comitis* is

Par is the Latin 'equal'; *passus* is 'step' or 'stride'. The phrase is used to describe any sets of moves that are made concomitantly. Thus 'The Americans and the Soviets should have removed their nuclear weapons from Europe *pari passu*.'

Virgil, in his great Latin epic, the *Aeneid,* traces the

adventures of Aeneas from his flight from Troy to his eventual landing in Italy where his descendants Remus and the eponymous Romulus, both suckled by a she-wolf, became the founders of Rome. The ablative plural of *passus* occurs in a celebrated passage that describes the boy-child, Julus, Aeneas's son, hurrying from the burning city of Troy in the wake of his father: *sequiturque patrem non passibus aequis* – 'and he follows his father in shorter steps' (i.e. because of his short legs he could not manage to move *pari passu* with his father).

Passo is the Italian 'step'. When Mussolini visited Hitler in 1937 he was overwhelmed by the sight of thousands of rigidly drilled German troops goose-stepping past him. He decided to introduce that step into the Italian army, calling it the *passo romano* – 'the Roman step', 'the firm, inexorable step of the legions for whom every march was a march of conquest'. Count Ciano quotes Mussolini as countering the military establishment's objection to his innovation: 'People say the goose-step is Prussian. Nonsense! The goose is a Roman animal – it saved the Capitol. Its place is with the eagle and the she-wolf.'

'companion', from which the title count is derived. Counts (*comtes* in French) were originally the companions of French kings and their territories were called counties. A paladin, from the Latin *palatinus* 'relating to the palace' was originally one of the twelve peers in Charlemagne's household but the word came to be applied to any knightly champion. A palatine, also from *palatinus*, was a nobleman, such as an elector of the medieval and early modern German empire, who exercised an almost kingly power over his territory (called a palatinate)

parliament
the legislature

Parler is the French 'to speak' and *parlement* (transliterated parliament in English) means 'speaking' or 'discussion' and by transference 'a meeting for discussion'. The earliest appearance in literature of *parlement* occurs in the eleventh-century epic, *Chanson de Roland,* where it simply means conversation. In the twelfth century we find that general assemblies of Italian cities are called *parlamenti*.

In England, which has had the longest continuous parliamentary experience, the first parliaments were meetings between the king and his barons to discuss the business of the king and the kingdom. Generally speaking, kings called parliaments not to promote participative government but to collect money to pay for their expenses. Those who owned or controlled most of the wealth of the country – the land and the produce of the land – were the lords and bishops, and they were the ones who were first summoned to parliaments. When the shires (counties) and the boroughs (cities and towns) became officially recognized communities, they were obliged to appoint representatives to attend the king in parliament to be told what their communities

parler
also gives us parlance, meaning a particular vocabulary and mindset, for example scientific parlance; and parley, meaning to discuss, often with an enemy under a truce

should pay. In time they became the major suppliers of subsidies to the king.

In parliament the lords and bishops met separately as a House of Lords. The commons – the knights of the shires (substantial freeholders) and the representatives of the towns and cities – met separately as a House of Commons (from the Latin *communis* meaning 'common', from which we also derive commune, communal, communist, communitarian and community).

communitarian
involves putting an emphasis in the development of state policies on the values that flow from communal structures and practices, such as solidarity and trust. It contrasts with liberalism, which places the individual at the centre of policy concern, and with Marxist communism and fascism, both of which sought to subordinate the individual and all communal structures to the requirements of a centrally developed *Weltanschauung*

Parliament's capacity to meet the king's need for money gave it a bargaining power that it used first to have grievances remedied and then to achieve the law-making power.

However, it was not until the fourteenth century that the House of Commons succeeded in turning itself from a congregation of petitioners into an assembly that had a part in law-making. Acts of Parliament became the joint products of King, Lords and Commons. The medieval terminology is still used: 'Whereas it is expedient … Be it therefore enacted by the King's most excellent majesty, by and with the advice and consent of the Lords Spiritual and Temporal and Commons in this present Parliament assembled, and by the authority of the same, as follows …' The monarch, though, was still what we today would call the government. Since the relationship of king and parliament was based on finance, kings could ignore parliament if they did not need subsidies. In times of peace kings often did not call parliaments because they could subsist on the produce of their own properties and on income from sources not controlled closely by parliament such as customs charged on imports.

petitioners
are people who make requests – they are seeking something. *Petere, petitum* is the Latin 'to seek'; a competitor is a rival, someone who seeks the same thing as you – *com* derives from *cum* 'with'; centripetal describes a tendency to move towards the centre the way a whirlpool does and derives from *centrum* 'centre' and *petere*; its opposite – centrifugal – means a tendency to move away from the centre and derives from *centrum* and *fugere* 'to flee' (thus a passing bicycle may splash you with mud because the revolving wheels create a centrifugal force). From *fugere* we also derive refuge, refugee and fugue (a musical form in which a theme seems to flee by being repeated a fifth above or a fourth below)

By the mid-seventeenth century parliament was challenging the monarch. After a civil war, it beheaded Charles I. Although the monarchy was restored in 1660, parliament soon succeeded in asserting its control over all sources of taxation. The formal assertion of parliament's control came with the enactment of the Bill of Rights in 1689. This embodied the conditions under which William and Mary were offered the English Crown: parliaments were to be held frequently, freedom of speech in parliament was guaranteed, laws could not be suspended without parliament's consent and parliament's consent was needed for the levying of money or the keeping of a standing army. Within parliament the House of Commons succeeded in asserting complete control over money matters. The House of Lords was denied the power to amend taxation bills and was loath to exercise its power to reject them – a power that in any event disappeared with the enactment of the Parliament Bill in 1911.

The next stage in the evolution of parliament came when the Commons gained control over the king's ministers (*minister* is the Latin 'servant'). In the reign of Charles II a committee of the Privy Council – the cabinet – had come into being. This informal group of ministers gradually became the *de facto* government.

Privy Council
In 1540 following the fall of Thomas Cromwell, Henry VIII reshaped his council. He gave it a fixed membership, a new structure and formal powers. It was also given a new name – the Privy Council – because it met in a room in the king's privy lodgings

When George I withdrew from government in 1717, one of the members of the cabinet was recognized as the group leader – the prime minister (*primus* is the Latin 'first', from which we also derive primitive, primitivism, primary, primal, premier and primogeniture – the feudal right of the first-born son to succeed to his father's offices and property). By the end of the century the king's government was fast becoming government on behalf of the king.

The ultimate victory of the Commons in its struggle with the king over his right to appoint and dismiss his government without reference to parliament was signalled by the resignation of Lord North, the prime minister during the American Revolution, after the House of Commons passed a motion to end the war. It can be said that the power of the king to control the policy of his ministers ceased in 1829 when George IV, after a prolonged struggle, finally gave his assent to the bill for the Emancipation of Catholics.

emancipation
means freedom from legal, political, social, intellectual or moral restrictions. It derives from the Latin e 'from', *manus* 'hand' and *capere* 'to take', and originally described the ritual by which Roman children became legally independent of their fathers

The early nineteenth century saw two other developments on the road to parliamentary democracy. During the 1830s the concept of ministerial responsibility with ministers answering to parliament for their departments developed. In the same decade the first Representation of the People Act was passed and the House of Commons was gradually transformed, by successive extensions of the franchise, into a generally representative chamber. Democratization took nearly a century. Women did not get full voting rights until 1928. The process also extended itself in the nineteenth century to local government, which was then extensively reformed.

The British are rightly proud when they proclaim Westminster 'the mother of parliaments', because the modern representative parliament is one of man's greatest inventions. However, it can hardly be said that the UK has parliamentary government. For a while in the middle of the nineteenth century this was the situation, but once mass politics arrived with the extension of the franchise, governments that could appeal directly to the people began to dominate parliament and the whole political process. By the end of that century cabinet government had arrived, that is a system in which governments have a monopoly of legislative initiative and parliament is reduced to appraising, amending and approving the bills and measures proposed to it by the government.

parochialism
an assertion of the primacy of local attitudes, perspectives, beliefs, culture, etc. against the larger world

Parochia is a late Latin word meaning 'parish', the smallest unit of ecclesiastical organization. Provincial derives from the Latin *provincia,* a large tract or region outside the capital or metropolis, controlled not by local officials but by a Roman official. A provincial attitude is wider than a parochial one but narrower than a metropolitan one.

partisan
pertaining to a supporter – usually a vehement one – of a party or cause

Pars, partis is the Latin 'part' or 'faction', from which we derive partisan as well as party and partial. Bipartisan means relating to two parties (*bi* derives from *bis* the Latin 'twice'.) A bipartisan policy is a policy supported by two (often otherwise opposed) parties.

pathos
a quality in a situation that moves one to pity; also a feeling of sympathy or pity

Pathos is the Greek 'suffering' and therefore 'feeling'. Writers often seek to create pathos. To heighten their effect they may resort to pathetic fallacy, a phrase coined by John Ruskin to describe the false attribution to inanimate nature of the feelings of a human subject. Pathos can slide into bathos, a ludicrous descent from elevated to ordinary matters, or from elevated to ordinary style in speech or writing (*bathus* is 'deep' in Greek). A writer may actually seek a bathetic effect. Oscar Wilde remarked of Dickens's description of the death of Little Nell in the ruin where she and her grandfather had made their home, 'One would have to have a heart of stone to read the death of Little Nell without laughing.' Alexander Pope in *The Rape of the Lock* proclaimed:

> Here thou, great Anna! whom three realms obey,
> Dost sometimes counsel take – and sometimes tay [tea].

The prefix *patho,* from *pathos*, indicates 'disease', which is often the cause of suffering. Pathology is the branch of medicine that deals with the origin and nature of disease, including the changes that occur as a result of disease (*ology* here means 'study of', from the Greek *logos* word', 'reason' or 'account'). A pathogen is any agent that can cause disease (*gen*, from the Greek *genēs* 'born', here indicates 'cause of'). The suffix *path* indicates either 'a practitioner of a particular method of treatment' – thus an osteopath seeks to heal by manipulating the bones (*osteon* is the Greek 'bone') – or 'a person suffering from a specific disease or disorder', such as a psychopath. A psychopath (*psychē* is the Greek 'spirit' or 'mind') is a person afflicted with a personality disorder characterized by a tendency to commit antisocial and sometimes violent acts and a failure to feel guilt for such acts. Sociopath – *socio* indicates 'social' or 'society' (from the Latin *socius* 'comrade') – is a synonym. A homeopath seeks to treat disease by using small amounts of drugs that, in a healthy person, would produce symptoms similar to those of the disease being treated (*homos* is the Greek 'same'), and an allopath seeks to induce a condition different from the cause of the disease – allopathy is the orthodox approach of doctors (*allos* is the Greek 'other' or 'different').

genēs
also gives us genealogy, gene, genetic, generation and genome

homeopathy
A German doctor introduced this system of medical practice about 1796 on the principle *similia similibus curantur* (Latin, 'like things are cured by likes')

If a person is indifferent to a situation he or she may be said to be apathetic (*a* is the Greek negative).

The Latin equivalent of *pathein* is *pati, passum* 'to suffer'. From it we derive passion, dispassion, passionate, dispassionate, compassionate, passive and impassive.

patrician
aristocratic

Pater, patris is the Latin 'father'. The *patricians* were the 'fathers' of Rome, the nobility. They were the senators who, after the expulsion of the kings, held all the power in Rome. The appointment of tribunes to represent the ordinary people (*plebs*) eroded their power to some extent. They were finally eclipsed by the appointment of emperors.

In modern usage it is apposite to apply the word to someone who lives in a republic but displays the appearance, manners or attitudes of an aristocrat.

patriot
one who loves, serves and defends his or her country

Patria is the Latin 'fatherland'.

A compatriot (*com* is derived from the Latin *cum* 'with') means a fellow-countryman.

patriotism
'Patriotism is your conviction that this country is the best in the world because you were born in it.' (George Bernard Shaw)

An expatriate is someone who lives outside his or her own country (*ex* is the Latin 'from' or 'outside').

Funds invested abroad and brought home are said to be repatriated (*re* is the Latin 'again').

A patrimony is an inheritance from a father or one's ancestors (it comes from the Latin *patrimonium,* a legal term for the will of a *paterfamilias* – a head of a Roman family; it denotes property inherited by an individual or an institution – thus the patrimony of St Peter refers to the property passed to a Pope by his predecessor).

Pavlovian
automatic, unthinking but artificially engineered

Ivan Petrovich Pavlov was a Russian physiologist whose experiments on the stimulation (*stimulus* is the Latin 'goad') of saliva in dogs by the ringing of bells led to the theory of conditioned reflex. A physiologist studies the processes of life in animals and plants (*physis* is the Greek 'nature'). A physicist studies physics, the branch of science concerned with the properties of matter and energy and the relationships between them. It includes mechanics, optics, electricity and magnetism, acoustics, and heat. Modern physics, based on quantum theory, includes atomic, nuclear, particle and solid-state studies.

acoustics
is the science of sound from the Greek *akouein* 'to hear'

pax Romana
the long period of peace and stability throughout the Roman world following the establishment of imperial power by Augustus

Pax, pacis is the Latin 'peace', from which we derive pacify, pacific and pacifism – *pax Romana* is literally 'the Roman peace'. Janus was the Roman god of doorways, depicted in art with two heads facing in opposite directions. In the forum in Rome there was a temple to Janus, the door of which was kept open in time of war and closed in time of peace. Augustus was greatly pleased when the Senate decreed the closing of the temple of Janus to mark the restoration of peace following his triumph over Antony and Cleopatra.

In the nineteenth century when the British empire ('on which the sun never sets' as the Scottish writer Christopher North observed) reached its zenith, the mandarins in Whitehall, steeped as they were in the ancient classics, discerned a *pax Britannica*. The world hegemony established by the Americans from the 1960s onwards, characterized by the avoidance of world war, led commentators to refer to a *pax Americana*.

A pacifist is someone who is opposed to war or who believes that all war is wrong. 'Overt "pacifism" – the word was coined in 1901 – was undeniably one of the early twentieth century's least successful political movements.' (Niall Ferguson, *The Pity of War*) When war psychosis grips a country, it is extremely difficult for pacifists to maintain their principled stance. Lytton Strachey, author of *Eminent Victorians*, was arraigned before a court for refusing to obey the call-up when World War I broke out. The prosecutor followed the usual line in such cases, namely that pacifists were cowards. 'Tell me, Mr Strachey, what would you do if you saw a German soldier attempting to rape your sister?' This question usually left pacifists snatching at such straws as 'I'd try to reason with him,' or 'I'd call the police.' Strachey, who was homosexual, convulsed the court with the reply, 'I should try and come between them.'

psychosis
from the Greek *psychē* 'soul' is a serious mental disorder characterized by such conditions as mental confusion, delusion or hallucination. The psychotic individual lacks insight concerning the nature of these symptoms believing them to be objectively true. Insight is a term used in psychiatry to describe the capacity to appreciate that one's disturbances of thought, feeling and behaviour are subjective and invalid. In neurotic conditions the individual retains insight into the nature of his symptoms, in psychosis the individual loses it

Janus, from which we derive janitor for a doorkeeper, gives us the name of the first month of the year – January (from *Januarius* 'relating to Janus') – a felicitous usage since the first month looks in two directions: back to the old year and forward to the new. Janus-faced describes someone two-faced or duplicitous (from the Latin *duplex, duplicis* 'double').

The Romans called the threshold of a doorway *limen, liminis*. Psychologists use the term subliminal (*sub* is the Latin 'below') for the level at which sensation is too faint to be consciously experienced. Hence the expression subliminal advertising.

sublime
from the Latin *sublimis* 'elevated', seems to be unrelated to subliminal. Freud used the term sublimation (from *sublimis*) for the directing unconsciously of the sex impulse into some non-sexual activity. Preliminary (something done before a main event) derives from the Latin *prae* 'before' and *limen*. To eliminate is to remove or get rid of (literally to turn away from the threshold, e being 'from')

A pedagogue was originally a tutor slave in a wealthy Greek or Roman family (*pais, paidos* is the Greek 'boy' and *agōgos* is 'leader' – compare demagogue and mystagogue). His duty was to guard the sons of the family from evil, both physical and moral, rather than to instruct them. In later Roman times the name was given to boy slaves who discharged a variety of personal services in palaces; later still these were called pages (from a corruption of pedagogue). We might say 'The primary school curriculum is strong pedagogically because it seeks, so far as is possible, to centre learning on the interests of the child, in line with modern education theory.'

pedagogic
relating to the principles and practice of teaching

A peninsula is a piece of land jutting into the sea – it is almost an island (*insula* is the Latin 'island', from which we also derive insular, insularity, insulate and isolate). Note that a narrow strip of land connecting two relatively large bodies of land is called an isthmus, from the

pen
peninsula, penultimate and penumbra – words whose prefix *pen* derives from the Latin *paene* 'almost'

Greek *isthmos* 'narrow passage' – thus the isthmus of Corinth, which joins the Peloponnesus to the rest of mainland Greece. (The eponymous Pelops was the son of Tantalus and grandfather of the two Greek leaders of the Trojan War, Agamemnon and Menelaus.)

Penultimate means last but one – the ultimate is the last (*ultimus* is 'last' in Latin).

Penumbra means the partly shaded area around a darkened object (*umbra* means 'shadow' in Latin; umbrageous as in an umbrageous oak means shady; to adumbrate is to foreshadow; an umbrella provides protection from rain; the euphonious Vallombrosa in Milton's famous reference in *Paradise Lost*, 'Thick as autumnal leaves that strow the brooks / In Vallombrosa,' derives from the Latin *vallis* 'valley' and *umbrosus* 'shady').

per se
intrinsically, in itself, as such

Per is the Latin 'through' or 'in'; *se* is 'itself'. Thus, 'Alcohol *per se* is not bad for you – too much of it is!'

persona grata
an acceptable person

Persona is the Latin 'player's mask'; *grata* means 'acceptable'. The phrase *persona grata* is used primarily in a diplomatic context where the person so typified is declared to be an acceptable diplomatic representative by the host country. Someone who is not acceptable or who becomes unacceptable (for example an official attached to an embassy who is discovered to be a spy) is declared *persona non grata* and has to leave.

dramatis personae
(Latin) means the characters in a play. *Drama, dramatos* is the Greek 'play'

In classical drama each player wore a mask (grave, terrifying, sleepy or humorous as the character being played required) called a *persona* because it was a thing through which the actor spoke (*per* is the Latin 'through', *sonare, sonatum* is the Latin 'to sound'). Gradually, persona came to mean the character being played and finally it got the modern meaning of individual or person.

The Swiss psychiatrist Carl Jung developed the psychological concept of the persona as a mask adopted by a person to present a particular image to others, often the one the public expects because of the person's role in society. The persona is the public personality. It often contrasts with the person's real or private personality: 'Nixon presented the persona of an affable, self-confident world leader but the tapes revealed the real Nixon – a bad-tempered, foul-mouthed paranoiac.'

Personality, the cluster of essential characteristics

that makes each of us what we are, is a major concern of psychologists. Is the neonate (newborn, from the Greek *neos* 'new' and Latin *natus* 'born') a *tabula rasa* awaiting the stamp of life's experience or does he or she already possess the elements of a personality type? Are certain characteristics genetically encoded? Is the human personality basically good and incorrigibly social as Rousseau and Rogers would maintain or is it more naturally inclined towards evil, as Freud would suggest, yet with the capacity to integrate different elements to achieve a self-realized whole?

paranoiac
means someone with an abnormal tendency to suspect or mistrust others, derived from the Greek *para* 'beside' and *noos* 'the mind', often used, as here, in a loose, non-clinical sense (*klinē* is the Greek 'bed'; clinical derives from *klinikos* 'pertaining to a [sick] bed'). Nous from *noos* is used for intelligence or *savoir faire* (French, 'the knowledge to do what is necessary', literally 'to know how to do')

Observably, personality, like plaster, is pretty stable over time. The great American psychologist William James, the brother of the novelist Henry James, said that by the age of thirty the character had set in most of us and would never soften again. (That age is set much earlier now.) While the nature versus nurture (from the Latin *nurire* 'to nourish') debate rolls on, research on identical twins suggests that in the development phase both genetic and environmental influences are at play, although the relative weighting to be given to each set is not settled.

Jung means 'young' in German, and is pronounced yung. James Joyce used this fact to work into the fabric of *Finnegans Wake* an irreverent reference to the fathers of modern psychology: pubescent girls were, he observed, 'yung and easily freudened'. (Pubescent means becoming sexually mature – *pubes* is the Latin 'a grown-up youth'; the *escent* suffix derives from a Latin form that indicates 'becoming', the process of change from one state to another: an adolescent is someone who is becoming an adult, an obsolescent instrument is one that is becoming obsolete.)

philanthropy
love of mankind as shown in disinterested service to the welfare of all

Philos is the Greek 'lover'; *anthrōpos* is 'mankind'. Institutions or wealthy individuals who donate money for schools, libraries, irrigation schemes, etc. in undeveloped countries could be characterized as philanthropic.

A person is disinterested when he or she has no personal advantage to gain from a situation; a person is uninterested when his or her attention is simply not engaged by a situation; a person may be interested and disinterested at the same time. A person who characteristically acts in the interest of others is said to be altruistic (derived from the Latin *alter* 'other', from which we also get alternative).

Phile is a particle derived from *philos* which, used as a suffix, denotes 'lover of' – thus Anglophile (admirer of England and things English), bibliophile (lover of books from *biblion,* the Greek 'book', from which we also get Bible, derived from Bublos, a Phoenician port Greece obtained its supplies of Egyptian papyrus from, as well as bibliography, a list of books or articles on a subject, *graphein* being the Greek 'to write'), and paedophile (a person with a pathological sexual attraction to children, *pais, paidos* being the Greek 'child').

Mis is a prefix derived from *misein,* the Greek 'to hate', which denotes 'hater of'. A misanthropist is a hater of mankind, a misogynist is a hater of women (*gynē* is the Greek 'woman'), a misandrist is a hater of men (*anēr, andros* is 'man'; but, anomalously, a philanderer means a womanizer – a lover of numerous women).

Androgynous is used to describe someone who has the characteristics of both a male and a female – who is epicene. It is often applied to a male with normal genitalia but secondary female features such as soft fair skin, a small pretty face and a gentle voice. Hermaphroditic is related, referring to more overtly ambiguous genitalia with apparent mix of both male and female properties. True hermaphrodism with dual genitalia is virtually non-existent. Hermaphroditos was the son of Hermes, the herald of the gods whom the Romans identified with their Mercury, and Aphrodite, the goddess of love whom they identified with their Venus and from whom aphrodisiac meaning sex stimulant is derived. Hermaphroditos and the nymph Salmacis grew together into the one person.

Phobia is the Greek 'fear'. Agoraphobia is a morbid fear of open spaces (*agora* is the Greek 'market-place', the equivalent of the Latin *forum*).

Claustrophobia is the fear of confined spaces (*claustrum* is the Latin 'enclosed space'). Since fear of people provokes hatred of them, Francophobe is the opposite of Francophile and means a hater of France and things French.

Homophobia is intense hatred or fear of homosexuals or homosexuality (*homo* here derives from the Greek component of homosexual).

Arachnophobia is fear of spiders (*arachnē* is 'spider' in Greek).

philistine
an uncultured, materialistic person

The Philistines, the ancient inhabitants of south-west Palestine, were the inveterate enemies of the Israelites (inveterate derives from the Latin *vetus, veteris* 'old' and means old, deep-rooted; the *in* prefix intensifies the sense; veteran is another derivative). Their god Dagon was therianthropic, being half-man and half-fish. The giant warrior Goliath whom the young David slew was a Philistine and so was Delilah, who robbed Samson of his strength by having his hair shaved off after she had lulled him to sleep in her lap. (The Philistines then seized Samson, put out his eyes and took him down to Gaza where they used him to turn the mill in the prison there – hence Milton's famous description of Samson, 'Eyeless in Gaza, at the mill with slaves.')

Philistine in its earliest usage signified the group enemy. It became associated with culture when, in the form *Philister*, it was used by German students as a pejorative term for townspeople and others outside the university, deemed to be therefore uncultured. It is said it first came into use in 1693 in Jena when a student was killed in a fracas between students and townspeople and the pastor, in his funeral sermon, used the text *Philister über dir, Samson* ('The Philistines are upon thee, Samson'). With the Industrial Revolution and the rapid growth of the middle-class, the word came to describe the materialistic values of that aesthetically insecure group. The French captured the same phenomenon in the term *mentalité d'epicier* (*epicier* is 'grocer' in French). The English borrowed *Philister* in the form philistine and the term was promulgated by Matthew Arnold, the poet and critic, in particular: 'Philistinism! – We have not the expression in English. Perhaps we have not the word because we have so much of the thing.' (*Essays in Criticism*) Arnold saw culture, which he defined as 'acquainting ourselves with the best that has been known and said in the world, and thus with the history of the human spirit' (*Literature and Dogma*), as the only means of saving Britain from Victorian materialism. His 'Dover Beach' is one of the nineteenth century's most anthologized poems.

fracas
from the French *fracasser* 'to shatter' is a brawl, a donnybrook (from the character of Donnybrook Fair held near Dublin until 1855), or a melee (from the French *mêlée*). An imbroglio, from the Italian *imbroglio* 'an entangling', describes a political or interpersonal situation of great confusion and complexity but has no connotation of violence

Philistinism has lost its class connotation. A public agency, whose ultimate owner is the people, that displays a lack of sensibility in the style of its buildings and furnishings, might now stand accused of being philistine.

philosophy
man's attempt to understand the world and his own existence in it by means of rational argument, discussion and debate

Philein is the Greek 'to love'; *sophia* is 'wisdom'. A philosopher is literally a lover of wisdom. Originally the Greek philosophers were simply called *sophoi* 'wise men' but Pythagoras, one of the greatest of them, felt that that title was too arrogant so he coined philosopher instead.

There are four major ways in which man seeks to understand the world and establish the things about it that are true. One is religion based on faith in doctrines that are usually derived from divine revelation, developed by a theology and sustained by public ceremonies and general obedience. Another is art, which in its various forms seeks to explore human experience and capture those things in it that seem perennial, perhaps eternal, perhaps true. Another is science, which addresses itself to that part of our world that can be physically grasped and tested. The fourth is philosophy, which addresses itself to the deep underlying issues that religion also addresses but aims to rely on human reason rather than faith to establish truth. While these ways may sometimes seem to conflict with one another, famously as in the case of science and religion, each produces a distinctive kind of knowledge; in combination they provide the polychrome forms of our inscape (inner field of vision, from the Latin *in* 'in' and *scape*, coined by Gerard Manley Hopkins by analogy with landscape, itself derived from the Dutch painting term *lantschap* 'region').

science
gave birth to scientific method – a method of investigation in which a problem is first identified and observations, experiments or other relevant data are then used to construct or test hypotheses that purport to solve it. Scientism may mean the application of, or belief in, the scientific method or, pejoratively, the uncritical application of scientific or quasi-scientific methods to inappropriate fields of study or investigation

Because philosophy seeks to understand the world using reason, its highest (metaphysical) concerns are with what exists, including what existence means (this is called ontology, from the Greek *on, ontos* 'being'), and what we can know, including what knowledge means (this is called epistemology, *epistēmē* being the Greek 'knowledge'). Since the defining characteristic of philosophy is that it asks the deep underlying questions, the word, which we have been using in its general sense, can also be applied in a specific sense to any activity – the philosophy of education, the philosophy of law, the philosophy of history, etc.

the philosopher's stone
for which alchemists searched, was believed to turn base metals into gold. Some alchemists thought magnesia was an ingredient of the stone

The Greeks are the people we look to for the beginning of philosophy. The two Greek philosophers Plato and Aristotle are probably the most influential philosophers that ever lived. It is said that everything written since is a footnote to their writing. For Plato philosophy was an attempt to articulate the wisdom inherent in the common beliefs of people. For Aristotle philosophy was an attempt to articulate the wisdom inherent in the phenomena of our everyday experience.

From these two philosophers two great schools of philosophy arose – Platonism and Aristotelianism. They influenced to varying degrees all philosophical and scientific thinking up to late medieval times. What we call modern science saw itself as a conscious break with Aristotle's thinking.

In the Middle Ages the Church sought to use philosophy to support religion by conflating (combining or blending, from the Latin *conflare, conflatum* 'to blow together') the two. Saint Thomas Aquinas, whose philosophy and theology are referred to as Thomism, was Aristotelian but used elements of Platonism. Aquinas sought to articulate his Christian vision of life predominantly in Aristotle's categories. The interplay between philosophical and theological thought has indeed been a continuous feature of Christian writing from the beginning. We find Stoic patterns of thought in St Paul, a strong existentialist impetus in much twentieth-century Christian life, and contemporary liberation theologians articulate their Christian vision in Marxist categories. Because of the profound way in which they discussed the central issues of philosophy the work of Plato and Aristotle is referred to as the perennial philosophy. It should not be surprising that in moral, political and certain areas of philosophic logic there is a revival of interest in Plato and Aristotle.

Following the Protestant Reformation and the decline in ecclesiastical authority over thought, thinkers turned to the use of reason alone as the means of establishing knowledge of the world. *Ratio, rationis* is the Latin 'reason'; rationalism is the term used to describe the approach of philosophers, starting with the Frenchman, René Descartes, who sought to apply reason with a mathematical rigour to the pursuit of knowledge. The German philosopher G.W. Leibnitz contributed an important distinction to rationalism: analytical statements can be demonstrated to be true or false by simply analysing them. Synthetic statements can be tested only

Aquinas
is the schoolman *par excellence*. A schoolman was a master in a medieval university versed in scholasticism – the system of philosophy, theology and teaching based on the writings of the Church Fathers and, from the twelfth century, of Aristotle. School derives from the Latin *schola* 'school', itself derived from the Greek *skholē* 'time spent in the pursuit of learning'. Scholastic means relating to schools, scholars (from *schola*) or education. A scholium is a commentary on a text, especially a classical one; a scholiast is a writer of such a commentary

it begs the question
is an expression used by philosophers to indicate a logical failure inherent in a proposition: it points out that the truth of the proposition is dependent on the acceptance as true of an unproven element in the proposition; it is sometimes incorrectly used as if it meant it provokes the question, that is to say, as if it raises the question of the truth of an element that is outside, and not inherent in, the proposition

by going beyond the terms and seeking evidence outside of them. Mathematics and logic were seen to consist entirely of analytic statements. They therefore were a source of certain knowledge. All statements about the world were seen as synthetic.

Empiricism was a reaction to rationalism. Empiricists asserted that all our knowledge of the world came through our senses and that therefore philosophy should concentrate on developing the means to handle and assess sense data.

The rapid success of modern science, based on Newton's physics, encouraged philosophers to think that the project of establishing an unassailable intellectual foundation upon which could be reared sound and complex systems to understand all of reality was a realistic one.

Albert Einstein, whose theories dethroned Newton's, changed that. To deal with the paradigmatic character of knowledge the Austrian philosopher Karl Popper proposed that, since all knowledge is provisional, the commonsensical approach would be to adopt propositions that can be rigorously tested, allow them to be subject to continual widespread criticism and change them as necessary.

placebo
a medicine given for psychological rather than physical effect

Placebo is a form of the Latin *placere* 'to please' and means 'I shall please'. People often expect a doctor to give them medicine even if he or she feels they do not need it. In order not to disappoint them, a doctor may prescribe a placebo. However, the placebo is a considerable resource in the development of medical treatment where quantitative testing of newly developed medicines is required. Placebo-controlled trials take place in which groups of patients receive the test agent or a similarly presented inactive substance.

People sometimes dourly characterize an attractive policy proposal made by a political opponent as a placebo.

A nostrum is a quack medicine, derived from the Latin *noster* 'our' – our own recipe. In ancient Rome Cato the Censor could be said to have had a nostrum to deal with Rome's fractious (irritable or unruly, from the Latin *frangere*, *fractum* 'to break', which also gives us fraction, fracture and fragment) relations with Carthage: he wound up every speech in the Senate with the phrase *'Carthago delenda est!'* (Latin, 'Carthage must be destroyed!')

platitude
a leaden, commonplace remark

Platus is the Latin 'broad' or 'flat'. It is not uncommon for one political party to attack another party's manifesto on the basis that it is full of platitudes.

plebiscite
a direct vote by the electorate on an important issue

Plebs is the Latin 'common people' (as opposed to the *patricians*). The *scite* formation derives from the Latin *sciscere* 'to consult'. *Referendum*, the Latin 'a thing to be referred' (to the people), is a synonym for plebiscite.

pleonasm
a redundant expression

Pleos is the Greek 'full'; *pleon* is a form of it that means 'fuller'. A pleonasm adds a word or part of a word to a word or phrase that already carries the meaning conveyed by the word or phrase. Bonus (from the Latin *bonus* 'good') means a payment made to workers that is additional to their regular pay. The expression added bonus is therefore a pleonasm. A prerequisite is something required as a prior condition (*pre* is Latin 'before' and *requisitus* from *requirere* is 'needed'). So a necessary (or essential) prerequisite is also a pleonasm. To plan means to work out a scheme to accomplish some purpose. It is always directed at the future – you cannot plan for the past or the present. The expressions to plan ahead or to preplan are therefore pleonastic. To divert (from the Latin prefix *di* 'away from' and *vertere* 'to turn') means to turn away from. The expression to divert away from is therefore pleonastic.

The word panoply (from the Greek *pan* 'all' and *hopla* 'arms') describes a full suit of armour worn by a hoplite, an ancient Greek heavily armed soldier and, by extension, is used to mean a brilliant array: 'The king received the victorious general in the Great Hall surrounded by the panoply of state.' The expression full panoply is pleonastic. So are the expressions a populist demagogue and a clandestine conspiracy (*clandestinus* is the Latin 'secret' or 'concealed').

Pleonasms are tautologous and should be avoided. However, as words lose their pristine sense, pleonastic expressions multiply and Leahy's Law comes into operation: 'If a thing is done wrong often enough, it becomes right.'

redundant
from the Latin prefix *red* 'back' and *undare* 'to flow' means flowing back and therefore overflowing – surplus to requirements; superfluous, from the Latin *super* 'above' and *fluere* 'to flow', and otiose, from the Latin *otiosus* 'idle' or 'functionless', would also serve; to inundate is to flood

plenus
is the Latin 'full'. From it we derive plenary meaning full or complete as in, 'She was given plenary powers to carry out the party's programme,' or 'The conference met in plenary session and then divided into workshops,' plenitude meaning fullness or completeness and plenum meaning a full session or a space completely filled with matter (as opposed to a vacuum, an entirely empty space, from the Latin *vacuus* 'empty')

pluralist society
a society that respects the culture and beliefs of the different groups and individuals within it

findere, fissum
also give us fission (the splitting of the nucleus of an atom), fissure (a cleft) and fissiparous (reproducing by splitting)

Plus, pluris is the Latin 'more'. Human society is fissile (tending to split, from the Latin *findere, fissum* 'to split') because pressing issues are constantly cropping up upon which people can strongly differ. Some states have tended to seek to maintain their unity by restricting the freedom of thought and action of all citizens and, where there were minority groups, by imposing the values of the majority on everyone, particularly through the provisions of their constitutions. Many Islamic states are confessional states (committed to a particular religious faith) and therefore the opposite of pluralist.

Until modern times most European states were confessional (thus, it was not until 1829 that Catholics were given the franchise in Ireland and Britain).

Liberal democratic thinking favours the separation of Church and State in the interest of freedom and tolerance (but this separation is often taken as synonomous with the separation of law and morality – see secularism).

Pluralism is a marked feature of modern Western societies that manifests itself in virtually all aspects of life – politics, religion, law, morality, economics and culture. In refraining from installing any one idea of the good life as ideal, it creates not only tolerance but also a productive interaction between people with different ideas and experiences that allows full range to the essentially questing nature of the human spirit. For criticism of certain pluralist tendencies see liberalism and secularism.

pogrom
an organized massacre of a minority group

Pogrom is the Russian 'destruction', which came into use in the late nineteenth century to describe the sporadic government-inspired attacks on Jews. To deal with the growth of nationalism among the many non-Russian peoples who had been absorbed in his empire the czar had decided on a policy of assimilation called Russification – the equivalent of the process of Anglicization taking place in Ireland at the same time. The Jews were attacked because they resisted assimilation.The fact that a Jewish girl was among the group of anarchists who assassinated Alexander II intensified the animus that found expression in the pogroms (*animus* is the Latin 'spirit' that in English usage means bad spirit or spite). Pogrom may be applied to attacks on any religious minorities in a community.

polemical
relating to heated dispute

Polemos is the Greek 'war' and so polemical suggests a certain fierceness in discussion or writing. Swift's *Drapier's Letters* was polemical. So was the debate conducted by Irish scholars in the 1940s about whether there was one Saint Patrick or two Saint Patricks. Apropos (from the French *à propos* 'to the purpose') of this controversy, the satirist Myles na gCopaleen observed that it was the singular achievement of the Dublin Institute for Advanced Studies, which had a School of Celtic Studies and a School of Cosmic Physics, to prove there were two Saint Patricks and no God.

Instead of taking a polemical approach one might find it more advantageous to take the opposite – an eirenic(al) or irenic(al) one (*eirēnē* is the Greek 'peace'). Irene, the Greek goddess of peace, was a favourite name for Byzantine princesses.

In a polemical discussion either side is likely to unleash a diatribe. A diatribe is a bitter, stinging denunciation (*dia* is the Greek 'through' and *tribein* is 'to rub'; tribadism, a lesbian practice, also derives from *tribein*). A diatribe originally, as in Plato, meant a discourse. It took on its rancorous character during the Reformation period. Someone may even deliver a philippic – a speech full of bitter invective, so called after the orations of the Athenian, Demosthenes, against King Philip of Macedonia, father of Alexander the Great, when he was establishing his hegemony over the Greek states exhausted by the internecine Peloponnesian War (internecine pertains to murderous conflict within a group: *inter* means 'between' in Latin and *necare* is 'to kill').

invective
means bitterly abusive denunciation, from the Latin *in* 'in' and *vehere*, *vectum* 'to carry', that is, to assail physically or as here verbally. Vehicle (a conveyance) and vector, which can mean among other things a carrier of disease, also derive from *vehere*, *vectum*

Political invective is often crude. Simon Schama in *Citizens* tells us about the treatment of Madame du Barry, Louis XV's last mistress, by the revolutionaries: 'One especially poisonous polemic called her "this barrel of infection; this drain of iniquity; this impure cloaca who not content with devouring the finances of France nourished herself on human flesh on the model of the anthropophagi".'

cloaca
means sewer, from the Latin *cluere* 'to purge'. In ancient Rome the *Cloaca Maxima* ('Grand Sewer') once flowed in open stream from the forum into the Tiber. Cloacal, as in cloacal humour, means relating to a sewer

politics
all that relates to the government of states

Polis is the Greek 'city-state' and *politikos* is therefore 'relating to the affairs of the state'. In democratic Athens every citizen (*politēs*) was expected to play an active role in governing the city by taking part in public debates, voting, holding public office, etc.

A politician is someone who takes an active part in politics. Everyone in a democracy should ideally be a politician (after the Athenian model). In practice the term is reserved for those who are active in political parties, particularly those who seek election to public office. Those who win elections are called public representatives.

A political party is a voluntary organization that seeks to gain popular support for a set of policies. A party with national appeal will have local party organizations in each constituency to influence the grassroots and mobilize support at elections. To win electoral support and keep it politicians in a democracy must be attentive to what ordinary people – the grassroots – are thinking about issues (grassroots originally applied to people living in rural areas).

to mobilize
is to put into motion, derived from the Latin *movere, motum* 'to move'; an automobile is a vehicle that can move itself – *autos* 'self' is Greek

Whatever interests politicians is political. Because of their nature, democratic politicians are likely to be interested in whatever interests significant numbers of people. Broadly speaking, the stuff of politics is woven from five threads.

Firstly, politicians are interested in order. The primary function of government is to establish and maintain order within the state and, with that end in view, to seek to secure political stability outside the state as well.

Secondly, politicians are interested in economic issues such as industrial development, agriculture, employment, imports, exports and infrastructure.

infra
is the Latin 'below' or 'beneath'. Infra dig (from the Latin *infra dignitatem*) means beneath one's dignity. Infrasound refers to sound-like waves that have a frequency below the audible (*audire, auditum* is the Latin 'to hear', which also gives us audience, audit, auditor, auditory, auditorium and audiovisual)

Thirdly, politicians are interested in social issues such as the welfare of the weaker groups in the state – the sick and the handicapped, the unemployed, the poor, the orphaned and the old (*socialis* is the Latin 'pertaining to friends or companions' and by extension 'to the community').

Fourthly, politicians are interested in cultural issues (the Latin *colere, cultum,* from which cultural derives, means 'to tend to' or 'to cultivate'; culture is sometimes used in a comprehensive sense to mean way of life, sometimes, as here, in a restricted sense to cover education, the arts, language and leisure activities, and sometimes in a more restricted sense still to mean the fine arts).

Fifthly, politicians are interested in institutional issues such as the organization of the public service, the efficiency of the courts and the functions of the local authorities (*instituere* is the Latin 'to make to stand' – an institution is anything that has been established).

In popular parlance, politics may also refer to any situation in which a group of people seeks to resolve peacefully the what, when, why, how and where issues, for example office politics. The word may be used in a somewhat pejorative sense to suggest that the motivation for actions taken against an individual or group is suspect.

Apolitical means uninvolved in politics – *a* is a Greek negative prefix. It also occurs in the word amoral. Moral (Latin *moralis*) in its general sense applies to someone who believes in the existence of laws that determine the goodness or badness of human behaviour – *mos, moris* is the Latin 'custom' or 'manner'. Amoral, the opposite of moral in its general sense, applies to someone who does not believe in the existence of such laws and who therefore holds himself or herself aloof from morality. Moral is also used in the restricted sense of virtuous – a moral person. Immoral, the opposite of moral in its restricted sense, means sinful or depraved – *in* is a Latin negative particle – before b, m or p it becomes *im* – thus also imbalance and improper.

Realpolitik is a German word meaning 'the politics of realism'. It marked a break with the traditional idea that politics was concerned with the pursuit of ideals such as the good or, since the Enlightenment, of values such as equality, freedom, justice. It was introduced in the mid-nineteenth century to contrast with the lack of realism of the German revolutionary liberals of 1848. It survived in usage because it captured the style of Bismarck's politics: Bismarck sought to assess what his opponents really wanted and based his moves on that rather than on what they said they wanted (because that would almost certainly contain elements they would be prepared to concede in the usual climax of politics – a compromise).

A political scientist is an academic who has qualified in the study of politics.

pornography
obscene descriptions or depictions

Pornē is the Greek 'prostitute'; *graphein* is 'to write'. Material on sex may be scientific, erotic (Erōs [gen. *Erōtos*] is the Greek god of sexual love called Cupid by the Romans), or pornographic. An academic context, e.g. medical, readily identifies the scientific. However, it

Eros
first appeared in art as a beautiful winged youth but in Hellenistic times he is depicted as a playful young boy with a bow and arrow to pierce the hearts of lovers. When he wooed and won the Princess Psyche they had a daughter Voluptas (Pleasure). A voluptuary is someone excessively given to bodily pleasure. Erotica are erotic writings

is difficult to distinguish between the erotic, which is also regarded as licit (such as occurs in love poetry and in the Bible, e.g. Song of Songs), and pornography, which is regarded as illicit. In a permissive age, such as ours, statues of nude subjects are regarded as a healthy celebration of the human form (as in classical times); in a puritanical period they may be fig-leafed. (Puritanical, derived from the Latin *puritas* 'purity', means strict in moral or religious outlook; the Puritans were the more extreme English Protestants of the sixteenth and seventeenth centuries who wished to purify the Church of England of most of its ceremony and other aspects that they deemed to be Roman Catholic.)

Moral relativism bedevils the debate on pornography. Pornography may, perhaps, be usefully distinguished by the fact that it seeks to give vicarious pleasure to the reader or viewer through subjecting some of those depicted to degradation (*vicarius* is the Latin 'substituted'). Such degradation dehumanizes. Dehumanization – the process the Nazis subjected the Jews and other minorities to – may lead to violence and murder.

posthumous
after the death of

Post is the Latin 'after'; *postumus* is a related word meaning 'coming after'; h was included in posthumous because of a mistaken association with *humare, humatum*, the Latin 'to bury' (from which we derive exhume, to disinter; *ex* is the Latin 'out' or 'out of'). Used of an author's book(s), posthumous means published after his or her death. Used of a man's son or daughter it means born after his death: 'Alfonso XII, meanwhile, died in 1885, at the age of twenty-eight, leaving a posthumous son, Alfonso XIII, for whom his mother, Maria Christina, ruled as Regent till 1902.' (Hugh Thomas, *The Spanish Civil War*)

postmodernism
a style and school of thought that seeks to cope with a sense that the values that sustained modernism have collapsed

Modernism is a term used to describe the range of intellectual and stylistic responses of artists from the end of the nineteenth century to the middle of the twentieth century to an awareness of a necessary divergence in the arts from tradition. The divergence was required by the radically altered view man held of himself as a consequence of Nietzsche's existentialism, evolutionary theory, Freud's psychoanalysis, and scientific development generally. It was characterized by such elements as surrealist, expressionist and abstract art, by atonalism in music, by interior monologues and concern for the action of the unconscious in the writings of Virginia Woolf and James Joyce, and by the functionalism and efficiency of high-rise glass and concrete structures in architecture.

modernism
In theology modernism was a movement in the Catholic Church to adapt Christianity to the implications of modern biblical historical and textual criticism. It was condemned by Pope Pius X in 1907

Modernism was a protean response to the vertiginous (from the Latin *vertigo, vertiginis* 'dizziness') scientific, cultural, political, social and economic changes of the twentieth century. Its predicament is caught by Yeats: 'Things fall apart; the centre cannot hold.' The things that weakened the modernist impulse were a realization that the future was not necessarily progressive and that absolute claims to certainty were not possible. Postmodernism (*post* is the Latin 'after') came into use not to suggest that modernism was finished but to indicate that in a world where standards of excellence and relevance could not be asserted as belonging exclusively to one movement, all movements had an equal claim. Contemporary artists are now free to employ the vocabulary of every art movement. This rich resonantal capacity has given the impression to some people that postmodernism is primarily concerned with pastiche. If the distinction between high culture and popular culture is no longer coercive, style rather than substance may tend to be emphasized.

postmortem
an autopsy

Post is the Latin 'after'; *mortem* is a form of *mors, mortis* 'death', from which we derive mortal, immortal, mortality and mortuary. Autopsy means a personal inspection from the Greek *autos* 'self' and *opsis* 'sight' and is applied to the dissection and examination of a dead body to determine the cause of death.

postscript (**PS**)
a message added at the end of a letter after the signature

Post is the Latin 'after'; *scribere, scriptum* is 'to write'. Kerry, in the remote south-west of Ireland is the most beautiful county in Ireland. The people of Kerry are renowned for their acumen, acuity (both words derive from the Latin *acuere* 'to sharpen'), or sagacity (from *sagire* 'to be astute').

There once was a tailor (*sartor* is the Latin 'tailor', from which we derive sartorial) who lived in a village in Kerry. He needed to replace his tailor's goose (a smoothing iron) and decided that if he ordered two from his suppliers in Dublin he would have enough to see him through the remainder of his career. However, what is the plural of a tailor's goose? Geese? Gooses? In Kerry to be guilty of a verbal error would be acutely embarrassing, to have it captured on paper would be insufferable – the tailor was aware of the Latin maxim *quod scriptum manet*. He thought deeply about the problem and after two days hit upon a solution. He wrote down his order: 'Dear Sirs, Please send me one tailor's goose.' Then he added a postscript: 'P.S. Since you are sending one goose you might as well send two.'

The plural of a tailor's goose is gooses.

error
Errare, erratum is the Latin 'to wander' and thence 'to err' – a human predisposition caught classically by Alexander Pope: 'To err is human, to forgive, divine.' (*An Essay on Criticism*). Erratum (plural errata) refers to a mistake in printed matter. Errant, erratic and erroneous are also derived from *errare*

praetorian guard
the personal guard of a Roman emperor or the group of aides surrounding any powerful politician

Prae is the Latin 'before'. A *praetor* was a Roman magistrate next in line to a consul; originally *praetor* (from *praeire, praeitum* 'to go before') meant 'headman' and *praetoria* meant 'headmanship'. Caesar Augustus, the first Roman emperor, established in Rome a praetorian guard of nine battalions of 500 men each to protect the emperor and act as his orderlies. Subsequently the power of the praetorian guard became notorious. On the death of the Emperor Caligula in 41 AD it was the praetorian guard that proclaimed Claudius emperor. When Claudius died suddenly in 54 AD, it was the praetorian guard that proclaimed Nero as his successor. When in 69 AD the Emperor Galba became unpopular with the soldiers because of his economies, the guard acclaimed his rival, Otho, as emperor, marched in upon the forum and unceremoniously lynched Galba without anyone raising a hand in his defence.

The source of the power of a praetorian guard lies in its ability to control access to the personage it protects. (Emperor, derived from the Latin *imperator* 'military commander', was assumed by Augustus as another non-royal title. Because of his pre-eminence among rulers and its adoption by his successors it became the premier royal title.)

guard
Custos, custodis is the Latin 'guard', from which we get custody, custodial and custodian. The word occurs famously in Juvenal, *Sed quis custodiet ipsos custodes*? (Latin, 'But who is to guard the guards themselves?') *Phylax, phylakos* is its Greek equivalent. In medicine a prophylactic (*pro* is the Greek 'before') is a drug or device used to prevent disease. It is also used as a synonym for condom

pragmatic
acting in response to practical needs as they arise

Pragma is the Greek 'act', from *prassein* 'to do'. Pragmatic is opposed to theoretical. It is frequently used of politicians either in a good sense to suggest they are practical, down-to-earth decision-makers or in a pejorative sense to suggest they are shallow, non-ideological and unprincipled. *Praxis*, also derived from *prassein*, means 'practice' and is often used by academics to contrast with theory. Marx, aware that a dichotomy between theory and practice raised the question of where the dynamic to achieve and sustain the theoretical ideal would come from defined praxis as the willed action by which a social theory becomes a reality. The praxis of the proletariat would result from the growing social consciousness created by their work and social experiences and their efforts to change them.

Parapraxis, from the Greek *para* 'abnormal' and *praxis*, was the word Freud used for what we call Freudian slips – minor errors in action such as slips of the tongue or pen or lapses of memory, caused, Freud said, by repressed unconscious thoughts. Joyce found parapraxis a comic device: in *Finnegans Wake* every time someone is about to reveal what exactly went on in the Phoenix Park they begin to stammer.

prerogative
a privilege shared with no one else

Praerogativa is the Latin 'the act of being asked first' (*prae* is 'before'; *rogare, rogatum* is 'to ask', from which we also derive interrogate). The Romans, who voted by tribes or centuries (from *centum* the Latin 'hundred'), had a custom of selecting by lot the tribe or century that would vote first. The other tribes and centuries followed the lead given by that tribe or century because they took the way the lot fell as an indication of the will of the gods.

president
the head of state, or the head of state and head of government, of a republic

Prae is the Latin 'before'; *sedere* is 'to sit'. The president is the one who occupies the chair of authority. The term, which appeared in the fourteenth century for the appointed governor of a province, was first used to describe the head of state and head of government of a republic in the United States of America when George Washington was appointed first president. The usage spread to the new republics of Latin America before becoming the general description of the head of state, or the head of state and head of government, of a republic. Spain's empire in Latin America, after enduring for three centuries, had splintered between 1810 and 1824 into what eventually became sixteen independent states with republican and constitutional governments.

Latin America relates to those regions of the Western Hemisphere south of the US that were conquered by people whose language was based on Latin – mainly Spanish and Portuguese.

Hispania was the Roman name for the Iberian

peninsula. In the US Hispanic (or Latino) describes a US citizen of Latin-American descent. Outside that context Hispanic means relating to Spain or Spanish.

prima facie
at first sight

Prima is a form of *primus,* the Latin 'first'; *facie* is a form of *facies,* the Latin 'appearance'. The expression is used in a legal context: 'When the police arrived, they found him alone in the house, standing over the body with a smoking gun in his hand. This provided them with a good *prima facie* case that he was the murderer.'

prince
a title applied to the male members of a royal family, apart from the king. A Crown prince is a king's eldest son, the heir apparent. A Prince Regent (regent comes from the Latin *regere, rectum* 'to rule' as does rector, direct, director and directory) is a prince who acts as king when the king or queen is either too young or incapacitated. Thus Regency London refers to London in the period 1810–20 when the Prince of Wales (later George IV) ruled in place of his mad father George III. The term prince is also applied to cardinals – princes of the Church – because originally each was head of a Papal State

Maecenas
a wealthy aristocrat and friend of Augustus, was the patron of Virgil, and of Horace, famous for his *Odes.* We use the expression a Maecenas for a munificent patron of the arts

The ancient Romans were once ruled by kings. The last of the kings, Tarquinius Superbus (the Proud), was so cruel that the Romans rebelled against him, expelled him and his family, and arranged that in future the government would be carried on by two officials called consuls, elected every year for a one-year term.

The conspirators who assassinated Julius Caesar (after whom July is named) in 44 BC sought to justify themselves on the grounds that he intended to make himself king. Octavian, Caesar's grand-nephew and adopted son, triumphed in the civil war that followed. The Romans rushed to heap honours on Octavian but he refused all titles except *augustus,* which means 'revered', *imperator,* which means 'emperor' (literally 'head of the army'), and *princeps,* which means 'first citizen' (it comes from the Latin *primus* 'first' and *capere* 'to take'). The word prince is derived from *princeps* and principal, meaning first in rank, is derived from the adjective *principalis* derived from it. Caesar Augustus, as Octavian was now called, went on to rule the Roman empire brilliantly for forty-five years as *princeps*.

In time, the term prince was applied to other sovereigns (in medieval times European kings were known as sovereign princes and it is as a sovereign that Christ is referred to as Prince of Peace and Satan as Prince of Darkness). Sovereign (someone who exercises supreme authority) derives from the French *soverain*, itself partly derived from the Latin *super* 'above'. Later, prince declined in prestige as a term and came to be applied to the sons of kings. Princess is applied to the daughter of a king.

The name Caesar Augustus in the adjectival form Caesaraugusta is found disguised in the toponym Zaragoza (in English Saragossa) and truncated in the form August in the name of the eighth month. A toponym is a placename, from the Greek *topos* 'place' and *onoma* 'name'.

The Greeks used *sebastos* 'revered' to translate the Latin *augustus*. The name Sebastianos (Sebastian) was their equivalent of Augustinus (Augustine). Sevastopol (in English Sebastopol), the great port and resort in the Crimea, derives from *sebastos* and the Greek *polis* 'city'.

privatization
the process whereby work previously done by public agencies is assigned to private firms or individuals

Privatization has two forms. One is where a public agency hires the services of a private company to do work that is, and remains, the public agency's responsibility. The other is where an activity, carried out by a public agency, is sold off completely to a private company or to a company quoted on the Stock Exchange. An example is British Telecom. That form of privatization is the opposite of nationalization: it is denationalization.

Privatization may be an attractive policy to a government because it may provide cash when cash is in short supply. It may reduce the government's running costs or increase the efficiency of organizations. Traditional socialists, who wish to see more rather than less work undertaken by the state, are ideologically opposed to privatization. Privatization may also be opposed on technical grounds – where, for example, it is believed the government is selling off an asset too cheaply.

Procrustean
forcing something to conform to a standard

Procrustes was a legendary Greek brigand who lived beside the road at Erineus near Eleusis in Attica. He lured travellers into his house on the promise of hospitality and forced them to lie on one of his two beds, the tall ones on his short bed and the small ones on his long bed. He made them to fit the beds exactly by using a hammer on the short ones and a saw on the tall ones. 'Thus, 'In higher education, history cannot be made to fit into the Procrustean bed of the tripartite division of disciplines into humanities, sciences and social sciences.' (*NYRB*, 29 June 2000)

discipline
means a field of study from the Latin *disciplina* 'instruction'

productivity
output per unit of input

Producere is the Latin 'to lead forward', 'to produce'; that which is produced is a product. Anyone who produces anything, for example, a writer who produces books, may be said to be productive. Productivity is commonly used in relation to industrial or commercial activity because the level of productivity of a firm is

commercial
derives from the Latin *cum* 'with' and *mercari* 'to trade'. A mercenary (from the Latin *merces* 'wages') is a man hired to fight for a foreign army. A *condottiere* (plural *condottieri*) was a leader, or sometimes simply a soldier, in a professional mercenary company in Europe in the thirteenth to sixteenth centuries (from the Italian *condotto* 'leadership', itself derived from the Latin *ducere* 'to lead' and *cum*)

vital to its survival. Private firms compete with one another. The greater their productivity the more cheaply they can offer their goods and services, and therefore the better they can compete.

Productivity is determined by the quantity and quality of the inputs (land, labour, capital) and the way they are managed. Is the labour force skilled and well-motivated? Is the machinery old or modern? Is the production process managed smoothly? These are the kinds of questions raised by the concept of industrial productivity.

Productivity agreements are agreements made between the workers and managers in an organization whereby the managers seek to increase productivity by changes in work practices or by the introduction of new machinery and the workers agree to this in return for higher wages or a betterment in working conditions, or both.

There are many kinds of work where productivity cannot be directly measured – much of the work of the public service is of this kind. Thus it is difficult to measure the productivity of a teacher. Teaching inputs can be measured – for example, the amount of time teachers spend preparing for class and the amount of time they spend in class. But how can one measure their output – education? People tend to settle for indirect measures such as the number of passes and honours achieved by the students. Indirect measures, however, can be misleading. Thus the examination system may reward those who have conformed most to the learning process in the schools rather than those who have increased their creativity, individuality and ability to think for themselves – the qualities most teachers feel are the proper objectives of education.

proletariat
low-paid wage-earners, the labouring classes

Proles means 'offspring' in Latin. The Romans used *proletarius* to describe someone who served the state not with wealth (taxes or a horse in time of war) but with offspring (to serve as soldiers). For Marx, the proletariat was the alternative to the capitalist class. The word is used to describe a key stage in Marxist revolution – the dictatorship of the proletariat, that is the assumption of power by (or at least on behalf of) the proletariat.

A member of the proletariat is called a proletarian. That word also serves as an adjective whose synonym is plebeian. George Orwell in *Nineteen Eighty-Four*, the novel he published in 1948, uses the diminutive 'the proles' as a dismissive term for his benighted lower classes.

The lumpenproletariat is the amorphous group of dispossessed and rootless individuals at the bottom of the social heap, despised by militant socialists because they have no capacity to engage in politics and promote revolution (*Lumpen* is the German 'rag').

amorphous
means without a definite shape – *a* is a Greek negative prefix, *morphē* is 'shape'

prolific
aboundingly productive

Proles is the Latin 'offspring'; the particle *fic* is derived from *facere* 'to make'. An ideas man in an organization may be described as prolific; and so may a sow. To proliferate or pullulate (*pullulus* is the Latin 'baby animal') is to breed abundantly.

promulgate
to make known to the public

The origin of the word is unclear. It is thought the Latin *vulgus, vulgaris* 'crowd' (from which we derive vulgar and vulgarity) is present in it in corrupted form. The word is important in law because justice requires that laws should be known to the public – promulgated – otherwise people would not know whether they were breaking the law or not.

mobile vulgus
from *mobilis*, the Latin 'moving' or 'fickle', and *vulgus* – 'the fickle crowd' – in shortened form gives us mob

propaganda
a deliberately distorted presentation of facts or doctrine to justify one's own actions or to weaken allegiance to one's opponents

Propagandum is a form of the Latin *propagare, propagatum* 'to multiply' or 'to spread' that means 'a thing to be multiplied or spread'. Its use in communications derives from the establishment in 1622 by the Catholic Church of a congregation (an office) concerned with spreading the Catholic faith (*de propaganda fide – fides* is the Latin 'faith'). The use of propaganda in war has given it a decidedly pejorative connotation (*pejor* is the Latin 'worse'). In war each side seeks to demonize the other. Propaganda, with its lies, distortions, half-truths and invective, is the means to do this.

In 1920 the Central Committee of the Communist Party in Russia established a Department of Agitation and Propaganda to manipulate the ideological responses of the masses. The term agitprop was coined to name its activity. The term is now applied generically.

prophet
a man through whom God expresses his will;

Pro is the Greek 'in place of'; *phētēs* is 'speaker'. A prophet was a man who spoke to the Jews on behalf of God. He told them what God's will was. Since a most

in popular speech a man who foretells events

effective way of establishing one's credentials as God's spokesman was to foretell the future, that was the function that came to be associated predominantly with a prophet. The word is also applied to a person who discerns the true character of events in the life of a religious community before others become aware of it.

Moslems regard Mahomet as The Prophet. The Koran says there have been 200,000 prophets of whom only six brought new laws or a new dispensation – Adam, Noah, Abraham, Moses, Jesus and Mahomet.

proscribe
to outlaw

Pro is the Latin 'before' or 'publicly'; *scribere* is 'to write'. The Roman authorities in the late Republic would proscribe their enemies, that is publish a list of their names. Those proscribed were labelled public enemies: a price was put on their heads so that they could be seized and killed by anyone; their property was confiscated. Caesar, when he crossed the Rubicon, was proscribed but he succeeded in routing his enemies.

The great statesman and philosopher Cicero was not so lucky. When he was proscribed in 43 BC he fled to his villa. His enemies tracked him down there and overtook him as he was being carried in a litter along the shaded walks down to the sea. Plutarch describes his death as follows:

villa
originally denoted a large house built on a Roman estate which, with its huddled workers' cottages, formed a natural rural centre – hence village from the French. The poor rustics and slaves attached to a villa were called villains; they eventually gained a reputation for being villainous

> The tribune, taking a few men with him, ran to where Cicero would come out. Cicero, seeing him hurrying through the woods, ordered his servants to set the litter down. Stroking his chin, as he was wont to do, with his left hand, he looked his murderers in the eye, his clothes covered in dust, his beard and hair unkempt, his face creased with strain. Most of those who stood about him covered their faces as the tribune advanced. Cicero stretched his neck out of the litter and the tribune struck. Cicero was sixty-four.
>
> The tribune cut off his head and, as Antony had stipulated, his hands too, for with those he had written his Philippics (the name he gave those orations he wrote against Antony).
>
> When these parts of Cicero were brought to Rome, Antony was holding an assembly to choose public officers. When he saw them he declared 'Now let there be an end to proscriptions!' He ordered the head and hands to be nailed over the rostra where the orators spoke. The people of Rome shuddered at the sight.

Nowadays harassed parents might declare 'Smoking should be proscribed', that is solemnly banned. Proscribe is distinguished from prescribe (to lay down rules, or, as in regard to medicine, to give directions for use).

protean
ever-changing

Proteus was an old Greek sea-god who had the gift of prophecy. He told you the future if you could catch hold of him. The trouble was he could change himself into different forms and so escape your grip. Homer tells how one of the Greek leaders, Menelaus, offended Pallas Athene when, after the fall of Troy, he refused to sacrifice to her – she had defended the Trojan citadel too long, he said. Angrily, the goddess sent storms that prevented him and his crew from reaching home.

sacrifice
derives from the Latin *sacrificium*, itself derived from the Latin *sacer* 'holy' and *facere* 'to make'. (The Greeks did not have a single word for sacrifice.) A libation (from the Latin *libare, libatum*) was a rite (Latin *ritus*) in which wine was poured out in honour of a deity

To find out how to break the spell Menelaus and three companions set out to capture Proteus. They disguised themselves in stinking seal-skins and lay waiting on the shore. At midday they were joined by hundreds of seals. Proteus himself then appeared and lay down to sleep among his flock.

Menelaus and his friends crept towards him and pounced on him. They held on to him firmly though he metamorphosed successively into a lion, a snake, a panther, a boar – even running water – and forced him to prophesy.

Proteus told Menelaus that his brother Agamemnon had been murdered and that he, Menelaus, must visit Egypt and propitiate (appease, from the Latin *propitiare, propitiatum*) the gods with sacrifices there. Menelaus followed this instruction and, when he had sacrificed, and erected a cenotaph to his brother, the winds changed and enabled him to sail home to Sparta. He arrived on the very day that Orestes avenged his father Agamemnon's murder by his faithless wife Clytemnestra and her lover Aegisthus.

Social problems are frequently protean. When a government department tackles one problem it often finds it creates another. Thus slum clearance tackles the problem of people who live in unsanitary conditions (*un* is a Latin prefix that negatives a word; *sanitas, sanitatis* is 'health') but it involves uprooting families and breaking the delicate web of relationships through which they often sustain one another emotionally and financially.

psephologist
one who studies voting systems and patterns

Psēphos is the Greek 'pebble'; *ologist* means 'student of' from *logos* 'word', 'reason' or 'account'. In classical Greece the Athenians were the great practitioners of democracy, albeit a limited democracy in which women and slaves had no say. Because they were relatively few in number and lived in a city, they could practise direct democracy – each citizen could vote on issues himself after listening to the arguments for and against, rather than have to elect a representative to act for him (indirect democracy). The voting procedure was simple. Each citizen was given a pebble and he voted by placing it in the appropriate urn.

In his *British Election of 1951* D.E. Butler tells us, 'I am indebted to Mr R.B. McCallum for the invention of this word [psephology].'

public
common to, or shared in by, all

Publicus is the Latin 'public', derived from *populus* 'people', from which we also derive populous, popular, populist and population. Public is applied in two major ways. Firstly, it may be applied to anything controlled or owned by the State – the public service, the public sector (as opposed to the private sector) or public property. Secondly, it may be applied to the people in general as opposed to private individuals. In this sense a public act is something done in public – in the open – as opposed to a private act (*privare*, *privatum* is the Latin 'to deprive' or 'to separate': *privatus* means 'separated').

public administration
the management of the affairs of the state including its subordinate institutions, or the study of it

Publicus is the Latin 'public', derived from *populus* 'people'; administration is derived from the Latin *administrare, administratum* 'to minister to'. Public administration is concerned with the work of government ministers and public servants. The subject of public administration is interdisciplinary, drawing upon other subjects such as law, politics, history, economics, sociology and management.

In the United States, the government is usually referred to as the administration. In the United Kingdom a prime minister's term of office is also described as his or her administration. People speak of Mrs Thatcher's third administration, for example.

Pyrrhic
describes a success won at so great a cost that the

About 300 BC a king called Pyrrhus ruled a small state in northern Greece. Courageous and ambitious, he dreamed of matching the success of Alexander the

Great. So when the city of Tarentum in southern Italy invited him to help them fight the Romans, he readily agreed. He landed in Italy with an army of 25,000 men and a herd of elephants.

victor is grievously weakened

The two armies clashed outside the town of Heraclea. The Romans fought fiercely until Pyrrhus ordered his elephants to be driven against their flanks. The Romans had never seen elephants before and, terrified by the screeching and roaring of the immense beasts, they panicked and fled. But the victorious Pyrrhus lost more men in the battle than the Romans. The Romans subsequently defeated him.

Q

qua
in the capacity of or precisely as

Qua is a form of *qui*, the Latin 'who' or 'which': 'The city manager attended the meeting not *qua* public official but as an interested citizen.'

quarantine
to isolate compulsorily or to detain in order to prevent the spread of disease

The first official quarantine was imposed by the Venetian doge (from the Latin *dux, ducis* 'leader', from which we also derive duke and ducal) in 1348 after the city death rate from bubonic plague had risen to six hundred per day (bubonic derives from the Latin *bubo, bubonis* 'the groin': the plague was characterized by inflammatory swelling in the groin or the armpit). The doge's council decided to isolate returning voyagers from the Orient and fixed on a period of forty days – *quaranta giorni* in Italian – simply because it was for such a period that Christ had been sequestered in the desert.

Another measure to control the spread of disease is to establish a *cordon sanitaire*, a sanitary zone maintained by a line of sentries posted to restrict entry into an area by infected or potentially infected people. The term was made famous by a French doctor Adrien Proust, the father of Marcel. In 1869 he travelled to Russia, Turkey and Persia to determine the routes by which cholera in previous epidemics had entered Russia and thereby Europe. He sought to have a *cordon sanitaire* (French, 'sanitary line', from a diminutive form of *corde* 'string') established that would encircle Europe and keep out the disease. The term is now sometimes used in a geopolitical sense to describe either a group of neutral states that keeps hostile states apart or a barrier that isolates a state other states consider dangerous.

An epidemic is a disease that attacks great numbers in a community at one time and that spreads from place to place (*epi* is the Greek 'among' and *dēmos* 'people'). If the disease strikes all the people, it is said to be a pandemic (*pan* is the Greek 'all'). If a disease is prevalent or regularly found in a people or area, it is said to be endemic (*en* is the Greek 'in'). Before contagion, that is, the transmission of disease by direct contact with an infected person or thing (from the Latin *cum* 'with' and *tangere, tactum* 'to touch'), was scientifically understood, doctors conceived of a miasma, a noxious exhalation of decaying matter, as the source of disease

Orient
derives from the Latin *oriens, orientis* 'rising [sun]' and therefore means the East. Since dawn allows one to fix a cardinal point (*cardo, cardinis* is the Latin 'hinge' and hence cardinal means of fundamental importance or chief) and provides the continuing light to fix the others, to orient is used in the general sense of placing oneself in a definite relationship to the points of the compass. The Latin *occidens, occidentis* means 'setting [sun]' and therefore the Occident is the West.

The French *levant* 'rising', from the Latin *levare* 'to raise', also means the East. The Levant is the coastlands of the eastern Mediterranean (Turkey, Syria, Lebanon and Israel). A levee, from the French *levée* 'raised', is a morning reception of visitors by a distinguished person (it was historically applied to the ceremony surrounding the French king's getting out of bed). A levee, also from the French *levée* in the sense of something raised, can also be any embankment, natural or artificial, on a river, especially the lower Mississippi, where French was for a time the dominant language (miasma derives from the Greek *miasma* 'pollution'). The randomness of disease was ascribed to the vagaries of the wind carrying the miasma (*vagari* is the Latin 'to wander'). An epidemiologist is a medical specialist who studies the occurrence, transmission and control of epidemics (the *ologist* suffix is from the Greek *logos*, here 'student of').

noxious
derives from the Latin *noxius* 'harmful'. Mephitic (origin obscure) is used to describe a foul pestilential smell

Veterinarians (from the Latin *veterinae* 'cattle' or 'beasts of burden': veterinarians are skilled in the diseases of animals) use the word epizootic for a disease that affects animals the way an epidemic affects people (*zōion* is the Greek 'animal', which also gives us zoo).

quark
a sub-atomic particle

In their exploration of the constituents of matter, nuclear physicists have had to develop a nomenclature. The central part of the atom – the nucleus (*nux, nucis* is the Latin 'nut') – is composed of protons (from the Greek *prōtos* 'first') and neutrons (from the Latin *neuter* 'neither'). The basic constituents of protons and neutrons are quarks; three quarks make a nucleon (from the Latin *nucleus*). It was the American physicist Murray Gell-Mann who came up with the name quark. A Joyce enthusiast, he recalled the line from *Finnegans Wake*: 'Three quarks for Muster Mark!' While quarks were originally thought to come in three types, the number is now known to be six.

quiddity
originally the essential nature of something but now a quibble

Quid is the Latin 'what'; the *ity* ending derives from the suffix *itas*, which is the equivalent of 'ness' in English: quiddity means whatness – that which makes something what it is. In proceeding with a rigorous analysis, philosophers must assure themselves that they understand the essential character – the quiddity – of the things they are discussing. However, by raising the question of the quiddity of everything, they exposed the word to its being seen as a delaying device – a quibble. In this pejorative sense the word occurs in the famous description of Cranmer's first eight years of study at Cambridge: 'he was nuzzled [trained] in the grossest kind of sophistry, logic, philosophy moral and natural (not in the text of the old philosophers, but chiefly in the dark riddles and quiddities of Duns and other subtle questionists)', quoted in *Thomas Cranmer* by Diarmaid MacCulloch.

quid pro quo
something given in return for something

Quid 'what' is a form of the Latin *quis*; *pro* is 'for' or 'in place of'; *quo* is also a form of *quis*. *Quid pro quo*, then, is literally 'what for what'. Politics is largely based on compromise. Before reaching a compromise one party may demand a *quid pro quo* from the other party before it gives up some privilege or position.

quintessential
relating to the pure concentrated form of a thing or idea

In their speculations about what the world is made of, the ancient Greeks (apart from the atomists) concluded that there were four basic elements (or essences) – fire, earth, air and water – which combined in various ways to make up everything that is. The Pythagoreans (the followers of the Greek philosopher Pythagoras) conceived of a fifth element – the quintessence – which they called ether (*quintus* is the Latin 'fifth'; *esse* is 'to be' and so the abstract noun *essentia*, from which we derive essence, means 'beingness'). Ether was the most refined element in creation – out of it the stars were made. Transferred to anything in existence, the quintessence is the purest and truest expression of the thing. Something heavenly or spirit-like may be said to be ethereal.

Element derives from the Latin *elementum* (of uncertain etymology) and denotes a fundamental component of something complex. Elemental means primal; elementary means simple.

Modern science has discovered the existence of 105 substances (of which 93 occur naturally) that consist of atoms with the same number of protons in their nuclei (plural of nucleus), which it calls elements. Elements are the basic building blocks of visible matter because they cannot be broken down further by any chemical process. They may combine to form compound substances (thus hydrogen and oxygen may combine to form water) and if they do so are in units called molecules (from the Latin *molecula*, a diminutive of *moles* 'mass'), which follow a precise formula for the number of combining atoms from each element (in water two atoms of hydrogen combine with one atom of oxygen to give a molecule of water, hence the formula H_2O). The visible world of the earth, living organisms and the stars and planets consists of these elements and their compounds. This ordinary matter makes up nearly 5 per cent of the universe. Over 95 per cent of the universe is made up of dark matter and dark energy, so called not because they are blackish or dim but because they are

oxygen
a colourless, odourless gas, is the most abundant element in the earth's crust. *Oxus* (transliterated *oxys*) is the Greek 'sharp' and the *gen* suffix, from the Greek *genēs* 'born', here indicates 'making'. Oxygen was originally believed to be a key element in acids (*acidus* is the Latin 'sharp') until hydrogen was found to play that role

completely unknown, being undetectible by our senses or instruments. They are known to exist only indirectly from their observed interference with gravity.

quixotic
lofty but utterly impracticable

Don Quixote is a satire by the sixteenth-century Spanish writer, Cervantes, on the chivalry and romance of the Middle Ages. The madly idealistic paladin Don Quixote sets out with his faithful squire, Sancho Panza, to rescue damsels in distress and, in one famous scene, tilts at a windmill.

Proposals from a political party are sometimes declared by their opponents to be quixotic.

quorum
the minimum number of people who must be present at a meeting before its proceedings can be taken as valid

Quorum is a form of the Latin *quis* and means 'of whom'. It derives from government commissions written in Latin (when Latin was the language of the European educated classes) where the following words would appear if, for example, a quorum of five were required: *quorum vos … quinque esse volumus*, 'of whom we wish that you … be five'. The purpose was thereby to designate the person (or persons) so addressed a member (or members) of an official body, without whose presence business could not go on. A *quorum* for meetings may be specified in the constitution of the body holding the meeting or it may be fixed by the members at their first meeting.

quota
the proportional part or share needed to make up a certain quantity or number

Quota derives from the Latin *quota pars* meaning 'the how manieth part' – *quot* means 'how many'. The word occurs notably in relation to the number of persons from a particular country that may be allowed to enter the US in any one year.

R

Rabelaisian
coarse and satirical

François Rabelais was the author of *Pantagruel* and *Gargantua*, two of the great books of European literature. They concern the exploits of the giant Gargantua, noted for his enormous capacity for food and drink (hence gargantuan), and his son Pantagruel, and are satirical masterpieces. Rabelaisian connotes extremely coarse humour but it should be appreciated that the writer, like Chaucer, merely reflected the earthy exuberance of his age. His dying words are said to have been, 'Bring down the curtain. The farce is over.'

exuberance
means full of vigour and high spirits from the Latin *ex* 'from' and *ubera* 'breasts'

radical
far-reaching, going to the root

Radix, radicis is the Latin 'root'. The term radical may be applied to the following kinds of people, among others: someone who always seeks to get to the root of a problem in the hope of solving it (a radical of this kind, for example, might analyze crime and conclude that poverty is the cause of crime and that crime, therefore, can be eradicated by abolishing poverty); someone who believes that his or her community or group has departed from its original ideals and should now be made to return to them (e.g. liberation theologians); someone who believes that present institutions and people are so corrupt that they must be totally changed (the atrocities of the Khmer Rouge proceeded from such radicalism); or someone who believes that there is a theoretical framework that can solve all problems (many left-wing politicians are radical in this sense).

A radical approach can be taken within all kinds of political positions (see also conservatism) and so one can speak of radical democrats, radical socialists, radical communists, radical conservatives, radical liberals, etc.

to eradicate
is to tear out by the roots, to stamp out (e is the Latin 'out'); to extirpate is a synonym, *stirps, stirpis* being another Latin word for 'root'

rapprochement
a re-establishment of harmonious relations

The word is French, meaning 'a coming together again'. In 1933 the United States gave official recognition to the Soviet regime, the last among the great powers to do so.

In his autobiographical work *The Invisible Writing* Arthur Koestler describes how he met African-American writer Langston Hughes in a remote part of Asiatic Russia just about that time. Hughes had come to Russia on the invitation of the leading Soviet film trust to script a film on the persecution of African-Americans. But by the time he reached Moscow a political *rapprochement* had come about between the USSR and the US. One of the American conditions for resuming normal diplomatic relations was that Russia should renounce its propaganda campaign among the African-Americans. Overnight the film project was dropped and the Russians asked Hughes to write a book on the cotton-growing regions of Asiatic Russia instead.

rationale
the set of reasons given to justify an action

Ratio, rationis is the Latin 'reason'. The power to reason differentiates man essentially from other animals: we expect a man or woman to act rationally and therefore to have a rationale for his or her actions. Rationalist refers to a tendency among many thinkers from the seventeenth century onwards to rely on reason alone to discover the basis for human society and the principles that should guide behaviour. In the *NYRB*, 29 November 2001, Aileen Kelly refers to 'the two dreams that have shaped modern Western culture: the Enlightenment's ideal of a rationally ordered society and the Romantic notion of the Promethean self-transformation of man'.

reactionary
someone who wishes for, or wishes to bring about, a return to an earlier political situation or a particular way of acting or thinking; someone opposed to radical political or social change

Reagere, reactum is the Latin 'to do in return', from which reaction is derived. The word entered political parlance this way. Isaac Newton in his *Principia Mathematica Philosophiae Naturalis* of 1687 set forth the three laws of motion, the third of which is the principle that to every action there is an equal and opposite reaction. It was his French admirers, especially Montesquieu, who applied the law to politics. During the French Revolution, reactionary became an antonym of revolutionary. During the nineteenth century its application became more general. By then, many thinkers believed social progress, by which they meant reform that would uplift the living conditions of the masses, was inevitable. Some felt that modern technology provided man with a cornucopia to finance perpetual progress. Others put their trust in dialectical materialism (which guaranteed progress!). They labelled as reactionary those who opposed or doubted such progress.

red-letter day
a very special day

In monasteries it was the practice to inscribe feast-days in red and other days in black in the calendar. Directions on the rituals to be followed in a ceremony were also inscribed in red ochre (Latin *rubrica*) and consequently the rules covering a ceremony came to be called the rubrics. This word has become secularized. Lawyers, for example, may use it to indicate the context in which they are discussing a topic: 'We'll take this under the rubric of tort.' Tort from the Latin *tortum* 'something twisted', which also gives us tortuous and torture, is a civil wrong arising out of an act or failure to act, independently of any contract, for which an action for damages may be brought.

referendum
a vote by the electorate on a political question referred to them

Referendum is a form of the Latin *referre* 'to refer' and it means a thing that must be referred (to the people). The referendum as a modern political device was introduced by the Swiss. It is the device favoured for changing constitutions (although some constitutions allow the representatives of the people to change the constitution, usually on the basis of a qualified majority).

For technical reasons the plural, referendums, is preferable to referenda.

remuneration
the reward or pay for work

Remuneration derives from the Latin *munus, muneris* 'gift'. (Munificent, meaning very generous, derives from *munus* and a form of *facere*, the Latin 'to make'.)

emolument
is related to the word to immolate (to sacrifice) through the Latin *mola* 'grindstone' or the product it produces – flour. Before the Romans sacrificed a victim, they sprinkled it with flour – immolated it

Emolument, meaning the fees or wages from an office of employment, derives from the Latin *emolumentum* 'the fee paid to a miller' (*emolere* is 'to grind') in feudal times.

A salary, meaning a fixed regular payment made by an employer for professional or non-manual work, derives from the Latin *salarium*, the payment made to Roman soldiers. *Salarium* derives from *sal* 'salt' (hence also saline): the most necessary thing to support human life was taken as representative of all others. Augustus introduced salaries for the governors of provinces and for senior military officers to keep them tightly dependent on himself.

manual
means relative to a hand or hands, or a book (held in the hand) from the Latin *manus* 'hand'.

Digital means performed with the fingers, *digitus* being the Latin 'finger' or 'toe', or displaying information as numbers (which were immemorially counted on fingers and toes)

A wage (from the Old French *wagier* 'to pledge') is a payment in return for work of a manual kind paid usually on an hourly, daily or weekly basis.

A stipend is a fixed regular sum paid as a salary or allowance, especially to a clergyman, derived from the Latin *stipo* 'contribution' and *pendere* 'to pay out'.

republic
a democratic state that is not ruled by a monarch

The word, derived from the Latin *res publica* (*res* 'thing' or 'affair' and *publica* 'public' – the public affair, commonwealth or republic), was first applied to Rome after the expulsion of King Tarquinius Superbus (the Proud) and the extinction of monarchical rule there. It was used to unite the Romans around the concept of a state ruled by two short-term elected consuls rather than a king. Since *publica* is a form of *publicus*, which derives from *populus*, the Latin 'people', democracy is inherent in the term republic.

The Roman Republic was so successful – it established an immense and stable empire – that it became the ideal of later republics. (Indeed, when Augustus inaugurated Imperial Rome he strove to maintain republican forms.) Furthermore the two great values of the Roman Republic – liberty, meaning both freedom from the arbitrary rule of despots and the right of the citizens to participate in government, and virtue, meaning the public spirit that disposed the citizen to pursue the common interest rather than his own personal interest – became part of republican theory.

values
are those things that in a particular context are thought of as being good; thus equality, justice and freedom are regarded as democratic values; value derives from the French *valoir* 'to be worth', which in turn derives from the Latin *valere* 'to be strong'

virtue
derived from the Latin *vir* 'man', originally meant manliness but now extends to moral excellence generally. Moralists distinguish four cardinal virtues (prudence, justice, fortitude and temperance) and three theological virtues (faith, hope and charity). In music a virtuoso is a consummate master of musical technique or artistry

Many states claim to be republics but in fact they are not. They may be dictatorships like Russia under Stalin or oligarchies like the historic Venetian Republic. Not all democracies are republics – there are democratic monarchies (for example, the United Kingdom of Great Britain and Northern Ireland, the Netherlands). Modern republicanism, the child of the American and French revolutions, is closely associated with democratic and egalitarian values (and claims to be more radically democratic than the ancient republics). Republicans, therefore, abhor distinctions between citizens based on titles of nobility: the French revolutionaries addressed Louis XVI as Citizen Capet (from his family name) before they guillotined him.

The republic of letters, from the French *la république des lettres*, means the world of ideas freely shared by writers. *Belles-lettres* (French 'fine letters') are literary works, especially essays and poetry, valued for their aesthetic rather than their informative or moral content. A belletrist is a writer of *belles-lettres*.

retro

retroactive, retrograde and retrospection share the prefix *retro*, the Latin 'behind' or 'backwards'

Retroactive means applying or referring to the past. Legislation that would seek to define a certain act as criminal and have the law apply retrospectively is inherently contrary to human rights principles.

Retrograde means tending towards an earlier worse condition. The Latin *gradi, gressum* means 'to go'.

Retrospection is the act of recalling things. The Latin *specere, spectum* is 'to look' (it also gives us inspection and spectacle). In art, a retrospective is an exhibition of an artist's work that shows development over time.

In lifestyle terms retro is used as an adjective that denotes something associated with or revived from the past – retro dressing, retro fashion.

revolution
a complete change

Volvere, volutum is the Latin 'to turn' and *re* is a Latin prefix meaning 'back' or 'again', from which revolution is derived. The words rotate (from the Latin *rota* 'wheel') and revolve are often used interchangeably but are distinguished in the statement 'The earth rotates on its axis as it revolves around the sun.' The idea of complete change that revolution now connotes came from an association with the image of the wheel of fortune on which men were thought to revolve, being one moment at the top of the wheel, the next at the bottom.

In politics, revolution denotes a complete change of government usually brought about by violence as in the American, French and Russian revolutions, or a radical transformation of the beliefs and mores of a people either by force or education. Pol Pot attempted such a revolution in Kampuchea as did the communists in Russia after 1917 when they sought to create a purely secular culture. In a social or economic context, for example the Industrial Revolution, there is no connotation of direct violence.

Romanticism
a movement in the arts that flourished in the late eighteenth and the early nineteenth centuries

the Hydra
was a hundred-headed poisonous serpent that lived in a swamp in Argos; Heracles's second labour was to kill the Hydra, a particularly difficult task because every time you cut off a head another one grew in its place

The movement has such variegated forms that it presents to a lexicographer (a writer of dictionaries, from the Greek *lexis* 'word' and *graphein* 'to write') as a Hydra. Instead of grappling with the word people tend to describe what it is a reaction against.

Romanticism is a reaction against neoclassicism, the dominant movement in European art after the rococo period, which sought to express once more the ideals of ancient classical art through order, proportion and unity of form. Romanticism in contrast placed the individual artist and his desire for self-expression at the centre of things.

Romanticism is a reaction against the Enlightenment. The Romantics felt that the cold reason of the Enlightenment had robbed Nature of her enchantment. Keats accused Newton of helping to 'unweave the rainbow' when he explained scientifically the spectrum of colours that make up white light. The Romantics were preoccupied with the remote – in time, place, or experience. The sense Romantics had of man's oneness with Nature led some of them in the direction of pantheism. It is easy to see Romanticism as a reaction against the Industrial Revolution too.

Romanticism is a cluster of attitudes and preferences (or predilections, from the Latin *prae* 'before' and *diligere, dilectum* 'to love'). As Lord Quinton puts it in *The Oxford Companion to Philosophy*:

> The Romantic favours the concrete over the abstract, variety over uniformity, the infinite over the finite, nature over culture, convention and artifice, the organic over the mechanical, freedom over constraint, rules and limitations.

convention
A convention is an assembly of people or a coming together of minds – an agreement; *con* is a Latin particle meaning 'with' and *venire, ventum* is 'to come' (it also gives us advent and adventure). A conference is a meeting for consultation, *ferre* being the Latin 'to bring'

Romantic derives from the French *romantique*, itself derived from the French *roman*. *Roman* originally referred to the vernacular language as opposed to Latin, the classical language used by the élite. It came to denote imaginative works, originally in verse and later in prose, written in the romance languages (the languages descended from Latin, chiefly French, Italian, Spanish, Portuguese and Romanian). Romance derives from the Latin *Romanice* 'in the romantic language' (compare the Latin *Anglice* 'in English'). Romances were originally accounts of adventures in places remote from everyday life, full of fantasy, gallantry and love; in popular speech a romance is a love story simpliciter.

A romantic comedy describes a book or film in which love is the main theme and where everything turns out well in the end.

royal road, the
the short and easy way of doing something difficult

The Persian kings built a splendid road between Sardis and Susa to ease communications within their empire. The Greeks were greatly impressed by the speed with which it allowed messages to be carried. The Royal Road, as it was called, became proverbial: Freud tells us, 'The interpretation of dreams is the royal road to a knowledge of the unconscious activities of the mind.' This is sometimes rendered 'Dreams are the royal road to the unconscious.'

The ancients believed that some dreams were significant and required an oneirocritic (an interpreter of dreams, *oneiros* being the Greek 'dream' and *kritēs* 'judge'; oneiric means of or relating to dreams). Freud in *The Interpretation of Dreams* enunciated the theory that dreams gave expression to infantile sexual wishes that had been repressed and that, if expressed in undisguised form, would so disturb the dreamer that he or she would wake up. Freud, therefore, distinguished between the manifest content of a dream and its latent content (*latere* is the Latin 'to lie hidden'). The latent content exposes the unconscious. Freud relished the bind in which his theory placed his enemies: 'they may attack my theories by day but they dream of them by night'.

Rubicon
when someone makes a fateful, irreversible move, he or she may be said to have crossed the Rubicon

victor
and victorious derive from the Latin *vincere, victum* 'to conquer'. A form of *vincere* occurs in Julius Caesar's famous laconic report to the Roman Senate on his exploits in the field: '*Veni, vidi, vici,*' – 'I came, I saw, I conquered.' Victorian means related to or characteristic of the reign of the British Queen Victoria

The Rubicon is a little river in Italy. In Roman times it marked the boundary between Italy and the province of Gaul (France and northern Italy). Its great moment came in 49 BC.

Julius Caesar, who had spent the previous nine years campaigning in Gaul, was leading his victorious troops towards Rome. He burned, so his enemies said, to set aside the Republic and establish himself as sole ruler. The Roman Senate ordered him to leave his army in Gaul and come to Rome alone – otherwise he would be proscribed.

When Caesar reached the Rubicon, he paused on the northern bank. As he pondered on how much was at stake, he became irresolute. But at last, throwing caution to the winds, he declared '*Jacta alea est!*' ('The die [or dice] is cast!' and led his troops across the Rubicon, formally breaching the constitution that forbad a provincial commander to bring his army back to Rome. He went on to take Rome.

A good plan seeks to omit all aleatory elements, that is, elements dependent on chance, from the Latin *alea* 'dice'. Artists, however, sometimes embrace aleatory elements in their work.

Ruritanian
relating to an imaginary European kingdom characterized by romance, adventure and intrigue

Anthony Hope, the pen-name of Sir Anthony Hope Hawkins, was the author of swashbuckling novels set in Ruritania, the fictional land he created in south-eastern Europe. *The Prisoner of Zenda,* the most famous of them, was filmed in 1937 with Ronald Colman, in 1952 with Stewart Grainger and in 1979 with Peter Sellers. The word is still current: 'We used to curse the Greeks for sheltering the Ruritanian King Zog.' (Louis de Bernières, *Captain Corelli's Mandolin*) *Rus in urbe*

(Latin, 'the country in the city') might be applied to a city building that incorporates rural features such as gardens with trees, flowers, fountains and streams.

In addition to indicating a country (as here), the *ia* suffix is used to name pathological conditions. Examples are diphtheria, a throat infection in which the air passages become covered with a leathery membrane (*diphthera* is the Greek 'leather'); bulimia, a condition of alternate over-eating and vomiting as a result of an obsession with weight (derived from the Greek *bous* 'ox' and *limos* 'hunger'); and anorexia nervosa, a loss of appetite and an aversion to food owing to emotional disturbance, often leading to catastrophic loss of weight (derived from the Greek negative *a* – *an* before a vowel – and *orexis* 'longing').

The *ia* suffix is also used as a neuter plural meaning 'things related to [the word to which it is attached]'. Thus marginalia means things (here notes) on the margins of a text (*margo, marginis* is the Latin 'margin'; to marginalize is to supply with marginal notes, but the word is also used to describe the deprivation of a person or group of civic capacity through such conditions as poverty, lack of education, physical or mental handicap). Militaria means things relating to soldiering such as swords, spears, banners and medals (*miles, militis* is the Latin 'soldier'). Genitalia or genitals (*genitalis* is the Latin 'relating to birth') means the sexual organs: the testicles and penis of a male and the labia (from the Latin *labia* 'lip-shaped folds'), clitoris and vagina of a female. Paraphernalia means miscellaneous articles or equipment (it originally meant the personal property of a married woman apart from her dowry, *para* being a Greek prefix indicating 'other than' and *phernē* being the Greek 'dowry'). Memorabilia (*memoria* is the Latin 'memory') means things that belonged to a dead person that serve as reminders of that person's life, such as family photographs, a set of golf clubs, theatre programmes, a monocle.

The *ia* suffix is also used to name botanical species – thus magnolia (after the French botanist Pierre Magnol), fuchsia (after the German botanist Leonard Fuchs), and forsythia (after the English botanist William Forsyth). Botany, the study of plants, is derived from the Greek *botanē* 'plant' and was founded by Aristotle's student Theophrastus.

marginalia
was introduced to English by Samuel Taylor Coleridge, the Romantic poet and critic, in 1819 when he published a collection of his annotations under the title *Marginalia*.

A gloss (from the Latin *glossa* 'an unusual word requiring an explanatory word') was originally a note written between the lines.

A scholium was originally a note written on the margins. Glosses and scholia (plural of scholium) are now used as synonyms for marginalia

S

sabotage
the carrying out of the destruction of strategic elements in a system to thwart someone else; the destruction of property or the disruption of a process in pursuit of some cause

Sabot is the French 'wooden shoe'. In the French railway strike of 1910 the workers prevented the operation of trains by cutting the wooden shoes that held the rails in place. (Strike in this sense is a pre-industrial term and derives from nautical experience: the first thing mutinous sailors did to assert their control was to strike, that is lower, the sails.) During World War II resistance groups throughout occupied Europe helped the Allies by numerous acts of sabotage against the Germans. An activist may be said to sabotage talks if at a delicate moment in the negotiations he or she reveals information deeply embarrassing to one or other of the parties. Sabotage is carried out by saboteurs.

sadomasochism
either the combination of sadistic and masochistic elements in one person, characterized by both aggressive and submissive periods in relationships with others or sexual practice in which one partner plays a sadistic role and the other a masochistic one

Sexology, the scientific study of sex and the relations between the sexes (*sexus* is the Latin 'sex', which also gives us sexual), was pioneered by the German Richard Baron von Krafft-Ebing in *Psychopathia Sexualis*. A neurologist (a student of the nervous system and its diseases, *neuron* being the Greek 'nerve') and psychiatrist, he coined the term sadist for someone who derives sexual pleasure from inflicting pain on another and masochist for someone who gains sexual pleasure from being subjected to pain, humiliation or domination by another.

The eponymous Marquis de Sade embraced hedonism as a youth – one of the great influences on his life was his uncle, the worldly cleric the Abbé de Sade, a voluptuary nicknamed the Sybarite of Saumane. The Marquis de Sade's licentious and orgiastic practices led to his being incarcerated (*carcer* is the Latin 'prison') for long periods, and gave him generous opportunities to write. He achieved notoriety with *Justine*, his first *succès de scandale*. His *magnum opus* was *120 Days of Sodom*.

succès de scandale
is a French phrase that means 'success due to scandalous matter'; a *succès fou* is a success marked by wild applause, *fou* being 'mad'; a *succès d'estime* is a critical rather than a popular or commercial success, *estime* being 'regard'

The eponymous Leopold von Sacher-Masoch was a minor nineteenth-century Austrian novelist who described the perversion (an abnormal means of obtaining sexual satisfaction, from the Latin *perversus* 'turned the wrong way') in *Venus in Furs*.

Sodom was the city in the Old Testament that God destroyed for its wickedness, traditionally taken to be homosexuality. Sodomy is the practice of anal intercourse. A sodomite is someone who practises sodomy.

A catamite is a boy kept for homosexual purposes and derives through the Latin Catamitus from the Greek Ganymedes (Ganymede), a handsome Trojan youth abducted by Zeus to Olympus to serve as the cupbearer of the gods. Ganymede appositely also names one of the Jovian moons.

samizdat
a system of clandestine printing and distribution in the former Soviet Union

Sam is the Russian 'self'; *izdatelstvo* is 'publishing'. A large volume of underground literature circulated throughout the USSR in the form of typescripts and photocopies. The work of leading writers such as Alexander Solzhenitsyn and Andrei Sakharov first appeared in this form.

samurai
the warrior caste that from the eleventh century to the nineteenth provided Japan's fighting and administrative élite

Samurai derives from the Japanese *saburau* 'to attend' (on one's *daimio*, a territorial noble). The samurai code, called *bushido* (Japanese, 'the way of the warrior'), stressed self-discipline, courage and loyalty and laid down that to die in the service of one's lord was the greatest honour a samurai could achieve. With chilling harshness, it required any samurai who failed to honour the obligations of military service to commit hara-kiri, a ritual in which the warrior disembowelled himself before witnesses (*hara* is the Japanese 'belly', *kiri* is 'cut').

The bushido ethic imbued Japanese militarism in the early part of the twentieth century, being perhaps most graphically exhibited in World War II in the kamikaze suicide missions in which Japanese pilots sacrificed their lives for the emperor by deliberately crashing their bomb-laden planes onto American ships (*kamikaze* is 'divine wind' in Japanese; it was traditionally applied to the wind that destroyed the ships of the invading Mongols in 1281).

scapegoat
someone who bears the blame that should attach to others

The Jews had a custom whereby on the Day of Atonement two goats, one for the Lord and one for the Devil, were brought to the altar of the tabernacle. There the high priest cast lots. The goat upon which the first lot fell was for the Lord, and it was sacrificed. The other goat was the scapegoat. The high priest transferred his own sins and the sins of all the people to it, by confession, and then drove the goat out into the desert and let it escape. When things go wrong for a group, such as a political party, they usually look for someone to blame – a scapegoat. Indeed scapegoating is now recognized as a basic tendency in human beings: it can intensify the sense of unity within groups while allowing individuals to shed responsibility for their own failures.

'The Scapegoat' is the title of a well-known painting by William Holman Hunt, one of the founders of the Pre-Raphaelites, a group of Victorian artists that also included Dante Gabriel Rossetti. *Pre* derives from the Latin prefix *prae* 'before'. Raphael was one of the masters of the classical Renaissance style. The Pre-Raphaelites took their inspiration from the naturalistic Italian painters who flourished before Raphael.

sceptre
symbol of imperial or sovereign authority

The Greek *skeptron* (Latin *sceptrum*) originally denoted a simple 'staff' or 'walking-stick'. Because a staff was used not merely to aid the steps of the aged and infirm but also as a weapon for defence or assault, the privilege of habitually carrying it became emblematic of position and authority. In ancient Persia whole classes of high-ranking officials and professionals were distinguished as the sceptre-bearing orders. In Homer and later Greek writers the sceptre is represented as belonging more to kings and princes. It descended from father to son. Those who bore the sceptre swore by it, solemnly taking it in the right hand and raising it towards heaven. As a symbol of authority the sceptre became a baton adorned with gold, silver or gems. The sceptre of the Roman kings, which after their expulsion descended to the consuls, was made of ivory and was surmounted by an eagle. Both Zeus and Jupiter were represented holding sceptres. Eventually the sceptre became a common element of the regalia of European monarchs.

ivory
was called *elephas, elephantos* by the Greeks. They sourced it either in India or north Africa. They often overlaid their cult statues with gold for the garments and ivory for the skin – a style called chryselephantine (*chrysos* is the Greek 'gold')

In *Richard II* Shakespeare famously apostrophizes England: 'This royal throne of kings, this sceptred isle'. In the modern Freudian world sceptre was to find an inevitable literary destiny as a phallic metaphor in Nabokov's *Lolita* ('the sceptre of my passion').

Apostrophize derives from the Greek *apo* 'away' and *strophē* 'a turning'. Its primary meaning, as here, is a turning aside to address an absent person or a personification of an inanimate being or an abstraction. Madame Roland, on her way to the guillotine in the Place de la Rèvolution in Paris, apostrophized the statue of Liberty that had been erected there: 'Oh Liberty, what crimes are committed in your name!'

An apostrophe is also – and more commonly – a

punctuation mark used to indicate the omission of a letter (she's for she is or she has) and also the possessive case (Tom's). In these senses it has a different etymology.

one
is the only pronoun whose genitive case ends in 's, as in 'One must defend one's interests.'

Scylla and Charybdis
monsters that commanded the opposite sides of a narrow channel in the Mediterranean – the Strait of Messina between the toe of Italy and Sicily – and so were a fearful hazard to sailors who in seeking to avoid the one were wont to be swept towards the other

In Greek legend Scylla was a canine monster with six heads and twelve feet. She would seize sailors, crush their bones and slowly swallow them. Charybdis, once a goddess, was metamorphosed by a baleful Zeus into a maelstrom that three times a day sucked in a huge volume of water and shortly spewed it out. Odysseus, on his voyage home from Troy, sought to give Charybdis a wide berth but in doing so sailed too close to Scylla. She suddenly appeared over the side of his ship, snatched six of his companions, one in each mouth, and made off with them to the rocks where she slowly devoured them. Odysseus had to ignore their screams and sail on.

Scylla and Charbydis still serve as a useful metaphor. Daniel C. Dennett in *Darwin's Dangerous Idea* seeks to indicate his approach to debate surrounding evolution: 'I have tried to navigate between the Scylla of glib dismissal and the Charybdis of grindingly detailed infighting …'

the Maelstrom
a powerful whirlpool off the coast of Norway, derives from the Dutch *maalstroom* 'whirlpool' and is used without a capital letter to mean any turbulent, confused situation

secular
not connected with religion, pertaining to the present world, occurring once every century or other long period of time

Secularis is a Latin word derived from *saeculum* 'age', 'generation' or 'lifetime'. According to the Etruscans, who ruled in Italy before the Romans, a *saeculum* was a space of time of 110 lunar years and therefore beyond the normal span of life. The beginning of each *saeculum* at Rome was announced by the pontiffs. To celebrate the event the *ludi saeculares* ('the secular games' – *ludus* is the Latin 'game', hence also ludicrous) would take place.

Modern centennials and millennia (*centum* is the Latin 'hundred'; *mille* is 'thousand') are accurately marked but the *saeculum* was not always celebrated punctually, because an impatient powerful leader might wish to blur the dates in order to be the one to preside over a *saeculum*. The most famous games were held in 17 BC at the request of Augustus. Horace was commissioned to write a poem to celebrate the occasion and it survives – the *Carmen Saeculare* (*carmen* is the Latin 'poem'). Before the games began, a herald proclaimed them throughout Rome summoning everyone 'to view such games as no one alive has seen before and no one alive will see again'.

pontiff
Latin *pontifex* – plural *pontifices* – from *pons, pontis* 'bridge' and *facere* 'to make sacrifice': according to one view the pontiffs were the pagan priests who originally made sacrifices on a bridge across the Tiber in Rome to unite the people living on either side

In common discussion secular contrasts with sacred (derived from the Latin *sacer* 'holy'). Secularism is a philosophy of life that precludes all religious and faith experience from relevance to public life.

Secularist attitudes may contrast or conflict with religious attitudes. Marx developed the most radical form of secularism in that he sought to reduce all faith experience to some aspect of worldly (economic, political, etc.) experience. The Russian communists embraced systematic secularism, closing churches and promoting atheism. Secularists hold that there should be no entwining of the State with religion.

Secularists regard religious faith as either false and irrelevant to secular life, or private and divorced from public life. The secular vision of life with its sharp demarcation between private and public derives from certain phases of the liberal movement. However, the distinction between the secular and the sacred goes back to the early days of the Church. In Christian Rome secular came to mean of this world as opposed to the next; secular clergy were those living in the world as opposed to those living, subject to religious rule, apart in monasteries. The latter were called the regular clergy.

regular
derives from *regula* the Latin 'rule'. A thing is said to be regular when it follows some rule, principle or pattern – thus regular clergy, regular shape, regular time, etc.

monastery
is from the Greek *monastērion*, derived from *monos* 'alone' and *ion*, a suffix indicating 'place', like the Latin *ium*.

Monos also gave us the Greek *monochos* 'monk'. The original monks lived alone in deserted places. Later they lived together in monasteries set apart from the people. The members of older religious orders, such as Benedictines and Cistercians, are monks. The newer religious orders of the thirteenth century, such as the Franciscans and Dominicans, chose to live with the people as their brothers (*fratres* in Latin) and their members were therefore known as friars, through the French *frères*. They lived in friaries

The State is concerned with the things of this life – it is secular. The Church is concerned with the redemption of mankind and therefore with all areas of man's experience in this life (*saeculum*), which it views *sub specie aeternitatis* ('from the perspective of eternity'; *sub* is the Latin 'under'; *specie* is a form of *species* 'viewpoint'; *aeternitatis* is a form of *aeternitas* 'everlastingness' or 'eternity'). The State claims authority over all its citizens. The Church, with its mandate from Christ to convert the whole world to the Christian way, claims a divine authority. The potential for conflict was considerable. In a particular case, should the Church's moral view of that case prevail or should that of the State? In a particular situation ought the State legislate in a certain way or not? The Church and State have therefore, over the changes of the ages, sought a *modus vivendi*.

The state into which the Church was born was the Roman empire. The Romans were tolerant of religious diversity but in order to bond every citizen to the state they insisted that the cult of Rome and the worship of the emperor that came to be associated with it should be observed by all. No religion that excluded such observance was tolerated. The only exception the Romans made was for the Jews whose monotheism ('Thou shalt have no other god but me') prevented them from engaging in polytheistic rituals.

At first the Romans did not distinguish between the Jews and Christians. By the time of the Emperor Nero, however, Christians *per se* were known in Rome. Indeed the accusation was made against the early Christians that they were atheists, presumably because they refused to join in the imperial cult. State officials came to appreciate that Christianity as an international monotheistic religion posed a threat to the empire and the state religion that bound it together. This consideration, as well as pagan and Jewish antipathy, led, over the next few hundred years, to sporadic persecution of the Church.

antipathy
means a settled aversion to, for, or between persons, derived from the Greek *anti* 'against' and *pathos* 'feeling'; sympathy is the capacity to share feeling with another (*syn* – *sym* before p – means 'with'); empathy is the capacity to enter into another's feelings and so fully understand him or her – a good actor has empathy with his audience (*en* – *em* before p – means 'in'); apathy is lack of feeling for or indifference towards (*a* being a negative prefix)

From the beginning there were, broadly speaking, two schools of thought within the Church over what attitude the Church should have towards the State. In the Apocalypse, Rome (the State) is called the beast, the great harlot, drunk with the blood of the saints. In St Paul we find what was to become the predominant Christian belief that the State exercises authority under God and should be obeyed. With the conversion of the Emperor Constantine (312 BC) the Church was granted the same privileges as the pagan religion (for example, it could hold property and its priests were excused from certain civic duties). Subsequently when paganism collapsed Christianity became the official religion of the empire.

Under the pagan system the emperor was the chief priest – the *Pontifex Maximus* – and was treated as divine. How should he be treated in a Christian system? Constantine and his immediate Christian successors were clear about that: they regarded themselves as God's lieutenants and exercised control over the Church. (Secular control of the Church is, as a result, called caesaropapism, from Caesar and *papa* or pope: it was exercised in modern times by the Soviet government over the Russian Orthodox Church.) This was not a satisfactory relationship from the Church's point of view because the Bishop of Rome, St Peter's successor, was Christ's Vicar.

It was Saint Ambrose, the Bishop of Milan, who first enunciated the principles upon which Church–

State relations should be based: in matters of faith the emperor must obey the Church, in secular matters the Church must obey the State. The most influential thinker on the subject was Saint Augustine who in his *City of God* sought to reconcile the conflicting role of the Christian as a political actor in the secular world and as a religious pilgrim whose vision transcends the here and now.

influential
means having a shaping effect upon a person or thing. It derives from the Latin *in* 'in' and *fluere, fluxum* 'to flow', which also gives us flux, efflux and effluence. Astrologers thought people's characters and destinies were affected by the ethereal fluid flowing into them from the stars – hence the concern to find out the star under whose influence one was born. A person whose speech flows smoothly is said to be fluent. The point at which two rivers meet to flow together is called the confluence (*con* is a Latin particle meaning 'with'). Affluent means wealthy as a result of goods flowing towards one

Under the feudal system that developed after the fall of Rome, kings were conceived of as deriving their authority from God (so they were crowned by bishops) and they were bound in conscience to rule in conformity with Christian principles and practices. As a consequence, a king excommunicated by the Church found himself not only a religious pariah but also a ruler whose people were no longer bound to obey him. The relationship between Church and State that developed under the feudal system was mutually supportive. Out of it secular theorists developed the concept of the divine right of kings, which flowered in the absolutism of Louis XIV in France and of Charles I in England. Out of it, too, came the pervasive influence of the Church and the elevation of the Pope to the position of international mediator *par excellence*.

mediator
means someone who seeks to reconcile opposing parties (*medius* is the Latin 'middle'; hence also intermediary)

The Protestant Reformation was the first great attack on the relationship: it divided the Christian world, and in many Protestant countries, particularly those influenced by the Lutheran reform, replaced the Pope with the monarch as head of the Church. (The Calvinists who for the most part flourished in city-states governed by councils of burghers established a form of Church government that reflected that of the cities.) The French Revolution was the second great attack on it: it replaced the authority of kings based on divine right with the authority of the people. These changes led to the development of modern pluralist societies.

secular control
in its extreme form, namely that the State should have control over the Church even in ecclesiastical matters, is called Erastianism, after the Swiss theologian Thomas Erastus

Where radical secularism has been established, religious personnel, practices and images have been banned from public life and places. Any moral vision derived from religious perspectives is excluded from public life and the only views allowed to have a bearing on social, political and legal affairs are the secularist ones. Secularism, then, is radically intolerant in regard to the criteria that may be used to judge the morality of State actions. It does not escape this criticism by its purported tolerance of private beliefs – these are only tolerated as long as they do not influence legislation.

Where Church and State have been closely allied, the demand for the separation of Church and State has been described by political activists as a demand for secularization. It could also be described as the demand for the autonomy of whole swathes of civic life. This demand, however, does not necessarily entail either radical secularism or the demise of religious belief and practice. It is part of what is implied in pluralism.

Even where radical secularism has not been established, sociologists speak of a process of secularization to refer to the decline in religious beliefs in a particular community and to a concomitant, almost exclusive concern with here and now issues.

separation of powers
the assignment of the primary powers of government to distinct and independent institutions

Ideally government should advance the common good. Historically tyrants have used the machinery of government to oppress the individual. Political scientists therefore have devoted much of their attention to the analysis of the powers of government and to the design of systems that will reduce the possibilities for their abuse. They have identified the primary powers of government as legislative, executive and judicial. They have concluded that by separating these powers, that is by assigning each of them to separate, independent institutions, a control is placed on their use. This doctrine was first elaborated by the French philosopher Montesquieu in his *Spirit of the Laws* and was embodied in the US constitution of 1787.

Under many democratic constitutions the legislative powers are assigned to the parliament, the executive powers to the government, and the judicial powers to the judiciary. In practice, the government usually dominates the parliament.

dominate
is derived from the Latin *dominare, dominatum* 'to rule over', from which we also derive dominant, predominant, domain, dominion, demesne, domineer and indomitable

Perhaps the greatest service performed by the doctrine has been to uphold the necessity of having an independent judiciary. The reason for the separation of the judiciary from the legislative and executive was provided by Montesquieu:

> Again, there is no liberty, if the judiciary be not separated from the legislative and executive. Were it joined with the legislative, the life and liberty of the subject would be exposed to arbitrary control; for the judge would be then the legislator. Were it joined to

the executive power, the judge might behave with violence and oppression.

To be independent a judiciary must be free from all extraneous pressures. Historically, when judges were the servants of kings, they could be dismissed at will for making decisions that were unfavourable to the executive.

shibboleth
a test word that betrays one's party or nationality; now usually used for a worn-out slogan

It is told in the Old Testament that the Ephraimites quarrelled with Jephthah who, gathering the men of Gilead together, fought and routed the Ephraimites. When the fleeing Ephraimites reached the river Jordan they were asked by Jephthah's guards to say the word shibboleth (which the Ephraimites pronounced sibboleth), and in this way were identified. Shibboleth has come to be applied to the cant or slogan typical of any group.

silhouette
a shadow-outline

parsimony
means, in a pejorative sense, niggardliness and, in a positive sense, economy in the use of resources; it derives from the Latin *parcere, parsum* 'to spare'. The law of parsimony obliges logicians and scientists to seek the least necessary cause to explain a phenomenon. It is called Occam's razor after the fourteenth-century English Franciscan who enunciated the maxims, 'Entities should not be multiplied beyond necessity,' and 'It is vain to do with more what can be done with less.' Thus to explain thunder one eschews such a high-powered hypothesis as that it is caused by an angry deity and seeks the cause in atmospheric conditions

The word comes from an eighteenth-century French minister for finance, Etienne de Silhouette, notorious for his parsimony. In order to replenish the state treasury he promoted all sorts of economy measures, such as the use of wooden snuff boxes instead of gold or silver ones. Indeed the term *à la Silhouette* came into vogue meaning on the cheap. Another measure he proposed was the buying of cut paper portraits instead of expensive painted miniatures. The word silhouette came to be applied to such portraits, and later to any shadow-outline filled in with black. Film-makers find the silhouette a useful device – it allows them to intimate the presence of someone without revealing who it is.

Chiaroscuro, from the Italian *chiaro* 'clear' and *oscuro* 'dark', is a method of presentation in painting that relies on varying degrees of shadow for its effect of varying degrees of spatial and imaginative depth. Rembrandt is the acknowledged master of the technique.

sinecure
a paid post for which there are no duties

Sine is the Latin 'without'; *cura* is 'care' or 'responsibility'. A *sinecure* is a traditional way of rewarding a political favourite.

sine die
until some other, unspecified date

Sine is the Latin 'without'; *die* is a form of *dies* 'day'. The expression is used in a legal or institutional context about a court, tribunal or meeting: 'The meeting adjourned *sine die*.'

sine qua non
an essential condition

Sine is the Latin 'without'; *qua* means 'which'; *non* is a negative. *Sine qua non* literally means 'without which not'.

Sisyphean
endlessly laborious

Keeping open a silting tidal channel might be called a Sisyphean task. In Greek myth Sisyphus was the founder of Corinth. He had a dark reputation as an untrustworthy knave. He was the putative father of Homer's hero Odysseus, who was believed to have inherited his cunning from him.

putative
means supposed or reputed, from *putare, putatum*, the Latin 'to think'

He fell foul of Zeus in this way. Zeus abducted (from the Latin *ab* 'away' and *ducere, ductum* 'to lead') Aegina, the daughter of the river-god Asopus. Asopus came to Corinth looking for her. Sisyphus knew what had happened but he said he would not tell Asopus anything unless the river-god undertook to supply the citadel of Corinth with a perennial spring (to allow it to hold out indefinitely under siege). When Asopus made a spring rise behind Aphrodite's temple, Sisyphus told him all he knew. Zeus, the hot-tempered lover, flew into a rage: he ordered his brother Hades (Death) to seize Sisyphus, carry him down to Tartarus and punish him for betraying the divine secrets. (Tartarus was believed to be so deep down in Hades that a bronze anvil would fall from Earth for nine days and nine nights before reaching it.) In the underworld Sisyphus was ordered to roll a huge stone up a hill and over the far side; but every time he reached the top the stone rolled back to the bottom.

Hades
ruled the underworld, also called Hades. He was also known as Pluto (The Rich One – compare plutocracy) because he owned all the gems and precious metals hidden beneath the earth. The most hated of the gods, he was gloomy and heartless

slogan
a pithy rallying-call or criticism of an opponent

The word is derived from two Irish words, *slua* 'crowd' or 'host' and *gairm* 'call' or 'shout' – a slogan was originally a war cry. Slogans, shouted, printed or scrawled on walls, seek to rally supporters or attack opponents. Graffiti are often slogans but not every graffito (singular form), e.g. 'Kilroy was here!', is. An Italian word, *graffito* is derived from the Greek *graphein* 'to write'.

social democracy
a philosophy of the State, society and the person that promotes radical democratization as the best way to achieve the socialist goal of a caring yet free society

Marx asserted that capitalists would violently resist any attempts by the proletariat to introduce socialism and that therefore revolution was necessary. The Social Democratic Party in Germany, founded in 1875, rejected this dogma. They were democratic socialists rather than revolutionary socialists, and were committed to a programme of gradual social reform to be achieved by constitutional means. With the failure of Marx's scientific socialism to predict modern social and economic evolution, social democracy has become the ascendant form of socialism.

Social democrats believe everyone should be involved as much as possible in deciding those issues that concern him or her. They would like to see all our institutions democratized, that is they would like to see all the decisions made by institutions arrived at by democratic means. This form of participatory democracy goes well beyond representative democracy, which gives the people the power to elect those who form the government and to change them periodically, if they wish.

Social democrats stress the social nature of the person, our mutual interdependence, our responsibility for each other and the responsibility of groups and society as a whole to foster the personal development of each member of society. It places great stress on equal educational opportunities. Social democrats stress harmony, dialogue and sharing as opposed to individualistic competitiveness and acquisitiveness. They see the State as intervening to promote wealth creation, to redistribute wealth, and to ensure equal social and cultural conditions for all. Unlike Marxists and many democratic socialists, they do not require that the means of production should be owned by the State. They favour in fact the mixed economy because it makes for a plurality of subordinate groups, with their own identity and culture, and the freedom to live their own form of life.

Social democracy might be contrasted nowadays with liberal democracy which lays great stress on the rights and freedom of individuals and the many pressure groups which they develop to foster their own interest (rather than that of society).

socialism
a body of political beliefs that stresses that men and women are social beings and achieve their full humanity in and through authentic relationships with others. Hence the stress on the responsibility of the community to meet

Socialis is the Latin 'pertaining to friends or companions' and by extension 'pertaining to society in general'. Social may be used to refer to any aspects of the life of a community. It contrasts with individual or private. In public affairs it may be applied to services provided by the state to meet needs, especially in the areas of housing, health and education. Socialism, which came into use as a term in the early nineteenth century, stresses the responsibility of the community to care for its members and opposes the competitive individualism favoured by liberals. In 1887 Ferdinand Tonnies advanced two German words to capture the sociological dichotomy: *Gemeinschaft* ('community') denotes a community organically bonded by kinship and neighbourly ties and *Gesellschaft* ('society') denotes an aggregate of individuals connected only by their material interests.

As the Industrial Revolution worked its way through Europe in the nineteenth century, it presented the grim prospect that the means of production (and therefore wealth) would be concentrated in the hands of fewer and fewer owners of capital and that the bulk of the population would be transformed into a proletariat forever struggling on subsistence wages. Socialism sought to contend with that development. It appeared first, therefore, in the three countries that were first to industrialize – France, Germany and Great Britain.

Socialists argued that industrial capitalism, by grossly over-rewarding the owners of the means of production and grossly under-rewarding the labour that made them productive, was fundamentally unjust, that by creating classes within society it perpetuated inequality, that by making the worker an extension of a machine it robbed him of his dignity, and that by rewarding self-interest it frayed the social ties that made cooperation possible.

Socialists demand communal action, which would make wealth and power serve the interests of all. For them, social equality and justice are the predominant values. Socialists have elaborated a great number of means by which their objectives might be achieved. Broadly speaking, two systems have been put into practice. The system employed in communist countries places the means of production and distribution into the hands of a central planning agency. The result, as is now evident, has been to stultify the economies of those countries. The other system is that employed in those Western European countries where socialist parties have gained power.

The work of early Labour governments in the UK may serve as an example. To bring industry into communal hands they used nationalization. To distribute the fruits of production equitably they developed the welfare state. To prevent large-scale private accumulation of wealth they imposed death duties and restrictions on gifts and inheritances. They invested surplus

the needs of its members. Some argue that this can be done only by public, that is, State, ownership of the means of production and public control of the free market of production and distribution (thus communists and democratic socialists); others argue that it can be achieved best by social moderation of the free market of production and distribution (thus social democrats)

state wealth in communal cultural and leisure amenities. However, such centralized socialism came under fire because of its failure to provide dynamic growth in the economy. Social democracy, with its reliance on the mixed economy, is increasingly being favoured.

Socialism is internationalist in sympathy – it sees workers everywhere as having a common interest in overthrowing capitalism – but in practice socialist parties, like the British Labour Party, may be nationalistic. Socialism expresses itself in many forms ranging from Marxism to social democracy. It is an important political movement in Western Europe. Indeed at the end of the twentieth century the variegated Socialist Group was the largest group in the European Parliament. Socialism that seeks to achieve its goals through the parliamentary, multi-party system – democratic socialism – contrasts with revolutionary socialism, which insists that socialism can only be achieved by force. Marxism, the only form of revolutionary socialism to be tried, stresses the role of the State controlled by the proletariat as an agent of transformation from capitalism to socialism. It regards socialism as only the penultimate stage in the progress to communism when the State will wither away and everything will be administered by experts. (Note that the USSR was the Union of Soviet Socialist Republics.)

social partners
the employers, trades unions, farmers, other major interest groups and government

consensus
meaning agreement, derives from *con*, a form of the Latin prefix *cum* 'with' and *sentire*, *sensum* 'to feel'; it denotes unanimity and therefore the expression general consensus is tautologous

Many modern democratic governments seek to rule by creating consensus in the community about how major social, economic, cultural and legal issues should be tackled. Such governments pursue consensus by involving the major interest groups, in particular the employers, the trades unions, the farmers and the non-commercial voluntary groups, in the making of policy. They invite them to submit proposals and meet with them to agree national plans. In view of the consensus being sought, these interest groups, along with the government, are called the social partners.

sophist
a person who uses clever or quibbling arguments that are fundamentally unsound

Sophistēs is the Greek 'wise man'. Sophists were originally teachers of rhetoric, a skill needed by the Athenian citizen to defend himself in court or to persuade his fellow-citizens to some course of action. The sophists believed that thinking is a technique that can be formalized, taught and learned by people. Their emphasis on technique and on winning an argument at all costs gave the term sophist its pejorative connotation. (Sophister is an old-fashioned form of sophist used most famously by Edmund Burke in *Reflections on the Revolution in France* where he says that because 'ten thousand swords' did not 'leap from their scabbards' to avenge the smallest insult to Marie Antoinette 'the age of chivalry is gone. That of sophisters, economists and calculators has succeeded; and the glory of Europe is extinguished forever.')

sophisticated
is applied to someone who is worldly-wise; applied to things, it means elaborate

soviet
a political assembly in the former Union of Soviet Socialist Republics

Sovet, transliterated soviet in English, is the Russian 'council' like the French *conseil* and the German *Rat*. In czarist Russia it was applied to any political or economic advisory body. In the Revolution of 1905 in Russia, workers' councils called soviets were formed out of strike committees. In February 1917, after the overthrow of the czar, workers' and soldiers' soviets mushroomed in Russia to take over all political, administrative and economic functions. The soviets in turn elected delegates to an All-Russian congress. Lenin and his Bolsheviks, with the slogan 'All power to the Soviets!', used the soviets to gain control of Russia in the October Revolution of 1917.

Each of the fifteen constituent republics of the USSR had a supreme soviet. Above these was the supreme soviet of the USSR itself.

Spartacists
a group of German revolutionary Marxists, founded in 1916 and called after Spartacus, the slave who led a revolt against the Romans (73–71 BC)

The Romans trained slaves to fight one another to the death as gladiators in the arena (*gladius* is the Latin 'sword'; *arena* is 'sand', which was strewn over the place where combats were held). Spartacus was among a group of gladiators who escaped from a training-camp in the Italian town of Capua. A charismatic leader and shrewd tactician, Spartacus succeeded in drawing thousands of other slaves, and even poor shepherds and herdsmen discontented with their lot, to his standard; he armed them and led them to victory against the forces sent out by the Senate against him.

Alarmed at the revolution spreading through the countryside, the Senate eventually appointed Crassus, one of their wealthiest and most influential men, to lead a large army against Spartacus. Crassus doggedly stalked Spartacus and his slave army, eventually defeating him. Plutarch, in his *Lives of the Noble Romans* (one of Shakespeare's sources) describes the death of Spartacus as follows:

> Before the battle began Spartacus's horse was led up to him whereupon he drew his sword and killed it on the spot, saying the Romans had plenty of fine horses which would be all his if he won the coming battle, while if he lost, he certainly would have no need of a horse. After this, in the battle itself, he made a bee-line for Crassus, thrusting through the weight of weapons and wounded soldiers. He failed to make it through to Crassus but managed to down two centurions, who fell on top of him. At last, deserted by those who were about him, he stood at bay, surrounded by the enemy. Bravely defending himself, he was cut to pieces.

The Spartacists worked for a proletarian revolution and became the nucleus of the German Communist Party. They opposed World War I. Their leaders, Rosa Luxemburg and Karl Liebknecht, were murdered in Berlin in 1919 by the right-wing Freikorps, the loosely organized movement of ex-soldiers who felt they had been betrayed in 1918, and who were one of the elements from which Hitler later drew support for his Nazi Party.

Marx hailed Spartacus as 'the most splendid fellow in ancient history'.

Spartacus is recalled in the ballet *Spartacus* by the Russian composer Aram Khachaturian and in a Hollywood film, *Spartacus*, in which Kirk Douglas plays the eponymous hero and Laurence Olivier plays Crassus.

spartan
exceedingly austere, in the manner of the ancient Spartans

The Spartans were the greatest warriors of ancient Greece. Their system of government depended on the existence of a form of serfdom. The serfs (from the Latin *servus* 'slave'), far more numerous than the Spartans, were called Helots. They were kept subdued through an efficient secret police service (*krupteia*) and the timely assassination of any promising Helot leaders. The country the Spartans controlled was in the Peloponnese and was called Laconia. Their city, Sparta, was the only unwalled city in Greece in classical times.

The Spartans built their whole lifestyle around their need to excel in war. They lived absolutely equal and communistic lives. Each Spartan had his plot of ground and a number of Helots to till it. The men lived in barracks and had their meals served at common mess-tables. They had no home or family life. They visited their wives by stealth and returned to barracks. They practised eugenics in this way. When a child was born the mother brought it to a hall where the elders sat to examine it. If it was healthy they said 'Rear it!' If not, it was exposed to die in a cleft of the mountain.

The education of the boys was aimed at making them excellent warriors. They followed a regimen that made them strong, able to bear pain, despise luxury and be resourceful (they were kept half starved so that they developed great skill in stealing food – something that could be critical in a protracted campaign by land). Their intellectual development was functional too – they were taught to answer questions briefly and to the point, so famously so that terse speech is still called laconic (from Laconia).

The Spartan government tended towards the aristocratic model. They and their allies engaged in a great war against democratic Athens and its allies (431–404 BC). The Spartans won but the war so weakened the Greeks in general that they could not resist the outsider, King Philip of Macedonia, the father of Alexander the Great.

Sparta was the militaristic state *par excellence*. Mothers and wives would say to their menfolk as they went off to war, 'Come back with your shield – or on it!' *Miles, militis* is the Latin 'soldier'. From it we derive military, militant (combative), militarism (a tendency to give excessive emphasis to military might and its use), militia (a body of people enrolled and trained as soldiers to serve as troops of the second line, such as the US National Guard and its reserve), and militate (against). (Note the distinction between militate and mitigate – to make or become less harsh – from the Latin *mitis* 'mild'.) The practices of the Spartans had a large influence on the thinking found in Plato's major work *The Republic*.

excellent
means surpassing, from the Latin *excellere* 'to surpass'. The word does not admit of degrees – a thing is excellent or it is not excellent: more excellent is a solecism. (However, custom allows the usage most excellent majesty.) Likewise, since unique (from the Latin *unus* 'one') means without a like, only a citizen of Soloi would say very unique. *Par excellence*, from the French and literally meaning 'by excellence', applies to something superior to all others of the same genre

luxury
derives from the Latin *luxuria*, which itself derives from the Latin *luxus* 'excess'. Sybaris, a Greek city in southern Italy, was so noted for its wealth that sybaritic became a synonym for luxurious or opulent (from the Latin *opulentus*). Sumptuary laws place taxes on luxuries (from the Latin *sumptus* 'cost', which also gives us sumptuous). In ancient times southern Italy was called *Magna Graecia* ('Great Greece') because of the number of colonies established by the Greeks there from about 800 BC on. It was an indefinite term that, for instance, was sometimes taken to include Sicily and sometimes not

miles gloriosus
(Latin, 'the braggart soldier') was a stock figure in classical literature. One of Plautus's comedies was titled *Miles Gloriosus*. That is why the Latin rather than the Greek form has come down in literature

Sphinx
in Greek mythology, a monster with the head of a woman, the body of a lioness, a serpent's tail and eagle's wings, that

The riddle was, 'What creature, with only one voice, has sometimes two feet, sometimes three, sometimes four, and is weakest when it has the most?' Oedipus guessed the answer. 'Man', he said, 'because as a child he crawls on all fours, as a young man he stands on his own two feet, and as an old man he leans upon a stick.'

proposed a riddle to travellers going to or coming from Thebes, and strangled those who could not solve it

The Sphinx was so incensed at Oedipus's acuity that she threw herself from the mountain into the valley below and was dashed to pieces. The grateful Thebans proclaimed Oedipus king.

Sphinx comes from the Greek *sphingein* 'to draw tight' or 'to throttle'. In biology, a sphincter (also from *sphingein*) is a ring-like muscle whose contraction closes an orifice (an opening, from the Latin *os*, *oris* 'mouth' and a form of *facere* 'to make').

In ancient Egypt, the Sphinx was a colossal sculpture of a recumbent lion with the head of a man, ram or hawk, thought by many to represent the pharaoh as the descendant of Ra, the sun-god, who sailed across the sky in a barge during the day, and who was represented by a ram or a hawk. Recumbent means reclining and derives from the Latin *recumbere*. A celebrated occurrence of it in literature is in Oscar Wilde's *The Importance of Being Earnest*. The formidable Lady Bracknell surprises Jack on his knees proposing to her daughter Gwendolen: 'Rise, sir', she commands, 'from this semi-recumbent posture!' *Recumbere* itself derives from another Latin word, *cubare* 'to lie'. From it we get incubate (to lie upon eggs, to hatch), incubus (a devil supposed to take the form of a man in order to have sex with women in their sleep – the prefix *in* means 'upon'; used in general for any oppressive person, thing or influence), succubus (a devil supposed to take the form of a woman in order to have sex with men in their sleep – the prefix *suc* is a form of *sub* 'beneath'), and concubine (a woman who cohabits with a man without their being married – the prefix *con* derives from the Latin *cum* 'with').

succubi
and incubi were among the subjects treated in *Malleus Maleficarum* (Hammer of Witches), the notorious manual produced by two Dominicans c.1486 for use in the crusade against witches

spoonerism
a transposition of the initial letters of the words in a phrase to humorous effect

The transposition creates a new sense to the ear. Examples are 'a shoving leopard' for 'a loving shepherd', 'you have hissed my mystery lectures' for 'you have missed my history lectures', and 'hags were flung out of the windows' for 'flags were hung out of the windows'. It is so called from its most famous exponent, the Rev. W.A. Spooner, an Anglican clergyman.

status quo
the existing situation

Status is the Latin 'state', 'condition' or 'rank in society'; *quo* is a form of *quis* meaning 'in which'. Conservatives characteristically wish to maintain the *status quo*. The *status quo ante* – the pre-existing situation (*ante* is the

Latin 'before') – is the state two parties in an inconclusive conflict may wish to return to. A status symbol is something its owner believes to declare his or her desirable rank in society. For many people a sports car is a status symbol; and throughout history another form of transport – the horse – was a status symbol.

symbol
comes from *symbolon*, the Greek 'token'. A symbol is an emblem, something taken by convention to represent something else

statute
an Act passed by parliament

Statutum is the Latin 'a thing established [by law]'. A statute is a law passed by parliament as opposed to a law arising from customary practice or the decisions of judges. The statute book is a notional volume listing all the laws passed by parliament, allowing one to say 'There is no such law in the statute book.' A provision described as statutory is one that proceeds from an Act. A statutory instrument is a set of detailed rules issued by a government minister under the general provisions of an Act. Parliament later examines these instruments, through one of its committees, to ensure they comply with the Act. By allowing the use of statutory instruments parliament avoids getting bogged down in the minutiae (small details, the plural of the Latin *minutia* 'smallness') of technical legislation.

Stock Exchange
the building in which people buy and sell stocks and shares or the association of people who engage in that business

Before the London Stock Exchange came into being in 1773, rich people often met in London coffee houses and put their money together to buy ships to send around the world to trade with other countries. When a ship returned after a successful voyage, the profits were shared out among the speculators in proportion to the amount they had invested in the ship. A merchant who had invested in a ship but wanted his money back quickly before the ship returned would go to the coffee houses to see if anybody wished to buy his share and, if they did, at what price. Other businesses, such as factories and mines, came to be financed in the same way.

The Stock Exchange was established to provide a single place where all the buying and selling of shares could be done efficiently.

efficient
means acting or producing with the least waste of effort or resources, from the Latin *efficiens* 'effecting'. Effective means producing a desired result *simpliciter*, from the Latin *efficere*, *effectum* 'to accomplish'

The Stock Exchange enables companies to raise money for expansion or to produce new products by selling shares in companies. It enables a government and its agencies to borrow money to build roads, hospitals, airports, etc. by offering securities on which a certain rate of interest is paid each year. Individual investors may be said to hold tranches (pieces, slices) of shares and stock (*trancher* is the French 'to cut', from the Latin *truncare,* which also gives us truncate – cut short).

People who save in such institutions as building societies, banks and insurance companies (as many as nine out of ten adults, it would seem) deal indirectly in the Stock Exchange because those institutions invest the money lodged with them in securities and shares. A smaller number of people deal directly in the Stock Exchange through professional advisers and dealers called stockbrokers.

fluctuate
means to vary or waver, from the Latin *fluctuare*, *fluctuatum* 'to rise and fall like a wave'. To oscillate is to swing from side to side regularly, from the Latin *oscillare*, *oscillatum* 'to swing'

The value of shares fluctuates as the trading experience of the various companies fluctuates. Speculators who seek a profit by selling a security in the hope of buying it back later at a lower price are called bears (and thus a bear market is one that would favour bears – a falling market). Speculators who seek a profit by buying a security in the hope of selling it later at a higher price are called bulls (and thus a bull market is one that would favour bulls – a rising market). A stag is someone who applies for new issues in the hope that they will rise immediately and provide an opportunity for a quick profit.

An index representative of industrial and commercial shares (such as the Dow Jones Index in America) indicates each day whether the market overall is rising or falling (*index, indicis* is the Latin 'the forefinger', which is used to indicate).

A gilt or gilt-edged security is one where interest and capital are guaranteed by a government. A blue-chip investment is one in the most highly regarded industrial shares (the term is American, derived from the highest valued chip used in poker).

stoic
indifferent to pleasure or pain; courageous in the face of danger or adversity

In ancient Athens there was a decorated portico (the Stoa Poikilē) famous for its historical and mythological pictures. Here in the fourth century BC a philospher called Zeno held lectures. His doctrine came to be called Stoicism from the name of the portico.

According to Zeno, the divine mind, which produced the cosmos, is itself present in every part of it. Man by his possession of reason shares in the divine nature. But his nature also has lower elements that often oppose his reason. Virtue consists in living at one with the divine mind, which expresses itself in and through the world, i.e. in living in accordance with the natural law, which is discoverable by reason. (This idea of a natural law was incorporated in the Roman and Christian legal systems. These systems were taken over by the barbarian kingdoms of Europe after the fall of Rome; as a result the Stoic natural law doctrine lies at the heart of the legal systems of Europe today.)

The Stoics placed great emphasis on doing one's duty. Because pleasure, praise, the fear of pain and death were obstacles to the performance of one's duty, the Stoics sought to make themselves indifferent to those conditions through stern, sustained exercises – through aesceticism in its original sense. An important tenet of Stoicism was that reason must manifest itself in action. Stoics, therefore, were politically active whereas Epicureans (followers of the philosophy of Epicurus), who sought happiness or pleasure, were politically inactive: the latter believed political activity would not normally contribute to the individual's happiness because it would not assist 'repose of the mind'. (Epicurean is frequently used to describe someone who single-mindedly pursues physical pleasure, that is as a synonym for hedonist, even though the Epicureans opposed excess.)

The Romans were strongly attracted to Stoicism because of its exhortation to contribute to the State. Indeed many of Rome's earliest heroes such as Brutus and Cincinnatus were later felt to have been natural Stoics before the Stoic philosophy was formulated in Greece – *avant la lettre* as the French put it (*avant* is the French 'before'). Some historians believe that Stoic qualities inherent in many early Roman leaders such as Appius Claudius, Fabius Cunctator and Cato the Censor played an important part in Rome's eventual supremacy. The Stoic qualities referred to would be pietas (love of God, country and family) and gravitas. Aeneas, the hero of Virgil's *Aeneid* and the ancestor of Rome's founders, is in essence a Stoic – thus while he dallies with Dido in Carthage awhile, his sense of duty soon drives him back to his ship to continue his arduous mission.

gravitas
is a general seriousness of outlook; *gravis* is the Latin 'heavy' – hence also grave and gravity. We still use gravitas in such expressions as 'He has not the gravitas to be a judge.'

Levis, the Latin 'light', is the opposite of *gravis*. It gives us levity, levitate and lever

For 500 years Stoicism was the most influential philosophy in the Mediterranean world. Its last great adherent – and possibly the best-known of the Roman Stoics – was the Emperor Marcus Aurelius. His *Meditations*, containing Stoic aphorisms, is regarded as one of the greatest books of all time. Among his thoughts are the following:

> Whatever this is that I am, it is a little flesh and breath, and the ruling part.

> And thou wilt give thyself relief, if thou doest every act of thy life as if it were the last.

In common usage, we might say of a man who endured with courage a series of calamities, 'He remained stoical throughout.'

strategy
the series of steps needed to win a campaign or other major objective

Stratēgos is the Greek 'general' so strategy is concerned, as a general is, with the overall objective. At a lower level of concern the general must decide the tactics (from the Greek *taktikos* 'fit for arranging') to be employed in gaining each strategic position. Thus to capture a strategic city he may decide to besiege it or to scale the walls; or he may come up with a stratagem just as the Greeks did when they built a wooden horse outside Troy, filled it with soldiers and left it – an irresistible trophy – for the Trojans to haul inside the city themselves. A general must also ensure that he has the logistical support to carry out his strategy. Logistics originally applied to the arrangements for the movement, supply, quartering and maintenance of a military force in the field. It derives from *loger* the French 'to quarter'. Logistic, derived from the Greek *logos* 'word', 'reason' or account, refers to the process of reasoning.

sub judice
before the courts

Sub is the Latin 'under'; *judice* is a form of *judex, judicis* 'judge'. When a matter is *sub judice* it is before the courts and therefore not yet decided. While a case is *sub judice*, the media must not discuss it so as to avoid prejudicing the legal process. If they did so, they would place themselves in contempt of court and subject to heavy penalties.

subpoena
a summons to appear in court

Sub is the Latin 'under'; *poena* is 'punishment'; a subpeona carries a threat of a fine or imprisonment. From *peona* we derive penal, penalize, penalty and penology.

sub rosa
in strict confidence

Sub is the Latin 'under'; *rosa* is 'rose'. For the Romans, Cupid was the god of love (*cupiditas* is 'desire'), represented in art as a cheeky, chubby, naked child (his mother was Venus, the goddess of love), often winged. In Renaissance art a putto (Italian *putto* 'little boy', plural *putti*), in the manner of the ancient representation of Cupid, may attend the gods or sometimes, winged and angelic, the Virgin Mary. Venus had many lovers and Cupid once gave Harpocrates, the god of silence, a rose as a bribe to keep quiet about his mother's indiscretions. Ever since, the rose has been a symbol of secrecy (as well as being associated with love). The ceilings of Roman dining rooms were often decorated with roses to remind guests to keep *sub rosa* what was said *in vino*.

in vino
is literally 'under the influence of drink' – *vinum* is the Latin 'wine'; *oinos* is the Greek 'wine' – an oenophile is a connoisseur of wine

Veneris is a form of Venus, from which we derive venereal, as in venereal diseases, i.e. sexually transmitted diseases (STDs) and *mons veneris* ('the mountain of Venus', *mons, montis* being the Latin 'mountain'), the cushion of fatty tissue in human females above the junction of the pubic bones. The external sexual organs are called the pudenda, especially those of women, derived from the Latin *pudere* 'to make [or be] ashamed', which also gives us pudor (in Latin *pudor*), the sense of shame, and impudent (disrespectful or impertinent, *in* being a Latin negative prefix). Venery means either the pursuit of sexual pleasure (from Venus) or the practice of hunting (from the Latin *venari* 'to hunt', which also gives us venison).

subsidiarity
the principle whereby a lesser body that is carrying out its functions efficiently and effectively should be allowed to continue to function by a superior body

Subsidiarius is the Latin 'supplementary', from *subsidium* 'assistance', which also gives us subsidy. Modern European history is largely the story of how certain dynasties succeeded in concentrating power in their own hands and thereby established the various states we know today. Central authority has a drive to increase its powers. Often, it tries to do this by absorbing or destroying lesser bodies, frequently on the grounds of efficiency. The principle of subsidiarity is a good appeal against centralism because it, too, is based on efficiency – the fact that service can be delivered best by those closest to the people or bodies to be served.

The term subsidiary is used in business – a subsidiary company – to describe a company operating its business with a significant degree of freedom and discretion but subordinate to the overall policies of an owning company.

sui generis
unique

Sui is a form of the Latin *suus* 'his', 'her' or 'its'; *generis* is a form of *genus, generis* 'kind' or 'class' – *sui generis* means 'of a class of its own'. The parthenogenetic birth of Christ was *sui generis*.

surrealism
a movement in literature and art, begun in France in the early twentieth century, which turning away from reason sought to draw its inspiration from the dream-world of the subconscious exposed by psychoanalysis

Surrealism derives from the French *surréalisme*, *sur* being 'above' and *réalisme* 'realism'. The term was coined by the *outré* (French 'going beyond what is proper', from *outrer* 'to pass beyond') poet and influential art critic Guillaume Apollinaire in 1917 – he applied it to his avant-garde play *Les Mamelles de Tirésias* ('Tirésias's Tits').

Surrealism developed from Dada (or Dadaism), a short-lived (1916–*c*.1922) international literary and artistic movement whose protagonists, reacting to the pomposity (vain display, from the Latin *pompa* 'procession') of traditional art, proclaimed in the *Dada* review their intention of replacing reason with madness. The surrealists sought something beyond quotidian reality. E.H. Gombrich observes in *The Story of Art*:

> Many of the Surrealists were greatly impressed by the writings of Sigmund Freud, who had shown that when our wakening thoughts are numbed the child and the savage in us takes over. It was this idea which made the Surrealists proclaim that art can never be produced by wide-awake reason.

Among the leading surrealists were André Breton, Marcel Duchamp (the inventor of ready-mades who gained notoriety by presenting a urinal – *urina* is the Latin 'urine' – entitled 'Fountain' and signed with the name R. Mutt, for exhibition), René Magritte, and Salvador Dalí whose cupidity (greed for money, from the Latin *cupidus* 'desirous') was captured in the anagram Breton made of his name: Avida Dollars. An anagram is a rearrangement of the letters in a word or phrase to make another word or phrase, from the Greek *gramma* 'letter' and *ana* indicating 'transposition'.

In common speech surrealistic means bizarre or weird.

sycophant
an ingratiating flatterer

At one time it was forbidden by law in Athens to export figs. Someone who laid information against another for exporting figs was called a *sukophantēs* (*sukon* is the Greek 'fig' and *phainein* is 'to show' or 'to expose'). It is not clear how the word came to have its modern meaning. Presumably the reason people often informed on others was to ingratiate themselves with the authorities. The Athenian justice system depended on citizens being keen litigants, intent on discovering infringements of the law and making sure judgments were carried out. However, we know that eventually the activities of sycophants became vexatious to the Athenians and they sought to curtail them.

litigate
derives from the Latin *lis, litis* 'lawsuit' and *agere* 'to carry on'. Someone with a penchant for litigation is said to be litigious

Oleaginous from the Latin *olea* 'oil', unctuous from *ungere, unctum* 'to oil' or 'anoint', obsequious (meaning obedient in a servile way) from *sequi, secutum* 'to follow', and ingratiating from *gratia* 'favour' are synonyms for sycophantic.

Phantasm (a fancied vision), fantasy, phantom and phenomenon (the appearance anything presents to the mind) are all derived from *phainein*. Epiphany, from the Greek *epi* 'upon', 'above' or 'on' and *phainein*, means the manifestation of a supernatural reality and is used to name the Church feast on 6 January that commemorates the manifestation of Christ to the three wise men from the East. James Joyce secularized the word by applying it to those commonplace events or objects that have a special, inexplicable radiance – which are epiphanic. Diaphanous also derives from *phainein*.

avatar
(from the Sanskrit) may be used for a manifestation. In Hindu temples images of the various protective powers of the god Vishnu, called *avatars*, are carved on the walls

A phantasmagoria is a swiftly proceeding series of fantastic images (it was the name given to a show of optical illusions in France in 1802) and derives from the Greek *phantasma* 'an appearance' and, probably, *agora* 'assembly'.

symposium
a formal academic discussion of, or set of papers on, a single topic, by a number of specialists

Sun is a Greek particle meaning 'with', transliterated *syn* – *sym* before a word beginning with p; *posis* is 'drinking'. A *symposium* – the Latin transliteration of the Greek *symposion* – was originally a Greek drinking party, heightened by agreeable conversation, music and dancing. The philosopher Plato liked to enliven his treatises by casting them in the form of dialogues (*dialogos* is the Greek 'conversation'). The setting for one of his most famous dialogues is a symposium – it is called *The Symposium* – thus beginning the formal connection between the word and a conference to present varying academic views about a topic.

A favourite amusement at symposia (plural form) was telling riddles. If you solved a riddle, you could expect a reward of a cake or a kiss. If you failed, you were likely to be condemned to drink in one breath a jug of wine, sometimes mixed with salt water. The Greek for a riddle *ainigma* transliterates into English as enigma.

symptom
any sign of change in the body that is associated with a particular disease

Symptom is derived from the Latin *symptoma*, which is itself derived from the Greek *sumptōma* 'chance' or 'occurrence'. Symptomatology is the study and classification of the symptoms of disease. Symptom and symptomatic, derived from it, can be applied generally.

A syndrome is any combination of symptoms that are indicative of a particular disease or disorder (*sun* is the Greek 'with'; *dromos* is 'course').

syndicate
a combination of people for some common purpose

Sundikos (syndic in English) is a Greek word that originally meant 'defendant's advocate' (*sun* is the Greek 'with'; *dikē* is 'justice'). It later came to mean an officer of government. A syndicate was a group of such officers entrusted with the affairs of a city or community – see Rembrandt's painting 'The Syndics of Amsterdam'.

Syndicate came to be applied especially to a combination that capitalists entered into for the purpose of prosecuting a scheme requiring large amounts of capital, often one having the aim of cornering the market in a particular commodity.

A syndicated column is an article carried by a combination of newspapers. In France the adjective *syndical* is applied to combinations of workers – trades unions. Syndicalism is a development of trades unionism that originated in France with the aim of putting the means of production into the hands of unions of workers.

T

tactile
relating to, affecting, or having a sense of, touch

The Latin *tactilis* itself derives from *tangere*, *tactum* 'to touch'. The fingers and the tongue are tactile organs. The tongue is also a gustatory organ (*gustare*, *gustatum* is 'to taste'). The eyes are the visual organs (*videre*, *visum* is 'to see'). The ears are the auditory organs (*audire*, *auditum* is 'to hear'). The nose is the olfactory organ (*olere* is 'to smell', *facere*, *factum* is 'to make'; redolent, from the Latin prefix *red* 'back' or 'again' and *olere*, means having the scent or smell of, or reminiscent or suggestive of, for example 'a big bare room redolent of Victorian charity'). Tangible, from *tangere*, means capable of being touched or felt, for example tangible evidence. Palpable, from *palpare*, *palpatum* 'to stroke', means able to be touched and is a synonym for tangible, for example 'The tension was palpable.'

tantalize
to tease or frustrate

In Greek legend, Tantalus was a great friend of Zeus, who often invited him to the Olympian banquets of nectar and ambrosia. Puffed up with pride, he betrayed Zeus's secrets and stole the food of the gods to share among his human friends. When Zeus found out, he punished him appositely. He sent him to Hades where he was suspended eternally from a tree that leant over a swampy lake. Consumed by hunger and thirst, Tantalus would feel the water of the lake rise to his thighs and then to his chin, but if he tried to slake his thirst, the water immediately retreated; he would feel the delicious fruit of the tree brush against his shoulder, but whenever he strained towards it, the wind blew it away from his lips.

A tantalus is a case in which bottles of alcohol are locked with their contents tantalizingly visible.

Ambrosia was the food of the Greek gods; it conferred everlasting youth and beauty. Nectar was their drink. Ichor (from the Greek) rather than blood (Greek *haima*) flowed in their veins. From *haima* we derive haematology (the branch of medicine dealing with diseases of the blood), haemophilia (an inherited disease involving the loss of the clotting ability of the blood), haemorrhage, haemorrhoids, anaemic (lack of blood; *a* – *an* before a vowel – is a negative), leukaemia (a disease caused by gross proliferation of white blood cells;

leukos is 'white') and septicaemia (blood poisoning, from *septikos* 'related to something rotten').

tautology
saying the same thing twice in different words

Tauto is the Greek 'the same'; *logos* is 'word', 'reason' or 'account'. 'They were looking for a panacea for all their troubles,' is tautologous and should read '... a panacea' *tout court*.

tele
telecommunications, telegram, telegraph, telepathy, telephone, telescope and television – these are all words whose common prefix *tele* means 'afar' in Greek

Telecommunications is the transmission of messages over long distances by electronic means – radio, television, cable, telephone, telegraph, etc. (*communicare* is the Latin 'to communicate').

Telegram is a written message received by telegraph (*gramma* means 'writing' or 'letter' in Greek).

Telegraph is an apparatus for sending messages or signals over long distances by electricity (*graphein* means 'to write' in Greek).

Telepathy is the act of communicating thoughts and feelings to another over a distance without the use of a telephone or other apparatus (*pathein* is 'to feel' in Greek).

Telephone is an apparatus for speaking to another over a long distance (*phōnē* is 'voice' in Greek).

Telescope is an instrument for making distant objects appear closer (*skopein* is 'to look at' in Greek). The Greek mathematician Giovanni Demisiani coined the word in 1611 when he proposed it to name the spyglass Galileo had brought along to a dinner party in Rome to show the guests the Jovian moons.

Television is an apparatus for receiving sound and pictures broadcast from a distant place (*videre, visum*, from which vision derives, is 'to see' in Latin).

theist
a believer in God

Theos is the Greek 'god'. Theism usually denotes a belief in a God who created the world, who rules over it, who is the saviour of mankind (*sotēr* is the Greek 'saviour'; soteriology is the doctrine of salvation), who has revealed Himself to mankind, and who commands religious devotion. The theistic God transcends the world because He is eternal and infinite. He is also immanent in the world. Theism has been used to embrace both monotheism and polytheism.

An atheist is someone who does not believe in God or who positively denies the existence of God (*a* is a Greek negative particle). An agnostic in religious matters professes not to know for certain whether God exists or not – and thus is distinguished from an atheist.

A monotheist is someone who believes in the existence of one god only (*monos* is the Greek 'alone' or 'single').

A polytheist is someone who believes in the existence of many gods (*polus* is the Greek 'many').

A pantheist is someone who believes God is an impersonal force that exists in all of nature (*pan* is the Greek 'all') and permeates it (*per* is the Latin 'through' and *meare, meatum* is the Latin 'to pass') but does not transcend it. Pantheists may identify God with the material world or the forces of nature. Someone who is willing to worship all gods may be called a pantheist.

Deism, from the Latin *deus* 'god', means belief in a Supreme Being on the basis of reason rather than revelation as found, for example, in Holy Scripture; deists distinguish themselves from Christians, as well as from believers in other religions, and atheists. Historically deism emerged during the Enlightenment as the minimalist belief position between traditional Christianity and free-thinking atheism. The deistic God is remote from mankind. For Voltaire he was 'the great clockmaker' who kept the clock that is the universe working more or less harmoniously.

theology
rational discourse about God and man's relationship to God, based on study of every source of knowledge about God

Theos is the Greek 'god'; *ology*, from *logos*, here means 'study of'. Theology involves the systematic study of every source of knowledge about God, but particularly of the sacred revealed writings, traditions and practices of a particular believing community. Its purpose is to enrich the life of that community and the lives of its members in their endeavours to achieve both communal and personal unity with, and witness to, God. Christian theology takes as its chief source God's revelation of himself in the Old and New Testaments and in Christ, and the Christian community's understanding of that revelation. Theology has been defined by Saint Augustine as 'faith seeking understanding'.

Dogmatic theology is the continual effort to re-articulate the basic truths about God in language that is appropriate to the believing community and in a way that integrates a developing understanding with the tradition of that community. *Dogma*, *dogmatos* is the Greek 'opinion' – in English a settled opinion, hence a

to integrate
means to combine various elements into a whole; disintegrate means to break a thing into pieces, *dis* being the Latin 'apart'; integral means whole, complete or forming a whole; an integer is a whole number (from the Latin *integer* derived from *in*, a negative particle, and *teger* from *tangere* 'to touch' – an integer is something untouched and therefore whole)

principle, a tenet (a belief, from the Latin *tenere* 'to hold'), or a doctrine laid down with authority; in everyday use dogmatic has a pejorative sense – thus a dogmatic person is someone who believes his or her opinions are incontrovertible. Dogmatic theology is also called speculative theology as opposed to practical theology or moral theology.

Moral theology is the same faith seeking understanding of the implications of these truths for the daily living out of the faith in God by the community and the person (moral is derived from the Latin *mos*, *moris* meaning 'custom' or 'conduct'; its Greek equivalent is ethical, from *ēthos* 'custom' – hence also ethics and ethos, used in English for the distinctive spirit of a group or people, and ethology for the study of the behaviour of animals in their normal environment). It tries to articulate in a theoretical way an account of those practices that will bring the community and the person into a deeper union with God.

articulate
means to express oneself coherently, achieved by joining statements together in a way that makes sense; *articulus* is the diminutive form of *artus*, the Latin 'joint'; *arthron* is the Greek 'joint', from which we derive arthritis, inflammation of the joints

The aim of theology, whether it is dogmatic or moral, is always understanding with a view to a life lived in union with God here and hereafter. (Different faiths have different theologies because their sources of knowledge about God are different but all theologies have as their common purpose the leading of persons towards union with God.)

Liberation theology is an attempt to articulate the demands of the Christian faith for a particular Christian community where its members and fellow human beings are the victims of oppression and degradation. It faces such practical issues as whether, and to what degree, Christians should involve themselves in radical, even revolutionary, endeavours to free themselves and their fellow-citizens from political, economic and social servitude. It developed in Latin America where great contrasts exist between the wealthy ruling classes and the oppressed masses. Liberation theology has created tension in the Catholic Church in Latin America and elsewhere, and has divided the Christian communities there.

servitude
tude is a Latin suffix indicating a 'state' or 'condition'; *servus* is 'slave' – servitude means slavery or subjection. Thus also fortitude (*fortis* means 'strong'), multitude (*multus* means 'many'), altitude (*altus* means 'high'), certitude (*certus* means 'certain'), pulchritude (*pulcher* means 'beautiful'), latitude (*latus* means 'broad'), longitude (*longus* means 'long') and solitude (*solus* means 'alone', from which we also derive solo and sole)

Some forms of liberation theology justify violence in the interest of justice and thereby come into conflict with the Vatican's proscription of violence. Some forms accept a Marxist analysis (on the principle that theological problems should be translated into economic and political ones) and thereby come in conflict with the Church, which rejects this kind of reductionist analysis. (Reductionism is a theoretical understanding of human affairs that commits one to a search for antecedent causes of a particular problem. These causes may be of a different character to the event to be explained or understood. Nonetheless, reductionists believe that unless those causes are understood the original complex problem cannot be properly understood and solved. *Reducere, reductum*, the Latin word from which reductionism derives, means 'to lead back'.)

However, not all liberation theologians are believers in violence or Marxism. *Liber*, from which liberation derives, is the Latin 'free'.

Third Reich
the Nazi regime 1933–45

Reich is the German 'empire' or 'kingdom'. It is related to the Latin *regere* 'to rule'. Reich is also related to the Hindi *raj* 'kingdom' and *rajah* 'king' or 'ruler' (the British government of India, 1858–1947, was known as the Raj).

The First Reich was the medieval Germany-centred Holy Roman Empire. The Holy Roman Empire, a revival of the ancient Roman empire of the west, came into being with the coronation (*corona* is the Latin 'crown', which is used in English for the circle of light around a luminous body, especially the moon) of Charlemagne as emperor by Pope Leo III in 800 AD. It fell into decline for a period but was revived by the coronation of the German Otto I as emperor in 962 AD. It continued in being until it was dissolved by Napoleon in 1806.

regere
is also the source of regime, meaning administration or course of treatment; regimen, meaning course of treatment; and regiment, meaning a large number in organized – regimented – groups. In John Knox's famous diatribe against the English Queen Mary, *The First Blast of the Trumpet Against the Monstrous Regiment of Women*, regiment means rule

The Second Reich was the German empire established by Bismarck in 1871, which ended with the abdication of Kaiser Wilhelm II in 1918.

Kaiser
was used by German speakers as the title for the Holy Roman Emperor, the Austrian emperor from 1804 and the German emperor from 1871

The Third Reich, inaugurated in 1933 when Hitler gained dictatorial powers following his appointment as chancellor, would last, the Nazis boasted, a thousand years. It lasted twelve.

A striking feature of Nazi style was the glowing ovations (from the Latin *ovatio*, from *ovare* 'to exult') Hitler received at massed rallies – a practice redolent of ancient Rome. The Romans publicly acclaimed their victorious generals in either of two processions: the triumph and the ovation. In a triumph the general entered Rome in a magnificent chariot drawn by four horses, preceded by the captives and the spoils of war. The magnificence of the display and the adulation of the crowds were so heady that a slave accompanied the general in the chariot to shout occasionally in his ear: '*Hominem memento te!*' ('Remember you are only a man!') In an ovation – a lesser triumph – the general entered the city on foot: he did not wear the gorgeous gold embroidered robe, nor did he carry a sceptre; and the ceremonies concluded with the sacrifice not of a bull but of a sheep.

The idea of a golden age of a thousand years occurs in the Apocalypse – it was the period Christ would reign on earth following His second coming; people who believe in such a doctrine, taken literally, are called millennialists or millenarians (*mille* is the Latin 'thousand') or chiliasts (*chilioi* is the Greek 'thousand'). Arthur Moeller van den Bruck applied the concept to the developing political state of Germany in his book published in 1923, *Der Dritte Reich* ('The Third Reich'), and the Nazis gladly seized upon it for propaganda reasons.

Third World
the underdeveloped countries

In 1955 a conference was held in Bandung in Indonesia attended by delegates from twenty-nine Asiatic and African states that were not attached to either the capitalist states under the hegemony of the US or the communist bloc states under the hegemony of the USSR.

G. Balandier, writing in French, hailed them as the representatives of the *Tiers Monde* and the term later came into use in English as the 'Third World'. *Tiers Monde* had been coined by the French economist Alfred Sauvy on an analogy with *Tiers État* ('Third Estate'): under the *ancien règime* only the First and Second estates – the clergy and the aristocrats – were regarded as politically significant. The Third Estate, which embraced the vast majority of French people, was regarded as impotent or nugatory (from the Latin *nugae* 'trifles').

Third World countries, which include many Latin American and African countries, are marked by an extremely low level of economic activity, dependence on one or a few primary commodities (food or minerals), a poor infrastructure, illiteracy, and poor social welfare and health services. Third World countries desperately need help from developed countries, often to meet disasters such as famine, flooding and earthquakes, but persistently to help them develop their own economies. The internationally accepted target for official (as distinct from voluntary) aid from developed

voluntary
means undertaken by free choice from the Latin *voluntas, voluntatis* 'will', which also gives us volunteer

countries is 0.7 per cent of gross national product (GNP). Some of the oil-rich Arab countries exceed the target, a few countries such as the Netherlands and Norway reach it, but the average response is 0.36 per cent.

and voluntarist (proceeding from the belief that the State should not interfere in the process of collective bargaining or in the operations of trades unions)

titanic
immensely strong

In Greek myth, at the beginning of all things Mother Earth emerged from Chaos and bore a son Uranus. Uranus fathered the Titans upon Mother Earth. The Titans were giants, the best-known being Cronus and Atlas. Cronus and his brothers attacked Uranus and killed him. Cronus then became the chief god. Subsequently Cronus had a son called Zeus who in turn engaged in a great struggle with Cronus and his brothers, eventually overcoming them. The Titans were banished and Zeus became the chief of the gods. Titanic, then, is aptly applied to a struggle between mighty forces – the struggle between the superpowers was titanic.

Atlas
was condemned by Zeus to the eternal labour of holding up the sky. He is often represented in art as bearing the earth on his shoulders. In the sixteenth century printed collections of maps often featured Atlas as a frontispiece. The Flemish geographer Mercator first used the term atlas for a collection of maps itself

Gigas, gigantos is the Greek 'giant', from which gigantic is derived. The struggle between the gods and the giants – called *gigantomachia* (*machē* is the Greek 'battle') – was a favourite subject of Greek art. *Giga*, derived from *gigas* and, attached to units of measurement, indicates immense multiples, for example gigawatts and gigabytes.

gē
the Greek for 'earth', lurks in giant (*géant* in French) because the giants, like Adam, came from the earth

The Cyclopses or Cyclopes (in Greek *Kuklops* 'round eye' from *kuklos* 'circle' and *ops* 'eye') were a race of giants who had a single eye in the centre of their foreheads. They lived barbarous lives in caverns by the sea. They were troglodytes – the Greek *trōglodytēs* means 'cave-dweller'. In one of the most famous episodes in the *Odyssey* Odysseus puts out the eye of the Cyclops Polyphemus with a burning stake ('the eye sizzled', says Homer). An episode is an interesting incident in a story and derives from the Greek *epi* 'upon' and *eisodos* 'a coming in'. Cyclopean is aptly applied to massive walls made from large, rough-hewn stones because the ancient Greeks associated that style of masonry with the Cyclopes. Agamemnon's palace in Mycenae, excavated by Schliemann, is a famous example of Cyclopean architecture.

spelaeum
the Latin 'cave' gives us speleology for the scientific study of caves

Colossal is a synonym for gigantic. It derives from the Greek *kolossos* (Latin *colossus*) 'giant statue'. The most famous colossus was the 'Colossus of Rhodes' – a bronze statue of the god Apollo that stood over one hundred feet high near the harbour. It was wrongly thought to have stood astride the entrance to the harbour allowing ships to pass full sail between its legs – hence Shakespeare's description of Julius Caesar 'he doth bestride the narrow world / Like a Colossus; and we petty men / Walk under his huge legs, and peep about'. It was one of the Seven Wonders of the World. The Colosseum in Rome was a huge amphitheatre – a building with tiers of seats around an open space like a modern football pitch – opened in 80 AD by the Emperor Titus. Beside it stood a massive statue of Nero as the sun-god, the colossus from which the building took its name. The Colosseum itself was colossal – it had seats for 45,000 spectators (*eum* is a Latin suffix denoting 'place' – compare museum). Both gigantic and colossal are aptly applied to physical things. Losses, too, may be gigantic or colossal (but not titanic or Cyclopean).

Lucullan
describes a lavish epicurean feast, after Lucullus, a first-century BC Roman general who was famous for his banquets

Gargantua, the Rabelaisian hero, was a giant with an enormous appetite. Gargantuan is aptly applied to a huge meal.

Hercules was a colossal son of Zeus. He was most famous for the twelve labours he performed: these would easily have defeated any normal man. His fifth labour, for instance, was to clean out the Augean stables in a single day. King Augeas of Elis, one of the wealthiest men on earth, had huge herds of cattle and flocks of sheep. But his stables, where he kept the animals, had not been cleaned out for years and the stench carried across the whole of Greece. Eurystheus, who set Hercules this task, cackled gleefully as he pictured the hero piling the noisome filth into a basket and carrying it away in a state of near asphyxiation … and then haring back for more. Hercules, however, made two gaps in the stable walls and diverted two neighbouring rivers so that they streamed through the stables and swept them clean. Herculean is aptly applied to a spectacularly difficult task.

A Lilliputian is the opposite of a giant. Lilliput was the country whose tiny inhabitants pinned Gulliver to the beach in Swift's *Gulliver's Travels*. Brobdingnag, a country of giants in the same book, gives us Brobdingnagian as another word for gigantic.

traumatic
pertaining to an emotional shock of such violence

Trauma is the Greek 'wound'. Psychoanalysts seek to treat traumata (plural form) – any powerful shock that may have long-lasting effects. In popular speech traumatic is often applied to elevate the effects of a relatively minor setback. The word trauma is also used by physicians to describe any severe physical injury. The Latin for 'wound' *vulnus, vulneris* gives us vulnerable (open to being wounded) and invulnerable.

that it causes recurrent psychological reactions

tribune of the people
a champion of the ordinary people

The Latin *tribunus* originally meant 'tribal commander'. In the early days of the Roman Republic there was a class struggle between the aristocratic party, who ruled through the consuls and the Senate, and the ordinary people, the plebs. The plebs eventually won the right to elect a number of representatives to protect them from abuse of power by the Senate and the consuls. These representatives were called *tribuni plebis*, 'tribunes of the people'. Tribune is now used of any informal defender of the people. It is probably derived from *tribus*, the Latin 'tribe', and would have aimed to lay claim to a primal legitimacy.

Caius Gracchus, one of the most famous tribunes of the people, was ranked by historians of Rome as a public speaker second only to Cicero. He asserted the rights of the plebs over those of the patricians to an unprecedented extent (from plebs we derive plebeian meaning pertaining to the lower class). When he slipped from power, he escaped the wrath of the Senate only by persuading his slave to stab him to death.

In modern times the word tribune is much favoured as a title for a newspaper: it promises the excitement of crusading journalism to its readers and of large circulation to its publishers.

In time the Roman tribunes acquired the veto over senatorial appointments and acted as judges in certain cases. It is from their legal functions that we get the word tribunal, meaning either a place where a case can be heard or a process of formal enquiry, as in 'The government has set up a tribunal of enquiry into the price of gas.'

triumvirate
any joint rule by three men

The term comes from the Latin *trium virorum*, '[rule] of three men', the genitive plural of *tres* 'three', and *vir* 'man'. Historically, it was used to describe the political alliance of Caesar, Crassus and Pompey, which was formed in 60 BC, and that of Antony, Lepidus and Octavian, which was formed in 43 BC. It is now used to describe any group of three men associated in some way.

France was ruled by a triumvirate, consisting of Napoleon, Sieyès and Ducos, following the collapse of the Directory in 1797. Napoleon, as first consul, was the formal head of the triumvirate and not simply *primus inter pares*. Sieyès, the great constitutionalist, had no influence with the army and Ducos, his ally, had no influence with anybody. Sieyès summed up the situation for his friends: *'Messieurs, nous avons un maître; il sait tout, il peut tout, il veut tout.'* ('Gentlemen, we have a master; he knows everything, he can do everything, he decides everything.') A plebiscite in May 1802 overwhelmingly confirmed Napoleon as first consul for life. A further plebiscite in 1804 overwhelmingly confirmed him as emperor of the French.

plebiscite
derives from the Latin *plebs* 'the ordinary people', and *sciscere, scitum* 'to decree' and means a direct vote by the people on an issue, first employed in the ancient Roman Republic. Referendum is a synonym for plebiscite. Because plebiscites were used to install or promote right-wing dictatorships in France under Napoleon and in some other states in Europe in the 1930s, referendum tends to be the favoured term nowadays

A troika (from the Russian *troe* 'a set of three') is a team of three horses abreast that draws a vehicle. It is a synonym for triumvirate. It was used to describe the three men who briefly shared the supreme power in Russia following the death of Stalin in 1953 – Malenkov, Khruschev and Bulganin. It is used by the European Union to describe the mechanism by which the Union is represented in external relations coming under the common foreign and security policy, namely, a group of three, one from the member state currently holding the presidency of the council, one from the member state that held it in the previous six months and one from the member state that will hold it in the following six months.

A duumvirate is joint rule by two men (*duo* is Latin 'two', *duum* is its genitive plural). When the ancient Roman Republic was set up in 510 BC following the expulsion of the last monarch, Tarquin the Proud, the executive power of the state was entrusted to two men called consuls. They held office for only one year and each had equal authority and functions. The Roman Republic was therefore ruled by a duumvirate. A diarchy is its Greek equivalent (*di* is the Greek 'twice' and *archein* is 'to rule').

A pentarchy is joint rule by five men. It is derived from the Greek *pente* 'five' and *archein*. The Directory was a pentarchy. The Latin-based equivalent of pentarchy, quinquevirate, is rarely used. *Quinque* is the Latin 'five', from which we also derive quinquennium, a period or cycle of five years, and *vir* is the Latin 'man'.

On analogy with pentarchy, tetrarchy may be used

to describe joint rule by four men (*tetra* is a Greek component indicating 'four').The Basilica San Marco in Venice features a sculptured group called the 'Tetrarchs'. It is said to represent the emperors Diocletian, Maximian, Galerius and Constantius. To help him rule the empire Diocletian had appointed Maximian as joint-emperor in 286 AD and Galerius and Constantius as sub-emperors in 292 AD. However, historically tetrarchy described one of the four political units into which ancient Thessaly was divided. In early imperial Rome it was used for the realm of a subordinate king (who was called a tetrarch). Thus chapter three of Saint Luke's Gospel begins: 'Now in the fourteenth year of the reign of Tiberius Caesar, Pontius Pilate being governor of Judea, and Herod being tetrarch of Galilee …'

subordinate ruler
Satrap was the title for the governor of a province in ancient Persia, called a satrapy. Satrap connotes a despotic subordinate ruler. Thus, 'He controlled Chicago directly himself but extended his power throughout the States by appointing satraps in each of the major cities — Danny Duck-toes Del Monte in New York, Peter-the-Painter Picasso in San Francisco, and so on.'

A heptarchy is either a body of seven (Greek *hepta*) men who hold office together or a state divided into seven regions, each of which has its own ruler. A heptagon is a polygon (from the Greek *polugōnon* 'a figure with many [*polus*] angles') having seven sides.

A decemvirate is a body of ten (Latin *decem*) men who hold office together. It was first applied to the men who codified the Roman law – the Laws of the Twelve Tables – between 451 and 450 BC. The ten men who formed the Committee of Public Safety, which under Robespierre imposed the Reign of Terror on revolutionary France, were known as the decemvirs. The Greek equivalent of decemvirate is decarchy, from the Greek *deka* 'ten', which also gives us decade (a period of ten consecutive years or a group or series of ten), Decalogue (the Ten Commandments), and decapod (any crustacean with ten feet – *pous, podos* is the Greek 'foot' – such as a crab, lobster or prawn).

decem
is also the source of December, the tenth month of the Roman calendar, and decimate – to destroy or kill a large proportion of – derived from the Roman punishment of killing every tenth man of a mutinous or cowardly troop

trompe l'œil
a painting or decoration designed to make one think the objects represented are real

Tromper is the French 'to deceive' and *œil* is 'eye'. Thus, the painter Jean-Siméon Chardin 'was, in fact, fond of toying with his signature, affixing it to surprising facets of the represented reality. In many of his early canvases, it is inscribed on the edge of a shelf as if carved there – a demure bit of *trompe l'œil*.' (*NYRB*, 10 August 2000)

type
archetype, daguerreotype, prototype and stereotype are words whose suffix

Archetype means the original model (*archos* is the Greek 'first' or 'chief' – hence archbishop and archenemy). It is usually applied to people: Cain is the archetypal fratricide. Jung introduced the concept of

type derives from the Greek *tupos* 'stamp' or 'model'

the archetype into psychology, giving it a special meaning. The myths and fairy tales of world literature contain definite motifs that crop up everywhere. These same motifs are met in the fantasies, dreams, deliria (plural of delirium, meaning violent excitement or emotion, from the Latin *delirare* 'to swerve from a furrow' and hence 'be crazy') and delusions of individuals living today. 'These typical images and associations are what I call archetypal ideas,' said Jung. 'They have their origin in the archetype, which in itself is an irrepresentable, unconscious, pre-existent form that seems to be part of the inherited structure of the psyche and can therefore manifest itself spontaneously anywhere, at any time.' While archetypes are not conscious their presence is felt by some as numinous, that is of ineffable spiritual significance. Jung said: 'All the most powerful ideas in history go back to archetypes. This is particularly true of religious ideas, but the central concepts of science, philosophy and ethics are no exception to this rule.'

A daguerreotype is a photograph taken using an early process invented by the Frenchman Louis Daguerre.

Prototype also means the original model (*prōtos* is also a Greek word for 'first'). It is usually applied to things. Before a new line of aircraft is put into production a prototype is built to test the design.

A stereotype is a fixed set of characteristics that is applied by convention to certain kinds of people. The stereotypical salesman is young, nattily dressed, excitable and fast-talking. *Stereos* is the Greek 'solid'. A stereotype was originally a solid plate developed in printing to ensure an even, clear image on all the sheets of printed paper. It was made from a cast of the moveable type (the type had to be movable so that different words could be made from its different letters). A solid has three dimensions – height, width and depth. Sound reproduced with three dimensions is called stereophonic (*phōnē* is the Greek 'voice' or 'sound').

U

Ultima is a form of the Latin *ultimus* 'furthest', 'final' or 'last' (hence also ultimate, *ultimo* meaning 'in the last [month]', and ultimatum, meaning a final unalterable demand). Thule is the name given by the Greeks and Romans to a cold, fog-bound island believed to lie north of Scotland. It became for them the proverbially utterly remote place – as Timbuktu did for the Victorians.

ultima Thule
the most distant place in the world

Ultra is the Latin 'beyond'; *vires* is a plural form of *vis* 'power'. Governments give specific powers to certain bodies – for example city councils – to carry out functions for the State. Cases often arise in the courts on the issue of whether or not these bodies have exceeded their powers in particular instances. A body that has so acted is said to have acted *ultra vires*; one that has acted within its powers is said to have acted *intra vires* (*intra* is the Latin 'within').

ultra vires
beyond one's legal authority

Unus is the Latin 'one'; *animus* is 'mind' or 'spirit'. People may be said to have arrived at a unanimous decision.

A magnanimous person is generous and noble – *magnus* is 'great'.

A pusillanimous person is characterized by a lack of courage or determination – *pusillus* is 'weak'.

An equanimous person acts with balance and composure, with equanimity – *aequus* is 'equal' or 'even'.

unanimous
in complete agreement

Scire is the Latin 'to know', from which the *scious* formation derives; *con* derives from *cum* 'with'; *un* is a negative prefix. In psychology the unconscious is the part of the mind that contains instincts, impulses and other elements that affect thoughts, actions and feelings but which are not available for direct examination because they are unconscious. Freud is sometimes hailed as the inventor of the unconscious but, in fact, the idea of unconscious mental processes is discernible from *c.*1700. Freud created brilliant models of how the unconscious works and produced tools to analyze the psychological dysfunctions rooted in the unconscious and to apply therapies that remove the pathogenic effects of repression. Jung developed the concept of the collective unconscious, a myth-producing level of mind

unconscious
the part of the mind not available for direct examination

collective
derives from the Latin *colligere*, *collectum* 'to collect'. Collectivism,

as employed by political scientists, is the principle of ownership of the means of production by the State or the people – hence collective ownership and collective farm

that evidence shows is common to all men (hence collective), where archetypes, a Jungian term for innate ideas or for the tendency to organize experience in innately predetermined patterns, operate on the experience of each individual.

unemployment
lack of paid occupation

Employer is the French 'to employ', derived from the Latin *implicare* 'to enfold', from which we also derive implicate and implication. People lay claim on some of the goods and services made available in a country each year through the payment of money. Most adults obtain money from a paid occupation that involves the production of goods and services: employment is the means most people have of making a living. A small number of people are wealthy enough not to need employment. Adults who are incapacitated or who cannot find employment may be provided for by the State (from taxes gathered from those employed and those who are rich), by relatives or by charity.

Unemployment – the word came into general use in the 1890s, thanks to the enquiries into industrial conditions made by Beatrice Webb and the Fabians – is a term covering the condition of those who would like a job but do not have one. We derive the numbers of unemployed from the labour force. The unemployment rate or rate of unemployment is the percentage of the labour force without a job.

The rate of unemployment is a more important measurement than the number unemployed because proportion allows one to compare one country with another in a meaningful way.

The term unwaged is sometimes used to embrace the unemployed, dependent groups such as the elderly, the young or the handicapped who are unemployed, and certain people who work but receive no pay such as those who work in the home.

universe
the whole of creation

order
from the Latin *ordo*, *ordinis*, is the opposite of chaos and means a state in which everything is arranged harmoniously. Primordial means existing from the beginning of order (*primus* is the Latin 'first')

The Latin equivalent of the Greek *cosmos* is *universum*, literally 'the whole thing', the totality of the physical world, in English the universe (*uni* is a Latin particle meaning 'one' and *verse* derives from *vertere*, *versum* 'to turn' – the universe is that which has been turned into one by divine order).

Universal is used to describe something that applies to everything or everything in a class, e.g. universal suffrage (as opposed to limited suffrage where, for example, only men or property-owners have the right to vote).

Universitas is the Latin 'the whole', which came to be applied to a society. University now denotes a learned society or institution that is authorized to confer degrees. There is a connotation of universality in the range of its interest in study. A polytechnic (from the Greek prefix *poly* indicating 'many' and *technē* 'art' or 'skill') is a third-level educational institution teaching many skills courses but not the range available in a university.

Ur
original

When scholars conceive of a common source for stories found in a number of literatures they refer to it as the Urtext. *Ur* is a German prefix that indicates 'first', 'original' or 'initial'. Philologists speak of an *Ursprache* (*Sprache* is the German 'speech') to refer to a proto-language (*protos* is the Greek 'first'). *Ur* is now used generally by textual scholars: 'Goethe worked on *Faust* for most of his life. A version of 1775–6, now known as the *Urfaust*, survives in a copy which was rediscovered only in 1887.' (*LRB*, 20 July 2000) *Ur* and *ur* are both used.

philology
means the study of language, from the Greek *philein* 'to love' and *logos*, here 'word'

utopian
pertaining to an imaginary state of perfection

Utopia (from the Greek *ou* 'not' and *topos* 'place') is the name of a book written by Sir (later Saint) Thomas More in 1516 that describes an imaginary island of that name where everything is perfect – laws, morals, politics, etc. Herbert Marcuse's *Eros and Civilization* is a modern example of the genre (*genre* was originally a French word meaning 'type' or 'kind', derived from the Latin *genus*, *generis*; a genus – plural genera – is a class of objects containing a number of subordinate groupings called species; generic means applicable to a whole group or class – general – and, applied to drugs, means not having a trademark). Utopian is often used to describe schemes that are well-intentioned but utterly unrealistic. However, Oscar Wilde in *The Soul of Man Under Socialism* insisted that 'a map of the world that does not include Utopia is not worth even glancing at, for it leaves out the one country at which humanity is always landing'.

a species
is defined by the fact that the members of it are reproduced sexually from other members

Dystopia, the opposite of utopia, is an imaginary state where everything is for the worst (*dys* is a Greek prefix indicating 'bad'). The most famous modern example is *Nineteen Eighty-Four* by George Orwell (the *nom de plume* of Eric Blair – Orwell is an estuary in Suffolk, England, where Blair was reared). The Orwellian world is a brutal totalitarian society where the individual is under constant surveillance ('Big Brother Is Watching You'), his mind is controlled by Newspeak ('War is Peace, Freedom is Slavery, Ignorance is Strength') and his prospects are numbingly bleak:

> If you want a picture of the future, imagine a boot stamping on a human face – for ever.
>
> Don't you see that the whole aim of Newspeak is to narrow the range of thought? In the end we shall make thought crime impossible, because there will be no words in which to express it.
>
> –George Orwell, *Nineteen Eighty-Four*

Here Orwell plumps for one side of the epistemological dilemma: are words antecedent (Latin *ante* 'before' and *cedere* 'to go') to thought or is thought antecedent to words?

V

vandalism
wanton destruction of property or other amenities

The Vandals were one of the fiercest of the barbarian tribes that fell upon the Roman empire in its decline – they sacked Rome in 455 AD. They were notorious for their delight in destroying churches, books and works of art. The word vandalism was coined in modern times by a French cleric to characterize the destruction of works of art by French revolutionary fanatics. It is used nowadays for the wanton destruction of property or amenities *simpliciter*. It may even be applied to the destruction of beautiful things or amenities by a public or private organization, for example the demolition of a historic building to make way for a car park.

verbatim
using exactly the same words

Verbum is the Latin 'word'. A verbatim report reproduces a speech word for word. A speech on nuclear energy is likely to refer *passim* (Latin 'here and there' or 'throughout') to radioactivity. The arguments in a good speech flow *seriatim* (Latin 'one after another', from *series* 'series') and there are no *non sequiturs* (conclusions that do not logically follow, *non sequitur* being the Latin 'it does not follow').

vernacular
native, indigenous (of language); concerned with ordinary buildings as opposed to those of great corporate bodies such as the Church or the State (of architecture)

Vernaculus is the Latin 'domestic':

> Besides Czech-language literature, already well developed by the fourteenth century, even before the Hussites' dramatic assertion of the vernacular, German writers thus left their mark, from medieval Minnesänger, or troubadours, through historical epics of the Romantic period and beyond.
>
> –*NYRB*, 21 October 1999

Architecture derives from the Greek *archos* 'chief' and *tektōn* 'builder'. Vernacular architecture relies on traditional forms, such as the thatched cottage in Ireland, and local materials. It avoids high style.

veto
the power to reject

The tribunes of the people in Rome had the power to prevent a judgment from being carried out. They exercised it by uttering the word *veto* ('I forbid' in Latin). The word entered the modern political vocabulary at the beginning of the French Revolution when the constitutional issue arose as to whether or not the king could veto the decisions of the national assembly. Indeed the revolutionaries referred to the king dismissively as Monsieur Veto.

The veto may be a formal power. In the United Nations' security council each of the five permanent members (China, France, Russia, the UK and the US) can exercise a veto to prevent the council from taking action on any matters other than procedural ones. In the European Union most of the decisions of the European council are made by a majority vote; in the voting the larger states have more votes than the smaller ones and a qualified majority is needed for a decision. On the most important and far-reaching questions, including the admission of new members, there must be unanimous agreement. That means that each member state in theory has a veto in regard to those issues. However, the EU tends to work in such a way that no single member state ever finds that the disadvantages arising from any one proposal decisively outweigh the basket of benefits it gets from membership.

viable
capable of maintaining independent life

Vita is the Latin 'life', from which is derived the French *vie*, the immediate source of viable. Originally applied to the foetus – a viable foetus is one that is capable of independent life – the word is now often transferred e.g. a viable project, a viable economy.

Via is the Latin 'way' or 'road'. In, for example, 'She came home from Germany via Amsterdam,' via means by way of. To take the *via media* is to take a middle course between two extremes – *media* is a form of *medius*, the Latin 'middle'.

A viaduct is a structure that carries a road or railway over a valley, formed by analogy with aqueduct, a structure built by the Romans to carry water – Latin *aqua* – over a valley.

The Romans called a paved road a *via strata* (*stratus* is the Latin 'laid down'). A stratum is a layer. Stratification – the *fication* formation derives from the Latin *facere, factum* 'to make' – is the laying down of *strata* (plural).

Stratigraphy (*graphein* is the Greek 'to write') is used by geologists for the study of the composition, relative positions, etc. of rock strata to determine their history, and by archaeologists for the study of a vertical section through the earth showing the relative positions of the human artefacts and therefore the chronology of successive levels of occupation.

Stratosphere is applied to the highest layer of the atmosphere and stratospheric connotes a great height. From *strata* we also derive street, the Dutch *straat*, German *Strasse* and Italian *strada*. However, stratocracy, meaning rule by an army, derives from the Greek *stratos* 'army' and *kratia* 'rule'.

vice versa
the other way round

Vice is a form of *vicis*, the Latin 'turn'; *versa* is a form of *vertere*, *versum* 'to turn'. The expression literally means the turn having been turned: 'The czar relied on the army and *vice versa*.' Vice, indicating acting in place of (as in vice-president), derives from *vicis*, as does vicissitude, meaning turn of fortune: 'He remained stoical in spite of all vicissitudes.'

Vichy France
that part of France (and its empire) not occupied by the Germans in 1940, which had a government whose seat was in the town of Vichy. The Vichy government collaborated with the Germans and disappeared with the liberation of France in August 1944

France was shattered by the German blitzkrieg of May–June 1940 – a *tour de force* (French, 'feat of power') that carried German forces up to the Channel and precipitated a British withdrawal through Dunkirk. France's leaders were left with two choices. They could acknowledge the German victory, seek an armistice (from *arma* the Latin 'arms' and *sistere* 'to stand still' or 'to stop') and negotiate a peace or they could flee metropolitan France and continue the war from the French territories overseas. The vast majority supported Marshal Philippe Pétain, the legendary defender of Verdun in World War I (*'Ils ne passeront pas!'* – 'They shall not pass!' – from his Order of the Day, Verdun, 26 February 1916), and made the first choice. A small number, led by General Charles de Gaulle, made the second. Pétain successfully negotiated a peace with the Germans who were initially content to occupy Paris and northern France, to control the Channel and the Atlantic coast and to have access to French agricultural and industrial production. (Up to 1942 the Germans needed only 30,000 men – less than twice the size of the Paris police force – to control France.) He also succeeded in commanding the loyalty of almost all the French territories overseas. He established his government in the town of Vichy.

Vichy is famous for its natural spring water. A southern mountain spa (derived from Spa in Belgium, whose medicinal mineral springs were discovered in the

emigration
Migrare is the Latin 'to go from one place to another', from which we derive migrate, migrant, migration and migratory. *E* is a Latin prefix meaning 'out of' – to emigrate is to move out of one

country into another. *In – im* before m – is a Latin prefix meaning 'in': to immigrate is to move into one country from another. The French *émigré* is a synonym for emigrant but often carries a connotation of someone forced to leave his or her native country for political reasons (like some French aristocrats during the Revolution)

fourteenth century) town, it had the spare accommodation to meet the needs of a bureaucracy. It was favoured before the southern cities because some, like Marseilles, were too close to the temptation of emigration and others were the power-bases of left-wing opponents of the Vichy regime.

The Vichy government never achieved its aims of negotiating the reintegration of France and of installing itself in Paris.

vigilantes
a self-appointed group of citizens who band together to maintain order in a community

Vigilare is the Latin 'to watch', from which vigilantes, originally a Spanish word, derives – vigilantes watch for criminals. But they also catch and punish them and thus usurp the proper functions of the police and the courts.

Vigilantes tend to appear whenever the law is failing to protect the community. They mete out justice in a rough and ready manner. In the absence of the formal processes of law, gross injustice is sometimes perpetrated.

virulent
extremely infective, poisonous, hostile

Virus is the Latin 'poison'. As an English word (plural viruses), it applies to any of a group of submicroscopic (*sub* is the Latin 'below' or 'under') entities consisting of a simple nucleic acid surrounded by a protein coat and capable of replication (a replica is an exact copy, from the Latin *replicare* 'to repeat') only within the cells of animals and plants.

Voltairean
in the manner of the Frenchman François-Marie Arouet who used the *nom de plume* Voltaire

A major playwright and novelist and a dazzling popularizer of philosophical and scientific ideas, Voltaire has come to embody the rationalism and liberalism that ushered in the modern world. He is the consummate *philosophe*. That word, originally French from the Latin *philosophus* ('philosopher'), is applied to the intellectuals in Europe and America who comprised the Enlightenment. Sceptical towards traditional thought, they held the characteristic attitude that the confidence we place in our beliefs should be proportionate to the evidence we can establish to support them. The traditional appeal to authority – *magister dixit* (Latin, 'the master said it') – was anathema to them.

Voltaire accepted the argument from design for God's existence: *Si Dieu n'existait pas, il faudrait l'inventer.* (French, 'If God did not exist, it would be necessary to invent Him.') As a Deist he did not believe in a provident God – unlike the German genius G.W. Leibnitz, who in his famous work *Theodicy* had declared that God had made the best possible world – for instance the benefits that flow from man's freedom are possible only at the risk of some evil. Voltaire satirized this in his novel *Candide ou l'Optimisme*. The young Candide sets forth sanguinely into the world with his tutor Dr Pangloss, whose motto is 'All is for the best in the best of all possible worlds.' They immediately encounter a string of disasters of every kind. Chastened, Candide myopically concludes '*il faut cultiver notre jardin*' (French, 'we must cultivate our garden'), echoing Epicurus.

Voltaire was reputed to have once said 'I disapprove of what you say, but I will defend to the death your right to say it.' However, the illiberality of *ancien régime* France (the system of government before the 1789 Revolution) meant that he himself spent twenty-seven years in exile. One of the places he stayed in was England where, on the execution of Admiral Byng in 1757 for his failure to relieve Minorca, Voltaire remarked that the English thought it was a good thing to kill an admiral from time to time '*pour encourager les autres*' (French, 'to encourage the others') – the first use of that expression. (The word admiral, which is found with minor variations in many European languages, carries echoes of Turkish naval power in the Mediterranean in the Middle Ages. It derives through Norman Sicily from the Arabic *emir-al*[*-bahr*] 'ruler of the sea'.)

Voltaire returned to France in 1778 and received the adulation of Paris. His death at the end of May that year became a semi-public event with everyone watching to see if he would succumb to the persistent pressure of a confessor who, to the very last, sought to persuade the old reprobate to accept the orthodox rite of absolution. Voltaire was reported as refusing to renounce the Devil: 'Is this a time to make enemies?' The story is *ben trovato*. Voltaire actually said 'Leave me to die in peace!', a formulation in itself exquisitely ironical.

provident
relates to God's foreseeing protection and care for His creatures, from the Latin *providere* 'to provide'

genius
is used of a person of exceptional and original capacity. The Romans believed every place had its guardian spirit – its *genius loci* (from Latin *gignere* 'to beget' and *locus* 'place'). The essential connotation of originality is carried in such expressions as the genius of the French and an evil genius

theodicy
from the Greek *theos* 'god' and *dikē* 'justice'; the word was coined by G.W. Leibnitz for a branch of theology dealing with the problems of physical and moral evil in a providential world

myopically
Myopia is shortsightedness, from the Greek *muein* 'to blink' and *ops* 'eye'. A synopsis (from the Greek *sun* 'with' and *opsis* 'view') is a summary; synoptic means relating to a summary; it is also used in relation to the Gospels of Matthew, Mark and Luke – the synoptic Gospels – which present the narrative of Christ's mission from a common viewpoint

vote
a registration in some agreed way of one's opinion about a candidate or on an issue

Votum is the Latin 'wish' or 'vow'. You cast a vote in an election by marking a ballot-paper and placing it in a ballot-box (ballot derives from the Italian *ballotta* 'little ball': little balls placed in an urn or box were used for voting). In democracies the law provides for universal suffrage, that is it enables everyone to vote (*suffragium* is the Latin 'vote'), for a secret ballot so that voters will not be intimidated (*timidus* is the Latin 'fearful'), and for the division of the State into constituencies so that representatives will be returned by the different parts of the State. To have the franchise, that is the right to vote, is the mark of a free man (*franc* is the Old French 'free').

The poll at an election is the total number of votes cast (poll derives from a middle Dutch word *polle* 'head' and by extension means 'the counting of heads'). Some voters spoil their votes from ignorance or in protest. The valid poll is obtained by excluding spoilt votes. (The word poll is also used in relation to attitude surveys – opinion polls – and poll tax or head tax.)

Those who do best at the hustings win the seats. The hustings was a temporary platform on which the nomination of parliamentary candidates was made before the Westminster Ballot Act 1872, and is now applied to any platform where election speeches are made and, by extension, to the election campaign generally.

vox pop
the opinions of people in the street

Vox, vocis is the Latin 'voice'; *populi* 'of the people' is a form of *populus* 'people'. *Vox pop* is a short form of *vox populi* 'the voice of the people'. (The Latin maxim *vox populi vox Dei* – 'the voice of the people is the voice of God' – has been used by leaders down the ages to cloak abject submission to the will of the mob.) *Vox pop* is often used in radio and television circles for a sequence in a report presenting the views of members of the public randomly chosen.

W

The New York Stock Exchange is located on Wall Street. Wall Street is used as a synonym for that stock exchange and by extension for the financiers and the financial specialists from the American business world who conduct their business there – the financial establishment.

Wall Street
the American financial establishment

Welfare means well-being. For our well-being we need to be able to avail ourselves of a wide range of services, from womb to tomb. The full-hearted welfare state seeks to provide such services as health, housing, education, unemployment assistance, family allowances, and widows', orphans' and old-age pensions.

The first notable step in welfare legislation was taken in Bismarck's Germany. Other European states followed. In Britain the welfare state, introduced at the beginning of the twentieth century by Lloyd George, was greatly advanced under Clement Attlee's Labour government from 1945–51. The extended system was based on recommendations in a report by the economist Sir William Beveridge, who had been commissioned to prepare it by the wartime coalition government.

Most modern states might be called welfare states, even the US (beginning with Roosevelt's New Deal), whose political culture favours rugged individualism and therefore self-sufficiency.

welfare state
a state in which the economic and social needs of dependent groups such as the poor, the sick and the elderly are met by the state

Welt is the German 'world'; *Anschauung* is 'perception'. *Weltanschauungen* (plural) may be fashioned by philosophy, religion or ideology but they also exist in the absence of formal intellectual structures in primitive societies.

Weltanschauung
the view of the world held by an individual or group

When the revolutionary government in Paris introduced conscription in 1793 to deal with the external threat, parts of the west of France – called La Vendée – revolted. The movement was taken over by the Royalists and it was from their emblem the *fleur de lys* (the white lily of the monarchy) that the largely guerrilla forces got their name the Whites. It was from them in turn that the Russian reactionary armies got their popular collective description. There was not, therefore, an eponymous relationship between White Russia (or

White Army
the czarist anti-revolutionary forces defeated by the communist Red Army in the Russian Civil War 1917–21

Byelorussia or Belarus), one of the fifteen constituent republics of the former USSR, located in the west close to Poland, and the White Army.

Whitehall
the centre of British government

Whitehall is a street in London where a number of important government offices are located, including the Treasury. The media use the term Whitehall to refer to thinking on policy (rather than political) matters at the highest levels of British government. Downing Street, a small street off Whitehall where the British premier resides and has executive and administrative offices, is used to refer to thinking on political matters at the highest level of government.

The Cenotaph is located in Whitehall.

White House
the official residence of the American president in Washington DC, the capital of the US

In 1790 a decision was made by the first US congress under the new constitution to establish a federal capital on the Potomac river. In a public competition to choose a design for the president's residence, an Irish architect from County Kilkenny who had settled in Philadelphia, James Hoban, was the winner. It is said that Hoban derived elements of his design from that of Leinster House, the residence of the Duke of Leinster in Dublin and now the seat of the Irish parliament.

Work on the new capital – including the president's house – went slowly and Washington never lived there. When the government finally moved to the new city in 1800, president Adams took up residence in the still unfinished building. The building was partly destroyed in the course of a war with the British in 1814. Afterwards, it was found impossible to clean the walls blackened by smoke, so Hoban suggested that the entire exterior be painted white. This solution was accepted – and gave the house its name.

White Paper
an official document presenting government policy decisions

The term – a colloquial one – is derived from British parliamentary experience. During the nineteenth century the practice arose of printing official reports, statistical and other government publications, which were to be presented to parliament, on white paper and of covering them in a heavier blue-coloured paper. Those publications became known as blue books. Short government policy statements did not need a special cover and were printed entirely on white paper. Such documents became known as White Papers. That term, from 1945 on, came to be applied officially to documents that contained government decisions on an area of public policy irrespective of the size of the document.

In 1967 the Labour government in Britain decided, in the interest of open and more participative government, to publish a consultative document (*The Development Areas: A Proposal for a Regional Employment Premium*) so that interested parties could make their views known before the government made its decisions. That document was issued with a green cover. Such consultative documents have ever since been called Green Papers.

X–Z

xenophobia
morbid fear and dislike of foreigners

Xenos is the Greek 'stranger'; *phobia* is 'fear'. Politicians sometimes whip up xenophobia to strengthen the internal cohesion of their countries – or to seek scapegoats.

zeitgeist
the spirit of the times

ostensible
means outwardly showing, from *ostendere*, the Latin 'to show'

derive
Rivus is the Latin 'river', *de* is 'from' – to derive is to draw from a source

perennially
means constantly – *per* is the Latin 'through' and *annus* is 'year', which in the form *ennial* also occurs in centennial and millennial

Zeit is the German 'time' or 'era'; *Geist* is 'spirit'. The term is often used in its ostensible sense. Thus, 'Jazz, illegal booze and playing the stock market – these manifested the *zeitgeist* of the 1920s in America.' But the word, derived from the writings of the influential German philospher Hegel, has a much deeper import.

Thinkers address themselves perennially to the problem of the meaning of human history. Does it follow a divine plan? Is it simply the process through which the fittest survive? Is it meaningless? Hegel believed the movement of history was dialectical (*dia* is the Greek 'through'; *lektikos* is 'spoken'). For Socrates and Plato the dialectic was simply a form of discourse designed to force people to acknowledge their true beliefs.

Hegel transformed the idea of dialectic to explain and understand the historical process. Each era of this process and each phase of development of each era generates its own negation (from *negare*, the Latin 'to deny': negation is a synonym for contradiction). A new era emerges when the synthesis of the positive and negative forces is realized. The *zeitgeist* captures the characteristics of the era in summary form. All that is good and true is preserved and enriched in the new era; nothing is lost. (Thus the Greeks discovered the principle of freedom but it was negated by further political developments, to re-emerge in a new and richer light in the French Revolution.) Contradiction is at the heart of reality; contradiction is the moving principle of the world and Reason is its agent. The subject of this historical process is Spirit (*Geist*) and through history it is seeking self-understanding. Man is the vehicle of this self-understanding and there can be no further development beyond man. Hence all expressions of the human spirit – religion, art, politics, philosophy – are expressions of, and a moment in, this endeavour by Spirit. History ends when Spirit, through the human spirit, will have achieved full self-knowledge, that is will have become Absolute Spirit.

Marx seized upon Hegel's idea of the dialectic for his theory of history. Since he did not believe in Hegel's notion of Spirit, he sought the explanation of the historical process in the dialectic between man and the material conditions of his existence. Marx's theory of history is therefore called dialectical materialism.

zenith
the highest point

Zenith derives from the Arabic *samt* 'way [of the head]'. Zenith is the point of the heavens directly above the observer's head. It is opposed to the nadir, the diametrically opposite point of the heavens – nadir means opposite to (the zenith). Both words attest to the primacy in astronomy attained by the Arabs in the ninth, tenth and eleventh centuries. The words often appear in connection with the lives of public figures and soldiers. Thus, 'This campaign marked the zenith / nadir of his career.'

The antipodes are either or both of two points or places situated diametrically opposite to one another on the earth's surface (*anti* is the Greek 'against' or, as here, 'opposite', and *pous, podos* is 'foot'). The Antipodes is used to refer to Australia and New Zealand.

Zionism
the Jewish movement to establish and develop a Jewish homeland in Palestine

Zion is a synonym for the Holy Land and so Zionism is an apt name for the movement that re-established the Jews in Palestine and continues to help the state of Israel by gathering funds and enlisting diplomatic support for it (mainly in the US) and promoting the emigration of Jews to it. Zionism is a movement that started with a secular objective but which, having attained it, has, under various pressures, both internal and external, acquired a surprisingly strong religious connotation.

Following the destruction of Jerusalem by the Romans in 70 AD, most of the Jewish population of Palestine fled abroad. It was only natural that a yearning to return to the Promised Land should be a feature of the culture of the Jews of the diaspora – they prayed for it three times a day. However, the first real steps to achieve the aspiration were taken when the Hungarian Jew Theodor Herzl, moved by the anti-Semitism revealed by the Dreyfus affair in France, convened the first World Zionist Congress in Basle, Switzerland, in

1897. Some Jews did not agree (as some still do not) with his strategy of setting up a Jewish homeland. They felt Jews should seek to be good citizens of the states they lived in – that they should assimilate. Most Jews felt it was necessary for their protection as a race to establish a state (though a small number of these felt the state need not necessarily be in Palestine).

Of those who felt a state should be established in Palestine, Herzl and his supporters felt the task was urgent, while others favoured a gradual building up of the Jewish population in Palestine by small-scale immigration first. (The total population of Palestine at the turn of the century was small. It built up rapidly thereafter with the immigration of Arabs from the surrounding states and of Jews from Europe.)

It was Chaim Weizmann and his followers who decided these issues. They won the Balfour Declaration in 1917, which committed the British government to support the establishment of a Jewish national home in Palestine. The British, who controlled Egypt, were expected to control Palestine if the Ottoman empire did not survive the Great War. As it happened, the Balfour Declaration was included in the mandate for Palestine given by the League of Nations to the British after the war.

The Declaration, however, had also contained a guarantee not to interfere with the civil and religious rights of the majority non-Jewish population of Palestine (the 500,000 Moslems and 60,000 Christians). Understandably, the Palestinian Arabs were opposed to Jewish immigration and the establishment of a Jewish state. The British found themselves in a difficult situation over a commitment made for propaganda reasons at a critical point in a war.

In 1924 America closed its door to mass immigration. This was a momentous event in the history of Zionism because it diverted the massive Jewish emigration from Poland and Russia to Palestine. (By 1931 the Jews in Palestine numbered about 175,000.) Another momentous event was the accession of Adolf Hitler to power in Germany in 1933: in spite of a restrictive immigration policy imposed by the British, the Jews in Palestine, swelled by those who managed to flee Nazi anti-Semitism, numbered about 400,000 in 1937. The Arabs then numbered about a million.

The Holocaust cost 6 million Jewish lives and reduced the world Jewish population by as much as a third, to 12 million. It built up an irresistible pressure for the establishment of a Jewish state through which the Jews could defend themselves. Immediately after the war Jewish refugees from Europe streamed into Palestine, most of them illegally. By 1948 there were a million Jews there.

Holocaust
the terrible destruction of the European Jews by the Nazis (*holokauston* is the Greek 'whole-burnt sacrifice', from *holos* 'whole' and *kaustos* 'burnt'; it came into use in this context around 1959). *Shoah*, the Hebrew 'destruction', is used as a synonym for Holocaust

The UN solution to the Palestine problem, at that stage erupting in violent clashes between Jewish guerrilla forces and the British, was partition. Partition was accepted by the Jews but rejected by the Arabs. In May 1948 the British withdrew and the Jewish leader David Ben-Gurion proclaimed the state of Israel. The Israelis beat off the attacks immediately mounted on them by the surrounding Arab states. Some half-a-million Arabs fled the Israeli-occupied territories: these displaced people and their children are at the heart of the Middle Eastern problem today. Indeed it is often said that the Palestinians have paid the penalty for Europe's, especially Nazism's, crimes against the Jews.

INDEX

The page numbers below indicate the fullest entry for each term.